VARIORUM COLLECTED STUDIES SERIES

Merchant Families, Banking
and Money in Medieval Lucca

Thomas W. Blomquist

Thomas W. Blomquist

# Merchant Families, Banking and Money in Medieval Lucca

Routledge
Taylor & Francis Group

LONDON AND NEW YORK

First published 2005 by Ashgate Publishing

Published 2016 by Routledge
2 Park Square, Milton Park, Abingdon, Oxon OX14 4RN
711 Third Avenue, New York, NY 10017, USA

*Routledge is an imprint of the Taylor & Francis Group, an informa business*

ISBN 9780860789710 (hbk)

**British Library Cataloguing in Publication Data**
Blomquist, Thomas W.
 Merchant families, banking and money in medieval Lucca. –
 (Variorum collected studies series)
 1. Merchants – Italy – Lucca – History – To 1500 – Sources
 2. Banks and banking – Italy – Lucca – History – To 1500 – Sources
 3. Contracts – Italy – Lucca – History – To 1500 – Sources 4. Lucca (Italy) –
 Commerce – History – To 1500 – Sources 5. Lucca (Italy) – Economic
 conditions – Sources 6. Lucca (Italy) – Social conditions – Sources
 I. Title
 330.9'4553

**Library of Congress Cataloging-in-Publication Data**
Blomquist, Thomas W.
 Merchant families, banking and money in medieval Lucca / Thomas W. Blomquist.
  p. cm. – (Variorum collected studies series)
 Includes index.
 ISBN 0–86078–971–3 (alk. paper)
 1. Merchants – Italy – Lucca – History – To 1500. 2. Banks and banking – Italy –
 Lucca – History – To 1500. 3. Money – Italy – Lucca – History – To 1500.
 4. Lucca (Italy) – Commerce – History – To 1500. I. Collected studies

 HF3590.L83B56 2005
 330.945'53–dc22

                                                            2004065779


VARIORUM COLLECTED STUDIES SERIES CS828

Dedicated to
my wife of forty-one years, Clelia Palmerio Blomquist,
to my son Charles M. Blomquist, LLD,
to my daughter Maria Blomquist Izzo
and to the memory of
Stuart Hoyt,
Vsevolod Slessarev
and
David Herlihy

# CONTENTS

## CONTENTS

This volume contains xvi + 278 pages

## PUBLISHER'S NOTE

*The articles in this volume, as in all others in the Variorum Collected Studies Series, have not been given a new, continuous pagination. In order to avoid confusion, and to facilitate their use where these same studies have been referred to elsewhere, the original pagination has been maintained wherever possible.*

*Each article has been given a Roman number in order of appearance, as listed in the Contents. This number is repeated on each page and is quoted in the index entries.*

# ACKNOWLEDGEMENTS

Grateful acknowledgement is made to the following people, institutions and publishers for their kind permission to reproduce the papers included in this volume: Medieval Academy of America, Cambridge, Mass. (I); The President of the Instituto Storico Lucchese, Lucca (II, III, IV, VII); Edizioni Scientifiche Italiane, Naples (V); Kent State University Press, Ohio (VI); Duane J. Osheim, Charlottesville (VII); Walter Friedman, Editor, *Business History Review*, Boston, Mass. (VIII); Yale University Press, New Haven (IX); Professor Luigi De Rosa, Editor, *Journal of European Economic History*, Rome (X, XI); Damien Dard, Librairie Droz S.A., Geneva (XII); Cambridge University Press, Cambridge (XIII); Casa Ed. Leo S. Olschki Publishers, Florence (XIV); Elsevier, Oxford (XV, XVI).

# FOREWORD

The sixteen articles that make up this collection were published between 1969 and 1995, and, with one exception – the piece on Raymond de Roover – all are based on the unpublished notarial documents housed in the *Archivio di Stato in Lucca* or in the *Archivio archivescovile* and the *Archivio capitolare* of the diocese of Lucca.[1] This archival documentation, being extensive in both its quantity and quality, can tell us much about life in the Middle Ages. When I began working with these notarial registers, their scope and significance proved far greater than what I had supposed. Although I had done my master's topic – "Lucchese Commercial Activities in Genoa, 1186–1226" – using unpublished Genoese notarial materials, and although I had read about the Lucchese and other notarial collections, I still had not comprehended the extent of the economic and social information that they contain. In this Foreword, I would like to make some observations on the notarial materials, together with a few remarks about the articles themselves.

The State Archive in Lucca houses the surviving registers of 41 different notaries and the Chapter Archive contains 37 cartularies for the thirteenth century.[2] Although the notaries worked in their homes and their offices, they also wandered about in the streets of their neighborhoods or villages, greeting and chatting with prospective clients, who often would give them some piece of business on the spot. Such business might be anything that could be put in contract form. The notary usually used a throwaway slip of paper to record the essentials of the matter at hand – the contracting parties, the essence of the deal,

---

[1] Generally speaking, I will not provide full footnotes in this Foreword, since the supportive material is already in one or more of the collected articles. For example, on the Lucchese notarial materials, see article II, p. 8, n. 4. For a more recent treatment, see also Andreas Meyer, *Felix et inclitus notarius: Studien zum italienischen Notariat vom 7. bis zum 13. Jahrhundert*, Bibliothek des deutschen Instituts in Rom, 92 (Tübingen, 2000).

[2] Lazzareschi, "L'Archivio dei notari dell repubblica lucchese," *Gli archivi italiani*, II (1915), pp.190–191, has provided a chronological list of thirteenth-century Lucchese notaries whose work has survived. For the chapter archive, see Giuseppe Ghilarducci, *Le biblioteche e gli archivi archivescovile e capitolari della diocesi di Lucca* (Lucca, 1969) and Andreas Meyer, "Der Luccheser Notar Ser Ciabatto und sein Imbreviaturbuch von 1226/1227," *Quellen und Forschungen aus italienischen Archiven und Bibliotheken*, 74 (1994), pp. 172–293.

the date, and the witnesses – and later, at his workplace, he redacted the contract in Latin, putting it in due legal form but with the stock formulas abbreviated, for which reason this shortened form was termed an *imbreviatura*. Such a record was then duly entered in the notary's *liber*, or cartulary. Usually these cartularies were organized chronologically, but sometimes a whole book was devoted to a single client or a specific location. In the thirteenth century, these entries in the notarial book were given the full faith of the law. And from them, if required, the notary could always draw up a final, formal, unabbreviated version on parchment, which could be given to all of the parties as a permanent legal record. Transactions such as wills, real estate deals, dowries, or anything else of which the contracting parties wished to have a permanent record, were engrossed on parchment. When these parchment copies survive, they are a boon to our documentation; I found those in the Archiepiscopal Archive especially valuable and have used them extensively in my studies. [3] Therefore, the abbreviated entries in the cartularies and the expanded parchment versions are the principal sources for the studies in the present volume.

Certainly the number of surviving registers is only a small part of all those that were produced, so we are dealing with only a fraction of an unknown quantity of the notarial writings of our period. Based upon the ratio of the population of Lucca and Pisa to the extant registers in the two cities, I have made an educated guess that ten percent of the notarial registers that were produced have survived.[4] From the Lucchese archives, Andreas Meyer has culled the names of some 80 notaries working in Lucca during 1220 and a different set of 200 names for 1273.[5] Accordingly, by the 1290s the number of Lucchese notaries would seem to have grown to about 240, since according to Lazzareschi some 24 of their books survive.[6] Moreover, Meyer's names and numbers reflect the dramatic demographic expansion of Tuscany as well as the growth of professionalism in the region during the thirteenth century.

Bias is another problem for the historian using the Lucchese notarial registers because they are biased in the sense that each of the notaries had his own particular clientele or geographical area, which gives each register its own

---

[3] See Duane Osheim, "The Episcopal Archive of Lucca in the Middle Ages," *Manuscripta*, 17 (1973), pp. 131–146.

[4] For a discussion of this problem, see Thomas W. Blomquist, "Trade and Commerce in Thirteenth-Century Lucca," unpublished doctoral dissertation, Dept. of History, University of Minnesota (Minneapolis, 1966), pp. 5–6, note 3.

[5] Meyer, *Felix et inclitus notarius*, pp. 321–334. See also his graph of the number of notaries through the thirteenth century on p. 328, as well as his list of notaries and judges through the same century on pp. 511–556.

[6] Lazzareschi, "L'Archivio dei notari" (n. 2, above).

distinctive character. For example, Ciabatto, the notary whose work is contained the in *LL* series of the Chapter Archive, focused his attention on the area of St. Martin's cathedral, where the money-changers plied their trade.[7] While Ciabatto certainly had customers other than the *campsores*, the changers were nevertheless his principal clients. Ciabatto's entries led me to write articles I and IX, in which I have offered some numerical, though only approximate, estimates. Another example of a specialized notary is found in the large cartulary of Bartholomo Fulcieri and his two sons. In over 500 folios devoted to the year 1284, it offers an extended example of documents dealing with the large-scale Lucchese international commercial-banking companies. This register enabled me to identify 22 companies and to recreate their membership for that year (article VIII, pp.172–178). Furthermore, using the 249 contracts in this register that deal with foreign exchange between Lucca and the fairs of Champagne, I was able to calculate the amounts of Lucchese and Provinois moneys that were traded in 1284 (article XI). My point is simply that each cartulary has is distinctive character, which must be taken into account when using its contents for quasi statistical analyses.

The only time in these articles that I have changed my mind about an interpretation concerns the relationship between the larger-scale mercantile-banking companies and their partners. In an early study, published in 1971, I had argued that during the 1270s, while many of these companies were growing, in order to supply capital or business skills, they took partners who were outsiders in the sense that they had no family or marriage ties to the original founding group (article VIII, p. 160). After working for many years with the merchant families and their companies – particularly the Riccardi, Guidiccioni, and Bettori – I came to believe, however, that the ties binding the companies were much stronger than I had once supposed. This new position (new at least for me) I summed up in article IV, in which I suggest that the companies were in fact closed to outsiders and that instead they were, in the economic and social field, something like the consorteria in the political arena. I would be the first to insist, however, that we need more research on this problem than has been done for Lucca and elsewhere.

Another issue deserving of comment is that of urban landlords in the countryside. Once again we are looking at the Ricciardi family, in this case two brothers who had interests in and around the village of San Pietro a Marciliano di Segromigno, about ten miles or so outside of Lucca (article V). Although Chris Wickham has done superb research on the problem of aristocratic investment in the Lucchese contado, he did not extend it beyond the twelfth century. Wickham does conclude, however, that the aristocracy was weak *vis-à-vis* the peasantry in

---

[7] For Ciabatto, see Meyer, "Der Luccheser Notar Ser Ciabatto" (n. 2, above).

the rural communes around Lucca.[8] This agrees with my study of the Ricciardi brothers in the period 1271–1300. I had concluded that those two brothers were the leading economic, social, and (probably) political powers in San Pietro, but that they nevertheless kept a low profile in the village. To be sure, they were the largest landowners in the region, but as far as I can see they did little but collect the rent. On occasion they financed the commune, but others did so as well. Their courtyard, or corte, was a place where the notary met many of his clients and where a good deal of business, both personal and public, must have been done. The Ricciardi were an impressive presence in San Pietro, but still they seemed content to allow their holdings pretty much to run themselves. Indeed this is just one case, although a most instructive one, and I would hope that in future similar cases will be investigated.

The articles dealing with money stem obviously from my work with banking. They were especially challenging. In one of them I endeavored to match up the private documents with the few public notices that we have in order to establish a new chronology for the appearance of the five Tuscan *grossi* (article XIV). Since there are very few indications of the intrinsic value of the local *denarii* upon which the groats were based, it is a tricky thing to put the numbers in place without forcing them. Nonetheless, I believe that I have come up with a plausible argument that Pisa was the first to mint the Tuscan groat, followed by Siena, Lucca, Florence, and Arezzo. Moreover, as their standard, all the Tuscan cities adopted Lucca's intrinsic value of its *denarius* in determining the worth of the groat. Subsequently, I have argued that the Florentines and Lucchese had continued the monetary reform of the *grossi* by striking gold coins that were to be the reality of the pound, or *libra*, in the money of account (article XVI).

One final word of explanation: the word "government" in the title of first group of articles refers only to article VII, which Duane Osheim and I cheerfully did together.

Lastly I would like to acknowledge the help, inspiration, and kindness that I have received over the years from so many people. I must go back to my high school days to remember Dr. John W. Wilhems who taught me Latin for five, sometimes grueling and sometimes exciting, years. While I was in graduate school at the History Department, the University of Minnesota, there were many particular friends: among them were Richard and Anne Place, John and Marian Gruenfelder, Thomas Kruger, John Christanson and John Barcroft. Among my faculty mentors were Stuart Hoyt, Ralph Giesey, god-father to my son, Tom B.

---

[8] Chris Wickham, *Communità e clientele nella Toscana del XII secolo: le origini del comune nella piano di Lucce* (Rome, 1995).

Jones, Karl Morrison, and, in the James Bell Ford rare book collection of the University library, Vsevolod Slessarev; all became very close. In the years since taking my Ph.D, David and Pat Herlihy, Robert Lopez, Archibald Lewis, Florence Edler de Roover, John Day, William Bowsky and Robert Reynolds afforded me special help and friendship. Two curators of the American Numismatic Society in New York, Joan Fagalie, also a god-parent to my son, and Alan Stahl, both became life long friends. In Lucca, in the State Archive, Dr. Domenico Corsi, the Director and the self-styled "Tiger of the Archive," whose temperament one always had to respect, ultimately became a helpful mentor. My thanks, as well, to Dr. Giorgio Tori, the current Director of the Archive, to Dr./Professor Antonio Romiti, the Director of the Istituto Storico Lucchese, to Professor Emilio Chistiani from Pisa and to Dom Giuseppe Ghilarducci in the Capitular Archive. Also in Lucca's archives in the late 1960's and 1970's, I met three Anglos who would become in their own rights distinguished scholars, Christine Meek, Duane Osheim and Michael Bratchel with whom I still stay in close touch lo these many years. In 1962, during my Fulbright year in Florence, I met my wife to be, Clelia Palmerio, her sister Maria and her family, and through them I met Mauro Senese, the novelist, opinion writer, adventurer and entrepreneur and his varied group including Dr./Professor Marissa Di Donato, Dr. Antonietta Passinese and Dr. Vilma Vetromile who adopted me into the wonderful ways of Tuscan life. Also in Florence, I met Richard Goldthwaite and Reinhold Mueller who each became to be very helpful. Closer to home, there was Professor Maureen Mazzoui, the co-editor with me of *The "Other Tuscany:" Essay in the History of Lucca, Pisa, Siena during the Thirteenth, Fourteenth and Fifteenth Centuries* and her husband Oliver Hoffron in Madison, Professors Jack McGovern and Jame Buundage in Milwaukee, and Professor Louis Robbert in St. Louis. In DeKalb, there is still George Freek, playwright and poet, and his wife Barbara; while at Northern Illinois University was William Beik and his wife Millie, James and Nancy Greenlie, James Peavler and then my close pal David Wagner and his wife Renie Adams with whom I have been through thick and thin. This volume would not have come into being without, Dr. John Smedley of Ashgate and Professor Richard, "Skip" Kay of the University of Kansas who suggested the book. Skip and I go way back to the earliest meetings of the *Midwest Medieval History Conference* and he has always been a true friend. He has read all of the articles, listed the slip-ups in the them, he has read through my additional writing for the volume and he has prepared the index. Special thanks to you Skip. Some of these people are now gone but I will remember each and every one of them for their help and friendship.

Taken as a whole, I believe that these articles have made an important contribution to our understanding of the social and economic history of Lucca, and hence of Tuscany and indeed western Europe as well. Looking back, I remember them as fun to do, and I hope that they will be profitable to my readers.

THOMAS W. BLOMQUIST

*Northern Illinois University*
*September 2004*

# I

# THE CASTRACANI FAMILY OF
# THIRTEENTH-CENTURY LUCCA*

The partnership controlled by the Castracani family ranked among the foremost international banking organizations of late thirteenth-century Lucca.[1] Members of the Castracani family first appear in the Lucchese notarial documents of about 1250 as money-changers, *campsores*. In succeeding generations they became increasingly identified with large-scale, international banking and finance. Thus, apart from the interest attaching to the family that produced Castruccio Castracani, lord of Lucca and would-be master of Tuscany, the history of the Castracani family's enterprises serves to illucidate the conduct, methods and organizations of early banking in Lucca, one of the major industrial and commercial centers of mediaeval Europe.

Among the mass of notarial documents housed in the *Archivio di Stato* and the *Archivio capitolare* of Lucca, there are numerous contracts relating to the activities of the members of the Castracani family through four generations spanning the last fifty years of the thirteenth century.[2] To be sure, the surviving notarial materials represent only a fraction of the original total, and with respect to the Castracani contain a regrettable lacuna for the decade 1274–1284, yet they are sufficient to permit a reconstruction of the main outlines of the family history from about 1250 until the family's expulsion from Lucca in January 1300.

The first of the Castracani family about whom we have direct evidence is one Castracane Rugerii whose name first appears in the sources in a document dated 1202.[3] On two other occasions, in 1218 and 1221, he again figures in the documents.[4] In July 1218 we find him handing over to Giovanni *domino et magistri templorum Rome et Tuscie et Sardinie* and *domino* Stefano, rector of the Church of St. Peter *de mansionis de Luca*, a piece of land with a house in Lucca valued at

* A portion of the research necessary for this study was accomplished in Lucca under a National Endowment for the Arts and Humanities Summer Stipend. The author wishes to express his gratitude to the Endowment.

[1] For the composition of various Lucchese partnerships active in the international field in 1284, see T. Blomquist, "Trade and Commerce in Thirteenth-Century Lucca," unpublished doctoral dissertation (Dept. of History, University of Minnesota, Minneapolis, 1966), pp. 147–158.

[2] E. Lazzareschi, "L'Archivio dei Notari della Repubblica lucchese," *Gli archivi italiani*, II (1915), 175–210 provides a catalogue of the cartularies in the state archive of Lucca. See also R. S. Lopez, "The Unexplored Wealth of the Notarial Archives of Pisa and Lucca," *Mélanges d'histoire de moyen-âge dédiés à la mémoire de Louis Halphen* (Paris, 1951), pp. 417–432. R. H. Bautier, "Notes sur les sources de l'histoire économique médiévale dans les archives italiennes," *Mélanges d'archeologie et d'histoire*, LVIII (1941–1946), 299–300 first pointed out the numerous references to the Castracani in the Lucchese notarial materials.

[3] G. V. Baroni, *Notizie geneologiche delle famiglie lucchesi*, Lucca, Biblioteca governativa, Ms 1102, fol. 7.

[4] *Archivio di Stato in Lucca, Santa Maria Corteorlandini*, 21 July 1218. The reference of 1221 is cited by F. P. Luiso, "Mercanti lucchesi dell' epoca di Dante," II, "Gli antenati di Castruccio Castracani," *Bollettino storico lucchese*, VIII (1936), 69.

£150 *pisanorum novarum* as partial payment for a debt of £200 Pisan owed the Templars. It was specifically added that Castracane was *insolvent* and unable to satisfy his debt in cash. In 1221 he was involved in a dispute with a former business associate, a dispute most probably linked to his insolvency of 1218.

Although leaving many important questions unanswered — Castracane's geographic and social origins, as well as the source of his original capital, for instance — our sources show this first authenticated member of the family engaged in business and possessed of urban property within the city of Lucca. Furthermore, the documents indicate that Castracane resided in *Curte Sancti Martini*, the area fronting on the Cathedral of San Martino, which was the traditional site of the money-changer's tables and thus suggest that he was at this early date a practicioner of the money-changer's art, the profession to which his descendents devoted themselves and which provided the basis of the family wealth.

By 1250 there were two existing branches of the family descending from this earliest Castracane.[5] His two sons, Pilio and Rugerio, were both to carve out successful careers as money-changers, and in turn their respective heirs succeeded in expanding their business operations into the field of international banking. However, the line established by Pilio Castracanis passed into relative obscurity when his son, Savarigio, died in 1284; leaving on his death a considerable fortune but no adult heirs.[6]

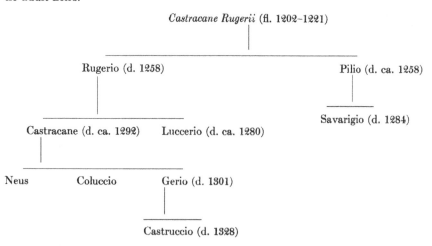

*Castracane Rugerii* (fl. 1202–1221)

Rugerio (d. 1258)                              Pilio (d. ca. 1258)

Castracane (d. ca. 1292)   Luccerio (d. ca. 1280)        Savarigio (d. 1284)

Neus        Coluccio        Gerio (d. 1301)

Castruccio (d. 1328)

---

[5] *Ibid.*, pp. 69–91 has shown that a second family bearing the patronymic Castracane had no connections with the line descending from Castracane Rugerii.

[6] Savarigio died between 17 August 1284 and 5 October 1284: see *Archivio di Stato in Lucca, Archivio dei Notari*, n. 14 (notary Nicolao Alamanni Clavari), fol. 64ᵛ, 17 August 1284, in which Johannes Morlani acts *procuratorio seu gestorio nomine pro Savariscio* and fol. 65, 5 October 1284 in which the same Johannes appears as *tutori filiorum et heredum quondam Savariscii Pilii Castracanis*. Johannes, himself a merchant-banker, as executor of the estate continued to invest in foreign exchange on behalf of his minor wards. Between 5 October 1284 and 11 April 1287 he purchased, through twenty separate transactions, a total of £3,900 Provinois payable at the fairs of

The other branch of the family consisted in the mid-thirteenth century of Rugerio Castracanis, his two sons, Castracane and Luccerio, and at least one daughter, Caracassa. Until 1258 and Rugerio's death, father and sons seem to have conducted their affairs jointly, but from then on Luccerio and Castracane appear to have followed separate business paths.[7] The former continued in the traditional, locally oriented business of the money-changer while the latter pursued his fortune through diversification and the exploitation of new business opportunities. Castracane's work culminated in the formation of the large-scale international banking organization of the last decades of the thirteenth century.

By the 1250's Rugerio and his sons had accumulated considerable real property, both urban and rural. The core of the Castracani holdings was in the urban quarter of San Martino, the area surrounding the Cathedral of Lucca, in which also were centered the activities of the Lucchese money-changers. In addition to owning at least six pieces of rental property in this part of the city in the 1250's, the family also maintained their residence there and kept stable facilities to support a flourishing livery business.[8] Interestingly, at least three of these properties were of recent acquisition, suggesting a consistent policy of investment in income-producing land. Other references to Castracani rentals of city property unfortunately do not provide precise information on the location of a given hold-

---

Champagne for the sum of £14,489 ls. 2d. disbursed in Lucca. These transactions are entered consecutively in the cartulary of the above cited Nicolao Alamanni Clavari, fols. 65–73ᵛ which suggests that only after completion of the transactions did Johannes have recourse to a notary. The notary no doubt made his redactions from the books supplied by Johannes.

In addition, the same cartulary, fol. 56, 19 January 1284 through fol. 62ᵛ, 1284 shows that Savarigio, perhaps sensing death, appointed various brokers (*sensalis*) to receive £4,900 Provinois due him at the fairs from Lucchese merchant bankers. For these credits he had paid in Lucca the total sum of £18,018 Lucchese.

Savarigio's career, beginning as he did as a second generation money-changer and expanding into the international field, offers a close parallel to that of Castracane Rugerii.

[7] See *Lucca, Archivo capitolare*, LL 31, fol. 147ᵛ, 24 Sept. 1258 for the first reference to *Castracane quondam Rugerii*.

[8] On the occasion of his marriage to Diamante Durassi in January 1250, Castracane handed over as *antefactum* title to a house and land valued at £50 Lucchese located *prope ecclesiam S. Stefani de curia Sancti Martini*: LL 24, fol. 70. In June 1250 Rugerio, Castracane and Luccerio bought a house, also near the church of San Stefano, in which they had been living (*in qua consueti sunt habitare*) for £4 annual rental: LL 25, fol. 105ᵛ. Rugerio and Castracane rented another house in April 1252 for £5 annual rental but reserved the use of the attached stable: LL 27, fol. 110. A rental contract dated 1252 makes reference to the letting of a house situated in San Martino and adjacent to *terre et domui Rugerii Castracanis et filiorum que quondam fuit Ugolini Rasine*: LL 27, fol. 22. In June 1257 Rugerio, on behalf of himself and his sons, added to the family holdings in San Martino through the purchase of a house from Ubaldo Cipolette which he then rented to the former owner for £3 per year: LL 31, fol. 21. In 1266 Rugerio and Luccerio leased a house in San Martino, acquired earlier from the sons of Carratelle, for an annual rental of £7 10s.: LL 33, fol. 72.

The information, though fragmentary, relating to the real estate dealings of the Castracani suggests that urban rents were rising sharply in the 1260's. In October 1270 for example, Castracane rented a house purchased from the sons of Aldibrandini under a four year lease for £8 per annum: LL 36, fol. 14.

ing, and it is therefore impossible to learn if we are dealing with a newly acquired property or with a new lease on one of the properties already mentioned.[9] In any event, the evidence is sufficient to demonstrate the tendency, common to mediaeval businessmen, to invest heavily in real estate.

The Castracani dealings in real property were not confined to the city alone. In the period covered by our documents they invested a significant amount of capital in rural as well as urban land. These rural holdings were geographically scattered and were composed both of farmland near Lucca and pasturage in the mountains. Luccerio, for example, in 1258 purchased a property from his cousin Savarigio Pilii Castracanis located in the western plain *ultra de Lunata*; he also held in his name land in *Colle Allpiane* which judging from the place name was situated somewhere in the lower Garfagnana.[10] And in the same year, 1258, Coluccio also gave three pieces of land located in Conpito on the plain to the Southwest of Lucca in perpetual lease while in 1270 he rented a house which he owned in Segromigno near the city.[11] Lands, held in the name of Castracane Rugerii, were among those in the contado near the bridge of San Pietro, devastated in 1269 by the Pisans.[12]

This list of rural properties would undoubtedly be longer if our sources of information were complete. The involvement of the Castracani in the *contado* is further illustrated by the references to their dealings in livestock. The contracts indicate a modest but regular investment in the husbandry of swine, goats and mules as well as a major capital outlay to support the livery business of the family.[13] The Castracani maintained at least one stable within the city from which they trafficked in the sale and rental of horses both riding animals and horses trained for war.[14] Some of these animals were no doubt quartered on the Castracani lands in the countryside while others were maintained through temporary partnership arrangements (*soccida*) with local peasants before they were brought to the city for sale.

In addition to land and livestock, from the late 1250's, Castracane Rugerii was actively engaged in iron mining, another sector of the rural economy. In 1255 and

---

[9] LL 26, fol. 103, 7 Aug. 1251; LL 32, fol. 71ᵛ, 26 Nov. 1259.

[10] LL 31, fol. 155, 13 Nov. 1258; LL 32, fol. 12ᵛ, 3 Feb. 1259. For the historical geography of Lucca and environs, see E. Repetti, *Dizionario geografico fisico storico della Toscana*, 6 vols. (Florence, 1833–1846).

[11] LL 31, fol. 137, 13 Aug. 1258; LL 36, fol. 3ᵛ, 11 July 1270. The latter house originally rented for £5 per year but in 1271 the rent increased to £6: LL 36, fol. 25ᵛ.

[12] LL 36, vol. 13ᵛ, 11 Oct. 1270: The commune assigned restitution amounting to 24s. in wood delivered to Castracane's home in Lucca *pro guasto et dampno facto et illato per pisanos apud pontem S. Petri*.

[13] LL 27, fol. 99, 7 May 1252; LL 28, fol. 24ᵛ, 4 Sept. 1253; LL 30, fol. 13, 6 Oct. 1256; LL 31, fol. 35ᵛ, 11 Aug. 1257; LL 31, fol. 161, 29 Dec. 1258; LL 32, fol. 50, 18 July 1259; LL 32, fol. 82ᵛ, 19 Jan. 1260; LL 32, fol. 102, 22 April 1260; LL 33, fol. 122ᵛ, 24 Oct. 1268; LL 33, fol. 134ᵛ, 11 Jan. 1269.

[14] For the sale of horses, see LL 30, fol. 80, 26 Sept. 1256; LL 33, fol. 116ᵛ, 19 Sept. 1268. See LL 32, fol. 51ᵛ, 23 July 1259; LL 32, fol. 109, 2 June 1260; LL 33, fol. 123, 24 Oct. 1284; LL 36, fol. 7, 16 Aug. 1270; LL 36, fol. 12, 25 Sept. 1270, for rentals of horses. On 17 May 1267 Luccerio rented out an *equus de armis* for a period of five and one-half months at a fee of £8: LL 23, fol. 90. In Feb. 1250 Castracane purchased a horse for a price of £29 6s.: LL 25, fol. 119ᵛ.

again in 1258 he entered into agreements with miners for the extraction of ore from a vein in Massa Pisana in which he held a one-fifth interest.[15] Iron mining continued as a major involvement of Castracane over the years. In 1287 and 1288 he leased substantial mineral rights in Versilia and Lunigiana.[16] It would seem that Castracane was acting on his own in these transactions. In 1297 his son Gerio was forced to defend his rights over these mineral leases against the claims of the Lucchese Commune with no mention made in the proceedings of any right held by Luccerio's heirs.[17]

The diverse economic interests in the *contado* of the urbanized Castracani demonstrate the close economic and social connections between town and country in the communal period. We cannot judge with certainty, on the basis of the surviving documents, what proportion of the total Castracani business activity dealt with real estate, animal husbandry, livery or mining. It would appear, however, that these interests were secondary to their financial and, later, commercial ventures. Of the total surviving notarial contracts relating to members of the Castracani family from the period 1250–1274, the overwhelming majority reflect a commitment to finance and related affairs. Whether acting jointly or individually, the Castracani were first and foremost money-changers, *campsores*, which in Lucca as elsewhere meant that they were bankers. As *campsores* they accepted deposits, made credit available in the form of loans, and settled accounts by in-bank transfer of clients' credits and liabilities. And it was success as a money-changer which provided Castracane Rugerii with the resources and no doubt the motivation to aggrandize his operations in the last quarter of the thirteenth century.

### I

The art of the money-changer was a venerable one in Lucca. The earliest evidence for the existence of a gild in mediaeval Lucca is the oath of the money-changers and dealers in spices (*speciarii*) dated 1111, enscribed on the portico of the Cathedral of San Martino where it can still be viewed today.[18] It was here, in the court of the Cathedral, that the early changers and dealers in spices set up their tables and stalls, and here was the physical heart of the Castracani business.

The individual *campsor* either owned or leased the ground, the table (*tabula, mensula*) and chair (*sedia*) from which he worked. In November 1252 Rugerio, Castracane and Luccerio jointly purchased a *tabula* and ground from one Bonifatio Ubertelli Baiori for the price of £15. This location had been in the possession of Bonifatio's ancestors for three generations, since 1172 when his grandfather

[15] LL 30, fol. 5, 4 April 1255; LL 31, fol. 108ᵛ, 15 April 1258. The vein was located *de monte montiolo Masse Pisane*.

[16] G. Sforza, "Castruccio Castracani degli Antelminelli e gli altri lucchesi di parte bianca in esilio," *Memorie della Accademia delle Scienze di Torino*, ser. 2, XLII (1892), 53.

[17] See *ibid.*, pp. 84–88, for the documents relative to Rugerio's defense before the priors *Soceitatum armorum lucani populi* in 1297 and 1298.

[18] E. Lazzareschi, "Fonti d'archivio per lo studio delle corporazioni artigiane di Lucca," *Bollettino storico lucchese*, IX (1937), 78. The text of the oath is translated in R. S. Lopez and I. W. Raymond, *Medieval Trade in the Mediterranean World* (New York and London, 1961), p. 418.

Baioro bought it from Rolando Passavantis.[19] Whether this purchase marks the entrance of the Castracani into the field of banking we cannot tell with certainty; only in the year 1254 did they begin to style themselves *campsores* with any frequency.

Near the Castracani table and next to the portico of the cathedral was the table belonging to Gerardo Arzuri which two years later, in 1254, was leased for 10 s. to the future partner of the Castracani, Guido Perfectucii.[20] Guido's *tabula* in turn adjoined that of Pilio Castracanis, brother of Rugerio.[21] The tables of the Castracani and their associates thus formed a little island where common affairs could be discussed and transactions concluded with a minimum of inconvenience.

In addition to the outdoor *tabula* at which much of their business was conducted, the Castracani also leased a shop, *apotheca*, from the Cathedral Chapter.[22] There no doubt they kept their supplies of cash, account books, and other items needed for the conduct of their business. The shop was also located in the cathedral square and therefore was conveniently close to the family *tabula* as well as the Castracani residence.

As money-changers the Castracani continued the original function of the profession, the on-the-spot exchange of one currency for an equivalent sum in another. This aspect of their business must, however, remain hidden from us, since it was carried on over-the-counter and consequently did not require the intervention of a notary. On the other hand, we have an abundance of contracts illustrating the credit aspects of the money-changers' art; that is, their banking function.

Unfortunately, the notarial contracts reveal little about the organization and coordination of the various Castracani enterprises. It is possible, however, to draw some tentative conclusions from our evidence. Until 1258 and Rugerio's death, the basis of the Castracani business structure was the family, and the family as a business organization functioned approximately like a holding company. The *tabula*, for example, was owned jointly by Rugerio, Castracane and Luccerio, but in order to bring about greater flexibility, both in terms of capital and manpower, they jointly and individually formed subsidiary partnerships with outsiders. However, towards the end of his life Rugerio seems to have turned active management over to his two sons. Thus, from October 1254 through 1256, the two Castracani brothers, Castracane and Luccerio, formed in succession three partnership arrangements for the practice of the *ars cambii* with the money-

---

[19] LL 27, fol. 18ᵛ, 10 Nov. 1252: *et qui locus obvenit quondam Baioro quondam Portachie ex compera inde facta a quondam Rolando quondam Passavantis ut apparet per cartam . . . cuius anni sunt MCLXXII.* The Passavante family were apparently considered of noble origin and members were always styled *dominus* in the sources.

[20] LL 28, fol. 150ᵛ, 24 Oct. 1254.

[21] *Loc. cit.,* . . . *qui est contra locum et tabulam quondam Pilii Castracanis.* The space purchased by the Castracani was separated from that of Gerardo Azuri by an isle: see the above cited LL 27, fol. 18ᵛ (note 19).

[22] LL 31, fol. 127, 13 July 1258; a shop leased in San Martino was described *ad latus apothece quam tenet Castracane a dicto capitulo . . . .*

changer Guido Perfectucii.[23] To the various partnerships Guido brought successively the capital sums of £350 in 1254, £400 in 1255 and £300 in 1256, a total
of £1050. The Castracani collectively contributed a total of £1840: £600 in 1254,
£600 in 1255 and £640 in 1256. These were short-term agreements, the first to
last only three and one-half months and the other two one year each. At the
termination of each contract the profits and losses were determined and divided
equally among the three principals.

1256 marks the apparent end of Guido Perfectucii's association with the Castracani. His place was taken by his brother Genovese, also a money-changer, who
until the 1270's occasionally cooperated with the Castracani in a series of short-
term partnerships devoted to the *ars cambii*. In the first of these, organized in
August 1257 for a period of six months, Castracane contributed £600, Genovese
£300 and Luccerio £200.[24] However, in a subsequent document the latter, Luccerio, stipulated that in fact he had brought nothing to the partnership. Nevertheless, he seems to have continued as a partner; perhaps compensating with his
labor for the failure to contribute capital into the enterprise.[25] Here, also, the
profits were divided equally among the partners.

Again in the following year another partnership was formed by the same parties for a period of six months, with the total capitalization set at £1200.[26] In this
case, however, profit and loss were shared according to the capital contributed.
Thus, Genovese received 5/12 on his £500 investment, Castracane 1/3 for his
£400 and Luccerio 1/4 for £300. Significantly, it seems that in addition to being
a distinct bookkeeping venture, this partnership also maintained its own table in
the money-changer's area where transactions were developed *apud mensulam
ipsorum*.[27] At the time that these subsidiary partnerships were in effect Castracane and Luccerio were also active in the operation of the family *tabula* as well
as in other ventures entered into individually.

We would, of course, be aided immeasurably if one or another set of books belonging to the *tabula* or to either of the brothers were available to shed light upon
the way in which these various enterprises were coordinated. However, the
sources clearly indicate that following Rugerio's death Castracane and Luccerio
struck out separately on their own. No contract dated after 1258 indicates that
they were acting jointly, and each seems to have maintained and managed his
own money-changing table. Furthermore, by 1271 we learn that both Castracane
and Luccerio were conducting at least a portion of their respective businesses
from separate counting houses.[28] It seems that of the two, Castracane enjoyed

---

[23] LL 28, fol. 146; 15 Oct. 1254; LL 30, fol. 93, 22 Oct. 1255; LL 30, fol. 107ᵛ, 3 Aug. 1256.

[24] LL 31, fol. 36, 8 Aug. 1257.

[25] LL 31, fol. 36, 23 Nov. 1257. Compensation for labor through an increased share in the profits
was a common feature of Lucchese partnership: see T. Blomquist, "Trade and Commerce in Thirteenth-Century Lucca," pp. 9–36. For numerous later examples drawn from the records of the Medici
bank, see R. de Roover, *The Rise and Decline of the Medici Bank, 1397–1494* (New York, 1966).

[26] LL 31, fol. 159, 21 Nov. 1258.

[27] *Ibid.: Actum Luce apud mensulam ipsorum quam habent in curia S. Martini ante ecclesiam.*

[28] Luccerio transacted business in *apotheca tabule ipsius Lucerii, apud apothecam suam cambii*:
LL 36, fol. 29ᵛ, 18 July 1271 and LL 36, fol. 27ᵛ, 10 Feb. 1271. Castracane, on the other hand worked

the greater success in their separate activities. Although Luccerio continued to engage in business in the 1270's, it was Castracane who had the vision to diversify and expand his operations; it was he who headed the mercantile-banking organization of the 1280's. Luccerio apparently contented himself with managing his *tabula* and dealing in land. In short, Luccerio turned his back upon the opportunities to expand and increasingly the business history of the Castracani family must focus upon the career of Castracane Rugerii.

After 1258 Castracane continued intermittently the relationship with Genovese Perfectucii. In 1259 the two men formed a partnership for the business of exchange with a capitalization of £1200;[29] and over the next decade they continued to act jointly in various ventures involving *ars cambii*.

In the early 1260's Castracane and Genovese became associated with a third *campsor*, one Baroccho Barocchi, who apparently had direct connections with the minting of money.[30] We cannot determine whether the Castracani were involved in the operation of the Lucchese mint, but the sources do show that as money-changers they were concerned with the flow of bullion.[31] In 1259 Castracane and six partners, two from Bergamo, financed the opening of a silver mine (*argentaria*) in the nearby Val d'Lima.[32] Some of this metal no doubt found its way to the mint but a portion, as well as gold and silver from other sources, was worked into leaves under Castracane's direction by smiths tied to him through exclusive contracts.[33] Luccerio, although apparently not linked by contract to

---

from *domo ubi moratur ad cambium, domo curie S. Martini in qua moratur ad tabulam, in domo campanilis Luce ubi detini* (sic) *cambium*: LL 36, fol. 41ᵛ, 17 Oct. 1271; LL 36, fol. 21, 8 Jan. 1271; LL 36, fol. 33, 1 June 1271.

[29] LL 32, fol. 42ᵛ, 4 June 1259. The contract has been published in R. S. Lopez, "The Unexplored Wealth of the Notarial Archives of Pisa and Lucca," p. 428 and translated in R. S. Lopez and I. W. Raymond, *Medieval Trade in the Mediterranean World*, pp. 195–96.

[30] On 3 Oct. 1266 Baroccho stipulated to Castracane, styled *socius corporalis*, that he had only £1200 in partnership with Castracane and Genovese rather than the larger sum indicated in the original notarial contract of partnership: LL 33, fol. 66. In 1259 Baroccho, in partnership with Bonaguido Gerardini, hired a moneyor to cut dies for *grossi*, *piccoli* and gold coins which were to be struck in Perugia: see E. Lazzareschi, "Fonti d'archivio per lo studio delle corporazioni artigiane di Lucca," p. 141. Judging from his will, LL 33, fol. 66ᵛ, dated 14 October 1266, Baroccho was a moderately wealthy man able to provide a total of £200 to a variety of religious and charitable institutions and £250 as future dowry for his daughter when and if she married. Castracane Rugerii was designated one of the guardians of Baroccho's children.

[31] In Genoa, by way of comparison, R. S. Lopez, *La Prima crisi della banca di Genova (1250–1259)* (Milan, 1956), pp. 27–29 has shown that the money-changers (*cambiatori*) at an early date controlled the Genoese mint. North of the Alps, too, the changers were the main purveyors of the mint: see R. de Roover, *Money, Banking and Credit in Mediaeval Bruges* (Cambridge, Mass., 1948), pp. 233–239.

[32] LL 32, fol. 78, 26 Dec. 1259.

[33] On 17 April 1259 Ugolino Guilielmi *magistri* promised that he would work all gold and silver with which Castracane provided him. He was to be paid at a rate of 7s. 6d. for each pound of silver: LL 32, fol. 32ᵛ. In August 1266 Castracane, Genovese and Baroccho formed a partnership with the gold beater Rubertino Bonaventure in which the latter was obligated to work into *foliis* all silver delivered to him by his partners at a salary of 7s. per *libra*. For working gold, Rubertino received compensation of 16d. for an ounce of twenty carats, 12d. for an ounce of twenty to twenty-three carats and for an ounce of more than twenty-three carats 8d. For this arrangement, see LL 33, fol. 16ᵛ.

any one smith, also traded extensively in bullion and wrought silver.[34] Evidently dealings in precious metals constituted a mainstay of the money-changer's business.

But the principal function of the mid-thirteenth century Lucchese money-changer was banking. We find the Castracani raising capital for their *tabula*, or more accurately *tabule*, by accepting funds in deposit. The terminology of the contracts varied; and we find *depositum seu accomandiscia, accomandiscia seu prestantia, mutuum seu prestantia* used indiscriminately to describe both demand or time deposits. The distinction was embodied within the contract. Time deposits specified repayment after a period which tended to vary between one month and a year, with six months the usual term of the time deposit. Demand deposits were payable upon request of the client, although a variant form resembling the modern continental *depôts à préavis* was also employed.[35]

The sums received in deposit by the Castracani were relatively larger than the loans which they made. Their deposits varied in amount from £20 to £300, but averaged £96, 6s. 6d. per individual deposit on the thirty-seven contracts surviving intermittently from the years 1254 through 1274; a significant figure, suggesting that depositors were drawn from the more affluent elements of society.[36] And indeed an examination of the list of depositors turns up the names of the noble Passavanti family;[37] various canons of the Cathedral Chapter;[38] Bartolommeo, a judge;[39] Alessio, son of *Dominus Antellus*;[40] *Dominus Albertinus*, who deposited a part of his minor ward's inheritance with Castracane;[41] and Guido, son of the late *Dominus Rubertus de Fucecchio*.[42] We also find a number of artisans, a stone-mason and a baker, as well as a notary represented among the creditors of the Castracani.[43] If this list is representative, it would seem that the capital channeled into the economy through the money-changers' banks in Lucca derived principally

---

[34] For Luccerio's sales of wrought gold and silver, see LL 33, fol. 122ᵛ, 23 Oct. 1268 (two ounces gold leaves, ten ounces silver in leaves); LL 36, fol. 31, 17 April 1271 (twelve ounces silver in leaves); LL 36, fol. 42, 23 Oct. 1271 (six ounces silver in leaves); LL 36, fol. 46, 17 Nov. 1271 (six ounces silver in leaves); LL 36, fol. 46, 17 Nov. 1271 (six ounces silver *battorati*). On 30 Oct. 1270 Luccerio bought six ounces of worked silver: LL 36, fol. 16ᵛ.

[35] For an example of demand deposit, see LL 36, fol. 3, 12 May 1270 in which Castracane promised payment *quandocumque sibi* (the depositor) *placuerit et ad suam requisitionem*. For *depôt à préavis*, see LL 36, fol. 39ᵛ, 8 Sept. 1271 in which repayment was to be made *a requisitione quam inde fuerit per se* (the depositor) *vel suum certum nuntium ad XV dies* . . .

[36] In order to construct a more complete series, contracts relating to both Luccerio and Castracane have been averaged together despite their separate operations after 1258. See LL 28, 30, 31, 32, 33, 34, 36 *passim*.

[37] LL 30, fol. 53, 8 March 1256; LL 31, fol. 115ᵛ, 16 May 1258; LL 32, fol. 53ᵛ, 31 July 1259; LL 32, fol. 123ᵛ, 8 Feb. 1260; LL 36, fol. 3ᵛ, June 1270.

[38] LL 36, fol. 3, 12 May 1270; LL 36, fol. 9, 10 Sept. 1270; LL 36, fol. 28ᵛ, 7 March 1271.

[39] LL 31, fol. 118ᵛ, 6 March 1258.

[40] LL 31, fol. 131, 17 July 1258.

[41] LL 32, fol. 71ᵛ, 28 Nov. 1259.

[42] LL 36, fol. 16ᵛ, 8 Nov. 1270.

[43] LL 36, fol. 39ᵛ, 8 Sept. 1271; *Jacobus quondam Alberegni de Como magister petrarum*: LL 33, fol. 19, 4 Oct. 1265; *Bonamicus pistor quondam Dolcimanni*: LL 33, 127ᵛ, 4 Dec. 1268; *Fara notarius quondam Paganelli Beccabove*.

from the upper and middle elements of society, and that the banks did not bring
together and direct into commerce to any significant degree the savings of the
more humble classes.

In addition to accepting deposits, the money-changers' *tabule* also performed a
clearing function by permitting clients' debtors to make payment in bank, crediting the amounts paid into the client's account. By way of example, we may cite a
contract of 1256 whereby Castracane Rugerii stipulated to the notary Savarigio
Ubaldi Rainerii that he, Castracane, had received on behalf of the notary £84
from the *sindicus* of Controne; £30 from the Commune of Lucca; £21 from
Bonaccorso de Batone; and £30, as partial payment of £100 due from Custor
Battosi, and that he, Castracane, was as a result in the debt of Savarigio for the
total of these sums amounting to £165.[44] The money-changers also debited their
clients' accounts as they settled debts on their behalf: for example, the obligation
of £140 which *Dominus Guilielmus*, canon of the Cathedral Chapter, acknowledged to Castracane for disbursements made on the former's behalf for expenses
connected with the hospital of the Chapter and debts owed to the Commune.[45]
Thus, the Castracani acted as fiscal agents for their clients — the above canon
was a frequent depositor — and it is likely, although we can offer no direct proof
from our sources, that they created credit by permitting clients to overdraw their
accounts.

A sizable proportion of the money-changer's working capital was deployed in
the form of short-term loans. If, as we have seen, depositors were from the upper
and middle social level, the borrowers, predictably, were mainly from the oppo-
site end of the social scale — primarily artisans and rural peasants. Basically,
there were two forms of loans granted by the Castracani, the simple unsecured
loan (*mutuum*) and loans disguised as purchase-sale made against the future delivery of agricultural produce. Of the former, unsecured loans, eighty-one contracts involving the Castracani have survived for the period 1250–1274, indicating
a total disbursement of £1830 4s.; or an average amount per loan of £22 12s.[46]
On the other hand, the thirteen surviving contracts involving future delivery of
crops averaged a mere £2 6s. 9d. per transaction.[47] Although contractually set up
as purchase-sale there is no indication that the Castracani trafficked directly in
grain or wine and it is therefore reasonable to assume that in Lucca as elsewhere
these represent simply a device to lend funds in the countryside at excessive rates
of interest.[48]

---

[44] LL 30, fol. 57, 7 May 1256.

[45] LL 36, fol. 6, 15 Aug. 1270.

[46] As with the deposit contracts, loans involving both Luccerio and Castracane have been averaged
together. See LL 28, 30, 31, 32, 33, 34, 36, *passim.*

[47] LL 28, fol. 79, 28 March 1254; LL 28, fol. 88ᵛ, 22 April, 1254; LL 28, fol. 90, 23 April 1254; LL
30, fol. 1, 24 Dec. 1254; LL 30, fol. 21ᵛ, 10 June 1255; LL 30, fol. 31ᵛ, 12 Feb. 1256; LL 30, fol. 31ᵛ
12 Feb. 1256 (no. 2); LL 32, fol. 12, 2 Jan. 1259; LL 32, fol. 37, 28 April 1259; LL 32, fol. 93ᵛ, 29
March 1260; LL 33, fol. 119, 14 July 1268; LL 36, fol. 27ᵛ, 18 Feb. 1271; LL 36, fol. 43ᵛ, 14 Nov. 1271.

[48] In the Florentine contado such loans brought 30% interest: D. Herlihy, "Santa Maria Impruneta: A Rural Commune in the Late Middle Ages," N. Rubinstein, ed., *Florentine Studies* (Evanston, Illinois, 1968), p. 262.

The money-changers were, however, properly circumspect concerning references to interest charges. Nowhere in the Lucchese materials is there mention of interest, and each *mutuum* contract explicitly stated that the borrower was obligated to return only the principal sum. But interest was certainly extracted at some point in the transaction. The most common means of doing this, if we may judge from Pisan sources, were by the add-on and discount types of lending whereby the borrower acknowledged a debt larger than the sum actually received in loan;[49] a practice which required the collusion of the notary and witnesses who in the formulae of the contract expressly stated that they were present and had in fact seen the sum in question change hands.[50] This wholesale and routine departure in Lucca from the usury doctrine of the church testifies to the ineffectiveness of these tenets in the market place.[51] There is no evidence that the Castracani or any of their colleagues in the money-changing guild were cited for violating the usury canons. We must conclude, therefore, that there was a conventional interest charge which was considered licit. In Genoa, as Professor Lopez has pointed out, bankers paid 10% on deposits and charged 20% on loans without running afoul of the authorities while in San Gimignano 20% interest charges were allowed by the communal statutes.[52] What the conventional charge was in Lucca we do not know, but it would seem that only a flagrant instance of gouging was likely to bring a money-lender into court.

## II

As we have seen, during the 1250's the Castracani engaged as a family in a variety of business enterprises, ranging from real estate to the joint operation of

[49] The *Archivio di Stato in Pisa, Sezione miscellanea, manoscritti* n. 58, kindly called to the author's attention by Dr Gero Dolezalek, preserves testimony taken in two usury suits heard before the Archbishops court in 1230. In the first the plaintiff stated that the lender had forced him to appear before a notary and swear that he had borrowed £26 when in fact he had received but £20, a return to the lender of 30%: *Archivio di Stato in Pisa: Sezione miscellanea, manoscritti*, n. 58; fol. 123ᵛ–124ᵛ. In the second case, the borrower claimed that he was forced to stipulate that he had received £7 in order to borrow £4: *ibid.*, fols. 100ᵛ–101. For the evidence from Pistoia, see A. Sapori, "L'Usura nel Dugento a Pistoia," *Studi di storia economica, secoli XIII-XIV-XV* (3rd ed., Florence, n.d.), I, 181–189.

[50] . . . *Coram me notario et testibus infrascriptis.*

[51] The essence of the Church's view of usury was that any return on a loan, *mutuum*, larger than the principal was usury. Numerous qualifications developed, to be sure, but profit on a *mutuum* remained tainted. Yet, the Lucchese evidence shows not only professional money-lenders such as the changers but also individuals from a broad cross-section of Lucchese society engaged in lending through the granting of *mutua* to their fellow-citizens. The point deserves fuller development, but for a similar situation in San Gimignano see E. Fiume, "L'Attivita usuraria dei mercanti sangimignanesi nell' età communale," *Archivio storico italiano*, CXIX (1961), 145–162, and the same author's *Storia economica e sociale di San Gimignano* (Florence, 1961), pp. 86–88. On the medieval ecclesiastical doctrine of usury, see B. Nelson, *The Idea of Usury* (Princeton, 1949), J. Noonan, *The Scholastic Analysis of Usury* (Cambridge, Mass., 1957), and the recent article of R. de Roover, "The Scholastics, Usury and Foreign Exchange," *Business History Review*, XLI (1967), 255–271.

[52] R. S. Lopez, *La Prima crisi della banca di Genova (1250–1259)*, pp. 34–35; E. Fiume, *Storia economica e sociale di San Gimignano*, p. 87, n. 286.

the banker's *tabula*. Following the death of Rugerio, however, Castracane and Luccerio apparently sorted out their affairs. Luccerio continued to devote himself to the art of the *campsor*, while Castracane began to widen and diversify his business activities.

In 1271 Castracane entered into his last partnership devoted exclusively to local exchange.[53] Again he allied himself with Genovese Perfectucii, but this time with a novel and significant modification, the participation of an outside investor who was neither of the immediate family nor a money-changer. The contract establishing this new arrangement describes Castracane and Genovese as *socii corporales*. We may understand this term to mean that they were active members of the partnership whose combined investment constituted the partnership capital, or *corpo*. Castracane contributed £2,000 to the venture, and Genovese brought £1,800. However, it was further stipulated that of Genovese's £1,800, £1,050 belonged to one Jacobo Sciaventis *de Burgo*. The partnership was to last a year and upon its termination the investor, Jacobo, was to receive 3/4 of the profit assigned pro rata on the £1,800 while Genovese gained the remaining 1/4. The silent partner, then, earned 3/8 of the total profits on his investment of slightly more than 1/4 of the total capital.

The inclusion of a passive partner from outside the family or the circle of professional money-changers as well as the disproportionate share of the profits accruing to the investor suggest the capital demands of a growing and expanding economy. The climate of economic growth afforded novel opportunities for the business man able to attract and organize capital. And during this period Castracene was indeed exploiting new investment possibilities. In 1270 he and Genovese financed, as investing partners, three Lucchese spice dealers in an African venture.[54] Under the terms of the agreement, two of the *speciarii* were to take up residence for five years in Carthage and Tunis, respectively, in order to superintend the buying and exporting of goods to the third *speciarius* who remained in Lucca to handle local distribution.

In the same year, Castracane and his partner, Genovese, also invested £100 with a travelling Lucchese merchant departing on a trip *super mare et in terra*,[55] and in 1271 Castracane placed merchandise valued at £65 in *commenda* with another Lucchese undertaking a voyage to Sicily.[56] Simultaneously, and by contrast, Luccerio was in partnership with a group of merchants engaged in general trade in Lucca.[57] Castracane Rugerii was evidently seeking new profit opportunities, and with diversification evolved a larger, more stable and versatile business organization.

[53] LL 36, fol. 37, 17 Aug. 1271.

[54] LL 36, fol. 13, 9 Oct. 1270.

[55] LL 36, fol. 7, 19 Aug. 1270. The travelling partner was to remain abroad for one year and upon termination of the agreement was to receive two-thirds of the profits.

[56] LL 36, fol. 42v, 22 Oct. 1271.

[57] LL 36, fol. 22v, 27 Jan. 1271: *Perfectus Sandonis et Sandone Arrigi et Bonacursus quondam Bonaiuncte Ronchi et Luccerius Castracane, mercatores et campsor . . . receperunt in compagnia et societate . . . a Rainone de Gallo quondam item Rainonis libras nonaginta . . . ad risicum et fortunam ipsorum . . . cum quibus possint lucrari Luce et eorum utilitatem facere. . . .*

Our documentation for the history of the Castracani resumes after a decade interruption with the cartulary of the notaries Bartolommeo, Tegrimo, and Fulcerio Fulcieri of the year 1284.[58] The Fulcieri, father and sons, catered extensively to the large-scale mercantile-banking community of Lucca. Their cartulary is consequently a mine of contracts relating to long-range trade and finance as well as the wills, land conveyances and other more personal transactions drawn up by prominent merchant bankers and members of their families.[59] Figuring often among the mercantile element engaged in international commerce and finance were Castracane Rugerii and his associates in an expanded business organization devoted to traffic in international banking.

Structurally the partnership through which the Castracani carried on their international operations remained essentially a family affair. In 1284 it consisted of at least seven partners; five of whom, Castracane, his three sons Gerio, Neo, Coluccio, and his brother-in-law, Durasso Durassi, were members of the immediate family.[60] But two seeming outsiders, Arriguccio Bocchadivacche and Buiamonte Turchii, had been added, the latter representing the partnership on a permanent basis at the Champagne Fairs.[61] Thus, by 1284, if not earlier, the small, locally oriented partnership had given way to an enlarged organization, including outsiders as partners, with at least one agent stationed abroad, and endowed with greatly increased capital resources.

Moreover, the nature of the Castracani business turned from the small short-term loans of the *tabula* to an almost exclusive concern with foreign exchange. It is instructive furthermore to note that by 1284 Castracane had dropped the appellation *campsor* in favor of *mercator et negotiator*, while no evidence survives to indicate that he continued to practice the money-changer's art. The transition from *campsor* to international banker was seemingly complete.

### III

It has been observed that mediaeval banking developed in close connection with the rise of international money-markets and the techniques of foreign exchange.[62] However, foreign exchange was in turn the product of long-range commerce and the attendent necessity of moving money and credit from place to place in order to facilitate payments for merchandise. Lucchese merchants as early as the turn of the twelfth century were skilled in the financing of commerce by recourse to foreign exchange.

---

[58] *Archivio di Stato in Lucca, Archivio dei notari, n. 15* (notaries Bartolommeo Fulcieri, Tegrimo Fulcieri, Fulciero Fulcieri).

[59] See T. Blomquist, "Trade and Commerce in Thirteenth-Century Lucca," pp. 148–49 for a description of the contents of this cartulary.

[60] For the partners of the Castracane organization, *ibid.*, p. 153.

[61] Buiamonte was named in each exchange contract of the year 1284 as receiver for the Castracane at the fairs. Permanent representation should be understood in the sense of continuous representation at the fairs and not the establishment of permanent branches.

[62] R. de Roover, *L'Evolution de la lettre de change* (Paris, 1953), pp. 24–25 notes the close connection between expanding commerce and the development of the exchange transaction.

Lucca, as an industrial center, was particularly dependent upon Genoa as port of entry for raw silk and dye stuffs to feed her burgeoning silk industry.[63] In order to expedite this traffic a group of Lucchese permanently resident in Genoa made it their business to advance Genoese funds to their co-nationals visiting Genoa to secure silk, dyes and other wares for export to their city. In return the visiting merchant handed over a notarial instrument in which he stipulated repayment of the Genoese funds in Lucca, usually within two or three weeks.[64] Thus developed a regular means to furnish the capital needs of merchants importing merchandise from Genoa.

Lucchese merchants were also in early and frequent contact, through the fairs of Champagne, with Northern Europe. In 1153 Genoa granted a reduction in the transit tolls upon their merchandise to Lucchese merchants passing through Genoese territory to and from the Champagne fairs.[65] On the northern journey Lucchese silks no doubt made up the bulk of the cargo, while the terms of the treaty specifically mention various qualities of northern cloth; these must have constituted the usual wares on the return leg of the round trip. In this early commerce the merchant customarily accompanied his merchandise and consequently was able to supervise on the spot its sale and the investment of the proceeds in cloth for export to Italy.

By the late twelfth century, however, merchants increasingly relied upon agents to handle their business at the fairs while they remained at home to manage their complex affairs.[66] In the following century these practices were institutionalized by the formulation of the large scale mercantile-banking organization which maintained permanent representation abroad through partners or agents.[67] Accompanying the growth of international commerce between Lucca and northern Europe was the development in Lucca of a money market based upon the Champagne fairs. Transactions in foreign exchange drawn upon markets other than the fairs are extremely rare in the Lucchese documents.

Although the primary function of exchange was the transfer of funds from one

---

[63] For the Lucchese in Genoa, see F. Edler, "The Silk Trade of Lucca during the Thirteenth and Fourteenth Centuries," unpublished doctoral dissertation (Dept. of History, University of Chicago, Chicago, 1930), pp. 116–123; T. Blomquist, "Lucchese Commercial Activities in Genoa, 1186–1226," unpublished master's essay (Dept. of History, University of Minnesota, Minneapolis, 1960); and M. Baldovini, "Santa Croce di Sarzano e i mercanti lucchesi a Genova (sec. XIII–XIV)," *Atti della società ligure di storia patria*, n.s., II (1962), 76–96.

[64] See T. Blomquist, "Lucchese Commercial Activities in Genoa," pp. 82–100 for the mechanics of this traffic. For abstracts of many of the relative documents, see A. Ferretto, ed., *Il Codice diplomatico delle relazioni fra la Toscana e Lunigiana a i tempi di Dante*, 2 pts., *Atti della Società Ligure di storia patria*, XXXI (1901–1903).

[65] The text of the treaty is published in C. Imperiale, ed., *Il Codice diplomatico della Repubblica di Genova*, I (Rome 1936), n. 1.

[66] R. D. Face, "The Techniques of Business in the Trade between the Fairs of Champagne and the South of Europe in the Twelfth and Thirteenth Centuries," *Economic History Review*, X (1957–1958), 427–438, has studied the increasing use of agency and improved methods of transportation in the traffic between Genoa and the fairs.

[67] R. de Roover, "The Organization of Trade," *Cambridge Economic History of Europe*, III (Cambridge, 1963), 70–76.

place to another, mediaeval dealings in foreign exchange were also by their very nature credit transactions. The buyer of exchange delivered funds in Lucca, and received from the seller a notarial instrument promising repayment at one of the Champagne fairs in an equivalent amount of money of Provin. But repayment at one or another of the fairs meant repayment at some time in the future and hence the buyer was in effect a lender, the seller a borrower with interest on the buyer's capital built into the rates of exchange.[68]

The Castracani organization was perhaps the most active Lucchese firm engaged in this business. Forty-nine of the 249 exchange contracts surviving in the cartulary of the Fulcieri — about one in every five — involved the Castracani partnership. They were primarily buyers of funds, paying out in Lucca over the course of the year, the impressive sum of £28,622. Lucchese in return for which they accumulated credits due in the North of £7,930 Provinois payable to their agent-partner, Buiamonte Turchii.[69]

Furthermore, we know from the information given in the notary's cancellation addended to the original cartulary entry that these transactions were in fact concluded in the north. These were not fictitious exchanges disguising illicit lending but were actually completed with the delivery of credit to Buiamonte Turchii representing the partnership in Champagne.[70]

At this point in the Castracani partnership's dealings in foreign exchange, our sources again prove wanting, for they shed no light as to how these extensive accumulations of capital were returned to Italy. A variety of alternate courses of action existed, of course, and each was no doubt exploited as business circumstances dictated. It was possible, for example, to invest in goods of northern manufacture for export south. Another possibility involved re-exchange, that is, buying Lucchese monies on the Champagne money market for delivery in Lucca. Or yet another option existed as the merchant-banker could resell his northern credits in Lucca by drawing upon the fairs.

Further, with respect to the movement of money and credit between Lucca and northern Europe, we should also observe that while Lucca and Champagne were the ultimate termini in this traffic, a number of intermediate transactions might take place before capital completed its round trip journey. A merchant-banker may have made his returns from Champagne, for instance, by drawing upon Genoa, using these funds to purchase raw silk which could then be exported

---

[68] R. de Roover, *Evolution de la lettre de change*, pp. 23–42 discusses the technical relationship between the mediaeval exchange transaction and the bill of exchange. For a discussion of the mechanics of the exchange transaction, see the same author's *Money, Banking and Credit in Mediaeval Bruges* pp. 52–55.

[69] For the pertinent documents upon which these figures are based, see *Archivio di Stato in Lucca, Archivio dei notari*, n. 15 (notaries Bartolomeo Fulcieri, Tegrimo Fulcieri, Fulciero Fulcieri), *passim*. and for a calendar of the same material, T. Blomquist, "Trade and Commerce in Thirteenth-Century Lucca," pp. 192–202.

[70] The notary cancelled the entries in his cartulary by drawing crossed diagonal lines across the face of each. He then added beneath the text or in the margin the information relevant to the satisfaction of the terms of the agreement. Thus is appended the information that the agent of a given buyer received payment in Champagne through the agent of the seller on such and such a date.

to and sold in Lucca. The variations on these possibilities were virtually without limit and in the absence of the books of the Castracani partnership we may only point out that they infrequently sold credits on the Lucchese market.[71] Nor is there evidence that they operated in the cloth or silk trade to any significant degree. The most probable conjecture, then, is that they dealt primarily in foreign exchange and made their returns by drawing in Champagne upon Lucca, traces of which business were recorded in a cartulary now lost to us.

The last notarial contract relating to the Castracani family in thirteenth century Lucca ushers upon the scene the sixteen-year-old *Castruccius filius emancipatus Gerii*.[72] Dated 1 August 1296, the contract refers to an earlier agreement entered into in France by Gerio Castracanis on the one hand and representatives of the Ricciardi partnership on the other. Perhaps the most powerful business organization of thirteenth-century Lucca, indeed if not of Europe, the Ricciardi by 1296 had fallen upon hard times.[73] Difficulties with their operations in England and France coupled with simultaneous demands by Boniface VIII for delivery of papal funds held in deposit placed the firm in dire need of capital.[74] To avert disaster the partners were recalling their loans where possible as well as negotiating for new funds. In all, Gerio, stipulating for himself, his brother and his son acknowledged that the three jointly would deliver to the Ricciardi at a future date in Lucca the rather considerable sums of £1,000 *tournois* and 1,000 gold florins. Apparently the Castracani were in sound financial condition in a time of general crisis for the Italian banking community.[75]

Unfortunately, however, our contract of 1296 offers no evidence on the fate of the Castracani partnership of 1284. In this agreement, Gerio, Coluccio and Castruccio acted jointly as individuals rather than as active members of a partnership and in the absence of specific evidence we can only speculate on the outcome of the organization of 1284. Castracane Rugerii, the guiding spirit behind the family's international banking business probably died at some time between 1292 and 1296.[76] His death, according to prevailing business practice, would have

---

[71] For the Castracani sales of credit *Archivio di Stato, op. cit.*, fol. 308, 27 May 1284; fol. 309v, 27 May 1284; fol. 92v, 7 Oct. 1284; fol. 464v, 27 Nov. 1284.

[72] *Archivo di Stato, Archivio dei notari*, n. 17 (notaries Alluminatus Parensi, Bonifazio Parenti, Nicolao Passamonte), fol. 94v.

[73] On the Ricciardi, see the study, based mainly upon Vatican sources of E. Re, "La Compagnia dei Ricciardi in Inghilterra e il suo fallimento alla fine del secolo XIII," *Archivio della Reale Società Romana di storia patria*, xxxvii (1914), 87–138.

[74] See *ibid.*, pp. 99–124 for the fall of the Ricciardi and pp. 108–109 for the lament of one of the Ricciardi partners in 1296: *semo in sie mala chondissione che in della fere di Champangna, la v'era tutta nostra civansa et di tutti merchadanti et la v'eravamo creduti et potevamo improntare C et CCᵐ milliaia di tornesi et piu, ogi semo a tale se vollesemo libre C di tornesi non se lle troveremmo et a Luccha non potremo chambiare C libre di tornesi se semo dottati.*

[75] The Bonsignore of Siena failed at the same time as the Ricciardi: see M. Chiaudano, "I Rothschild del duecento: La Gran Tavola de Orlando Bonsignore," *Bullettino senese di storia patria*, n.s., II (1935), 119–123. The policies of Philip IV with respect to Italian bankers also caused serious difficulties for the Florentine banking community: See note 78.

[76] His name does not appear in the sources after 1292. See *Archivio di Stato in Lucca, Fregionai*, 1 July 1292.

made necessary the reorganization of the partnership.[77] But whether it was reconstituted along existing lines or liquidated we cannot tell. We do know from the above mentioned dealings with the Ricciardi that Gerio was in France in the 1290's, yet whether he was there as a member of a partnership or acting independently is unclear. It is, though, tempting to suggest that Gerio and Coluccio anticipated the policies of Philip IV so unfavorable to Italian bankers in France and by retrenching succeeded in protecting their international banking interests.[78] How clearly they foresaw the political and social upheaval which rocked Lucca at the end of the century is a moot question.

In the split between Blacks and Whites which erupted into the open in Lucca in 1300, virtually the entire Lucchese international mercantile-banking community adhered to the conservative and aristocratic White faction.[79] With the triumph of the Blacks many of the great merchants chose exile abroad; others remained in Lucca to be branded as *casastici et potentes* shorn of full political rights.[80] Although the Castracani were not specifically named in the list, included in the Statute of 1308, which named those houses considered magnatial, Gerio and his brother Coluccio fled Lucca and the popular regime; the one for Ancona, the other for Pisa.[81] The explanation for their absence from the list of the proscribed may be that they were subsumed under the rubric *omnes et singuli di domo Antelminellorum*, the house of the noble Antelminelli with which Castruccio Castracani later claimed a collateral relationship.

Nothing in the sources, however, indicates that the Castracani of thirteenth-century Lucca were considered of noble extraction. Nor do the sources suggest that they were active in politics. They were instead men of business and the

---

[77] For this as well as other aspects of partnership law in thirteenth-century Italy, see A. Sapori, "Storia interna della compagnia mercantile dei Peruzzi," *Studi di storia economica*, pp. 665–669.

[78] Philip's financial problems were exacerbated by the outbreak of war with England in 1294 and to raise revenues he resorted to forced loans under threat of confiscation, tallages, and embargoes which weighed heavily upon Italian bankers in France. Most harmful, however, was the crown policy of currency debasement. For the effects upon Florentine banking interests of these measures, see G. Arias, *Studi e documenti di storia del diritto*, p. 17. J. Strayer, "Italian Bankers and Philip the Fair," *Economy, Society and Government in Medieval Italy*, D. Herlihy, R. Lopez and V. Slessarev, eds., published as nos. 1 and 2 of *Explorations in Economic History*, VII (1969), 113–121 develops the view that Philip's relations with the Italians were cordial through the 1290's but provides no assessment of the consequences to the Italian's economic position as a result of the above policies. See also E. Miller, in *Cambridge Economic History of Europe*, III, 304–305; E. Grundzweig, "Les incidences internationales des mutations monétaires de Philippe le Bel," *Moyen Age*, LIX (1953), 117–173; as well as M. Prestwich, "Edward I's monetary policies and their consequences," *Economic History Review*, XXII (1969), 406–416.

[79] For the events of 1300 in Lucca, see the contemporary account in B. Schmeidler, ed., *Tholomei lucensis annales, Monumenta germaniae historica, Scriptores rerum germanicorum*, n.s. VIII (Berlin, 1930), 318–319. For the list of those branded *casastici et potentes* by the popular regime, see S. Bongi, L. Del Prete, eds., *Statuto del Comune di Lucca dell' anno MCCCVIII* (Lucca, 1867), pp. 241–244.

[80] F. P. Luiso, "Gli antenati di Castruccio Castracani," pp. 74–79 has argued that many on the proscribed list remained in Lucca without serious handicap. However, the list of 1308 clearly states that no member of the *popolo* could be condemned by testimony of a *casastici*.

[81] G. Sforza, "Castruccio Castracani degli Antelminelli e gli altri lucchesi di parte bianca in esilio," pp. 59–60.

counting house with interests remote from the aristocratic concerns and values of the noble Antelminelli who still retained vestiges of feudal jurisdiction in the *contado* and whom the sources invariably style *dominus*.[82] Perhaps it was the polarization of Lucchese society in the 1290's and the emergence of the Antelminelli as leaders of the conservative Whites that led the Castracani to assert a real or fancied blood tie with this noble clan. Only after the death of his father in Ancona in 1301 did Castruccio join the revanchist Antelminelli and their group in Pisa, where he also combined with his uncle in a business partnership.[83] Nor did Castruccio adopt the patronymic *de Anterminellis* until his arrival in Pisa and this possibly to enhance his prestige not only within the aristocratically oriented Lucchese community in exile but also with the Italian Ghibelline faction generally.[84]

We may on the basis of our evidence concur with Macchiavelli that Castruccio was of ignoble birth.[85] Indeed Castruccio Castracani was the grandson of a self-made financier who had successfully capitalized upon the opportunities afforded enterprise in an expanding economic and business climate.

This brief historical sketch has attempted to indicate what the sources reveal about the thirteenth-century ancestors of Castruccio Castracani and what in turn their history suggests about the evolution of the techniques and organization of early banking. We have seen an example of the transition from locally oriented money-changing operations to the arena of international banking. But were the Castracani unique in making this transition? Did other members of the Lucchese money-changer's fraternity gravitate to large-scale banking? Is there, in short, a sociological as well as a technical connection between money-changing and large-scale mercantile-banking? Future research in the Lucchese materials will, it is hoped, provide fuller answers to these and other questions.

---

[82] The Antelminelli numbered among their ranks in the 1250's at least three judges, Bonus, Armannus and Davinus as well as one notary, Savarigio: see LL 27 and 28, *passim*. See LL 25, fol. 38, 30 April, 1250 for the rental by Davinus of one sixth of the fishing rights which he possessed in Lake Massaciuccoli to the *camerario communis et universitatis de Massaciuccori*. Ubaldus Antelminelli served in 1285 as captain of the Bolognese *popolo*: see U. Dallari, "Podestà e capitani del popolo lucchesi in Bologna," *Miscellanea lucchese di studi storici e letterari in memoria de Salvatore Bongi* (Lucca, 1931), p. 31.

[83] G. Sforza, "Castruccio Castracani degli Antelminelli e gli altri lucchesi di parte bianca in esilio," pp. 88–89 has published a Pisan document dated 1304 in which Coluccio and Castruccio appointed a procurator to recover their merchant books from an employee (*factor dictorum*).

[84] Coluccio, in the document cited in note 83, appears as *Coluccius quondam Castracanis de Anterminellis de Luca*. Castruccio appeared as *Castruccius quondam Rogerii Castracanis de Anterminellis de Luca* in a document of 1313; *ibid.*, pp. 88, 104.

[85] Niccolo Machiavelli, *Vita de Castruccio Castracani e altri scritti storici minori*, E. Barelli, ed. (Milan, 1962), pp. 43–44: *non ebbe più felice nè più noto nascimento.*

NOTE: Since the above article went to press, the Pisan material cited in note no. 49 has appeared in G. Dolezalek, *Das Imbreviaturbuch des Erzbischöflichen Gerichtsnotars Hubaldus aus Pisa. Mai bis August 1230*, Köln-Wien, 1969: see no. 4, pp. 89–93 and no. 22, pp. 106–107.

# II

## LINEAGE, LAND AND BUSINESS, IN THE THIRTEENTH CENTURY: THE GUIDICCIONI FAMILY OF LUCCA

On 1 August 1296 twelve partners of the Ricciardi company, « Societas Ricciardorum », assembled in the organization's home office in Lucca and elected another colleague, the absent Conte Guidiccioni, as the new director (« capud », « gubernator », « magister ») of the partnership (¹). Conte's elevation to the directorship of one of Medieval Europe's most powerful mercantile-banking institutions marks a climax in the rise of the Guidiccioni wi-

(*) An earlier version of this paper was presented to the Tenth Conference on Medieval Studies, Western Michigan University, May, 1975. The archival research was supported at various times by a fellowship from The American Council of Learned Societies and grants from the American Philosophical Society, The Dean's Fund and the Graduate School Committee on Research, Northern Illinois University: to each I am indebted. I also wish to express my thanks to David Herlihy, Harvard University; Daniel B. Smith, The University of Kentucky; and to my colleagues William Beik, Ann Congdon, James Greenlee and Benjamin Keen for their helpful comments as the paper passed through various stages to completion.

(1) The Document is discussed and published in full in THOMAS W. BLOM-QUIST, « *Administration of a Thirteenth - Century Mercantile - Banking Partnership: An Episode in the History of the Ricciardi of Lucca* », *Revue internationale d'histoire de la banque*, VII (1973), pp. 1-9.

thin the Ricciardi company and corresponding loss of control by the Ricciardi family ([2]). This prominence of the Guidiccioni within the Ricicardi business organization first attracted my attention to the family. A rather cursory excursion into the sources soon made it evident that the surviving material bearing upon the history of the thirteenth-century Guidiccioni not only told much about the connection with the Ricciardi enterprise but might also reveal a good deal about the composition and structure of the family as it evolved through some four generations into an increasingly complex patriarchal lineage. In the following essay I shall set out, so far as the sources will allow, the history of the Guidiccioni in the thirteenth century with particular emphasis upon the family's collective behavior in forging a network of social and economic relationships designed — and quite consciously so — both to protect and advance the Guidiccioni position within the often turbulent environment of communal Lucca ([3]).

The information upon which this study is based is drawn mainly from the notarial materials housed in the State, the Archiepiscopal and Capitular Archives of Lucca ([4]). These notarial deeds,

---

(2) On the Ricciardi, see RICHARD W. KAEUPER, *Bankers to the Crown*: *The Ricciardi of Lucca and Edward I* (Princeton, 1973) and EMILIO RE, « *La compagnia dei Ricciardi in Inghilterra e il suo fallimento alla fine del Secolo XIII* », *Archivio della società romana di storia patria*, XXXVII (1914), pp. 87-138. For the personnel of the Ricciardi company; KAEUPER, *Bankers to the Crown*, pp. 56-59 and THOMAS W. BLOMQUIST, « *Commercial Association in Medieval Lucca* », *Business History Review*, XLV (1971), p. 175.

(3) Survey histories of Lucca in the Middle Ages are GIROLAMO TOMMASI, *Sommario della storia di Lucca*, published as *Archivio storico italiano*, X (1846), and AUGUSTO MANCINI, *Storia di Lucca* (Florence, 1950).

(4) For a description of the Lucchese notarial materials housed in the *Archivio di Stato in Lucca* (hereafter ASL) see ROBERT S. LOPEZ, « *The Unexplored Wealth of the Notarial Archives of Pisa and Lucca* », *Mélanges d'histoire de moyen âge dédiés à la mémoire de Louis Helphen* (Paris, 1951), pp. 417-432. EUGENIO LAZZARESCHI, « *L'Archivio dei Notari della Repubblica lucchese* », *Gli archivi italiani*, II (1915), pp. 175-210 catalogues the cartularies. On the archiepiscopal and chapter archives, see ROBERT H. BAUTIER. « *Notes sur les sources de l'histoire économique médiévale dans les archives italiennes* », *Mélanges d'archeologie et d'histoire*, LVIII (1941-1946), pp. 299-300; GIUSEPPE GHILARDUCCI, *Le biblioteche e gli archivi arcivescovili e capitolari* (Lucca, 1969) and DUANE OSHEIM, « *The Episcopal Archive of Lucca in the Middle Ages* », *Manuscripta*, XVII (1973), pp. 131-146.

surviving in both rough draft cartulary form as well as in the final parchment redactions, can be supplemented by the massive genealogical compilations, often preserving traces of documents now lost, of the niniteenth-century Lucchese scholar and antiquarian G. V. Baroni (⁵). Taken together, these sources provide a unique picture of the birth, as it were, of a lineage and of the ways in which its early members laid the social and economic foundations that ensured its survival through the later Middle Ages into the modern era.

### The Guidiccioni and the Ricciardi Partnership

The evidence bearing upon the early history of the Guidiccioni is suggestive but inconclusive. The first references to the ancestors of the thirteenth-century family are in the folio pages of Baroni's genealogy. He reports *sub nomine* Guidiccioni that in 1175 a Geraldo Guidiccioni sold land on behalf of the Abbot of the Lucchese monastery of San Michele in Guamo; that Aldibrandino Guidiccioni was consul in Genoa in 1182; and in 1212 that an Uberto Guidiccioni accompanied Guinigio Guinigi, member of another Lucchese family destined for mercantile eminence in the later thirteenth century, on an embassy to the Court of Frederick II (⁶). But these references cannot be independently confirmed. True, Genoese sources indicate that Lucchese held consul-

---

(5) The Baroni genealogies are contained in thirty-nine folio volumes housed in the *Biblioteca Statale di Lucca* (hereafter BSL) as GIUSEPPE VINCENZO BARONI, *Notizie genealogiche delle famiglie lucchesi,* mss. nos. 1101-1139. The Guidiccioni references are in BSL, BARONI, *ms. no. 1115.* The folios have been paginated and re-paginated with confusing results, I am therefore citing Baroni under the appropriate year.

(6) BSL, BARONI, *ms. ns. 1115;* years 1175, 1182, 1212. In general I have italianized proper names, using the Italian *del fu* for the Latin *quondam* with the genitive, « son of the late » and *di* when the genitive indicates « the son of » in the Latin.

ships in Genoa from time to time, but there is no indication that an Aldibrandino Guidiccionis ever held such a post ([7]).

The information about the Guidiccioni becomes more abundant as we move into the thirteenth century. The earliest document mentioning the family that can be consulted directly is dated 29 July 1227 and refers to the swearing of an oath of fealty to the Bishop of Lucca by the men (« homines ») of Verrucola in the mountainous Garfagnana ([8]). Among the participants listed we find one « Artusco Guidiccionis »; and, although his name appears only this once in the sources, his presence on this occasion confirms the impression derived from later material that the Guidiccioni hailed from Garfagnana. Because of the single minded way in which the family is known to have pursued a consistent policy of building up its collective holdings and influence in Verrucola at a later date, it is quite likely that it already had a foothold in the locale. This document of 1227 buttresses the conclusions that the first Guidiccioni were rural tenants of the Bishop in Verrucola and that they were relatively new to the city ([9]).

The first member of the family that can be identified with any assurance is Aldibrandino del fu Guidiccioni, son of the otherwise obscure individual who gave his name to the subsequent lineage; and it is Aldibrandino's career that first links his family to the commercial enterprise of the Ricciardi.

The beginnings of the Societas Ricciardorum and its rise to the pinnacle of international trade and banking are, like the origins of the Guidiccioni, inevitably obscure. A document of 1231, does serve to reveal the partnership in embryonic form. On 17

---

(7) For example, in the years 1182, 1184, 1189 and 1197 Obertus Lucensis served as one of the Genoese Consuls of Justice: L. T. BELGRANO and CESARE IMPERIALE, eds., *Annali genovesi di Caffaro e dei suoi continuatori*, II (Rome, 1901), pp. 16-17, 19, 71.

(8) *Archivio arcivescovile*, * A, no. 92, 29 July 1227.

(9) DUANE J. OSHEIM, *An Italian Lordship: the Bishopric of Lucca in the Middle Ages* (Berkeley, Los Angeles, London, 1977), pp. 58-64 discusses similar oaths taken to the bishop by men of other rural communes.

March of that year, Gottifredo Conecti and Perfetto del fu Graziano, « brother of Ricciardo », acting for themselves and « for all their partners » sold to Morettino Ughi a credit which they held against Ugolino del fu Bonitho di Lotterio, in the amount of L 13 7s 7d, due on the sale of raw silk ([10]). Interestingly, Morettino Ughi was related by marriage to the Volpelli family and quite possibly to the Di Poggio, two families that were to play an important role in the subsequent history of the Ricciardi company ([11]).

The document of 1231 referring to the partnership of Gottifredo and Perfetto unfortunately does not provide the names of their other partners. In another document, hower, dated 1241, we read of a second partnership which in all probability was a continuation of the earlier one. On 30 September Guglielmo Roscimpelli, for himself and for Ricciardo Graziani, Orlandino Arnolfi and Peregrino Sexmondi, his partners, « and for all their other partners », stipulated to the treasurer of the Lucchese episcopate that he had been repaid the L 135 lucchese which the partners had advanced to the Bishop of Lucca in Rome ([12]). This document, then, places the partnership in Rome at precisely the time when the papacy began to transact its banking business regularly through Italian merchant-bankers ([13]). Furthermore, it establishes

---

(10) ASL, *Archivio gentilize, Archivio Guinigi,* no. 1, 17 March 1231.

(11) ASL, *Diplomatico, S. Maria Corte Orlandini,* 12 February 1239: Gherarduccio del fu Volpello appointed his brother-in-law Morettino Ughi de Fondoro; his brother, Francesco; Tegrimo de Podio and Bonaventura del fu Volpello guardians of his son Labro.

(12) *Archivio arcivescovile,* +F, no. 78, 30 September 1241.

(13) GLENN OLSEN, « *Italian Merchants and the Performance of Papal Banking Functions in the Thirteenth Century* », DAVID HERLIHY, ROBERT S. LOPEZ, VSEVOLOD SLESSAREV, eds., *Economy, Society and Government in Medieval Italy* (Kent, Ohio, 1969), published as *Explorations in Economic History,* VII (1969), nos. 1 and 2, pp. 43-63, argues that Italian merchants were transferring papal collector's funds to the *camera* at the end of the twelfth and beginning of the thirteenth centuries. The title *campsor domini papae* appears in papal documents in 1232: WILLIAM E. LUNT, *Papal Revenues in the Middle Ages,* I (New York, 1934), p. 51; E. JORDAN, *De*

the early connection of the Roscimpelli, Sexmondi and Arnolfi families with the enterprise which in a transaction of 1247 was for the first time styled the « Ricciardi Company ». In this latter reference, of which only Baroni's summary survives, one Opitone — most probably Opizo Malisardi — acting in the name of Aldibrandino Guidiccioni and Bandino del fu Lucano Bugianensis of the « Compagnia dei Ricciardi » handed over a sum of Venetian money to the procurator of the Bishop of Trapani ([14]). At this same time, Aldibrandino was either in or on his way to Champagne to represent the partnership at the fairs, where in 1245 he acted as procurator in an exchange transaction for another Lucchese ([15]). Consequently, Aldibrandino was in France when Renerio Maghiari and Peregrino Sexmondi — the same Peregrino, incidentally, of 1241 — arrived in England on behalf of the Ricciardi and he was thus in the forefront of the partnership's first penetration into the markets of Nothern Europe ([16]). Aldibrandino did not remain for long North of the Alps. In 1249 he was back in Lucca where he seemingly remained more or less continuously and where, as we shall see, he assumed the leadership of the family Guidiccioni ([17]).

The Ricciardi partnership around the mid-thirteenth century was embarking upon the formation of the European-wide commercial and financial network that was to guarantee its prosperity in

---

*mercatoribus camerae apostolicae saeculo XIII* (Rennes, 1909), p. 9 and GINO ARIAS, *Studi e documenti di storia del diritto* (Florence, 1901), pp. 75-114.

(14) BSL, BARONI, ms. no. 1115; year 1247. I am assuming « Compagnia dei Ricciardi » to be the Italian rendering of « Societas Ricciardorum » in the original document.

(15) ASL, *Diplomatico, S. Maria Corte Orlandini*, 6 December 1245.

(16) KAEUPER, *Bankers to the Crown*, p. 5: in June 1245 « Reyner of Lucca and Peregrino his partner » sold about L. 50 worth of cloth to Henry III. That these two were in fact Renerio Maghiari and Peregrino Sesmundi is confirmed in a letter of 1254 in which Henry obligated himself to « Peregrino Sesmundi, Bartolomeo Bendini, Reynerio Senaci, Henrico Saraceni, Luco Natali et sociis suis civibus et mercatoribus de Luca ».

(17) BSL, BARONI, ms. no. 1115; year 1249: Aldibrandino del fu Guidiccione bought land in Capannori from Renerio, Ubaldo and Orlanduccio Di Poggio for L. 32.

the later part of the century. By 1250 the incipient international enterprise, as we have seen, had contacts in Rome; had moved into Northern France and England; and, if the dealings with the Bishop of Trapani are an indication, may well have been operating overseas [18]. In terms of personnel, the partnership consisted of an increasing number of associates to deal with this expanding business [19]. From Lucca we can recover only the four names indicated in 1241, to which must be added those mentioned in 1247; Perfetto Gratiani, who in 1245 we also find borrowing capital from the banks of the Lucchese money-changers [20], Opizio Malisardi, Bandino del fu Lucani and Aldibrandino Guidiccionis. At the same time, operating for the partnership in England and Nothern France were Lucas Natale, Enrico di Podio, Baroncino Gualterii, Renerio Maghiari, Peregrino Sexmondi, Enrico Saraceni and one Percivalle Gerarduci [21]. We thus arrive at a total of thirteen partners working for the Ricciardi with seven of these stationed abroad.

The founders of the company were apparently the brothers Perfetto and Ricciardo, the sons of Graziano Ricciardi, and Gottifredo del fu Conecto. These had presumably put up the largest share of capital and provided the leadership for the ventures of 1231 and 1241. As a result, the organization became identified with the patronym they shared; it was known as « The Partnership of the Ricciardi ». In subsequent generations, however,

---

(18) On the Lucchese movement into Northern Europe, see BLOMQUIST, « *Commercial Association* », pp. 161-163. For Lucchese trade with Sicily in the twelfth century, see DAVID ABULAFIA, *The Two Italies: Economic Relations between the Norman Kingdom of Sicily and the Northern Communes* (Cambridge, 1977).

(19) See the list of Ricciardi partners in KAEUPER, *Bankers to the Crown*, pp. 56-59.

(20) On 27 January and 4 March, Perfetto Ricciardi del fu Graziano borrowed respectively L. 100 and L. 200 from the money changer Gerardo Azuri: *Archivio capitolare, LL.* 20, fols. 13 and 25v. Also on 27 January Perfetto borrowed another L. 150 from the changers Soldano, Gerardo and Uguccione Maghiari: *Ibid.*, fol. 57.

(21) KAEUPER, *Bankers to the Crown*, pp. 5, 55-57.

only the line descending from Ricciardo Graziani stayed active in the company. Indeed, Perfetto Graziani's branch had virtually died out in the male line by 1289 ([22]). And, although the company kept its headquarters in the house belonging jointly to « Dominus Andrea condam Domini Parenti Ricciardi » and his cousins Filippo and Ricciardo del fu Renerio Ricciardi, all three of whom were involved in the partnership in 1286, Ricciardi family members apparently played only a minimal role in company affairs in the last decades of its existence ([23]). No Ricciardi took part in Conte's election to the directorship of the partnership in 1296, indicating that the members of this family had withdrawn from the firm. Those partners who did participate in the proceedings were apparently at some pain to secure approval of Conte's elevation from all associates present at the time in Lucca, even to the point of

---

(22) See ASL, *Diplomatico: Fregionaia,* 4 July 1280 in which Maria, the wife of « Dominus Arrigus de Colle » formally approved a sale of land by her husband and renounced all claims against the parcel that she might have in right of her dowry: in the renunciation Maria had the approval of her nephew « Domini Peri quondam Connecti quondam Perfecti Ricciardi » whom she described as her only relative (« cum dicat se nullum alium habere propinquorum »). This branch seems to have focused upon estate management in the countryside around Segromigno: ASL, *Archivio dei notari,* no. 7 (Giovanni Gigli), fol. 5v, 26 August 1263 was drawn up « Segrominii in Curia Perfecti Ricciardi ». Although Perfetto was alive in 1263, there is no evdence that he or his heirs took an active part in the affairs of the commercial company that he helped to found. One entire section of the notary, Giovanni Gigli's cartulary for the years 1271-1320, A.S.L., *Archivio dei notari,* no. 7, consisted of the « Liber rogitorum mei Johannis Gygli notarii de negotiis Dominorum Peri et Ricciardi germanorum quondam Domini Conecti Perfecti Ricciardi factus et compositus anno Domini MCCLXXI ». The « book » is made up of contracts redacted in the course of Piero and Ricciardo's rural affairs. The line did, however, maintain social ties to the city and the world of commerce. Ricciardo's first wife was Maria, daughter of Leo Sexmundi, a partner of the Ricciardi Company: ASL, *Archivio dei notarii,* no. 7 (Giovanni Gigli), fol. 120, 17 July 1307. Piero's son, « Freduccius filius quondam Domini Pieri filii quondam Domini Conecti Ricciardi de Contrata S. Andree was married to Narduccia, Paganuccio Guidiccioni's daughter, and he was a neighbor of the Guidiccioni in San Andrea: BSL, BARONI, ms. no. 1130; year 1302.

(23) ASL, *Archivio dei notari,* no. 17 (Alluminato Parensi), fol. 94v, 1 August 1296: « Actum Luce in domo dicti Andree condam Domini Parentii Ricciardi et Dominorum Filippy et Ricciardi condam Domini Raynerii Ricciard ubi socii tenent eorum apothecam ».

seeking out Giovanni Symonetti and Guidiccione Guidiccionis in their homes and attaching their respective agreements in the form of two codicils, to the notarial deed solemnizing the event. Had the three Ricciardi still been associated with the firm they assuredly would have participated in this critical incident ([24]).

1296, however, was a year of crisis for the company and in all likelihood Conte's succession to the directorship represented the wresting of power from an old and patently unsuccessful leadership. In this time of trouble, the three Ricciardi may have been forced out or, perhaps seeing the handwriting on the wall, they prudently retired from affairs voluntarily. Yet, inspite of the absence of the Ricciardi from the organization, the partnership continued to meet in the Ricciardi house, retained the company style « societas Ricciardorum » and kept the company seal as a badge of corporate identity ([25]). These retentions suggest someting of the hold of tradition and the loyalty of the partners to the firm.

Throughout its life the Ricciardi partnership maintained a decidedly social character. Although legally straight partnerships, the Ricciardi and the other international mercantile-banking organizations, because of the practice of successively renewing partnership agreements, developed a corporate identity that transcended particular and temporary partnership arrangements ([26]). This sense

---

(24) BLOMQUIST, « Administration of a Thirteenth-century Mercantile-Banking Partnership », p. 9.

(25) For the company seal, see the example cited by MARIO CHIAUDANO, « Le compagnie bancarie senesi nel Dugento », in the same author's Studi e documenti per la storia del diritto commerciale italiano nel secolo XIII (Turin, 1930), p. 38, in which a partner of the Ricciardi in England authenticated a document of procuration by affixing his seal and that of the partnership with the words: « E io Rainieri sopradito con la mia mano abo jiscrito quie di soto e messo lo mio sugelo con quelo de la compagnia ».

(26) Armando Sapori makes the argument that when an old partnership was dissolved and a new one formed the company name, debits and assets were carried over to the new association. As far as third parties were concerned, there was no interruption in the continuity of the institution: they need only have been assured that they were dealing with a bona fide representative of the partnership bearing the company name at the time

of corporateness, as in the case of an emerging lineage, was most clearly expressed in the importance attached to a company name, which was carried over without a break in continuity from one formal contractual partnership agreement to the next [27]. The admission of new partners, the departure of old, the distribution of profits or re-capitalization required the dissolution of the current pact and the formation of a new partnership contract [28]. Yet, whatever the contractual arrangement, the Ricciardi partners of the moment faced outsiders as the united Societas Ricciardorum.

Another feature confirming the corporate nature of the partnership was the evident continuity in terms of personnel. To be sure, individuals from beyond the circle of families initially active in the Ricciardi were subsequently brought into the enterprise; but additional probing in the sources frequently reveals that these persons, seemingly having no social ties to Ricciardi partners or their families, in fact, were bound in some way to one or another of the families represented in the organization. For example, the Tadolini were related by marriage to the Ricciardi and were joined with the Malisardi in a consortium, the « domus filiorum Tadolini » [29]. Another consortium allied the Onesti with the Ricciar-

---

a particular transaction was carried out. See Sapori's two articles « *Storia interna della compagnia mercantile dei Peruzzi* » and « *Le compagnie mercantili toscane del dugento e dei primi del trecento* », in his *Studi di storia economica (secoli XIII-XIV-XV)*, 2nd ed., II (Florence, n. d.), especially pp. 659-665 and 803-805.

(27) For this point, see RAYMOND DE ROOVER, « *The Organization of Trade* », *Cambridge Economic History of Europe*, III (Cambridge, 1963), III (Cambridge, 1963), pp. 76-79 and SAPORI, « *Storia interna della compagnia mercantile dei Peruzzi* ».

(28) For the formation of successive Ricciardi partnerships, see KAEUPER, *Bankers to the Crown*, p. 7, note 27.

(29) Orlando Ricciardi was the brother-in-law of Rocchigiano del fu Gottifredo Tadolini: BSL, BARONI, ms. no. 1115; year 1253. On 24 December 1299 «Gerardinus condam Domini Soffredi Tadolini» and «Parentus condam Ardiccionis Malisardi» were consuls of the « Domus filiorum Tadolini »: ASL, *Diplomatico, Archivio dei notari*, 24 December 1299.

di ([30]). Finally, we shall see shortly that the Guidiccioni were connected to the Broccoli family by consortial and neighborhood ties and that they were linked to the Buggianesi by kinship.

Although the evidence does not reveal the degree of relationship uniting the Guidiccioni and Buggianesi, such a kinship bond would go far in explaining the close social and economic link between the two families revealed in the later thirteenth-century document ([31]). In 1253 Bartolomeo del fu Cimaccho and Paganino Guidiccioni, each representing other principals in the affair, launched a lawsuit against the heirs of Bonagiunta Mai over « a certain portion of houses and lands located in Lucca in the contrada of Cantonbretti » ([32]). Bartolomeo represented himself and Lazzaro Buggianesi in the matter while Paganino spoke for himself and his brother Aldibrandino and for Aldibrando del fu Ugolino Paganini. The defendants, heirs of Bonagiunta Mai, were Gemma, the wife of Orlando Ricciardi and daughter of Bonagiunta; and Rocchigiano del fu Gottifredo Tadolini who was the respondent for himself and for his children by Marchesina, Bonagiunta's other daughter. At issue was the property that Bonagiunta had inherited from one Ubertello del fu Pagano on condition that if the former should die without male offspring eighteen years of age or over, the inheritance would revert to Bandino Cimacchi and his sons, to the sons of the late Guidiccione and to those of Paganino Guidiccioni. Indeed, Bonagiunta had expired without adult male issue and the consuls of the Court of San Cristoforo decided in favor of the plaintiffs. The dispute shows the Guidiccioni, Cimacchi, Buggianesi and Mai connected by a distant kinship tie and these families

---

(30) ASL, *Curia San Cristoforo;* no. 3, fol. 92, 1266; when Tancredo Onesti died he was attended by « ... consortes scilicet Dominus Orlandus Ricchardi... ».

(31) BLOMQUIST, *Administration of a Thirteenth-Century Mercantile-Banking Partnership,* p. 9: in a codicil to the principal document, « Johanne Symonetti quondam Bonifatii Sexmundi concurred in the election of Conte Guidiccionis as head of the Ricciardi. Apparently Giovanni and his sons, all partners of the Ricciardi, formed a distinct branch of the Sexmundi taking their patronym from Simonetto.

(32) BSL, BARONI, ms. no. 1115; year 1253.

were in turn linked to the Ricciardi and Tadolini through marriage. Although the Cimacchi apparently went their own way in the course of the century, engaging in international mercantile-banking as partners in the Cardellini Company ([33]), « Societas Cardellinorum », the Guidiccioni, Buggianesi and Tadolini families all participated in the Ricciardi partnership.

Were our sources more abundant, they would doubtless yield more examples of similar social bonds that welded the members of the Societas Ricciardorum together. But the evidence at hand seems sufficient to warrant the conclusion that the Ricciardi Company was in fact a long term alliance for commercial ends between families descending from the early partners in the enterprise, an alliance that was augmented by recruiting new members from other families which were through blood, marriage, consortial or neighborhood ties already linked to the group. I would assume that admission to partnership status of an individual lacking these ties must have been rare. In other words, despite its legal status as a simple partnership, the Ricciardi enterprise appears to have been similar functionally to the consortial organizations into which families of the Lucchese urban elite commonly banded together ([34]). I am suggesting here that the large-scale international *societas* differed from a consortium (in Lucca called *consortatus*) only in that its purpose was to engage in commerce and finance rather than to provide political and social refuge for its members.

Thus, although not a strictly closed family organization, the late thirteenth-century international company had a social dimension reinforcing purely economic considerations ([35]). As a business

---

(33) For the composition of the Cardellini Company in 1284, see BLOMQUIST, « *Commercial Organization* », p. 174.

(34) For the consortium in Lucca, see below.

(35) It is generally accepted that medieval partnership, « compagnia » or « societas » has its origins in family arrangements for the investment of a portion of the familial patrimony in commerce and that gradually these partnerships lost their identity with one family: see ROBERT S. LOPEZ and IRVING RAYMOND, eds., *Medieval Trade in the Mediterranean World* (New

alliance, however, the Societas Ricciardorum was highly successful. The company presumably was an effective instrument in building each constituent family's liquid assets. The Guidiccioni, beginning with Aldibrandino, evidently derived a considerable part of their movable resources from the profits earned by the company in international commerce and banking. The increase in their capital as well as the availability of credit allowed the Guidiccioni in turn to studiously invest in real estate: it was the resulting stable foundation of property that enabled them and other families associated with the Ricciardi to weather business failure and the recurring periods of bad economic times characteristic of the Later Middle Ages ([36]).

## The Evolution of the Guidiccioni Lineage

The architect of the foundations of Guidiccioni economic prosperity — a prosperity that goes far toward explaining the longevity and solidarity of the evolving Guidiccioni lineage — was Aldibrandino Guidiccioni. As we have noted, he was one of the earliest adherents to the nascent Ricciardi partnership and himself had done a brief stint in Champagne on behalf of the company. Aldibrandino was the head of an extended family until his death

---

York, London, 1955), pp. 185-211 for a discussion with illustrating documents of this phenomenon. FRANCO NICCOLAI, *I consorzi nobiliari ed il comune nell'alta e media Italia* (Bologna, 1940), p. 63 and JACQUES HEERS, *Le clan familial du moyen-âge* (Paris, 1974), pp. 230-231, have called attention to the parallels between the noble consortium and commercial partnerships. ROBERT DAVIDSOHN, *Storia di Firenze*, tr. G. Miccoli, VI, (Florence, 1965), pp. 365-378 discusses the importance of the family in Florentine mercantile-banking companies.

(36) For the Lucchese economy in the fourteenth century, see the two studies by CHRISTINE MEEK, « *The Trade and Industry of Lucca in the Fourteenth Century* », *Historical Studies: Papers Read before the Irish Conference of Historians*, VI (1965), pp. 39-58 and *Lucca 1349-1400: Politics and Society in an Early Renaissance State*, (Oxford, 1978). See also LOUIS GREEN, « *Lucchese Commerce under Castruccio Castracani* », forthcoming in *Actum Luce*: I am grateful to Professor Green for allowing me to consult the typescript of this article.

around the yiear 1282 ($^{37}$). Although it is quite likely that before his brother, Paganino's, demise shortly before 1265, the two lived together with their wives and offspring under one roof as an extended fraternal family, the documents in fact make only two brief references to Paganino during his lifetime ($^{38}$): all we can be sure of is that in 1265 Aldibrandino presided over a household consisting of himself; his three sons, Paganuccio, Parensio and Conte; Parensio's sons, Adoardo and Bindo; and five nephews, the sons of the deceased Paganino. Of these nephews — no mention is made of daughters — two, Guidiccione and Ricciardo, had obtained their respective majorities ($^{39}$). The remaining three were Aldibrandino who was sixteen, Tomasino fifteen and the infant Parensio. Thus the household of the Guidiccioni comprised at this time eleven males, an unknown number, if any, of daughters, spouses, and a suitable contingent of servants ($^{40}$).

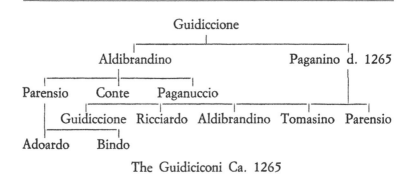

The Guidiciconi Ca. 1265

(37) BSL, BARONI, ms. no. 1115; year 1282, refers to Paganuccio, son of the late Aldibrandino (« Paganuccius filius quondam Aldibrandini »).

(38) *Ibidem;* years 1233 and 1253.

(39) *Ibidem;* year 1265.

(40) For the employment of servants, see ASL, *Archivio dei notari,* no. 17 (Alluminato Parensi), fol. 8, 7 January 1296: fol. 80, 9 June 1296: fol. 108, 18 August. Also fol. 30, 30 July 1296 for the will of Maria del fu Rodolfo, « olim de Pulliano provincie Garfagnane famula olim Paganucci condam Alderini Guidiccionis ».

Unfortunately the records reveal very little about Guidiccioni marriage unions; for example, we do not know the name of Aldibrandino's wife, although we do have the identity of the wives of three Guidiccioni males. Aldibrandino's son, Paganuccio, was first wed to an otherwise unidentified Giulia by whom be fathered Francesco and then to Agnesa, daughter of « Domino Gerardo di Garfagnana Luogo di Gragnana ([41]). One of Aldibrandino's nephews, Guidiccione was married to Mathilda, daughter of Orlando di Giorgio Medici, whose family held lands in the urban neighborhood of Cantonbretti, where the Guidiccioni were to concentrate their urban property holdings ([42]). The other married nephew, Ricciardo, was allied through his spouse, Contessa, with the Testa family, a family destined to play a significant part in the life of the important Lucchese mercantile-banking company of the Bettori ([43]). Although each of the Guidiccioni males, with the exception of Adoardo and Bindo, actively served the Ricciardi partnership, it was not until the early fourteenth century, when the fortunes of the Ricciardi company had gone into serious decline, that we find the Guidiccioni and Ricciardi families connected by marriage. A document of 1302 describes Marduccia, daughter of Paganuccio and thus Aldibrandino's granddaughter, as the wife of « Freduccio *quondam* Pieri *filius* Conecti Perfecti Ricciardi » scion of a branch collateral to the Ricciardi of mercantile promi-

---

(41) BSL, BARONI, ms. no. 1115; year 1298: Agnessa is described as the widow of Paganuccio and the « figlia di quondam Gerardo di Garfagnana ». ASL, *Archivio dei notari,* no. 17 (Alluminato Parensi), fols. 101-106v.: « Domina Angnezina uxor condam dicti Paganuccii » acted as guardian for her minor sons at the division of a portion of Paganuccio's estate which included « ... totius dotis condam Domine Giullie olim matris dicti Ceccori... ».

(42) BSL, BARONI, ms. no. 1115; year 1265 refers to « Domina Matilda di detto Guidiccione e figlia quondam Orlando di Giorgio Medici... ».

(43) *Ibidem,* year 1307 for « Contessa vedova quondam Ricciardo Guidiccioni figlia quondam Lunardo Teste ». See BLOMQUIST, « *Commercial Association* », p. 174, for the Testa and the Bettori Company.

nence ([44]). Fragmentary as these references to Guidiccioni marriage connections are, they nonetheless reflect the various fronts upon which members of the Guidiccioni family sought to advance their collective interests: they were allied to a noble family of the Garfagnana, indicating their interest in the country side; with a neighboring urban property holder; and with a family that was prominent in the Lucchese mercantile-banking community. Matrimonial ties were an obvious means to consolidate and extend the family's social network and to expand its circle of influence.

The extended household headed by Aldibrandino around 1265 was, of course, subject to the inexorable mechanism of the generational cycle. We can observe the emergence in the 1270's of the fraternal family descended from Paganino as a distinct line under the headship of Guidiccione, the eldest brother ([45]). When Aldibrandino died in 1281, his place as head of the fraternal family was taken by his eldest son Paganuccio who presided over a household that included his two nephews, Adoardo and Bindo ([46]). Upon Paganuccio's death in 1296 his surviving brother, Conte, assumed the tutelage of the nephews ([47]). But despite this inevitable branching out into two households the thirteenth-century Guidiccioni display a consistent solidarity as brothers, sons, nephews and cousins worked together for the benefit of the larger family.

---

(44) BSL, BARONI, ms. no. 1130; *Ricciardi,* year 1302.

(45) In all purchase-sale contracts Guidiccione acted as procurator for his brothers. Apparently he remained in Lucca while Ricciardo and Tomasino were abroad.

(46) After his father's death, Paganino acted, as did Guidicicone, as procurator for his brother and nephews in property transactions: see BSL, BARONI, ms. no. 1115; *Guidiccioni, passim.* Also ASL, *Archivio dei notari,* no. 17 (Alluminato Parensi), fol. 2, 3 January 1296 for mention of the « domo nova magna dicti Paganuccii et fratris et nepotum ».

(47) For Conte acting for himself and his nephews, BSL, BARONI, ms. no. 1115; *Guidiccioni, passim.*

Aldibrandino's Line

Paganino's Line

Birth and death were, of course, the ultimate determinants of family size and organization. But for the Guidiccioni, as no doubt for other families engaged in international business, another less dramatic element influenced family structure at any particular time. All Guidiccioni men were active in the Ricciardi company, and the exigencies of business kept many of them away for extended periods of time. For example, Aldibrandino's nephew, Ricciardo, was in England much of the time between 1279 and 1301, and in th 1280's he was the most important member of the Ricciardi company operating there ([48]). Thus, for twenty-two years Ricciardo was more or less — he was in Lucca in 1284 and in 1296 — continuously absent from his native city and his family. The career of Ricciardo's younger brother, Tomasino, is quite similar. He first ap-

---

(48) KAEUPER, *Bankers to the Crown*, p. 15.

pears in the English documents of the year 1273, when he would have been only twenty-three years old. In England he played a significant role in the Ricciardi's northern English branch located at York and in 1290 Edward I dispatched him on a mission to Rome. He is last mentioned in the English sources in the year 1301 [49]. Tomasino, then, would seem to have spent much of his life between the ages of twenty-three and fifty-one abroad in the service of the Ricciardi. Other Guidiccioni also make their appearances in the English documents relating to the company. Adibrandino's nephew and namesake was in England in 1278, although probably for a relatively short stay [50]. Somewhat later, Marchesino Guidiccioni, the son of Aldibrandino's eldest offspring Paganuccio, also appeared in England between the years 1293-1297 [51]. Another of Aldibrandino's descendents operating in England on behalf of the Ricciardi partnership was Nieruccio, called Renerio in the English documents, the son of Conte Guidiccionis, who was active abroad between 1285 and 1290 [52]. Conte Guidiccionis himself was « in partibus Francie » in 1296 when his co-partners in the Ricciardi elected him director of the company [53]. Another member of the Guidiccioni one « Guido Guidiccioni », likewise appeared among the Ricciardi operating in Northern Europe. This was in all probability Guidiccione whom we have already encountered as the head of the Guidiccioni line developing from Paganino. Although he is mentioned in connection with the Low Countries in 1287 and 1297 his visits there must in fact have been brief [54].

---

(49) *Ibidem,* pp. 15, 42.

(50) *Ibidem,* p. 56.

(51) *Ibidem,* pp. 15, 56.

(52) *Ibidem,* p. 56.

(53) BLOMQUIST, « *Administration of a Thirteenth-Century Mercantile-Banking Partnership* », p. 8.

(54) KAEUPER, *Bankers to the Crown,* p. 58. Although the English sources place him in the Low Countries in 1279, Guidiccione was in Lucca on 16 June 1279 when he bought a piece of property: ASL, *Diplomatico: Archivio dei Notari,* 16 June 1279.

The effects of these lengthy absences abroad upon domestic attitudes are easy to imagine yet impossible to measure with any precision. Undoubtedly one result of a prolonged sojourn abroad such as Ricciardo's twenty-two year tour north of the Alps was that his two children, Guiduccio and Ciambene, were raised by their mother in the bosom of an extended fraternal household presided over by their uncle Guidiccione. And, as we have seen, Ricciardo and his brothers had themselves been reared, along with their cousins, in the extended family directed by their uncle Aldibrandino. Growing up in a large family setting was an experience common to all Guidiccioni children of these generations: the second generation matured under the tutelage of Aldibrandino, the third in an extended fraternal ambient created as new lines, each under the leadership of the eldest brother stemmed from the main branch. However, the continuing cohesion of the expanding Guidiccioni cognate group suggests the subordination of newly emergent lines to the wider patriarchal lineage which remained the fundamental action group in advancing the Guidiccioni fortunes.

Identity with the larger family was affirmed specifically as each member, through the form of his name, identified with Guidiccione, the common ancestor. Guidiccione's first generation offspring, Aldibrandino and Paganino, were styled in the documents by the simple patronym, expressed in the Latin genitive form, as in « Aldibrandino Guidiccionis » ([55]). The second generation, Aldibrandino's sons and nephews, likewise employed their father's name to identify themselves; for example, « Tomazinus *condam* Paganini Guidiccionis » ([56]). This practice was continued in the third generation, as when Aldibrandino's, grandson was referred to as « Ceccorus *sive* Francescus *condam* Albertini (i. e. Aldibran-

---

(55) See *inter alia* ASL, *Diplomatico, S. Maria Corte Orlandini,* 6 December 1245.

(56) Among numerous examples, see ASL, *Archivio dei notari,* no. 15 (Bartolomeo Fulcieri, Tegrimo Fulcieri, Fulciero Fulcieri), fol. 33, 21 January 1284.

dini) Guidiccionis » in 1299 at the time he and his two minor brothers claimed their inheritance from their recently deceased father's estate ([57]).

At the same time, we can see the name of the common ancestor gradually emerging as a surname for all his descendents. Furthermore, Guidiccioni operating in England on behalf of the Ricciardi partnership apparently associated themselves, through the use of the Latin genitive form of Guidiccione's name, immediately with the lineage: we read, for example, of « Richard Guidichonis », « Thomasinus Guidichum » and « Reynerius Guidichonis » in the English documents ([58]). And in the necrology of the Lucchese monastery of San Michele in Guamo, we find entries not only for « Aldibrandinus Guidiccionis » and his brother « Paganinus Guidiccionis », both of which names employ the standard Latin patronymic, but for Aldibrandino's two sons, Parensio and Paganuccio, as well ([59]). In the latter citations, identification is by reference only to their grandfather Guidiccione; a certain indication of the transformation of the common ancestor's name into the family name. This expression of common origins by means of a surname was unquestionably the result of a heightened familial self-consciousness and pride, as well as a means of strengthening affective ties and a sense of family solidarity at a time when the extended family was evolving into a more complex, multibranched lineage.

More concrete evidence of increasing familial awareness on the part of the Guidiccioni comes to us in the form of a family crypt constructed in 1290 in the chapel of Santa Maria del Soccor-

---

(57) ASL, *Archivio dei notari,* no. 17 (Alluminato Parensi), fol. 101, 19 August 1299.

(58) *Calendar of the Patent Rolls Preserved in the Public Record Office: Edward I, 1272-1281* (London, 1901), pp. 354,356, 425 and EMILIO RE, « *Archivi inglesi e storia italiana* », *Archivio storico italiano,* ser 6, I (1913), p. 280.

(59) ASL, *Raccolti speciali; Monastero di San Michele in Guamo,* I, fols. 7, 16v, 18v. I am indebted to Professor Duane Osheim of the University of Virginia for supplying these references.

so adjacent to the Lucchese church of San Frediano. The burial place is marked by two tombs, of which the one to the right bears the following inscription in rhymned vernacular:

DISCE[N]DE[N]TI DI SER ALDIBRA[N]DINO ET DI SUO FRATEL

PAGANINO. GIACENO I[N] QUESTO LAVELLO. P[ER] LORO F[A]C[T]O

SI BELLO. DICTI FILLIUOLI GUIDICCION[I]. P[RE] GHIAMO

DIO CHE LOR P[ER] DONI. QUESTA E P[ER] LI MASCHI F[A]C[T]O.

ET P[ER] LE FEMINE L'ALTRO IN MCCXC. AIUTILI LA VERGINE S[AN]C[T]A ([60]).

We could hardly wish for more eloquent testimony of the sense of family identity — or to the perceived need to maintain that sense of identity — than this monument and the sentiment expressed in the epitaph. Particularly, there is the studied effort to link irrevocably together the two lines represented by Aldibrandino and Paganino, to link in effect the family's past, the family's present, and future. For the emphasis upon the bond between the two dead brothers clearly evoked the kinship of their « discendenti » now united as the « Guidiccioni sons ».

The decision to construct a family tomb most probably developed within family councils. The descendants of Aldibrandino and Paganino had evolved into affiliated branches and the building of the tomb commemorating the ancestral brothers undoubtedly required the approval of the members of both lines devolving through them from Guidiccione. Moreover, arrangements for the up-keep of the monuments were needed and this inevitably would have required a continuing monetary assessment against all « descendenti »: a levy which could have been assessed only after all affected Guidiccioni had given their consent. No documentation survives to shed light upon the building and management of the family tomb, although notarial deeds recording other events similary touching the Guidiccioni lineage as a whole show all adult

---

(60) The inscription is published in PACCHI, *Ricerche storiche,* p. 132, note 17 and ISA BELLI BARSALI, *Guida di Lucca* (Lucca, 1970), p. 192. I am following the latter's transcription.

males registering their individual approval. The adherance of
Guidiccioni absent from Lucca at the time any such decision was
ratified was customarily secured by one or more of their brothers
acting as agent or agents for the missing kin. Through this use
of agency, family members away from Lucca participated legally,
if vicariously, in family affairs. Examples of the scrupulous na-
ming of all adult males, whether physically present or represented
by a procurator, most often involve joint purchase of property by
the lineage. We should reasonably assume that no less delibera-
teness, nor less unanimity of purpose was devoted to the decision
to erect and maintain a family sepulchre — a permanent reminder
of the singularity of the « filluoli Guidiccioni » — than we find
in the handling of other decisions regarding common property.

\*

L'A. ha studiato la famiglia Guidiccioni sulla base dei documenti
notarili conservati nei vari archivi lucchesi. Si dimostra l'importanza notevole dei membri della famiglia nell'ambito della compagnia dei Ricciardi,
mettendo in luce i legami fra i due gruppi sulla base del noto fenomeno
del *consortato*. La compattezza del gruppo familiare è dimostrato attraverso
l'indagine dei singoli componenti la famiglia, che trae il suo cognome da
un avo comune attorno al 1290.

\*

L'A. a étudié la famille Guidiccioni d'après des documents notariés,
conservés dans les divers archives lucquois. On démontre l'importance con-
sidérable des membres de la famille dans le cercle de la compagnie des
Ricciardi, mettant en évidence les liens entre les deux groupes d'après le

fameux phénomène de l'association. L'union du groupe familial est démontrés à travers la recherche de chaque membre de la famille qui prend son nom d'un ancêtre commun autor de 1290.

Der Autor hat über die Familie Guidiccioni auf Grund der in den verschiedenen Archiven von Lucca aufbewahrten notariellen Dokumenten Nachforschungen aufgestellt. Die grosse Bedeuting der Familienmitglieder im Bereiche der Gruppe der Ricciardi wird gezeigt und dabei die Verbindung zwischen den zwei Gruppen auf Grund des gut bekannten Vorgangs der Vermählungen ans Licht gebracht.

Der Zusammenhalt der Familienangehörigen wird durch eine Nachforschung über die einzelnen Familienglieder bewiesen, deren Nachname auf einen gemeinsamen Ahnen zurückgeht und aus den Jahren um 1290 stammt.

# III

LINEAGE, LAND AND BUSINESS, IN THE THIRTEENTH
CENTURY: THE GUIDICCIONI FAMILY OF LUCCA *

### The Guidiccioni as an Economic Unit

The Guidiccioni family was not only a strong social entity,
but also functioned as an economic unit of considerable force.
Economically the family moved on a variety of fronts. Although
ultimately property proved the nexus that bound the family group
together over time, it was commercial profit derived from the
family's involvement in the Ricciardi company that made real investment on a significant scale possible.

Throughout the thirteenth century, from Aldibrandino on,
Guidiccioni were taken one after the other into the firm. For a
son to follow in his father's footsteps, however, was hardly rarity
in the world of the Lucchese mercant banker. We find, for exam-

---

\* *La prima parte di questo articolo è stata pubblicata in Actum Luce,*
*1980 n. 1-2.*

ple, descendants of the earliest partners—the Roscimpelli, the Sexmondi, Buggianesi and Di Poggio—listed among the Ricciardi partners at the end of the thirteenth century ([61]). What distinguishes Guidiccioni men is the consistency with they carved out careers in the company. Unlike the Ricciardi family which in the second generation descending from Perfetto and Ricciardo had seemingly given up an active role in the partnership, none of the thirteenth-century Guidiccioni abandoned the world of international commerce and banking ([62]). Such consistency argues strongly for the existence of a conscious family economic policy; and, the regularity with which that strategy was implemented implies a high level of familial discipline and solidarity.

When Conte stepped up to the director's office in 1296, the Ricciardi company was already in serious difficulty ([63]). In fact, it is most probable that this promotion was part of a general administrative shakeup intended to bring in fresh leadership to deal with the problems that had plagued the company since 1294 ([64]). But whatever the circumstances of Conte's assumption of the Ricciardi directorship, he and his colleagues failed to restore the company to sound financial health; in the first decade of the fourteenth century the once proud Societas Ricciardorum was reduced to a

---

(61) KAEUPER, *Bankers to the Crown*, pp. 56-59.

(62) Apparently Adoardo and Bindo, sons of Parensio di Aldibrandino Guidiccionis did not join in the Ricciardi partnership. However, in 1314 they along with « Coluccius quondam Tomasini Guidiccionis et Guiduccius quondam Ricciardi Guidiccionis et Coluccius eius filius et Guidiccius et Maginellus germani filii Mazini Guidiccionis were described as « publici negotiatori » indicating some involvement in commerce: BSL, BARONI, ms. no. 1115; year 1314.

(63) For the following discussion of the Ricciardi decline; KAEUPER, *Bankers to the Crown*, pp. 209-251 and RE, « *La compagnia dei Ricciardi* ». On the Italians in England in the late thirteenth century, see MICHAEL PRESTWICH, « *Italian Merchants in Late Thirteenth and Early Fourteenth Century England* », *The Dawn of Modern Banking*, Center for Medieval and Renaissance Studies, University of California, Los Angeles (New Haven, London, 1979), pp. 77-104.

(64) BLOMQUIST, « *Administration of a Thirteenth-Century Mercantile-Banking Partnership* », pp. 6-7.

handful of partners trying to sort out and wind up the firm's tangled affairs.

The immediate cause of the Ricciardi decline was the liquidity crisis created when Edward I and Philip the Fair both seized Ricciardi assets in their respective realms in 1294. These misfortunes in and of themselves would problably not have been fatal had they not been accompanied by simultaneous demands from Pope Boniface VIII for repayment of papal funds held on deposit by the Ricciardi. The company simply could not raise sufficient funds to offset the losses incurred through the royal confiscations and the interruption of normal business, yet at the same time come up with the 80,000 gold florins due the papacy ([65]).

The monetary damages suffered by the company as a result of Philip's arrest of Ricciardi partners and his confiscation of their goods cannot be calculated. But most crippling must have been the Crown's assumption of debts owed the Ricciardi within the realm and the cessation of their financial dealing at the Fairs of Champagne where, as one partner put it in 1296, the company previously « could borrow one million, two hundred thousand pounds tournois and more » ([66]). This quotation gives some idea of the capital sums with which the Ricciardi were accustomed to deal.

Although nothing is known of the partnership's profit structure prior to the difficulties issuing from the events of 1294, the yield on the partner's capital and labor must have been considerable ([67]). Because of their number, Guidiccioni considered as a group would have received a percentage of these earnings larger than that accruing to any other single family. Actually, of course, profits were distributed pro rata to individual partners, but Gui-

---

(65) KAEUPER, *Bankers to the Crown*, p. 233.

(66) RE, « *La compagnia dei Ricciardi* », pp. 108-109.

(67) SAPORI, « *Storia interna della compagnia mercantile dei Peruzzi* », pp. 672-673, calculates the return upon invested capital to the Peruzzi of 1300 to have been 15.4%. ROBERT DAVDSOHN, *Storia di Firenze*, pp. 390-391, estimates the average annual profit of the Strozzi Company in the years 1318-1339 at 13.6% .

10

diccioni came together frequently to pool their liquid resources in order to construct a common patrimony based upon joint ownership of property.

In trying to demonstrate the economic structure of the Guidiccioni and to follow the intricacies of the economic relations between family members, we are seriously handicapped by the loss of the personal books and contracts which Paganuccio had deposited before his death with the local Franciscans. In 1296 Francesco retrieved his dead father's records from the Chancellor of the convent and this material apparently became a part of a Guidiccioni family archive which Dr. Domenico Corsi, the retired director of the State Archive of Lucca, has informed me is now lost [68]. Baroni did, however, have access to this archive and he has abstracted from « a book in parchment » [69] — the same volume described by another Lucchese scholar, A. N. Cianelli in 1816 « as an ancient book of contracts pertaining to the most noble and respected house of the Guidiccioni » — a series of property transactions entered into by Aldibrandino and his heirs. [70]. Baroni's account in conjunction with the surviving notarial deeds, reveals, if only in outline, the pattern followed in constructing the Guidiccioni estate.

---

(68) ASL, *Archivio dei notari*, no. 17 (*Alluminato Parensi*) fol. 86, 20 July 1296: the material was described as « unum librum in quo sunt aliqui quaterni cartarum bambacis scripti et partim non scripti. Item duos quaternos cartarum bambacis qui scripti sunt pro parte et pro certa parte non que omnia erant in quodam sacculo. Item unum farsenum privium pictum et clausum et leve quod erat in predicto sacculo cum predictis rebus. Item unum sacchum novum in quo sunt multe carte in quibusdam taschettis de redditibus dicti condam Paganuccii qui taschetti erant otto ».

(69) Baroni's calendar deals only with Aldibrandino's line. The entries are taken from a « book in parchment in the ''Archivio Guidiccionis'' ». It seems inevitable that this book was among the « libri » deposited by Paganuccio.

(70) A. N. CIANELLI, « *De' conti rurali nello stato lucchese* », *Dissertazione duodecima* of *Dissertazioni sopra la storia di Lucca* in *Memorie e documenti per servire all'istoria della città e stato di Lucca,* III (Lucca, 1816), pp. 180-181. Both Cianelli and Baroni exerpt the same document of 1281, indicating they both were working from the same material.

However to think of the Guidiccioni estate as one, easily definable coherent block of property transmitted intact through the generations is to oversimplify the issue of the family's communal property. It is necessary, I believe, to consider tho economic relations existing between family members in terms of an intricate network of interlocking rights over property shared in various degrees by Guidiccioni men. Furthermore, as the lineage grew in complexity, as subordinate fraternal families assumed a distinct identity, new clusters of property rights among brothers, sons and nephews also appeared. Fundamentally, all Guidiccioni of the thirteenth century despite the degree of consaguinity were united by property bonds, but these were of differing intensity and levels, ranging from property held wholly or in part by the entire lineage, through property shared by extended fraternal branches down to individual patrimonies passed on undivided to one's heirs and finally to the specific legacy bequeathed by a father to each of his sons. Division through successive generations of common property rights of the lineage would increasingly diminish any given individual's share of the common patrimony. On the other hand, the property ties joining fraternal families would assume a correspondingly greater, more immediate, significance to the individual, especially for members of more remote branches.

The property rights shared by all members of the lineage can be traced back to Aldibrandino and his strategy of acquiring real estate in such a way as to build up the family's position in three main geographic regions: the locale of Cantonbretti (Castrum Bretti), a neighborhood primarily within the urban district of San Andrea, but which extended into the contiguous quarter of San Salvatore in Mustolio; the rural community of Capannori and environs, located about four miles to the East of Lucca; and, Verrucola, a mountainous redoubt situated in the alps of Garfagnana.

It would appear that Aldibrandino and Paganino maintained their patrimonies separately. We have no record of their buying property jointly. Following the death of his brother, Aldibrandino was constrained to mingle his property with the patrimony of his five nephews. In 1265 he purchased for L 50 one-seventh of the undivided legacy, consisting of a house and land in Cantonbretti

12

as well as lands in Capannori that Paganino had left to his sons ([71]). Judging from the property that Paganino bequeathed to his sons, it is evident that by the time of his death the Guidiccioni had secured a foothold in Cantonbretti and the rural region of Capannori. Indeed, as early as 1233 Paganino was so closely identified with the former area that he was referred to as « Paganinus quondam Guidiccionis de Cantonbretto »; ([72]) just as some years later Aldibrandino was referred to as « Dominus Aldibrandinus quondam Guidiccionis de Cantonbretto » ([73]). Cantonbretti was to remain the geographical center of Guidiccioni holdings in the city of Lucca not only in the thirteenth century but through succeeding centuries as well: here the family continued to buy land, houses and towers; and, as we shall see, carefully nurtured connections with their neighbors. Indeed, today the Piazza Guidiccioni and the magnificent sixteenth-century Palazzo Guidiccioni, housing the State Archive of Lucca, stand on the ground of medieval Cantonbretti.

Guidiccione himself — or an even earlier forebear — in all likelihood was influenced to settle in that area of the city by the presence there of the noble clan of the Gerardinghi of Garfagnana. We have speculated earlier on that the Guidiccioni originated from Verrucola in the Garfagnana where the noble Gerardinghi, « Domus Gherardinorum », held sway as territorial lords ([74]). It is plausible that the first of the Guidiccioni to immigrate to the city would have located in the shadow of a powerful rural neighbor. The possibility that the Guidiccioni settled in Lucca under the wing of the Gherardinghi suggests an interesting larger question regarding the influence of these « rural family clans » upon the pattern of urban settlement by immigrants of lesser so-

---

(71) BSL, BARONI, ms. no. 1115; year 1265.

(72) *Ibidem*, year 1233.

(73) PACCHI, *Ricerche storiche*, Appendix, pp. 34-36, document no. 31.

(74) For the Gherardinghi, see GIOACCHINO VOLPE, *Toscana medievale* (Florence, 1964), p. 335; CIANELLI, « *De' conti rurali* », pp. 177-182 and PACCHI, *Ricerche storiche*, pp. 88, 116, 132.

cial status: to what degree did the presence of a rural noble consortium in the city serve to attract newcomers from the consortial
rural territories? We may speculate that when the Gherardinghi,
who apparently remained essentially rural in their interests — and
probably in their attitudes as well — took up residence in Lucca,
they acted as a magnet attracting later arrivals from their lands in
the Garfagnana. No definitive proof that this occurred appears in
the available sources. Be that as it may, it appears that once established in Lucca the Guidiccioni turned their attention back to Garfagnana, where by the end of the century they had gained a preeminence within the rural consortium of the Gherardinghi as well as
control, exercised in the name of the Lucchese Commune, of Verrucola. In other words, we have here an exception, albeit a relatively minor one, to Jacques Heers' recent hypothesis that the rural family clans directly and enduringly influenced the course and
form of medieval urban development [75]. According to Professor
Heers, one aspect of this influence was the ascendency of the
rural family clans within the urban quarters in which they first
settled: the clans dominated urban areas in much the same way
that they dominated their rural domains [76]. The presence of the
Gherardinghi in Lucca may well have drawn population from the
country to the city as recently as the first half of the thirteenth-century—up to this poind heer's argument seem valid—but it is equally
certain that the upstart Guidiccioni, fueled by success as international merchants and bankers, became the principal force in Cantonbretti. In fact, the single reference that I have found to the
existence of an urban court, or closed courtyard, belonging to the
Gherardinghi is dated 1273 and makes mention of a « court called of the Gerardinghi' », « corte che si dice dei Gherardinghi' » [77]: by the latter part of the thirteenth century the active

---

(75) HEERS, *La clan famial,* pp. 150-166.

(76) *Ibidem,* especially pp. 157-162.

(77) *Ibidem,* pp. 154-157 for the urban courts. The reference is in BSL,
BARONI, ms. no. 1115; year 1273.

presence of this noble clan in the city would appear to have been only a memory.

Aldibrandino continued to expand his holding in San Andrea and in Capannori, a policy adhered to by later generations of Guidiccioni. In 1255 he bought land with a house and common wall in the contrada of San Andrea, from Gemma, the wife of Orlando di Corrado Ricciardi, for L 328 ([78]). This transaction was followed in 1259 by the purchase of an additional house and land in the same quarter from Gemma for 200 ([79]). And, in 1263 he bought part of a house in Cantonbretti and property in Capannori for L 215 ([80]). These notices are all that survive of Aldibrandino's urban buying in the period before Paganino's demise, but the focus upon the contrada of San Andrea is patently clear.

The same consistency is very much in evidence in Aldibrandino's acquisitions in the countryside where he concentrated almost exclusively on Capannori. In 1249 Aldibrandino bought land there from members of the Di Poggio and Perfetti families L 32 ([81]). In 1258, 1259, 1262, and 1265 he acquired land in Tofori, a village near Capannori, through four transactions worth L 44 29s., 50s., L 20 14s. and L 7 10s. respectively ([82]). In 1259 he secured lands in San Vito di Tempagnano, two miles to the west of Capannori, for L 80 ([83]). The year 1263 witnessed two more purchases of lands in Capannori proper; the first from the Malaspina family for L 443 10s., the second for L 50 from Dominus Ubaldo Bargecchia del fu Guglielmo dei Gherardinghi and Ugolino del fu Nuccollone dei Gherardinghi, both acting as procurators for Ugolino's sister([8a]).

--------

(78) *Ibidem,* year 1255.

(79) *Ibidem,* year 1259.

(80) *Ibidem,* year 1263.

(81) *Ibidem,* year 1249. For the geography of the Lucchese contado, see EMANUELE REPETTI, *Dizionario geografico fisico storico della Toscana,* 6 vols. (Florence, 1833-1846).

(82) BSL, BARONI, ms. no. 1115; years 1258, 1259, 1262, 1265.

(83) *Ibidem,* year 1259.

(94) *Ibidem,* year 1263.

And in 1265, Aldibrandino acquired land in Picciorana, also near Capannori, for L 122 ([85]). Again, in 1265, he acquired « all the lands » held by one Bongiattoro of Marlia for the sum of L 50 ([86]). The location of this latter property was unspecified, but given the pattern of rural buyng established by Aldibrandino we way assume that it was in or near Capannori.

In the movement of the Guidiccioni back into the Garfagnana, Aldibrandino initially opted to deal directly with the collective territorial lord of Verrucola, the « Domus Gherardinghorum », rather then attempt the difficult task of assembling a solid block of land out of numerous smaller purchases. Over three generations, the Guidiccioni, armed with liquid capital, succesfully insinuated themselves into the « Comune et Universitas Gherardinghorum ».

The first step in this infiltration occured on 2 November 1261, when « Dominus » Gherardetto Blanco, Podestà, or head of the Gherardinghi, acting with the consent and according to the will of eighteen of his fellow consorts « Comunis et Universitatis Gherardinghorum » appointed another member of the consortium, Saladino del fu Ghiberti, as procurator to arrange the sale of one-twentieth of all rights possessed by the Gherardinghi in the Garfagnana to « Dominus Aldibrandinus quondam Guidiccionis de Cantumbretto » and « to his heirs and successors » ([87]). Furthermore, Saladino was empowered to negotiate the sale price but was istructed to use the good offices of « Dominus » Gherardino, canon of the Cathedral Church of San Martino in Lucca, as an arbiter in determining a mutually satisfactory arrangement.

The next day, following this preliminary arrangement, Saladino sold the one-twentieth of the Gherardinghi rights « in Verucola Gherardinghorum et Bibbiana, Mechiana et S. Romano, Nagio et Bollio, Petrognano et Silicagnana, quae terrae sunt de Curria Verucolae praedictae, et in Silico, Capraia et Bargecchia, Monte

---

(85) *Ibidem*, year 1265.
(86) *Ibidem*.
(87) PACCHI, *Ricerche storiche*, Appendix, pp. 34-36, document no. 31.

16

et Torrite, et Summacologna » to Aldibrandino and his heirs ([88]). In addition, Aldibrandino and his heirs were made consorts of the Gherardinghi (« quatenus Dominus Aldibrandinus, et ejus heredes etc. de cetero sint Gherardinghi, et Gherardinghorum, et dicti Comunis et Universitatis etc.. »).

In 1281, shorly after Aldibrandino's death the Guidiccioni augmented their position within the « Domus Gherardinghorum », by further purchase of Gherardinghi rights. The reference to this transaction comes from the pages of A.N. Cianelli's *Dissertazioni sopra la storia Lucchese* ([89]). Although the transcription is unfortunately incomplete, it indicates that in April 1281 « Aldobrando del fu Compagni de Verrucola Gherardinghorum », acted as procurator in the purchase of one-seventy-seventh of all rights held by the Gherardinghi in unspecified localities, but evidently in the Garfagnana, on behalf of his principals « Paganuccio et Conte germanis filiis quondam Aldibrandini Guidiccionis et pro Adoardo et Bindo eorum nepotibus filiis quondam Parentii Germani ipsorum Paganuccii et Contis et dicti Aldibrandini». We do not know the cost of this acquisition; but, when added to Aldibrandino's purchase in 1261, it gave the Guidiccioni a share of slightly over 5-1/2% in the Gherardinghi patrimony.

Somewhat surprisingly, Paganino's line was not included in the above arrangement; only Aldibrandino's direct heirs and his nephews took part. But this situation was altered four years later when yet another sale of Gherardinghi dominium in the Garfagnana to the Guidiccioni was consummated ([90]). On this occasion, the exact fraction of the total Gherardinghi rights was not stated — Baroni uses the phrase « una porzione » — but the sale price is given at 1,800 gold florins, or approximately, L 3,457 lucchese. Not only was Paganino's line represented but the Buggia-

---

(88) *Ibidem.*

(89) CIANELLI, « *Dei conti rurali* », pp. 180-181.

(90) PACCHI, *Ricerche storiche,* Appendix, pp. 38-39, document no. 34 and BSL, BARONI, ms. no. 1115; year 1285.

nesi family, who as we have seen were linked by kinship to the Guidiccioni, likewise participated jointly in the purchase. Domenico Pacchi in his historical study of the Garfagnana includes as an appendix the contract solemnizing the transaction; but, as he says, « solo in piccola parte ». Among other omissions, he fails to give the full list of buyers, choosing instead to provide only the names of the principals present on the occasion while representing those they acted for with « etc ». as in « vendiderunt...... Paganuccio q. Aldibrandi Guidiccionis ementi etc. » Although communicating only the barest detalis, Baroni's summary of the same document does list the purchasers as follows:.... « vendono a Paganuccio del quondam Aldobrandino Guidiccioni pro se e pro Conte suo fratello e pro li suoi nepoti figli del quondam Paranso suoi fratelli, e a Bartollotto del quondam Buggianesi Bandini pro se e pro Rainerio e Lazario suoi fratelli, e a Tomasino del quondam Paganino Guidiccioni, e a Cionello figlio di Ricciardo del quondam Paganino compranti pro loro e pro Ricciardo padre di Cionello e pro Guidiccione fratello di detto Tomasino e Ricciardo ». Thus the two fraternal branches of the lineage were represented as distinct entities, as were the Buggianesi: each, according to Pacchi, answering for a discrete one-third share, « pro tertia Parte », of the total purchase.

Following this arrangement, the Gherardinghi formally, if in the case of Aldibrandino's line redundantly, accepted each of the principals named in the preceding into the « consortato », to use Baroni's rendering, « della Casa Gherardinga ». Thus, even if we exclude Paganuccio and Conte from our count on the grounds that they were already consorts by virtue of being Aldibrandino's heirs, nine new adherents were added at one fell swoop to the Gherardinghi community. It is true that the total number of consorts was probably larger in 1285 than it had been in 1261 when Aldibrandino first bought into the Gherardinghi, and that we do not know what percentage of the total Gherardinghi wealth was held by the Guidiccioni. Nevertheless, the sudden influx of nine new members who were also allied with the two existing Guidiccioni consorts surely gave these newcomers a preponderance of influence—reminiscent of their position vis-a-vis the Ricciardi partnership

—within the larger « Commune et Universitas Gherardinorum ». And, according to a series of four revealing documents from late 1280's this urban bloc among the rural nobles did not hesitate to use its weight.

In the first of these documents, dated 31 May 1287, Paganuccio, acting for himself and for his brother Conte; Guidiccione, likewise stipulating for himself and for his two brothers Ricciardo and Tomasino, as well as for his nephews Cionellus and Guiduccius, Ricciardo's sons; along with Lazzaro del fu Buggianese who spoke for himself and his brother, Bertolotto; all acting on their own behalf as well as for their consorts in the « Domus Gherardinghorum » (« ... et tam pro se ipsis quam etiam pro omnibus consortibus eorum qui sunt de domo Gherardinghorum ») appointed two procurators to look after their rights and the rights of the Gherardinghi (« ... suorum et consortium Gherardinghorum ») in the Garfagnana or elsewhere (« manutenendum omnem eorum jurisdictionem Garfagnane et ubiqumque » ([91]). In this instance we can observe the Guidiccioni performing, with no express delegation of either podestarial or procuratorial power, as a discrete sub-group within the larger consortial whole.

The apparent authority of the urban Guidiccioni and their allies, the Buggianesi, to act on behalf of the Gherardinghi becomes even more explicit in another document, similar to the one above, redacted on 12 June 1288 ([92]). Here Guidiccione del fu Paganino « de Guidiccionibus » stipulating for himself and as procurator for his brothers Ricciardo and Tomasino, acting along with Bartolotto del fu Buggianese and the brothers Cionello and Guiduccio, Ricciardo's sons, appointed Lazzaro del fu Buggianese as their procurator to collect from the consuls of the Communes of Silico, Capraia and Barghecchia « provincie Garfagnane » the sum of L 75 which had been awarded « nobilibus et consortibus

---

(91) ASL, *Archivio dei notari*, no. 18 (Alluminato Parensi), fol. 9v, 31 May 1287.

(92) *Ibidem*, fol. 126.

duos Gherardinghorum » by the appeals judge of Lucca. Following this declaration, Paganuccio and Conte, acting for themselves and their nephews Adoardo and Bindo also ratified in a separate codicil Lazzaro's appointment. Once more there is no suggestion of any delegation of authority that allowed the urban block to act in this fashion for the entire consortium.

Although the above examples of the unique relationshp of the Guidiccioni to the rural « domus Gherardinghorum » do not specify the excact legal standing of the former within the larger corporate proup, by 1288, they had gained control of the chief executive office of the consortium. On 25 May 1288 « Cionellus filius Ricciardi Guidiccionis », in his capacity as podestà of the Gherardinghi, (« potestas domus nobilium Gherardinghorum »), endowed Aldobrandino del fu Compagno with procuratorial powers to deal on behalf of the consortium with the consuls of the Communes of Silico, Capraia, and Barghecchia, probably regarding the dispute that resulted in the judgment referred to above (⁹³).

As yet a futher indication of the Guidiccioni position vis-a-vis the Gherardinghi, Cionello was allowed to succeed himself as podestà for the second half the year 1288. On 5 August Bertolotto and Lazzaro di Buggianese; Guidiccione di Paganino who was stipulating for himself and his absent brothers Ricciardo and Tomasino; and Conte del fu Aldibrandino Guidiccioni stated that they had heard and knew of (« audita et intellecta est ») the election of « Cionello filio dicti Ricciardi » by the nobles of the Gherardinghi as Podestà for the last six months of the year (⁹⁴). Having recorded this fact, the principals then went on to vow that they ratified Cionello's earlier election carried out by their rural consorts. Finally, in two codicils added to the main body of the document, Adoardo, Bindo and Paganuccio subsequently added their assent to the election « just as Bertolotto and the others did above ». Once again we find a clear distinction made between the urban Guidic-

---

(93) *Ibidem*, fol. 118.
(94) *Ibidem*, fol. 139.

cioni and their rural counterparts in the consortium: in this instance by what appears to have been the right of final approval in a twostage electoral process of the head of the Gherardinghi.

The last thirteenth-century document to deal explicitly with the Guidiccioni and the Gherardinghi not only illustrates further the Guidiccioni penetration of the Garfagnana and their accumulation of power in the region but illuminates as well the social and economic solidarity of the lineage. On 25 July 1296 representatives of the now three fraternal branches of the family, «Guidiccione (et) Ricciardus germanii filii condam Aldebrandini Guidiccionis (et) Cecchorus filius Paganuccii condam Aldebrandini Guidiccionis (et) Adoardus condam Aldebrandini Guidiccionis qui sunt omnes de civitate lucana» with the concurrence of the Podestà and the Captain of Lucca declared in a notarial deposition that they, the Guidiccioni, were to hold Verrucola in the name of the Lucchese commune from 1 October next for the full year following [95]. Thus, the representatives of the three fraternal groups were brought together and collectively they spoke for the united lineage. Moreover, it is significant that only the Guidiccioni took part in this arrangement: their allies, the Buggianesi, whom we have witnessed buying into the Gherardinghi with them were apparently excluded from this action. It seems to have been strictly a family affair.

But why would the rural Gherardinghi consorts permit this veritable incursion of urban merchants, albeit merchants with strong ties to the Garfagnana, into their number? The primary reason was undoubtedly money: the Guidiccioni had liquid capital available while Gherardinghi wealth was in the form of control over land and people in a relatively poor high mountain region of the Lucchesia. The initial purchase by Aldibrandino in 1261 may well have been triggered by the cash demands placed upon the Gherardinghi as a result of the crusading tithe due in 1260 from the

---

(95) ASL, *Curia dei ribelli e de' banditi,* no. 1, fol. 14.

churches under their patronage ([96]). It is unfortunate that we have no firm figures regarding the amounts paid by the Guidiccioni for their entrance into the rural consortium: the only sum mentioned, 1800 florins, was for an undisclosed portiom of the Gherardinghi patrimony and it is consequently impossible to assess the monetary yield to the consortium from these sales. Yet, while we may be sure that cash was an important factor, purely fiscal considerations between Guidiccioni and Gherardinghi were undoubtedly conditioned by the traditionally turbulent political situation in the Garfagnana.

The rural nobility of the region existed in a world of conflicting jurisdictional claims involving at various times and in varying degrees the Empire, the papacy, Pisa, the episcopate of Lucca and the Lucchese Commune ([97]). In these confused conditions, the rural nobility were frequently successful in playng one side off against the other; but the late thirteenth century Lucca had more or less gained recognition of her authority in the Garfagnana ([98]). Thus faced with a growing Lucchese presence in the region, it seems likely that the Gherardinghi would have been receptive to opening their ranks to an urban group that could well have served as a mediating influence between the consortium and the city of Lucca. But whatever the reason, the unique involvement of the Guidiccioni with the rural house of the Gherardinghi left these urban merchants with a well established economic and political base in the Garfagnana.

And while these events were unfolding in the mountains, the Guidiccioni were busily at work consolidating their landed posi-

---

(96) See Pacchi, *Ricerche storiche,* p. 131 and Appendix, pp. 31-34, document no. 29 for the assessments levied on the churches in Loppia, Galliano, Fosciano of the Garfagnana. The total tithe for the Garfagnana came to L. 5,501.

(97) *Ibidem,* pp. 127-140 deals with the political situation in the Garfagnana. See also Cianelli, « *Dei conti rurali* », pp. 81-245.

(98) In addition to the above, see Domenico Corsi, « Le ”*Constitutiones Maleficorum*” della Provincia di Garfagnana del 1287 », *Archivio storico italiano,* CXV (1957), pp. 347-370.

tion in Lucca proper as well as extending their contado holdings. Continuing the analysis of the documents summarized by Baroni, we find references to thirty-five real estate transactions concluded by the Guidiccioni between the year 1270, when Aldibrandino engineered the first joint purchase of property by the etended family, and 1291 when the documentation runs out. It must be remembered, however, that these exerpts were taken from « the ancient book in parchment » mentioned above that Paganuccio had maintained. They consequently reflect exclusively the dea· lings of the line descending from Aldibrandino while the other branch appears only in transactions involving the whole lineage. Nevertheless, despite the undue emphasis upon the doings of Aldibrandino and his heirs, the material reveals that the emergence of distinct fraternal family sub-groups did not preclude the continued unity and solidarity of the wider patriarchal lineage.

A breakdown of these thirty-five purchases shows that ten were concluded by Aldibrandino alone or by one or another of his sons acting for him ([99]): twelve were transacted after the death of their father and brother, Parensio, by either Paganuccio or Conte acting jointly for themselves and for their nephews Adoardo and Bindo ([100]). The remaining thirteen contracts reveal the whole lineage purchasing property jointly on four occasions ([101]); the lineage acting together through the consortium that included the Buggianesi six times ([102]); and the consortium buying in alliance with outsiders three times ([103]). Thus, one-quarter of these acquisitions were made by the lineage functioning as a unified economic entity, a level of frequency demonstrating the vitality of the larger family.

These same records when examined from a geographical perspective indicate eleven purchases that added to the holdings

---

(99) BSL, BARONI, ms. no. 1115; years 1272, 1274, 1276 (3), 1277 (2), 1279 (2), 1280.
(100) *Ibidem*, years 1281, 1284 (3), 1287, 1288 (3), 1289 (2), 1290, 1291.
(101) *Ibidem*, years 1270, 1273, 1282, 1286.
(102) *Ibidem*, years 1275, 1276 (2), 1277 (2), 1285.
(103) *Ibidem*, years 1280 (2), 1284.

in San Andrea ([104]); seven augmented the Guidiccioni presence in Capannori ([105] ; and another seven increased the presence in Garfagnana ([106]). The only departures from the design set down early on by Aldibrandino were three urban acquisitions ouside the quarter of San Andrea and four in the contado outside the region of Capannori ([107]). The locations of three pieces were unspecified in Baroni's epitomies ([108]).

The new purchases in Capannori were all made either by Aldibrandino or, after his death, by his sons and nephews. Likewise, six of the seven additions in Garfagnana were the exclusive work of Aldibrandino's branch. To what degree, if at all, Paganino's line, under Guidiccione's guidance, practiced a similar geographical specialization in increasing the fraternal patrimony is not clear. Only three documents survive to indicate the independent economic behavior of this group; but, they suggest that its possessions in the country were rather scattered. On 16 June 1279 Guidiccione bought four pieces of land and a house with its appurtenances in Schiava, a village near Viareggio, for L 106, and in 1296 he sold one-half of a piece of land in Soriano for the meager sum of L 11 8s. ([109]). In the same year Tomasino, now back from England, rented out for half the yield land located in Lunata to the East of Lucca near Capannori ([110]). Evidently Paganino's line was less concerned with investment in the contado than were Aldibrandino and his immediate offspring: although the former was heavily committed in Garfagnana through acquisitions of the lineage.

---

(104) *Ibidem,* years 1270, 1273, 1276 (2), 1277 (2), 1280 (2), 1282, 1284 (2).

(105) *Ibidem,* years 1274, 1276, 1277, 1279, 1288 (2), 1290.

(106) *Ibidem,* years (1284 (2), 1286, 1287, 1289 (2), 1290.

(107) *Ibidem,* years 1276 (2), 1277, 1279, 1280, 1284, 1289.

(108) *Ibidem,* years 1272, 1275, 1282.

(109) ASL, *Diplomatico, Archivio dei notari,* 16 June 1279.

(110) ASL, *Archivio dei notari,* no. 17 (Alluminato Parensi), fol. 169v, 8 December 1296.

24

In the city as in the turbulant Garfagnana, the Guidiccioni operated as a collective economic unit. Of the eleven acquisitions of property made by them between 1270 and 1291 in the San Andrea quarter, fully ten involved the whole lineage and the sole exception is unusual in other respects. In 1276 Aldibrandino received land and a house in Cantonbretti in settlement of the L 244 owed him by Rainero Ricciardi and Andrea di Parensio Ricciardi ([111]): a transaction suggesting that the Ricciardi were experiencing a cash shortage which in turn could explain their diminished role in the Ricciardi company in the 1280's. And in Lucca as in the Garfagana, the lineage operated not only as an entity but also through another corporation, the urban consortium which they had formed with the Buggianesi family at sometime around the mid 1270's.

### The Guidiccioni and Urban Consortia

With few exceptions, indeed, the thriteenth-century Lucchese merchant-bankers banded together into various corporate groups called « consortatus » ([112]). Though this movement was typical in the medieval Italian city, in Lucca the term « consortatus » (and the related « consors », consort) was apparently applied to two different types of consortial relationship.

---

(111) BSL, Baroni, ms. no. 1115; year 1276.

(112) A random sampling in the documents of ASL, *Archivio dei notari,* no. 15 (Bartolomeo Fulcieri, Tegrimo Fulcieri, Fulciero Fulcieri), reveals the following references to urban consortia: fol. 388v, 4 August 1284, « in domo dicti Sallientis (Salliente di Jacobo Melanensis) et consortum »; fol. 85v, 3 October 1284, « in domo dicti Bartholomei (Bartolomeo del fu Orlando Bettori) et consortum »; fol. 206, 16 March 1284, « in curte Dominorum Rustichelli Allucii et consortum »; fol. 243, 5 April 1284, « in domo dictorum Fedini et Albertini (Fedino and Albertino del fu Cecio Callianelli) et consortum »; fol. 68, il December 1284, « in domo suprascripti Uberti (Uberto Mangialmacchi) et consortum »; fol. 65, 5 October 1284, « in domo suprascripti Bernardini (Bernardino Manni) et consortum »; fol. 474, 30 November 1284, Nicolao and Landuccio del fu Arrigo Moriconis « pro se ipsis et omnibus consortibus » rent out a shop.

The first of these, which the 1308 Statute of the Commune of Lucca calls « consortium of the towers » («consortatus turrium») was a formal corporation patterned after the rural noble consortium such as that of the Gherardinghi, complete with its own governing statute and elected magistrates ([113]). As the name would imply the most important and most visible element of these associations was the communally owned tower or towers to which the membership could repair in time of civil strife or utilize in their own affairs (« negotium »). The « consortatus turrium » brought together non-related individuals, family groups, or combinations of both in an alliance for mutual protection and self-help in a manner, as we have argued above, not unlike that of long-term commercial partnership ([114]).

The second sense in which the term « consortatus » is employed in the Lucchese source refers to the consortial bond uniting relatives: the Statute of 1308 mentions «patrimonial consort» ([115]). These two kinds of consortial ties — the one created by mutual agreement of the parties, the other based upon kinship — were, however, not necessarily mutually exclusive and the claims of a tower consort could apparently overlap or conflict with those of a patrimonial consort, i.e. a relative ([116]). The Guidiccioni were involved in both kinds of consortial relationship.

---

(113) SALVATORE BONGI, LUIGI DEL PRETE, eds., *Statuto del Comune dell'anno MCCCVIII* (Lucca, 1867), Book 5, chapter 62, p. 281: « De consortatus turrium ».

(114) These Lucchese associations are similar to the « tower societies » of contemporary Florence: see P. SANTINI, « *Società delle torri in Firenze* », *Archivio Storico Italiano*, ser. 4, XX (1887), pp. 25-58, 178-204 and the comments of FRANCIS W. KENT, *Household and Lineage in Renaissance Florence: The Family Life of the Capponi, Ginori, and Rucellai* (Princeton, 1977), pp. 3-15, distinguishing between the tower societies on the one hand and familial « consorterie » on the other, See also HEERS, *Le clan familial*, pp. 190-202.

(115) BONGI, DEL PRETE, *Statuto*, Book 5, chapter 64, p. 283: « ... contra ipsum suum consortem de patrimonio... ».

(116) *Ibidem*, pp. 281-283 deals with situations in which consortial and familial obligations conflict.

Fortunately, the constitution of a Lucchese tower consortium, « statuta, ordinamenta et capitula constitutionis domus filiorum Corbolani et consortum », has survived to provide a specific indication of the nature of these collective associations ([117]). The statute reveals a membership of twenty drawn primarily from four families; the Corbolani, Del Veglio, Cerlotti and Truffe. But the consortium also included individuals such as Vanello di Bolgarino Stefani as well as the father and son team of Jacobo di Stefano del fu Bonaventura, none of whom had discernible ties to the main families. Evidently the Corbolani family dominated the organization which carried its name, yet there is nothing to indicate that all consorts were bound by kin ties.

The self-sufficiency towards which these organizations strove in shown in the clauses of the Corbolani statute. Perhaps the most revealing specifies that in the event of discord in Lucca (« quod si contingerit Luce vel in civitate lucana rumorem esse... ») the consul, or in his absence the treasurer, was to assemble as many members as he could locate quickly in order to deliberate whether they wished to go to the aid of the communal government of Lucca, whether they wanted to support individually their friends or whether they should follow some other course of action « et ibi deliberare inter se quod facere habeant, an servire Communi Lucano, an quilibet servire amico suo, an omnes ire ubi iudicatum fuerit inter se ». This rather cavalier attitude toward the Commune was echoed in still other provisions of Corbolani governance. Consorts, for example, were forbidden from seeking redress in Communal courts against fellow members in causes involving less than L 25: rather they were required to take complaints to the consul of the consortium (« Et teneantur omnes predicti consortes... se de aliquo consorte non reclamare nec reclamum facere de aliqua re vel causa aut facta usque in summam librarum viginti quinque ad aliquam Curiam Lucane civitatis vel coram aliquo iudice; potius

---

(117) SALVATORE BONGI, « *Statuto inedito della casa de' Corbolani* », *Atti della Reale Accademia Lucchese di Scienze, Lettere ed Arti*, XXIX (1886), pp. 471-487.

teneantur omnes se reclamare coram Consule eorum...»). Any sort of quarrel or disagreement («discordes seu litigantes») between consorts was likewise to be heard and resolved peacefully («per amicabilem compositionem») by the consul who also had the authority, indeed the duty, to levy a range of fines upon members for various specific offenses, such as verbally abusing or striking other members. Towards outsiders the consortium put forth a united and pugnacious front: if any consort should learn of another consort having come to blows with a third party, he must report it immediately to the consul, or in his absence, to the treasurer, who was constrained to assemble the membership to discuss what recourse to take («Et teneatur quilibet consors... quod si sciverit aliquem de consortibus devenire cum aliqua persona ad manumissiones vel percussiones, denuptiare ea incontinenti ipsa die qua scriverit Consuli vel Camerario, si Consulem non invenirit. Et tunc Consul vel Camerarius, scitis predictis, teneatur eius iuramento incontinenti congregare aut congregari facere omnes consortes, quos habere potuerit, et super predictis diligenter considerare aut diliberare, prout, eis videbitur expedire».). Such a procedure, of course, smacks of the vendetta, and the Communal authorities must have viewed these private organizations with considerable wariness if not outright alarm; even the popular regime that came to power in 1301 was reluctant to move directly against them ([118]).

The Corbolani statute does not deal with the subject of Communal property already in the hands of the consortium at the time

---

(118) It is apparent from the chapters of the statute of 1308 that communal authorities were more concerned with bringing these private associations under some measure of control than they were with destroying them. For example, BONGI, DEL PRETE, *Statuto*, Book 5, chapter 62, pp. 281-283, specifies that if a consort complained to the Podestà of Lucca of discord within a consortium, that official was to administer the *sacramentum consortatus* to the offending consorts. Chapter 63, p. 283 forbids the alienation of consortial property without the approval of one's fellow consorts. Chapter 64, pp. 283-284 gives the Podestà the right to levy a L. 100 fine on a consort guilty of destroying consortial property. Compare the power to regulate the internal life of the urban consortia claimed by the commune with the autonomy explicit in the Corbolani statute discussed above.

the document was redacted, although the association apparently possessed houses, lands and at least two towers in the three urban quarters, « contrade », verging upon the church of San Salvatore in Mustolio in the heart of the city. But two clauses show the importance that members attached to creating a kind of territorial integrity in the neighborhood where they were established. The first of these declares that any member of the consortium who learned that a piece of property in one of the three contrade was for sale, or likely to be (« .... quod aliqua domus seu casa vel turrus aut possessio aliqua trium Cappellarum vel aliqua earum Cappellarum vendatur vel vendi velit... »), must immediately apprise the consul, who was required to assemble the members, inform them of his thoughts on the matter, and then execute whatever policy (presumably whether or not buy the property in question) the assemblage should decide upon.

The second of the two clauses indicates that the consortium had a sort of collective option to buy up any property in the contrade which a consort owned privately but wished to sell. Again, anyone of the consortium having such knowledge was to so inform the consul who was to bring together the membership for discussion leading to the purchase of all or a part of the property. Clearly, consorts held property in their own right, or in right of their families, in the urban locales where their consortia were based, and it follows that an urban tower consortium brought together neighbors who pooled a portion of their property and/or liquid assets in order to increase their security and potential strength within a specific quarter of the city. But I would suggest that, as the case of the Guidiccioni illustrates, participation in a consortium was for many mercantile families only one of a number of ways through which the united family sought social, economic and political advantage.

The first reference to the Guidiccioni and a consortium occurs in connection with the appointment, in 1288, of Lazzaro Buggianesi as procurator by the Guidiccioni and by Bertolotto Buggianesi to deal with the Communes of Silico, Capraria and Barghecchia in the Garfagnana ([119]). The document was redacted in Lucca « in the tower of Paganuccio Guidiccionis and consorts » («Actum Luce in turri Paganuccii Guidiccionis et consortum »). The document does not, however, indicate whether or not Bertolotto and Lazzaro were consorts of the Guidiccioni, it only states that the contract was drawn up in the tower owned jointly by Paganuccio and his unnamed consorts. The first evidence explicity linking the Guidiccioni and Buggianesi in an urban association as opposed to their co-consortial status in the rural Gherardinghi consortium, dates from 1296 ([120]). Yet, the close cooperation of the families in property matters from the mid-1270's onward argues strongly for the earlier existence, probably circa 1275, of an urban consortial agreement between the two.

All told, relying on Baroni's recapitulations, the Guidiccioni lineage and the Buggianesi acting jointly purchased six pieces of property in the city ([121]), and there are three cases of the two families buying urban real estate together with third parties ([122]). In 1257 Aldibrandino, acting for himself and his nephews Ricciardo, Guidiccione and Tomasino; along with Lazzaro Buggianesi, stipulating in his own right and that of his brother, bought property in an unnamed location from Renerio Ricciardi and his nephew Andrea for an undisclosed sum ([123]). This was probably the house and tower in San Andrea referred to in a document of 1314 which specified that the property had formerly belonged to Andrea Ricciardi and his consorts but « now is said to be of the sons of Guidiccione » ([124]). The remaining five consortial purchases similarly

---

(119) See above note 92.

(120) ASL, *Archivio dei notari,* no. 17 (Alluminato Parensi): fols. 24v, 7 February 1296; 43, 11 March 1296; 46, 16 March 1296.

(121) See above note 102.

(122) See above note 103.

(123) BSL, Baroni, ms. no. 1115; year 1275.

(124) *Ibidem,* year 1314. « ... domum muratam et solariatam ponitam Luce in dicta contrata S. Andree que coheret ab una parte vie publice et ab alia parte domui et cothui turris que fuit Domini Andree Ricciardi et consortum et dicitur esse filiorum Guidiccionis... ».

involved possession in San Andrea. In 1267 two transactions
brought the consortium lands and houses in Cantonbretti for
L 450 and an unspecified sum respectively ([125]). The next year land
and a house at a price of L 225 and a one-half share of a house for
the large sum of L 2,925 were added to the fold ([126]). Finally, in
1280, Paganuccio, Conte and Guidiccione, the latter obligating
himself and his brothers Ricciardo and Tomasino, with Bartolotto and Lazzaro Buggianesi bought a one-half share in lands, a
house and a tower from « Dominus » Nicolaus del fu Michele
Broccoli for L 5,500 ([127]).

This last purchase witnesses the Guidiccioni and their consorts,
the Buggianesi, moving on yet another front, the neighborhood,
to extend their network of social contacts ([128]). As a consequence of
Aldibrandino's policy, a policy tenaciously adhered to by his descendents, the Guidiccioni already had a secure base of property
in the quarter of San Andrea. Yet, in 1280, acting with their
patrimonial consorts, they reached out to strengthen their relations
with the neighboring noble house of the Broccoli — a noble house
that was also involved in the Ricciardi Company ([129]). It is entirely
possible that the above sale and the establishment of comunal
ownership of a house and tower brought into existence a formal
tower consortium, involving the Broccoli on the one hand and the

---

(125) *Ibidem,* year 1276.

(126) *Ibidem,* year 1277.

(127) *Ibidem,* year 1280.

(128) For the social significance of neighborhood ties, see HEERS, *La clan
familial,* pp. 137-177. See also DIANE O. HUGHES, « *Urban Growth and
Family Structure in Medieval Genoa* », *Past and Present,* 66 (1975), pp. 3-28
and « *Kinsmen and Neighbors in Medieval Genoa* », HARRY MISKIMIN,
DAVID HERLIHY, A. L. UDOVITCH, eds., *The Medieval City* (New Haven
and London, 1977), pp. 95-111, for the social function of the neighborhood
in medieval Genoa. For the family and neighborhood ties in Renaissance
Florence, KENT, *Household and Lineage,* pp. 227-292 and CHRISTANE KLA-
PISCH, « *Parenti, amici e vicini: il territorio urbano d'una famiglia mercantile nel XV secolo* », *Quaderni storici,* XXXIII (1976), pp. 953-982.

(129) KAEUPER, *Bankers to the Crown, p.* 58 one Reiner Broccholi was
in England for the Ricciardi in 1282.

Guidiccioni patrimonial consortium on the other. Although no direct proof survives to bolster this supposition, according to the Statute of 1308, a tower consortium could be temporary in nature and an individual could even belong simultaneously to more than one such association. In other words, the sine qua non of a tower consortium was joint possession of a tower. When such communal ownership can be shown to have existed, as it can in the case of the Guidiccioni and their consorts the Buggianesi and the Broccoli, I beliere that we may postulate with confidence the presence of a tower consortium similar to that of the Corbolani.

In the same year, 1280, we find another example of the Guidiccioni sharing property rights with the Broccoli. In this instance, Nicolao del fu Michele Broccoli, the seller in the first transaction, participated with the Guidiccioni and the Buggianesi in acquiring a one-half share of land in Cantonbretti valued at 400 from Viviano Broccoli ([130]). Clearly, the social bonds created by physical proximity in the city and by membership in the Ricciardi venture were made more tangible, more specific, as a result of these transactions.

But the Guidiccioni were hardly finished with binding themselves more closely to their neighborhood. They were ready to seize, it would seem, any and every opportunity to increase their real presence in San Andrea. What they were doing is, in fact, reminiscent of the provision in the statute of the Corbolan consortium calling for the consorts to buy up any property in their neighborhood that should came on the market. In 1284 a group of buyers, all inhabitants of San Andrea, formed a kind of syndicate and purchased from the notary Bonacorso Doscii an eleven-twelfth portion of a house located in the neighborhood ([131]). We know from the description of the location of a house sold by the Guidiccioni in 1314 that all of the twenty-three buyers named in the above contract owned contiguous properties in San An-

---

(130) BSL, BARONI, ms. no. 1115; year 1280.

(131) *Ibidem,* year 1284.

drea ($^{132}$). The Broccoli are curiously missing, but the group numbered, in addition to the Guidiccioni and Buggianesi, members of the Ricciardi, Borgognoni and Medici families as well as a dyer, Alluminato del fu Comparetto. Here we have an example of neighbors banding together to shore up the ties of physical proximity in a fashion not unlike that in which the family or a consortium reinforced solidarity by acting together economically. With their considerable wealth and connections, the Guidiccioni were certainly a dominant force in the quarter of the city that they had literally tried to make their own. When one of the family died, we can well imagine that the funeral proceedings were attended by a throng of « consorts... neighbors and relatives » such as we read assembled at the burial of Noradino del fu Onesti some years earlier ($^{133}$).

### The Guidiccioni in the Later Middle Ages

In the course of the latter half of the thirteenth century, the Guidiccioni family evolved from the extended household of Aldibrandino's time into a complex and powerful lineage firmly entrenched in both city and countryside. They were connected through formal consortial associations with the noble Gherardinghi of Garfagnana; with their kin, the Buggianesi, and possibly the Broccoli, in the city; through the Ricciardi partnership with Lucca's major mercantile-banking families; by marriage with other families drawn from a variety of social strata; and by property held communaly with their friends and neighbors in San Andrea. Such a medley of relationships could only have resulted from a rational, self-conscious policy of familial aggrandizement.

The success of these strategies is attested to by the Guidiccioni family's subsequent prominence and prosperity. Members of the

---

(132) *Ibidem,* year 1314.

(133) ASL, *Curia San Cristoforo,* no. 3, fol. 94, 1266.

family continued in succeeding centuries to take part in international business, although seem lingly not on the grand scale of their thirteenth-century ancestors ([134]). Other Guidiccioni carved out careers in politics ([135]). While in the sixteenth century the family produced three bishops and a cardinal — sure evidence of wealth and influence ([136]). Certainly as the lineage grew more complex over time, collateral branches perished or fell upon hard times. Yet, the evidence brought together on sixteenth-century Lucca by Marino Berengo indicates a high level of cohesion not only among the Guidiccioni but among the other principal Luc-

---

(134) BSL, BARONI, ms. no. 1115; year 1304: « Adoardus et Bindus germani filii quondam Parentii Guidiccionis et Coluccius quondam Tomasini Guidiccionis et Guidiccius quondam Ricciardi Guidiccionis et Coluccius eius filius et Guiduccius et Maginellus germani filii Guidiccionis Mazini Guidiccionis are described as "publici negotiatores" »; indicating some involvement in commerce. In 1322 Nieruccio and Coluccio, Conte's sons, purchased in partnership with Chello di Allexio Interminelli 12 libs of « sendala » for L. 102: GREEN, « Lucchese Commerce », note no. 59. In 1371-72 Francesco Guidiccioni was involved in the silk trade in Lucca and a decade later he brought his three sons Betto, Nicolao and Conteinto the venture: PAOLO PELÙ, I libri dei mercanti Lucchesi degli anni 1371 - 1372 - 1381 - 1407, Preface by Gino Arrighi (Lucca, 1975), pp. 35, 111. Nicolao and Marco Guidiccioni were members of the Lucchese merchant community in Bruges in 1293-94: EUGENIO LAZZARESCHI, ed., Libro della comunità dei mercanti lucchesi in Bruges, Preface by Armando Sapori (Milan, 1949), pp. 192-194, 228, For a Guidiccioni commercial company active in Antwerp in the sixteenth century, ibid., p. XXXIII, note 3. There is nothing in the evidence that I have seen from the late Middle Ages to suggest the unanimous dedication of family members to trade such as we have observed for the thirteenth-century Guidiciconi.

(135) MANLIO FULVIO, Lucca: le sue corti, le sue strade, le sue piazze (Empoli, 1968), pp. 78-80; Francesco di Nicolao Guidiccioni was a member of the governing board, the « Anziani », in 1371; in 1456 Piero di Francesco Guidiccioni was elected to head, as « Gonfaloniere », one of the political and military wards into which the city was divided; Francesco Guidiccioni served as ambassador to Venice in 1484 and in 1487 he was a member of a commission to reform the gabelle. Between 1501 and 1520, Guidiccioni men occupied thirty-six seats in the Lucchese General Council and in the same period the family held positions in the influential College of « Anziani » eighteen times: MARINO BERENGO, Nobili e mercanti nella Lucca del Cinquecento (Turin, 1965), pp. 27-28 and p. 30, note 1.

(136) FULVIO, Lucca, pp. 78-80: Alessandro I, Bishop of Lucca; Alessandro II, Bishop of Lucca; Giovanni, Bishop of Fossombrone; and Bartolomeo, Cardinal.

chese families as well ([137]). Indeed, Berengo cites the Guidiccioni
as an example of the « Lucchese familial spirit » ([138]).

The astute creation of a landed patrimony upon which the
family could fall back in periods of economic recession or political
turmoil strikes me as a key ingredient in the Guidiccioni formula
for longevity as a distinct family group. And the accumulation
of land was in turn the consequence of a half century of enterprise in international commerce and banking. In forging and maint-
ainging the reality of a large cohesive family as the basic institution
through which its members sought their identity and material
well-being, the early Guidiccioni were acting within, and giving
strength to, an ideal of familial unity that would continue to be
a critical force in Italian social history well beyond the end of
the Middle Ages ([139]).

---

(137) BERENGO, Nobili e mercanti, p. 32, « nella classe dirigente lucchese
la famiglia non si frantuma mai ». For the Guidiciconi coat of arms, ELIO
BERTINI, Le grandi famiglie dei mercanti lucchesi, Preface by Niccola Car-
ranza (Lucca, 1976), p. 83 facing.

(138) BERENGO, Nobili e mercanti, p. 51.

(139) On the continued strength of familial unity and identity in the late
Middle Ages, see KENT, Household and Lineage, passim. DAVID HERLIHY,
« Family Solidarity in Medieval Italian History », HERLIHY, LOPEZ, SLESSA-
REV, eds., Economy, Society and Government, pp. 173-184 argues that while
the property bonds uniting the family weakened in the late Middle Ages,
heightened moral ties gave a new kind of solidarity, an increased self-
consciousness, to the family. See also the same author's « Mapping Households in Medieval Italy », The Catholic Historical Review, LVIII (1972),
pp. 1-24 and « Family and Property in Renaissance Florence », MISKIMIN,
HERLIHY, UDOVITCH, eds., The Medieval City, pp. 3-24. It seems to me
that for thirteenth-century Lucca the degree of nuclearization of the family,
at least the merchant family, remains an open question.
With regard to the status of the family in Renaissance Florence, mention
must be made of the views of RICHARD GOLDTHWAITE, Private Wealth in
Renaissance Florence: A Study of Four Families (Princeton, 1968) and
« The Florentine Palace as Domestic Architecture », The American Historical
Review, 77 (1972), pp. 977-1,012 who holds that the family disintegrated
as a social force in late 1 fourteenth and fifteenth century Florence.
For the continued influence of the family in the organization and conduct
of Italian business in the sixteenth century, see MICHAEL E. BRATCHEL,
« Italian Merchant Organization and Business Relationships in Early Tudor
London », The Journal of European Economic History, VII (1978), pp. 5-32.

IV

## LA FAMIGLIA E GLI AFFARI: LE COMPAGNIE INTERNAZIONALI LUCCHESI AL TEMPO DI CASTRUCCIO CASTRACANI

Lucca, nel 1284, fu la sede di 22 società impegnate nel commercio e nella finanza internazionali ([1]). Di queste 22 compagnie, quelle che portavano il nome delle famiglie Battosi, Bettori, Cardellini, Guinigi, Onesti, Paganelli, Ricciardi, Scorcialupi furono tra le più importanti nel commercio europeo della loro epoca ([2]). Grazie alle ricerche di Gino Arias, Mario Chiaudano, Robert Lopez, Federigo Melis, Leon Mirot, Yves Renouard, Raymond de Roover, Armando Sapori e André Sayous fra altri emeriti studiosi, conosciamo abbastanza bene come le società mercantili-bancarie erano concepite e come operavano alla fine del tredicesimo secolo e al principio del quattordicesimo

---

(1) T. BLOMQUIST, *Commercial Association in Thirteenth-Century Lucca*, in *The Business History Review*, XLV, 1971, pp. 173-177.

(2) *Ibidem*, p. 161.

secolo (³). Malgrado, però, l'importanza dei mercanti-banchieri lucchesi per lo svolgimento del commercio e finanza internazionali, i suddetti non sono stati oggetto di uno studio approfondito. Nella seguente relazione vorrei quindi — quanto le fonti lo consentono — esaminare la composizione sociale di due compagnie: quella della famiglia dei Ricciardi e quella dei Battosi, attive nel tredicesimo secolo, nell'intento di chiarire la natura di queste organizzazioni e capire meglio la struttura della società comunale che le produsse (⁴).

Le grandi compagnie italiane nella tarda metà del Duecento si svilupparono nelle città interne della Toscana e Lombardia. Il professore Armando Sapori ha illustrato le fasi del loro sviluppo da un nucleo famigliare (⁵). Ma verso la metà del tredicesimo secolo si espanse l'opportunità economica, la quale condusse i membri della famiglia a cercare capitali supplementari introducendo persone al di fuori del nucleo originale nelle venture commerciali — persone che non avevano legami di consanguinità col gruppo famigliare. Nello stesso tempo, vennero a regolare l'impresa con contratti formali che specificavano la durata della società, il capitale apportato, la distribuzione dei profitti e delle perdite ed altri dettagli.

---

(3) Cfr. le bibliografie in A. SAPORI, *Studi di storia economica: secoli XIII-XIV-XV*, terza edizione, 3 voll., Firenze, 1955-1967; II, pp. 1115-1186 e III, pp. 595-625.

(4) Sulla mercatura lucchese, v. T. BINI, *I lucchesi a Venezia: alcuni studi sopra i secoli XIII e XIV*, 2 voll., Lucca, 1853-1856; S. BONGI, *Della mercatura dei lucchesi nei secoli XIII e XIV*, in *Atti della Reale Accademia Lucchese di Scienze, Lettere ed Arti*, XVIII, 1868, pp. 1-55; L. MIROT, *Études lucquoises*, Paris, 1930; T. BLOMQUIST, *The Dawn of Banking in an Italian Commune: Thirteenth Century Lucca*, in *The Dawn of Modern Banking*, Center for Medieval and Renaissance Studies, University of California, Los Angeles, New Haven-London 1979, pp. 53-75; F. EDLER, *The Silk Trade of Lucca during the Thirteenth and Fourteenth Centuries*, PhD. Dissertation, Department of History, University of Chicago, Chicago, 1930.

(5) A. SAPORI, *Le compagnie mercantili toscane del Dugento e dei primi del Trecento*, in *op. cit.*, II, pp. 765-808 e *Storia interna della compagnia mercantile dei Peruzzi*, in *ibidem*, pp. 653-694.

Legalmente — sempre secondo Sapori — le compagnie internazionali italiane furono società in nome collettivo; così, la scadenza dei rapporti con i compagni, o la morte o la rinuncia di uno dei membri, significò la fine del patto sociale ([6]). Dopo una tale scadenza, i già soci erano liberi *de iure* di perseguire i loro interessi economici dove desideravano. In realtà, però, la maggior parte dei soci se non tutti, delle sciolte società normalmente si riaggruppavano e formavano una società nuova. Questa nuova impresa trasportava l'attivo e il passivo della precedente e regolarmente ne conserva il nome. In tal modo, l'esistenza di ogni compagnia mercantile-bancaria internazionale consisteva in una serie di patti sociali consecutivi. Nonostante le riorganizzazioni ripetute, le compagnie italiane mantenevano una notevole stabilità, in termini di personale, che durava frequentemente per varie generazioni ([7]).

Questa interpretazione del Sapori e di altri studiosi è fondata sulla base delle situazioni fiorentine e senesi; ma la documentazione lucchese rivela condizioni pressoché simili nella storia delle grandi compagnie. Infatti direi, senza forzature, che le compagnie lucchesi possono essere descritte come alleanze di lunga durata tra famiglie, alleanze formatesi con lo scopo di operare negli affari internazionali. In questo senso, le compagnie lucchesi possono essere paragonate alle consorterie nelle quali l'élite urbana approdò come rifugio sociale e politico.

Il più forte sostegno di questo punto di vista appare nella storia della Compagnia dei Ricciardi, *Societas Ricciardorum,* che fu economicamente fra le più potenti compagnie italiane del tardo

---

(6) Per una discussione della struttura legale delle compagnie v. T. BLOM-QUIST, *Administration of a Thirteenth-Century Mercantile-Banking Partnership: An Episode in the History of the Ricciardi of Lucca,* in *Revue internationale d'histoire de la banque,* VII, 1973, pp. 1-9.

(7) Y. RENOUARD, *Les relations des papes d'Avignon et des compagnies commerciales et bancaires de 1316-1378,* Paris, 1948, p. 45, seguendo Sapori, ha scritto: « Si bien qu'entre ces compagnies successives, absolument indépendentes l'une de l'autre, un lien de continuité apparait néanmois dans cette représentation des plus anciennes par la plus récente. Cette continuité est réelle... ».

tredicesimo secolo ([8]). Le origini dei Ricciardi e la loro ascesa all'apogeo del commercio e della finanza internazionali sono, come quelle di altre compagnie lucchesi dell'epoca, annebbiate nell'oscurità dei tempi. Cionostante, le fonti suggeriscono che la *Societas Ricciardorum* si sviluppasse sul tronco di una società formata nel 1231 fra Gottefredo Conetti, Perfetto Graziani e *omnibus suis sociis* ([9]). Sfortunatamente, il documento non rivela l'identità degli altri soci. Ma, in un altro documento datato il 30 Settembre 1241, Guglielmo Roscimpelli, per se stesso, e per Ricciardo Graziani, Orlandino Arnolfi e Pellegrino Sesmondi, suoi soci, e per tutti gli altri soci, confermò con atto pubblico di essere stato pagato con L. 135 Lucchesi, che i suoi soci avevano prestato al Vescovo di Lucca in Roma ([10]). Il primo riferimento al nome della *Societas Ricciardorum* appare in un contratto, riesumato nel diciannovesimo secolo dal genealogista ed antiquario G.V. Baroni, datato l'anno 1247, nel quale un certo « Opithone » — senza dubbio Opizo Malisardi — nel nome di Aldibrandino Guidiccioni e Bandino del fu Lucano Buggianesi della « *Compagnia dei Ricciardi* » consegnò una somma di denari veneziani al procuratore del Vescovo di Trapani ([11]). Allo stesso tempo, Aldibrandino Guidiccioni andava a Champagne a rappresentare la *Societas Ricciardorum* nelle grandi fiere ([12]). Anche nello stesso periodo, e precisamente nell'anno 1247, Renerio Maghiari e Pellegrino Sesmondi allargarono l'influenza dei Ricciardi in Inghilterra, là dove i soci ricciardiani serviranno Edoardo I come « banchieri della corona » ([13]).

---

(8) Per la storia della Compagnia dei Ricciardi, v. R. KAEUPER, *Bankers to the Crown: The Ricciardi of Lucca and Edward I*, Princeton, 1973.

(9) ARCHIVIO DI STATO LUCCA (d'ora in avanti abbreviato in ASL), *Archivio Guinigi*, N. 1, 17 Marzo.

(10) ARCHIVIO ARCIVESCOVILE LUCCA (abbreviato AAL) F, N. 78, 30 Settembre 1241.

(11) BIBLIOTECA GOVERNATIVA LUCCA (abbreviato in BGL), Lucca, ms. 1115, year 1247.

(12) ASL, *S. Maria Corte Orlandini*, 6 Ottobre 1245.

(13) R. KAEUPER, *Bankers...*, p. 5.

Verso la metà del Duecento, dunque, la compagnia dei Ricciardi si era impegnata a creare una rete commerciale e finanziaria europea che garantì la sua prosperità fino alla fine del secolo. Con l'anno 1250, la Compagnia internazionale nascente, come abbiamo visto, aveva contatti con Roma; si era infiltrata nel nord della Francia e dell'Inghilterra; e, se i rapporti con il Vescovo di Trapani hanno un significato, aveva legami anche con l'*oltremare*. Comunque, quello che qui c'interessa, è la struttura personale, piuttosto che la storia dell'espansione delle operazioni Ricciardiane, benché anche questo sia un tema molto importante. La continuità straordinaria delle famiglie rappresentate per almeno tre generazioni nella Società dei Ricciardi mi ha portato, sotto questo punto di vista, a riguardare la natura quasi consorziale delle compagnie bancarie-mercantili lucchesi del tredicesimo secolo.

Nel ricostruire la lista dei soci della *Societas Ricciardorum* al principio troviamo Guglielmo Roscimpelli, Ricciardo Graziani, Orlandino Arnolfi e Pellegrino Sesmondi della società del 1241; a questi dobbiamo aggiungere i compagni, già ricordati nel 1247, Opizo Malisardi, Bandino del fu Lucano Buggianesi e Aldibrandino Guidiccioni. Allo stesso tempo, incontriamo Lucas Natale, Enrico di Poggio, Baroncino Gualtierii, Renerio Maghiari, Pellegrino Sesmondi, Enrico Saraceni ed un certo Percivalle Gerarducci che lavoravano per la Società in Inghilterra e nella Francia del nord [14]; mentre Guido Panico si trovava a Genova [15]. Come risultato, si possono contare almeno quattordici compagni dei Ricciardi verso il 1250, di cui otto di loro all'estero.

E' importante riconoscere che i membri dei Buggianesi, dei Guidiccioni, Maghiari, Panico, Ricciardi, Roscimpelli e Sesmondi costituirono il centro originale della Società dei Ricciardi. Di questi primi nuclei famigliari, solo gli Arnolfi sembrano essersi

---

(14) *Ibidem,* pp. 56-57.

(15) R. DOEHAERD, *Les relations commerciales entre Gênes, la Belgique et l'Outremont d'après les archives notariales génoises aux XIIIe et XIVe siecles,* 3 voll., Bruxelles-Rome, 1941, II, p. 531, 977.

ritirati. Gli eredi e i parenti dei primi soci continuarono invece a lavorare per la Compagnia fino al fallimento della organizzazione al principio del quattordicesimo secolo.

Questo modello di coerenza sociale diviene più chiaro quando arriviamo ai nomi dei diciassette soci che nel 1286 accordarono la procura a due dei loro colleghi, Federigo Saraceni Incallocchiati e Nicolao del fu Bonaccorso Mignosii ([16]). Incontriamo tre Ricciardi, quattro Guidiccioni, due Roscimpelli, due Buggianesi, un Maghiari ed un Panico ricordati fra gli altri socii abitanti in quel tempo a Lucca. Labro Volpelli, rappresentante, al tempo, della Compagnia era o in Inghilterra o presso la Curia papale ([17]). Questo documento del 1286 dimostra la partecipazione continua nella *Societas Ricciardorum* di quattordici soci originali o dei figli loro. A questi devono essere aggiunti i nomi di Barchetta da Barga e Ricciardino del fu Domino Bonifazio Gottori, i quali, con Bertollotto Buggianesi, rappresentarono la Società alle fiere di Champagne nell'anno 1284 ([18]). Con l'inclusione dei Di Poggio (due dei quali rappresentavano la Società a Genova nell'anno 1260) e delle famiglie Tadolini e Broccoli, l'elenco dell'alleanza che si chiamò *Societas Ricciardorum* è completo ([19]). Tra i soci che si riunirono in Lucca il 1° Agosto 1296 per ratificare l'elezione di Conte Guidiccioni come direttore e Matteo Gottori come tesoriere della Società, non c'era neanche un socio estraneo alle famiglie suddette ([20]).

La lealtà della famiglia alle particolari compagnie bancarie-mercantili internazionali è forse illustrata nel migliore modo possibile dal rapporto fra la famiglia dei Guidiccioni e la Società dei Ricciardi ([21]). Abbiamo notato qui sopra come Aldibrandino

---

(16) G. ARIAS, *Studi e documenti di storia di diritto*, Firenze, 1901, p. 157.

(17) KAEUPER, *Bankers...*, pp. 87, 89.

(18) T. BLOMQUIST, *Commercial...*, p. 175.

(19) *Ibidem*.

(20) T. BLOMQUIST, *Administration...*, pp. 8-9.

(21) Per quello che segue sulla famiglia dei Guidiccioni v. T. BLOMQUIST, *Lineage, Land and Business in the Thirteenth Century: The Guidiccioni Family of Lucca* in *Actum Luce*, IX, 1980, pp. 7-29.

Guidiccioni fu uno dei primi aderenti alla nascente organizzazione, che sarebbe divenuta poi la *Societas Ricciardorum*. I tre figli suoi, Parenzio, Conte e Paganuccio coi suoi nipoti, Guidiccione, Ricciardo, Aldibrandino, Tommasino, Parenzio e Marchesino (quest'ultimo figlio di un nipote) entrano successivamente tutti quanti al servizio della Società. Potrebbe essere stata meno forte la tradizione alla partecipazione e alla lealtà ai Ricciardi data dai Guidiccioni che fra i Ricciardi, Buggianesi, Maghiari, Panico, Roscimpelli, Sesmondi, Volpelli ed altre famiglie suddette che fecero parte, attraverso gli anni, della *Societas Ricciardorum?* Mi pare di no.

La Compagnia Ricciardi portò, certamente, nella Società persone estranee al gruppo originale famigliare. Ma ulteriori ricerche rivelano frequentemente che questi individui, non avendo apparenti legami sociali con soci della Compagnia dei Ricciardi o con le loro famiglie, erano infatti collegati in qualche modo all'una o all'altra persona delle famiglie già rappresentate nell'organizzazione ricciardiana. I Tadolini, per esempio, erano imparentati attraverso matrimonio ai Ricciardi e si erano associati coi Malisardi in un consorzio urbano, la *Domus filiorum Tadolini* (22). Un altro consorzio collegò gli Onesti coi Ricciardi (23). Le famiglie Guidiccioni, Buggianesi e Cimacchi erano unite da lontani legami di parentela ed ognuna di queste famiglie di tempo in tempo era legata ai Ricciardi e ai Tadolini attraverso matrimoni (24).

In questo modo, così, la dimensione sociale della Società dei Ricciardi fu rinforzata dalla rete di parentele, di vincoli matrimoniali e consorziali che cimentarono ulteriormente le famiglie partecipanti.

Rimane, a questo punto, da domandare se la storia della Compagnia dei Ricciardi sia tipica di altre compagnie interna-

---

(22) *Ibidem*, p. 16.

(23) *Ibidem*, pp. 16-17.

(24) *Ibidem*, pp. 17-18.

zionali lucchesi. L'evidenza su questo argomento è un po' vaga, ma le informazioni disponibili indicano che le strutture delle altre società si conformarono al modello dei Ricciardi.

Non è mia intenzione di catalogare qui il personale di tutte le rimanenti compagnie lucchesi. Piuttosto, come altro esempio del fenomeno in discussione, vorrei esaminare in breve la storia della *Societas Bettorum*. Se accettiamo l'ipotesi di Sapori per la prima evoluzione delle compagnie italiane esposta sopra, sembrerebbe che la Compagnia dei Bettori si fosse sviluppata sulle attività commerciali di Orlando Bettori e dei suoi tre figli: Lanfranco, Bonaccorso e Giacomo.

Il primo riferimento all'organizzazione dei Bettori appare in un documento genovese del 7 Marzo 1253, nel quale Ugolino Testa — i cui discendenti ebbero un ruolo significativo nella storia susseguente delle Società dei Bettori — ed i suoi soci furono designati come agenti del mercante senese Roffredo Bramanzoni alla fiera di Bar-sur-Aube ($^{25}$). Questo stesso Ugolino, nel 1256, insieme a Guglielmo Faitinelli — un membro di un'altra famiglia che aveva una prolungata associazione con la *Societas Bettorum* — era fra sedici mercanti-banchieri lucchesi che rinnovarono un contratto d'affitto per una casa di pietra in Troyes; una casa completa con stalla, con magazzino e camera da letto che evidentemente serviva da residenza collettiva per le loro varie operazioni alle fiere di Champagne ($^{26}$).

Per tutto il secolo, i Bettori mantenevano la loro presenza nel nord della Francia e da questa posizione geografica seguirono i soci della Compagnia dei Ricciardi in Inghilterra ($^{27}$). Il primo

(25) R. DOEHAERD, *Les relations...*, II, p. 425, 785.

(26) F. BOURQUELOT, *Études sur les foires de Champagne*, 2 voll. in *Mémoires présentées par divers savants a l'Académie des Inscriptions et Belles-Lettres*, Paris, 1865, I, p. 166; L. MIROT, *Études lucquoises: la colonie a Paris du XIIIe au XVe siècle in Bibliotheque de l'École des Chartes*, LXXXVII, 1927, p. 52; E. CHAPIN, *Les villes des foires de Champagne des origins au début du XIVe siècle*, Paris, 1937, p. 110; F. Edler, *op. cit.*, p. 95.

(27) R. KAEUPER, *Bankers...*, pp. 22, 44, 48, 219.

a rappresentare la Compagnia dei Bettori nell'avventura inglese
fu un certo Piero Ugolinelli che arrivò in Inghilterra verso il
1255 ([28]). Durante il regno di Edoardo I, il numero dei soci
della Compagnia nell'Inghilterra era salito a sei. Questi erano
Giacomo Bettori, Lanfranco Bettori, Teobaldo Malagallie, Lotto
Ugolinelli, Nicolao Testa e Stefano Pitotelli ([29]). La permanenza
di Lanfranco e Stefano nel Nord sembra comunque che fosse stata
di breve durata. Infatti, nel 1273 si trovavano di nuovo a Lucca
dove nel Febbraio, insieme a Cecio Faitinelli, accettano L. 300
lucchesi *in societatem et compagniam* da parte della Società dei
Bettori ([30]). Anche il viaggio di Giacomo Bettori in Inghilterra
fu breve e, tornato in Lucca nel Marzo 1273, il suo nome risultò
segnato in una lista dei soci Bettori compilata *in apotheca filiorum
Bettorum* come si legge in un contratto di procura riguardante
la medesima Compagnia ([31]). Gli altri soci, aggiunti a Lanfranco
e Giacomo, presenti a Lucca a quel tempo erano Bonaccorso
Bettori, Piero Ugolinelli (anche lui tornato dall'Europa setten-
trionale), Caccianemico Overardi, Rabbito del fu Ugolino Testa,
Bruneto del fu Domino Albertini, Ubaldo Malagallie e Stefano
figlio di Giovanni Pitotelli.

Quando questi nomi sono paragonati con quelli dei soci
della Compagnia dei Bettori operanti in Lucca nel 1284, troviamo
la presenza continua dei Bettori, dei Faitinelli, degli Ugolinelli
e dei Testa ([32]). I Malagallie sono stranamente assenti dalla
lista, ma nell'anno 1284 potrebbero essere stati benissimo al-
l'estero per affari. La stessa cosa può essere vera nel caso di
Caccianemico Overardi e Burneto del fu Domino Albertini che
erano anche loro esclusi dalla lista dei soci nel 1284. Dall'altra

---

(28) *Calendar of Patent Rolls, 1232-1313*, 9 voll., London, 1893-1913,
*Henry III (1247-1256)*, p. 404.

(29) *Ibidem*, Edward I (1272-1281), pp. 214, 553-554.

(30) ASL, *Archivio dei Notari*, n. 12 (notaio Paganello di Fiandrada), f. 26,
17 Febbraio 1273.

(31) *Ibidem*, f. 28, 1 Marzo 1273.

(32) T. BLOMQUIST, *Commercial...*, p. 175.

parte, Duccio Bonaccorsi era, con ogni probabilità, figlio di Bonaccorso Bettori piuttosto che un nuovo venuto non meglio identificato.

In questo modo troviamo testimonianze della stessa continuità famigliare nella struttura della *Societas Bettorum,* come già abbiamo osservato a proposito della *Societas Ricciardorum.* Sfortunatamente, lo stato delle mie ricerche m'ha costretto a trattare solo degli esempi delle Compagnie dei Ricciardi e dei Bettori. E' chiaro, comunque, che le altre compagnie internazionali, quelle dei Battosi, Cardellini, Guinigi, Onesti, Paganelli, Scorcialupi ecc. erano ognuna composte probabilmente con affiliazioni a lungo termine fra famiglie particolari lucchesi. Così, come ho suggerito sopra, l'entrare nel mondo lucrativo del commercio e finanza internazionale era difficile, se non impossibile, per persone mancanti di legami a questo gruppo, relativamente piccolo, di famiglie economicamente potenti.

Questa situazione economica e sociale, mi sembra sia connessa agli eventi che si verificheranno nel quattordicesimo secolo in Lucca [33]. Il carattere sociale ristretto delle compagnie internazionali lucchesi costituì una barriera *de facto* al movimento economico e sociale, e effettivamente limitò la penetrazione popolare nei ranghi del patriaziato cittadino [34]. Vorrei affermare che il perdurare di un clima economico espansionistico come esisteva, per lo più, durante il tredicesimo secolo giovò a reprimere i risentimenti sociali. Di conseguenza, gli uomini delle basse classi furono capaci di soddisfare le loro ambizioni nelle sfere fiorenti dell'industria e del commercio locali o regionali.

Comunque, con il generale livellamento dell'economia nell'ultimo decennio del tredicesimo secolo, punteggiato in Lucca

---

(33) Per il tumulto tra le fazioni dei Bianchi e Neri v. B. SCHMEIDLER, ed. *Tholomei lucensis annales, in Monumenta germaniae historica, Sriptores rerum germanicorum,* n.s. VIII, Berlin, 1930, pp. 318-319.

(34) Su questo argomento v. S. BERTELLI, *Oligarchies et gouvernement dans la ville de la Renaissance, in Journal of the Social Sciences,* 15, 1976, pp. 601-623 e S. Cohn, *The Laboring Classes in Renaissance Florence,* New York, 1978.

dal fallimento dei Ricciardi, Bettori e dalla scomparsa di altre
compagnie mercantili-bancarie, il risentimento economico e sociale
scoppiò ugualmente con violenza ([35]). Con la vittoria della fazione
popolare dei Neri, quasi tutti i membri della comunità mercantile
e bancaria lucchese furono segnati con il marchio di *casastici et
potentes* e furono tagliati fuori dai diritti politici ([36]). Alcuni
di questi proscritti — fra i quali i Castracani — scelsero l'esilio
con la speranza di rivendicarsi nel futuro piuttosto che subire
l'umiliazione nel rimanere in Lucca ([37]). Concludendo, è permesso
pensare allora che la struttura del commercio e della finanza
internazionali lucchesi fosse un fattore importante per l'ascesa
di Castruccio Castracani al potere sulla sua città natale?

(\*) Vorrei ringraziare tanto *The American Council of Learned Societies*
quanto J. Carroll Moody, Chairman, Department of History, James Norris,
Dean, College of Liberal Arts and Sciences e Jon Miller, Associate Dean
of the Graduate School, Northern Illinois University per la loro assistenza
finanziaria che ha reso possibile il mio viaggio a Lucca per il Convegno
castrucciano dell'ottobre 1981. Vorrei anche ringraziare i dottori Antonio
Romiti, Mario Seghieri e Giorgio Tori e gli altri colleghi dell'Istituto Storico
Lucchese per la loro ospitalità generosa e cordiale durante il mio soggiorno
in Lucca. Finalmente, con piacere, ringrazio Clelia Palmerio Blomquist
per l'aiuto nella traduzione italiana della mia comunicazione presentata al
Convegno.

(35) Sull'economia dell'ultimo decennio del tredicesimo secolo v. *inter alia*
D. HERLIHY, *Medieval and Renaissance Pistoia: The Social History of an
Italian Town, 1200-1430*, New-Havem - London, 1967. Per il fallimento delle
compagnie dei Ricciardi e Bettori v. KAEUPER, *Bankers...*, pp. 209-251. Per
l'economia di Lucca nella prima metà del Trecento v. L. GREEN, *Il commercio lucchese ai tempi di Castruccio Castracani*, in *Istituto Storico Lucchese,
Atti del primo convegno di studi castrucciani: Coreglia Antelminelli
21 Maggio, 1978*, Lucca, 1981, pp. 5-19; C. MEEK, *The Trade and Industry
of Lucca in the Fourteenth Century*, in T. Moody, ed., *Historical Studies*,
VI, London, 1968, pp. 39-58 e *Lucca 1369-1400: Politics and Society in
an Early Renaissance City-State*, Oxford 1978, pp. 30-47.

(36) Per la lista dei proscritti, v. S. BONGI-L. DEL PRETE, *Statuto del
Comune di Lucca dell'anno MCCCVIII*, Lucca 1867, pp. 241-244.

(37) T. BLOMQUIST, *The Castracani Family of Thirteenth-Century Lucca*, in
*Speculum*, XLVI, 1971, pp. 459-476.

# V

## CITY AND COUNTRY IN MEDIEVAL TUSCANY: THE RICCIARDI FAMILY AND RURAL INVESTMENT IN THIRTEENTH-CENTURY LUCCA

The countryside of thirteenth-century Lucca, just as the rural areas of Florence and Siena, proved a magnate in attracting capital from the central city; yet, despite the evident importance of this phenomenon - and its relevance for the wider question of the relations between the medieval communes and their respective *contadi* - a great deal remains to be learned about the flow of urban capital to the Lucchesia in this relatively early perlod[1]. In this brief paper I would like to look, by way of a case study, at the involvement in the country of a branch of the Ricciardi family, founders of the *Societas Ricciardorum*, the Ricciardi Company, perhaps thirteenth-century Europe's most powerful international mercantile-banking organization, and to evaluate the impact, or lack thereof, of its behavior upon the economic and social structure of at least one area of the Lucchese *contado*[2].

---

[1] On the Lucchese countryside see D. OSHEIM, *An Italian Lordship: The Bishopric of Lucca in the Late Middle Ages* (Berkeley and Los Angleles, 1977), especially pp. 86-115; "Rural Population and the Tuscan Economy in the Late Middle Ages", *Viator*, 7 (1976), pp. 329-346; "Countrymen and the Law in Late Medieval Tuscany", *Speculum*, 64 (1989), 317-337: P. J. JONES, "An Italian Estate, 900-1200", *The Economic History Review*, 7 (1954-55), pp. 18-32; L. A. KOTELNIKOVA, "L'Evoluzione dei canoni fondiari dall'XI al XIV secolo in territorio lucchese", *Studi Medievali*, ser. 3, 9 (1968), 601-55: A. MAZZAROSA, *Le pratiche della campagna lucchese* (Lucca, 1846); C. SARDI, *Le contrattazioni agrarie del Medioevo studiate nei documenti lucchesi* (Lucca, 1914). For the evolution of Tuscan agriculture between the thirteenth and fifteenth centuries see the volume published by the UNIONE REGIONALE DELLE PROVINCIE TOSCANE; *Contadini e proprietari nella Toscana moderna. Atti del Convegno di studi in onore di Giorgio Giorgetti*, Vol. I, *Dal Medioevo all' età moderna* (Florence, 1979).

[2] For the Ricciardi Company see E. RE, "La compagnia dei Ricciardi in

128

There have fortunately survived in the *Archivio di Stato* in Lucca a considerable number of notarial documents that can shed light upon the rural dealings, primarily in and around the Parish of Segromigno, of the branch of the Ricciardi descending from Graziano Ricciardi through Perfetto, Perfetto's prematurely deceased son, Conetto, to his grandsons and heirs, Domini Pero and Ricciardo, in the period spanning the years roughly from 1263 to 1300[3].

The nucleus of what was to become the Ricciardi Company was formed in the early 1230's. In a document dated 17 March 1231, we read of a partnership involving Gottefredo Conetti and Perfetto del fu Graziano that sold a credit of L 13 which they held against one Morettino Ughi due on the sale of raw silk[4]. By the beginning of the following decade, this core had expanded to include, Ricciardo del fu Graziano, the above Perfetto's brother, Guglielmo Roscimpelli Orlandino Arnolfi, Peregrino Sesmundi and "all their other partners"

Inghilterra e il suo fallimento alla fine del secolo decimoterzo", *Archivio della Società di Storia Patria*, XXXVII (1914), 87-128: R. W. KAEUPER, *Bankers to the Crown: The Ricciardi and Edward I* (Princeton, 1973) and T. BLOMQUIST, "Administration of a Thirteenth Century Mercantile Partnership: An Episode in the History of the Ricciardi of Lucca", *International Review of the History of Banking*, VII (1973), 1-9.

[3] Critical to the present paper are two chartularies of the notary Giovanni Gigli: Archivio di Stato in Lucca (ASL), *Archivio dei notari*, nos. 6 and 7. These have recently been restored and re-paginated. Thus foglio lv becomes page 2, foglio 2r page 3 and so on. I will follow the new pagination. Register no. 7 covers the 49 year span from 1271 to 1320 and is headed "Liber rogitorum mei Johannis Gygli notarii de negotiis Dominorum Peri et Ricciardi germanorum quondam Domini Conecti Perfecti Ricciardi factus et compositus anno Domini MCCLXXI. The "book" is made up largely of contracts redacted in the course of Pero and Ricciardo's rural affairs. The line did, however, maintain social ties to the city and the world of commerce. Ricciardo's first wife was Maria, daughter of Leo Sesmundi, a partner of the Ricciardi Company: ASL, *Archivio dei notari*, no. 7, p. 220, 17 July 1307. Pero's son, Freduccio del fu Domino Pero del fu Domino Conetto Ricciardi de Contrada S. Andrea was married to Narduccia, daughter of Paganuccio Guidiccioni, also a partner of the Ricciardi: Biblioteca Statale di Lucca, ms. no. 1130, year 1302.

[4] ASL, *Archivio gentilize, Archivio Guinigi*, no. 1, 17 March 1231.

(*et omnibus aliis eorum sociis*)[5]. Such growth apparently required an infusion of working capital, for in 1245 Perfetto borrowed the sizable sum of L 450 Lucchese from local money-changers; an interesting strategy since recourse to the changers' bank betrays a reluctance on Perfetto's part to convert real property into liquid capital[6]. And at this time he and his brother, Ricciardo, apparently possessed significant holdings in Lucca; while in all likelihood they were investing heavily in the country as well.

In the first half of the thirteenth century, Perfetto along with his nephews, Parenzio and Renerio di Ricciardo, owned a house and tower in common in the urban quarter of San Andrea[7]. The three also shared possession of other houses and a tower, virtually next door in the same quarter with Uberto del fu Bononcontro Botriocchi which they had bought from one Berullo del fu Provinsale[8]. Perfetto owned at least one other house that we know of in the city[9]. And he also donated the land upon which the Franciscans were to build their earliest church in Lucca and where Ricciardo, his brother, was buried in 1249[10].

This urban real estate passed directly to Perfetto's grandsons upon his death in about 1270. Pero and Ricciardo inherited one of the houses in San Andrea next to the other that went to the heirs of Parenzio[11]. When in 1274 Pero and Ricciardo divided some of their

---

[5] Archivio arcivescovile of Lucca, + F, no. 78, 30 September 1241.

[6] On 27 January and 4 march, 1245, Perfetto del fu Graziano borrowed respectively L 100 and L 200 from the money-changer Gerardo Azuri: Archivio capitolare in Lucca, LL 20, fols. 13 and 25v. Also on 27 January Perfetto borrowed another L 150 from the changers Soldano, Gerardo and Uguccione Maghiari: *Ibid.*, f. 57.

[7] G. MATRAIA, *Lucca nel milleduecento* (Lucca, 1843), no. 369.

[8] *Ibid.*, no. 370.

[9] *Ibid.*, no. 213.

[10] M. PAOLI, *Arte e committenza a Lucca nel Trecento e nel Quattrocento* (Lucca, 1986), pp. 197-98 and I. BELLI BARSALI, *Guida di Lucca* (Lucca, 1953) pp. 145-46.

[11] On 6 January 1297 Ricciardo and his nephews, Freduccio, Perfettuccio and Cionello, settled a dispute which in part involved shares in a house in S. Andrea "que coheret ab una parte terre quondam filiorum quondam Domini Raynerii

urban property, Ricciardo received a house in the Contrada of Sant'Anastazio while Pero garnered three pieces of land within the Contrada of Santa Maria Forisportam[12]. The brothers continued to coreside in a house and tower in the Contrada of San Cristoforo which they also shared with their urban consorts[13]. Although the composition of the Ricciardi *consorteria* is not known, it undoubtedly included members of the branch of the family descending from Ricciardo. This house and tower was the centerpiece of the brothers' possessions, although we shall see that Perfetto also bequeathed a sizable rural patrimoney centered in and around Segromigno, most likely the family's place of origin, located some 16 kilometers north-east of Lucca[14].

It seems a fair conclusion that some, or at least, part of, the capital utilized to expand the rural holdings derived from Perfetto's share of the early Ricciardi Company's profits[15]. Although Pero and Ricciardo dealt in scattered pieces of land around Segromigno - S. Piero a Vico, Temapagnano, and Capannori, for example - the bulk of land passed on to them by their grandfather was in S. Pietro a Marcigliano and it was here that the brothers naturally focused the major part of their activities in the countryside.

The *Capella Sancti Petri ad Marcillianum*, about ten miles or so from Lucca, nestled at an altitude of 292 meters up against the steep and wooded slopes leading to the mountains of Le Pizzorne to the north and descended some two kilometers southward to the present day Segromigno a Monte where at 140 meters above sea level is situated the impressive Romanesque perish church of San Lorenzo[16].

---

Ricciardi et Domini Andree Parentu...": ASL, *Archivio dei notari*, no. 7, p. 206.

[12] *Ibid.*, p. 10.

[13] *Ibid.*, p. 33, 5 May 1272.

[14] For Segromigno, E. REPETTI, *Dizionario geografico fisico storico della Toscana*, 5 vols. (Florence, 1833-1845) V, 487-88. Also C. SARDI, *La Pieve di Segromigno* (Lucca, 1908).

[15] For references to Perfetto's continuing purchases of land, ASL, *Archivio dei notari*, no. 7, *passim*.

[16] F. 105 *della carta d'Italia*, *Istituto Geografico Militare*. For S. Lorenzo, C. SARDI, *Segromigno*.

Although the territorial extent of the *Comune et Universitas Capelle Sancti Petri ad Marcillianum* cannot be determined, it did number 66 households, according to an *estimo* drawn up by three locally elected *extimatores* in 1264[17]. From a second surviving estimate of relative wealth within this rural commune, redacted three years later, we learn that the community had grown by some five households[18]. Utilizing the higher number of the two household counts and applying David Herlihy's multiplier of 4.65 souls per rural household we may calculate a population in San Pietro of roughly 330 in the 1260's[19]. This was then a fairly good sized rural community. Given the rare mention of outlying houses in the leases made to peasant tenants between 1271-1300 by Pero and Ricciardo, we may assume that the inhabitants of San Pietro for the most part lived in a nucleated village environment nearby the rectory of San Pietro a Marcigliano[20].

The entire Popolo (*plebatus*) of Segromigno, probably coterminus with the ecclesiastical parish, constituted within the Lucchese

---

[17] The survey was conducted by local *estimatores* chosen by the community assembled in the courtyard of the rectory of San Pietro a Marcigliano and the results redacted in ASL, *Archivio dei notari*, no. 6, pp. 64-66 on 7 April 1264.

[18] *Ibid*, p. 417.

[19] D. HERLIHY, *Medieval and Renaissance Pistoia* (New Haven and London, 1967), p. 61. The multiplier of 4.65 is derived from average rural household size in the Pistoiese contado in 1427. G. CHERUBINI, *Una communità dell'appennino dal XIII al XV secolo: Montecoronaro dalla signoria dell'Abbazia del Trivio al dominio di Firenze* (Florence, 1972), 59, is quite vague in arriving at a population *di forse* 300 for Montecoronaro in 1274 but his multiplier of 3 for an estimated adult male population ("un centinaio") would seem to be quite conservative. Charles de la Ronciere, "Solidarites familiales et lignageres dans la campagne toscane au XIV S.: l'exemple d'un village de Valdelsa (1280-1350)" in *Civiltà ed economia agricola in Toscana nei secc. XIII-XV: problemi della vita delle campagne nel tardo medioevo* (Pistoia, 1981), 125, has found that between 1270 and 1330 in Petrognano in the Valdelsa the average couple had 2.3 children above the age of 12 years. This gives a multiplier of 4.3 per head of household.

[20] Fourteen houses, or *podere*, are mentioned in the documents recording Pero and Ricciardo's rural dealing between 1271 and 1300. See ASL, *Archivio dei notari*, no. 6, 11 march 1263 for a document redacted in what I understand to be the village common: "Actum in praticu dicte Capelle". *Ibid.*, p. 9, 28 March 1264 for a reference to the communal oven.

administrative structure of the *contado* a *Podestaria* with a *Podestà* elected annually in the urban Church of San Michele in Foro sent out to represent the city's jurisdiction[21]. The *Podestaria* subsumed the rural communes of the parish, such as San Pietro a Marcilliano or San Andrea, each of which seem to have enjoyed a good deal of autonomy in dealing with local affairs as long as they did not contravene the laws and decrees of the central city. San Pietro elected its own consuls, two in number, for what was probably an annual term[22]. They were aided by an unknown number of councillors (*consiliarii*)[23], who presumably served on a rotating basis, and a herald (*preconis*)[24]. The community assembled in the courtyard of the Rectory of San Piero a Marcigliano *per suonam campanne more solito* where they deliberated matters of common interest[25]. The enabling document authorizing the election of two *extimatores* to revise the estimo assessments, for example, emanated from an assembly of the commune that met on 5 August 1264 where 58 heads of household, or 88% of the 66 eligible heads, gave their approval[26]. On a more routine matter, the appointment of two procurators on 23 June 1267 - in this case the current consuls, Bonaventura Moricone and Carbone Arrigi, - less than half, 34 of the 71 householders eligible (48%) showed up[27]. Evidently the agenda had a direct bearing upon the degree to which the community participated in ordering its affairs. Still, the few glimpses that survive of the rural commune in action reveal a high degree of organization and cohesiveness that no doubt stood its members in good stead in putting forth a united front in its relations with the outside world.

---

[21] S. BONGI, L. DEL PRETE, (eds.), *Statuto del comune di Lucca dell' anno MCCCVIII* (Lucca, 1867), p. 69.

[22] ASL, *Archivio dei notari*, no 6, p. 12, 26 October 1263; Bonavia del fu Arrigo and Bonaventura del fu Moricone were consuls at that time.

[23] *Ibid*, p. 437, 23 July 1267: "Convocatis consulibus et consiliariis...", Capelle S. Petri ad Marcillianum.

[24] *Ibid.*, p. 414.

[25] *Ibid.*, p. 437: "in platea ecclesie S. Petri ad Marcillianum de Sugromineo...".

[26] *Ibid.*, p. 61.

[27] *Ibid.*, p. 437.

Perfetto, Pero and Ricciardo, although citizens of Lucca, were intimately intertwined within the economic and social fabric of San Pietro a Marcigliano. For better or for worse, they were a presence to be reckoned with. Peasants coming together in the courtyard of Perfetto's home in San Pietro to have their dealings recorded by the notary Giovanni Gigli are mentioned in 1263[28]. This rural residence was no doubt the *domus vetera* referred to in the division of a portion of their common rural patrimony effected by Pero and Ricciardo in 1271[29]. The "old house" and its surrounding lands were linked by a road to the rectory of S. Pietro a Marcigliano to the east, and by another *via*, to a connected farm *(ad poderem domus vete)*. In any event, the old house with its courtyard, outbuildings and adjacent farm must have dominated the landscape in the heart of the village nearby the rectory and it clearly suggests that the Ricciardi had deep roots in San Pietro. By 1278 Ricciardo had completed construction of an addition to his part of the house, indicating that while the brothers technically were co-resident they, with their families, at least in the country in fact lived in clearly defined separate quarters[30].

The *domus vetera* also constituted a secondary administrative and storage depot for Perfetto's, and after his death, Pero and Ricciardo's management of their rural holdings. While the brothers evidently spent a fair amount of time in San Pietro, most of their business involving the country was conducted from the house and tower in Lucca[31]. Of 84 transactions involving their rural affairs, 33 were concluded *in turre dictorum germanorum* - or *in domo dicti Domini Peri* (or *Ricciardi*) *et consortum* when they acted individually - 23 were settled in Giovanni Gigli's house in Lucca and another 17 were resolved in various other locations in the city. Only 11 were finalized in San Pietro[32]. Of the new leases entered into by Pero and Ricciardo between 1271 and 1300 specifying where the commodity rents were

[28] *Ibid.*, p. 10, 26 August, 1263.
[29] ASL, *Archivio dei notari*, no. 7, p. 17.
[30] *Ibid.*, p. 85, 25 September 1278.
[31] *Ibid.*, *passim.*
[32] *Ibid.*

to be delivered by the lessee, 18 call for hauling to Lucca and 14 to Segromigno. There is, however, a noticeable distinction between the types of produce travelling to the city and to San Pietro. In all 551.75 staia of grain (347 st. wheat and 204.75 st. of millet) were earmarked for annual delivery to Lucca while 209.5 staia (146.5 st. wheat and 63 st. millet) were destined to remain in Segromigno and 305 staia of must wine were also handed over there annually. No wine was collected in the city directly from Pero and Ricciardo's peasant tenants. This should not be taken to mean that no wine was consumed in the city but rather that it was preferable to ferment and age wine in facilities located in the country. Processed grain on the other hand, and especially wheat, was a readily saleable commodity on the urban market and surpluses could easily be converted to cash in the city.

Apart, however, from these newly leased pieces of land, Pero and Ricciardo shared the rural patrimony that they had inherited from their grandfather[33]. In all, this joint estate consisted of 128 separate agricultural rents and the lands from whence they came. When in 1271 the brothers divided a part of these holdings, Ricclardo received 58 rents and Pero 70. In actual income, Ricciardo received 618 staia of wheat, 390 staia of millet, 845 staia of must wine, 103.5 pounds of olive oil, 5.5 staia of chestnuts, 4.5 staia of fodder and 7s. 3d. in money payments. He also retained the right to build an extension onto the *domus vete* which, as we have seen, he had done by 1278. Pero's share amounted to 726 staia of wheat, 266.25 staia of millet, 867 staia of must wine, 92 pounds of olive oil, 12 staia of chestnuts, 1 staio of figs, 4s.2d. in money and one unfortunate hen. The grain rents alone could take care of a lot of people.

The 2,100.25 staia of grain accruing annually to Pero and Ricciardo would have, according to Enrico Fiumi's estimate of 1 staio filling the cereal needs of one person for a month, accommodated 175 individuals[34]. It is evident that were all the rents regularly delivered as

---

[33] *Ibid.*, pp. 1-17 for the division.

[34] E. FIUME, "Economia e vita privata dei fiorentini nelle rilevazioni statistiche di Giovanni Villani", *ASI*, CXI (1953), pp. 207-208.

per agreement Pero and Ricciardo could easily feed their families, retainers and help, with more than enough left over to sell on the market. If, however, we approximate the potential income to be had from disposing of all the grain available to them in 1271, we find that Ricciardo would have received L. 317 and Pero L. 348, less expenses[35]. To be sure, these are not inconsequential sums but they tend to pale beside the L. 1,000 that Pero invested with the urban dyers Luparello del fu Bencivene Lamarense and his nephew Gualterio del fu Paraduccio Lamarense in 1280[36]. It would seem that while farming could insulate the Ricciardi against famine, even turn them a profit, and their large-scale ownership of land gave them something to fall back upon in case of hard times, estate management was not their principal economic concern.

The Lucchese *contado* by the thirteenth century had become highly fractionalized in tenurial terms[37]. While citizen landlords such as the Castracani, the Guidiccioni and Ricciardi families or ecclesiastical entities such as the Episcopate or the Cathedral Chapter could acquire considerable land in the aggregate, for the most part it was dispersed in small scattered holdings, *petia terre* or *petie terrarum*, described in the sources by location, such as *Sancti Petri ad Marcillianum in loco dicto Allafossa* and so forth, with the names of contiguous landowners and/or public roads or paths, *via publica or semitola*[38]. Rarely is the size of the plot given, although when areas are indicated, the piece seems to have been about an acre or so. When Pero and Ricciardo split their patrimoney

---

[35] There is an unfortunate lack of information on the movement of prices in medieval Lucca. These estimates are based on averaging the citations in Osheim, *An Italian Lordship*, pp. 154-55.

[36] ASL, *Archivio dei notari*, no. 7, p. 120, 23 January 1281.

[37] L. A. KOTELNIKOVA, "L'evoluzione"; OSHEIM, *An Italian Lordship*; P. J. JONES, "An Italian Estate".

[38] For the Castracani see T. BLOMQUIST, "The Castracani Family of Thirteenth Century Lucca", *Speculum*, XLVI (1971), 157-77. On the Guidiccioni, the same author's "Lineage, Land and Business in the Thirteenth Century: The Guidiccioni Family of Lucca," *Actum Luce*, IX (1980), pp. 7-28 and XI (1982), pp. 7-34. For the lands of the Episcopate and Chapter, see the preceding note.

in 1271, they divided, as we have seen, 128 rents from lands scattered in and about Segromigno. In 122 cases the location of the land providing the rent is given. Of Pero's 69 rents, 41, or nearly 60%, were in Segromigno and of these 27 were in *Capella Sancti Petri ad Marcillianum.* Others were in nearby Capannori, Lammari and so on. Ricciardo's 53 rents, identifiable geographically, came from 28 holdings, with nearly 53% of his total, in Segromigno and 25 concentrated in San Pietro. In human terms, Pero had to deal with 75 tenants and Ricciardo with 87[39]. In the document detailing these rents, there is mention of but two unitary farms and the list of new leases turns up but two more, plus the podere domus vete[40].

Even these *podere* were not all unitary farms in the strictest sense of the term but were cobbled together from a number of separate but nearby pieces of land. For instance, on 19 July 1287 Margarita, Pero's widow, for herself and her minor children, along with Nepto, another son, who had obtained his majority, let in perpetuity a *podere* consisting of a house and lands *in confinibus corporis plebis Segrominei in loco dicto Palliciano* to Giacomo del fu Fancelli of Segromigno, his wife Berta and their two offspring, Bonaventura and Giovanni, at an annual rent of 130 staia of wheat[41]. The family was obligated to live in the house (*ad standum in dicta domo*) but they could not store hay, straw or wood within. Indeed the tenants were bound to construct a shed (*casana*) at their own expense for that purpose. The point here is that the seven *petie* of land constituting the *podere* were scattered about in the locale of Palliciano and were bordered by the pieces of other peasants and *vie publice* or *semitole*. Three pieces in fact butted against other lands of Pero's heirs yet obviously no effort had been made to incorporate the latter into this holding.

---

[39] These figures are based upon the tenants owing the brothers rents in 1271. I have assigned only a value of two when the holders were described as *filii et heredes* and thus these numbers probably undercount the actual size of the Ricciardi tenantry.

[40] In the division of 1271 the late Riccomo Signorelli held *poderem et terras* from Perfetto and the farm at the time was probably worked by his heirs. Bonaventura de Soria occupied *totum illum poderem et terras*. For the two podere among the leases from 1271-1300, see ASL, *Archivio dei notari*, no. 7, p. 38 and p. 165.

[41] *Ibid.*, p. 165.

Another example of the dispersion of lands may be adduced from a perpetual lease consisting of 18 distinct *petie* located in San Pietro made by Ricciardo on 14 November 1277 to Vitale del fu Giovanni Guardi[42]. These 18 pieces, owing an annual rent of 100 staia of must wine, 10 staia of wheat and 6 pounds of oil, were situated in 16 different localities. In two instances only, were pieces in the same locale: two pieces were contiguous in the place called *Pietulle* and two were next to one another In *loco dicto In carmia*. Again it is interesting to note that when two pieces were contiguous, no effort was made to combine them into one *petia* even though they were held in perpetuity by the same tenant.

Morcellization was clearly the rule. The other leases made by the brothers Ricciardi were of one or two pieces scattered about the nearby landscape. Of course, from the landlord's point of view, as long as the fixed rents were delivered as agreed, any inconvenience to the peasant caused by having to trudge from one field, meadow or wood to another was irrelevant.

All but two of the leases made by Pero and Ricciardo between 1271 and 1300 were perpetual rents (*per tenementum et locationem perpetuam*)[43]. And for the most part they would appear to have established a durable relationship between landlord and peasant. Revocation of leases occur with relative infrequency in the documents. In all, only five "foreclosures" took place. When they did happen, however, they could seemingly be drastic. On 14 December 1278 Benettone del fu Paterno returned to Pero all lands which he had held from Perfetto and currently held of him, i.e. Pero, since he was in arrears for a modest 82 staia of wine - a bit more than the annual rental of 72 staia[44]. What provoked this we cannot know, but in addition to his leasehold, Benettone also lost all his movables and equipment *(massaritias)* and renounced any claim to his costs for improvements to the holding (*omnem jus et millioramentum*). In a similar case, on 5 September 1299 Giovanni del fu Jacopo Acceptanti, after a suit in the *Curia Foretani*, the Lucchese court established to adjudicate disputes between citizens and countrymen, was also forced to return the

---

[42] *Ibid.*, p. 68.
[43] *Ibid.*, p. 31 and 58.
[44] *Ibid.*, p. 87.

lands which he leased from Ricciardo[45]. On the other hand, two restitutions for back rents involved but one piece of land each[46]. And in one Pero, on 23 January 1278, was given a piece of land in lieu of 300 staia of wine. Immediately, however, he leased out the same parcel to the delinquent at an annual rent of a mere 12 staia of wine[47].

In general then, accomodation rather than dispossesion seems to have been the guiding principle when a tenant fell behind in the rent. In three instances, tenants were allowed simply to make a cash settlement, albeit most likely with a penalty of some sort, for the overdue rents. For example, on 8 April 1272 Pero and Ricciardo agreed that Giovanni del fu Guascone could settle up on behalf of Amata, daughter of Giovanni del fu Arringhetto, the back rent of 8 pounds of olive oil [which had accumulated on an annual rent of 3 pounds oil] owed by the late Giovanni and his heirs for a lump sum payment of L 24[48]. In another instance, Giovanni del fu Acurzio was allowed to pay L 7 in two installments within a year on arrears of rent in wine[49]. Then, on another occasion, a peasant was given five years to pay L 12 for overdue rent[50]. In one final citation of difficulty between the Ricciardi and a tenant, Bonaiuncta del fu Bononcontro and his son from Antraccole were made to pay L 3 because they had failed to live on the land leased from Ricciardo[51]. They were, nevertheless, allowed to remain on their holding with the proviso that Ricciardo could evict them whenever he wished but at his own expense. Of course, when landlords extend credit to tenants, the question of terms arises. Did the brothers habitually charge exorbitant rates of interest to bail out their tenants? This we cannot tell but the infrequent signs of problems and the rare instances of financial arrangements hint at a fairly stable relationship between the Ricciardi and their tenants. The peasantry enjoyed tenurial security as long as the goods

---

[45] *Ibid.*, p. 221. For the workings of the Curia Foretani see D. OSHEIM, "Countrymen and the Law".

[46] *ASL, Archivio dei notari,* no. 7, p. 185 and p. 199.

[47] *Ibid.*, pp. 76-77.

[48] *Ibid.*, p. 33

[49] *Ibid.*, p. 39.

[50] *Ibid.*, p. 36.

[51] *Ibid.*, p. 53.

were delivered more or less on time. Given the ubiquitous use of the fixed rent, it was, however, the tenant who bore the brunt of bad harvests. Yet hard times in the country could be mitigated by the patience, if not necessarily generosity, of urban landlords more interested in stability than fleecing.

It seems to me that here we are at the heart of the matter. The Ricciardi apparently were content to allow their rural holdings pretty much to run themselves. Faced with a fractionalized countryside and the prospect of dealing with a small regiment of individual peasants, they eschewed any concerted effort at creating more efficient unitary farms: *appoderamento* would not appear to have been high on their agenda. When the opportunity presented itself - as in the leases forged between 1271 and 1300 - the brothers unswervingly stayed with the perpetual rent over the more flexible short term lease. Such a preference may, of course, have been influenced by the external element of stagnant population growth and the periodic difficulty of finding reliable tenants to work the land.

Also the cohesiveness of the peasant community itself, expressed in its communal organization, may have acted as a brake upon altering traditional tenurial relationships. In the final analysis, however, I am strongly inclined to the view that the citizen rural landowner preferred above all stability, continuity of production and a minimum of aggravation to a commitment of time that could be devoted to more profitable or pressing affairs. Land provided security and a measure of prestige but it was not an overwhelming economic concern for the urban investor. In short, while the Ricciardi of Perfetto, Pero, Ricciardo and their heirs were a looming presence in Segromigno, their practical impact upon the structure of this part of the *contado* was ultimately negligible. Indeed, the Lucchesia would have to await some two more centuries for a full-fledged poderial system to emerge[52].

---

[52] C. SARDI, *Le contrattazioni*, p. 171, places the creation of large farms in the Lucchesia in the sixteenth century. S. Polica, "An Attempted 'Reconversion' of Wealth in XVth Century Lucca: The Lands of Michele di Giovanni Guinigi", *The Journal of European Economic History*, 9 (1980), 655-699, shows the difficulties one armed with urban capital faced in overcomming the fragmentation of the Lucchese countryside.

TABLE 1 - *Land Transactions of Perus and Ricciardus q. Domini Conecti Perfecti Ricciardi: 1271-1300*

| year | S. Piero a Marciliano di Segromigno | | | Pieve di Segromigno | | | Cappella di S. Colombano di Segromigno | | | Tempognano | | | S. Casciano | | | Lucca | | | Other | | |
|---|---|---|---|---|---|---|---|---|---|---|---|---|---|---|---|---|---|---|---|---|---|
| | rent out | buy | sell | rent out | buy | sell | rent out | buy | sell | rent out | buy | sell | rent out | buy | sell | lease out | buy | sell | rent out | buy | sell |
| 1271 | (PR1) | | | (R1) | | | (PR6) | | | | | | | | | | | | | | |
| 1272 | (PR8) | | | | | | | | | | | | | | | | | | | | |
| 1274 | (R1)(PR2) | (PR1) | | (P1)(P1) | | | | | | (PR1) | | | | | | | | | | | |
| 1275 | (R4) | (PR1) | (R1) | | | | | | | (R1)(R1) | | (R1) | (PR2) | | | (PR1) | | | | | |
| 1276 | | (P1) | (R1) | | | | | | | | | | | | | (PR1) | | | | | |
| 1277 | (R13) | | (P1) | | | | | | | | | | | | | | | | | | |
| 1278 | (PR1)(P1)(R1) | (P7)(R1) | | | | | (R1) | | | | | | | | | | | | (R1)(P1)(R1)(R1) | | (R1) |
| 1280 | (PR4) | | | | | | | | | | | | | | | | | | | | (P2) |
| 1281 | (P4) | | | | | | | | | | | | | | | | | | | | |
| 1282 | (P3) | | | | | | | | | | | | | | | | | | | | |
| 1283 | (PR1) | (R1) | | | | | | | | (R1) | | | | | | | | | | | |
| 1285 | | | | | | | | | | | | | | | | | | | (R1) | | |
| 1287 | (R1) | | | (R/HP1)(HP7) | | | | | | | | | | | | | | | | | |
| 1294 | | (P1) | | | | | | | | | | | | | | | | | (R1)(R1)(R1)(R1) | | |
| 1295 | | | | | | | | | | | | | (R1) | | | | | | | | |
| 1296 | | (HP2) | | | | (R1) | | | | | | | | | | | | | | | |
| 1299 | (R8) | | | (R8) | | | | | | | | | | | | | | | | | |
| 1300 | (R2) | | | | | | | | | | | | | | | | | | | | |
| Total No of Transactions | 16 | 8 | 3 | 6 | | | 2 | | | 4 | | | 2 | | | 2 | | | 9 | | 2 |
| Total Pieces of Land | 55 | 15 | 3 | 19 | | | 7 | | | 4 | | | 3 | | | 2 | | | 9 | | 3 |

Legend:  1) P=Perus  2) R=Ricciardus  3) HP=Perus' Heirs  4) Number=Pieces of Land

FIGURE 1 - *The Ricciardi Family in the Thirteen Century*

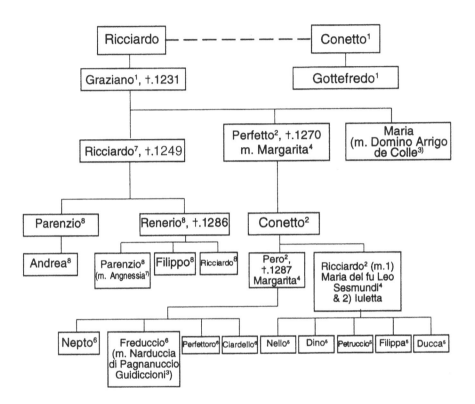

SOURCES:

1. ASL, *Archivio Gentilize, Archivio dei Guinigi*, no.1
2. ASL, *Archivio dei Notari*, no. 7, (Notary Giovanni Gigli) f.1, passim.
3. ASL, *Diplomatico, Fregionaia*, 4 July 1280.
4. Giovanni Gigli, f.9 v (old pagination).
5. *Ibid.*, f. 242.
6. *Ibid.*, f. 103 v (old pagination).
7. M. PAOLI, *Arte e committenza a Lucca nel Trecento e nel Quattrocento* (Lucca, 1986), pp. 197-98.
8. ASL, *Diplomatico, Archivio dei Notari*, 28 April, 1305.

# THE DRAPERS OF LUCCA AND THE MARKETING OF CLOTH IN THE MID-THIRTEENTH CENTURY

Despite the importance of the development of the woolen industry to the economy of the High Middle Ages, the processes by which cloth was marketed locally to the consumer remain largely obscure. We are, to be sure, relatively well informed about the merchandising of cloth in distant markets—the penetration of northern cloth in Mediterranean markets, for example[1]—yet the distributive channels through which woolens travelled after leaving the hands of importer or local manufacturer are still unknown.[2] That such a lacuna should exist is due primarily to the fact that traffic in cloth at the consumer level was based upon over-the-counter cash sales and has subsequently left few traces in contemporary records.

The State Archives of Lucca, however, preserve an extensive run of notarial acts of the year 1246 which help to fill this gap.[3] The evidence is fragmentary, for we are dealing with the partial production of one notary, Filippus Notti, spanning only a seven month period; yet these contracts serve to reveal one further step in the process of placing cloth in the hands of the consumer and also underscore the economic interdependence between a growing urban center, Lucca, and her neighboring countryside in the thirteenth century.

The notarial contracts deal with a part of the business carried on by a group of cloth merchants, referred to as *pannarii* in the Lucchese sources,[4] a segment of whose trade derived from credit sales developed among a group of buyers hailing from the countryside. Most of the latter in their turn dealt directly in the retail distribution of cloth in the Lucchese *contado*.[5] The cartulary of the notary Filippus Notti contains among its seventy-five folio pages 117 contracts for the purchase-sale of woolen cloths reflecting the credit business of fifteen partnerships of Lucchese drapers in the period from January 3 to July 30, 1246.[6] In the main these sales were small, averaging on a total volume of 1,108 *bracchiae* Lucchese a bit less than 10 *brac.* in quantity and 1 pound 14 sol. 5 den. in value for each transaction.[7] The smallest sale involved 4½ *brac.* of peach colored *(persi)* Florentine cloth while the largest in terms of quantity consisted of 12 pieces of both dyed and undyed cloth *(barracani albi et tinti)* and 6 *brac.* Florentine woolens sold to two inhabitants of the rural commune of Montecalvoli.[8] The majority of the recorded sales were, however, nearer in quantity to the above averages. All transactions were based upon short term credit; payment due usually within a month and seldom exceeding two months.

The 141 individuals appearing as buyers in the contracts were all residents of the *Lucchesia*, the Lucchese *contado*. They came from all corners of the surrounding countryside to the shops, *apothece,* maintained by the various drapers and their partners in Lucca.[9] From the Valdarno and Valdinievole to the southwest, the upper Valley of the Serchio, Garfagnana and the Valle della Lima to the northeast, and from the lower Serchio and Camiore to the northwest, as well as from the western *contado* bordering upon Pisan territory, men of the country sought woolen cloth in the city.[10] They usually made their purchases jointly, in temporary partnerships of two or three individuals from the same rural locale, and a draper's shop on most working days must have had a decided rustic flavor as buyers and witnesses crowded about the draper negotiating sales and settling old debts.

In general it would seem that the contracts reflect a wholesale rather than a retail trade; that is, it would appear that most of the cloth purchased in the city was intended ultimately for resale in the country. Although there are a number of obvious exceptions, such as the sales of tailored articles of clothing which were clearly destined for consumption by the buyer,[11] the credit nature of the transactions and the rural clientele involved lead to the conclusion that the majority of buyers appearing in the contracts were in fact rural peddlers. A credit transaction, of course, presumes the intent to repay, and in the case of these rural customers this meant a second journey from the country to Lucca. Had the draper's credit customers been buying solely to satisfy their own needs they undoubtedly would not have obligated themselves to undertake such a journey. Rather, they would have paid cash for their purchases, thus avoiding the inconvenience of an arduous trip. Nor, on the other hand, would a draper, were he selling retail, have been likely to advance short term credit, with all the risks involved, to individuals dwelling in some cases miles away from Lucca.

Furthermore, although none of the individuals appearing as buyers of woolen cloth was mentioned in more than one of the surviving contracts, it is nevertheless evident from the language of the documents that these men were regular visitors to the urban cloth shops. Thus, on April 5, when one Belluomo from Villorbano promised to pay the draper Ranuccio Ughieri 14 sol. 6 den. on or before the end of May as the price of 5¼ *brac.* of cloth, he also stipulated that he would also pay those monies owed from earlier transactions with Ranuccio ("... alios denarios quos se in alia parte dare debere confitetur").[12] The record of this earlier business, preserved no doubt in another cartulary, has been lost to us, yet reference to such business conclusively establishes that our rural buyers were not infrequent visitors to Lucca and the urban drapers.

In all probability such rural merchants shopped about, buying small lots of woolens from a number of drapers with whom they maintained regular credit accounts. They also may have visited the shops of other merchants and artisans in the city, acquiring their pack of merchandise in much the same way that *mercanti ambulanti* today replenish their stock at the weekly market held in Lucca. For their part, urban drapers regularly extended credit to these merchants of the country who marketed their cloth in the rural communes, parishes, *castelli, rocche,* and farms of the *contado* before returning to the city to settle their accounts and to acquire new merchandise.

The shop of the Lucchese draper was the focal point of distribution for cloth of both foreign and local origin. Among the foreign stuffs, Florence provided the most popular of those cloths distributed in the *contado.* Florentine woolens of various qualities figured in 28 contracts reflecting the sale of 146.2 *brac.* traded at an average price of 6 sol. 5 den. per *brac.*[13] Cloth of Verona also weighed heavily in the rural Lucchese market. Veronese woolens, the most popular type was known as *santellore,* were on the average somewhat cheaper than those of Florence; 121.5 *brac.* were sold through 26 transactions and brought a median per *brac.* price of 4 sol. 8 den.[14] Nearer to Lucca, cloth of Bolognese manufacture, figuring in only one sale, traded at a price of 2 sol. 8 den. per *brac.*[15]

The documents unfortunately throw no light upon the means by which Lucchese drapers acquired their supplies of foreign cloth. To judge from the almost continuous mention of individual drapers in the contracts, it would seem that they were a sedentary lot. One contract tells us that the partners Bonagiunta Bonansegne and Rainerio Bonacase kept a mule for use in their business.[16] However, the beast was probably employed in conveying the partners about the immediate *contado* rather than in long distance commerce. On the other hand, the existence of facilities for foreigners doing business in Lucca suggests that at least a part of the drapers' foreign goods were purchased locally from visiting merchants.[17] It is also probable that a portion of their stock was secured directly in the city of manufacture but more likely that Lucchese merchants imported Lombard cloth wholesale from Genoa, a major distribution point of Lombard production.[18] French woolens, which had only a minor significance in the rural Lucchese market, were in all likelihood purchased in Lucca from Lucchese importers operating in Genoa or at the fairs of Champagne.[19]

The rural market was most favorable to the cheaper cloths of local manufacture. Northern stuffs, for example, selling at a price half again that of Florentine woolens figure in only six of our contracts.[20] On the other hand, the woolen most frequently purchased by rural buyers was an inexpensive cloth known as *baracanus*.[21] In all, the sources show the sale of 356 *brac.* of both finished and unfinished baracans traded at the modest price of 1 sol. 4 den. for each *brac.*[22] Although the place of origin of these goods was not specified, it may be assumed from this very ommission that they were the products of local looms and the Lucchese finishing industry.

Of the organization of the Lucchese woolen industry in 1246 little is known. There is sufficient but scattered evidence to postulate the working of wool in Lucca at least from the beginning of the thirteenth century.[23] However, the relatively late date at which the weavers of Lucca formed a guild (the earliest certain reference to a guild of weavers is dated 1320) implies that the weaving industry was correspondingly slow in locating in the city.[24] Of the various crafts associated with the processes of converting raw wool into finished cloth, only the dyers had a formal guild organization in the thirteenth century.[25] In 1246 most of the local production apparently derived from looms situated in rural households.

The relationship of the drapers to the manufacture of woolen cloth remains unclear. Although some drapers, as Bonagiunta and Rainerio,[26] may well have travelled about the *contado* in order to organize the production of cloth, it would seem that woolens were brought to the city from the country by a group of middlemen cloth salesmen. These merchants, performing much the same economic function as the *lanarii, pannarii,* and *merciadrii* of contemporary Pisa, found a regular outlet for their cloth in the urban shops of the drapers.[27]

Involved in four of the six contracts reflecting wholesale purchases of woolen cloth by drapers was one Bonaccorso Adiuti who lived in Parlascio, a rural area in the Valdarno noted for the early production of woolen cloth.[28] Also furnishing cloth wholesale were a resident of the suburb, *Caput burgi,* and a Florentine merchant.[29] The cloth in each instance was dyed, a fact which in part explains why these entrepreneurial middlemen did not directly exploit the rural market for woolens. It was necessary to bring the cloth to the urban dyers for finishing, and once in the city the cloth salesmen found the urban drapers affording them a regular outlet for their goods. They no doubt preferred this steady market to the uncertainties of merchandising their cloth retail in the *contado.* Similarly, the drapers would seem to have preferred to acquire their cloth of local manufacture from middlemen rather than deal directly with the numerous household weavers of the country. However, there may well have been another factor. Each of these transactions was based upon credit, and thus the drapers were able to balance their own credit sales against those sums owed their suppliers.

The above sketch, based as it is upon fragmentary evidence, can present only a partial picture of the local distribution of cloth in Lucca. Yet the documents reveal the specialization characteristic of this commerce—drapers, middlemen suppliers, wholesale importers, weavers, dyers, and rural merchants all operating in a particular area of the local cloth trade. Our material also suggests something of the complexity of local business and the sophistication of the techniques employed in its conduct. The extensive use of credit, for example, implies an advanced method of keeping books. A business run on credit of necessity involves planning, that is to say a business rationale existed even at this modest level of medieval enterprise. In addition, the importance of the developing Italian woolen industries clearly emerges from a study of the contracts, showing Florence, Verona, and Bologna the seats of a cloth industry organized for export to distant markets. Finally, the documents reveal a clear picture of the city as the focal point of distribution to a significant consumer market in the surrounding country. If the *contado* was a source of foodstuffs and raw materials, it was also a market for the expanding industrial and financial resources of the city.

## NOTES

1. For the distribution of northern cloth in the Mediterranean, see especially R. L. Reynolds, "The Market for Northern Textiles in Genoa, 1179-1200," *Revue Belge de Philologie et d'Histoire*, VIII (1929), pp. 831-851; "Merchants of Arras and the Overland Trade with Genoa in the Twelfth Century," *idem*, IX (1930), pp. 495-533; "Genoese Trade in the Late Twelfth Century, Particularly in Cloth from the Fairs of Champagne," *Journal of Economic and Business History*, III (1931), pp. 362-381; H. Laurent, *Un grand commerce d'exportation au moyen-âge: la draperie des Pays-Bas en France et dans les pays mediterranéens, XIIe-XVe siècle* (Paris, 1935); R. Doehaerd, *Les relations commerciales entre Gênes, la Belgique et l'Outremont d'après les archives notariales aux XIIIe et XIVe siècles* (3 vols., Brussels-Rome, 1941); and A. Schaube, *Storia del commercio dei popoli latini del mediterraneo sino alla fine delle Crociate*, tr. P. Bonfante (Turin, 1915).

2. A. Sapori, *Le marchand italien au moyen-âge* (Paris, 1952), pp. 24-26 contains a brief bibliography of the major works dealing with the woolen industry. More recently, see the discussion of the wool industry in thirteenth-century Pisa in D. Herlihy, *Pisa in the Early Renaissance: A Study of Urban Growth* (New Haven, 1958), pp. 150-159 and Maureen Fennell Mazzaoui, "The Organization of the Fine Wool Industry at Bologna in the Thirteenth Century," unpublished Ph.D. dissertation, Bryn Mawr College, 1966.

3. On the notarial archives of Lucca, see R. S. Lopez, "The Unexplored Wealth of the Notarial Archives of Pisa and Lucca," *Mélanges d'histoire du moyen-âge dédiés à la memoire de Louis Halphen* (Paris, 1951), pp. 417-443, and E. Lazzareschi, "L'Archivio dei Notari della Repubblica lucchese," *Gli Archivi Italiani*, II (1915), pp. 175-210.

4. F. Edler, *Glossary of Medieval Terms of Business: Italian Series, 1200-1600* (Cambridge, Mass., 1934), p. 202 defines the *pannaro* as a retail merchant of imported cloth. This definition based upon the fourteenth-century statute of the court of Lucchese merchants is somewhat misleading for the earlier period. Although it is undoubtedly true that the greater part of the business of a Lucchese *pannarius* of the thirteenth century was retail, he nevertheless generated a considerable trade among the peddlers trafficking in the country.

5. The term *contado* is herein used as a geographical rather than a juridical expression to include all territories beyond the city *(civitas)* and immediate environs *(burgus)* considered by the Lucchese to be in their sphere of influence. For the territorial organization of the Lucchese state, see G. Tommasi, *Sommario della storia di Lucca*, in *Archivio Storico Italiano*, X (1847), pp. 140-142, and S. Bongi, ed., *Inventario del Archivio di Stato in Lucca*, (Lucca, 1876), II, pp. 342 ff.

6. Archivio di Stato in Lucca; Archivio dei Notari, Filippo Notti (1246), reg. 1, no. 1. The Lucchese drapers, and the location of their shops when known, were: (1) Bencipse quondam Rainolfi and Riccardus Raimundini *(in domo que fuit quondam Archiepiscopi de Benevento)*; (2) Matheus Orlanduccii; (3) Jacobinus Villiani Civithi *(in domo filiorum Arrigi Frangelaste)*; (4) Rainerius Benencase and Bonaiuncte Bonasegne *(in domo fili-*

*orum Aimerigi Mosche)*; (5) Marchianus quondam Bonaccursi, Ubaldus quondam Bonaiuncte Ferandi, Cecius quondam Rodolfi and Albichus Rodolfi *(in domo que fuit quondam Archiepiscopi de Benevento)*; (6) Jacobus filius Bartholomei, Gottefredus quondam Arrigi Baldinocti and . . . . . . ite quondam Vecchii; (7) Bandius Ferolfi and Nicolaus quondam Uberti; (8) Ranuccius quondam Guidi Ugherii; (9) Ubertus Columbani, Marronghinus quondam Rainaldi and Bugianese quondam Uberti *(in domo que fuit Archiepiscopi de Benevento)*; (10) Deodatus quondam Guillielmi Rambecci *et gemini*; (11) Jacobus Lunardi; (12) Caccialumbardus quondam Guidi Caccialumbardi and Johannes quondam Bonaventure *(in domo filiorum et heredum quondam Mori Mordecastelli)*; (13) Bandinus quondam *Aldibrandini Aimelline*; (14) Bonaverus quondam Meliorati; (15) Jacobus Notti.

7. *Bracchia* was a linear cloth measure equivalent to an arm's length, but varying slightly from one Italian city to another; see F. Edler, *Glossary,* p. 15. In Lucca four *bracchie* made one *canna.*

8. Fil. Notti, fols. 6, 24v.

9. The drapers would seem to have rented rather than owned their shops within the city. The only contract for the rental of an *apotheca* is Fil. Notti, f. 20v. Ranuccius quondam Guidi rented a shop *"in angolo turris"* belonging to Aldibrandinus quondam Mariani, his brothers Orlanduccius and Rubeus Rubei, and his sons, for the comparatively high annual rent of 8 pounds. The drapers would also seem to have located in the same general area, as for example the three shops "in domo que fuit Archiepiscopi de Benevento."

10. The below listed localities appear in the contracts. In parentheses are the number of contracts in which each is mentioned. I have retained the original case and spelling of the documents. Batone (2), Bonanno Montis S. Julie (1), Bozano (1), Camaiore—loco Tramestari, plebano de loco Peralle (5), Cantignano (1), Capella S. Giorgii (1), Capella S. Laurentii ad Vacchole (1), Capella S. Martini in Colle (1), Capella S. Michaelis de Villorbano (5), Capite burgi (2), Carraia (1), Cassano (1), Castagnone (1), Castro Vetrii, Castro novo plebani Conputi (3), Ceraliano Rocche Govertelli (1), Cercilliano (1), Conputo de Loco Colli (1), Controne (3), Decimo de Loco Roncato (4), Ecclesia S. Blasii de Aldepascio (1), Ecclesia S. Marie de Pellagio Vallis Lime (1), Francca (1), Hospitale S. Alluccii (1), Lamari (1), Lopellia (1), Limano Vallis Lome (1), Massa Pisana (1), Matraia (1), Montecalvoli (4), Monte Chiatri (1) Montefalcone (6) Moriana de Loco Factorii (1), Mocanno (1), Nave (1), Pescalia (1), Porcari (1), Porta S. Donati (1), Porta S. Petri (1), Pedona (1), Prato S. Columbani (1), Putholo (3), S. Casciano de Vico Rube (1), S. Gennuario (1), S. Johanne de Scheto (1), S. Giorgio (1), S. Martino in Fredano (1), S. Maria ad Colle (1), S. Maria de Paganico (1), S. Michele de Scheto (2) S. Petro Salaii (1), S. Prospero de Marlia (1), Seano (5), Scelinario Plebis Mostesi Gradi (2), Vallarni (1), Valle Nebule (1), Viritiano (1), Vurno (3).

11. See Fil. Notti, f. 32v for the sale of a woolen shirt to one Moricone de Carraia, intended for his son Gualfredus, for the sum of 25 sol. In this case the buyer stipulated that he had received the shirt and indeed Gualfredus was wearing it (". . . . et gonella vergata qua indorsa habebat suprascriptus Gualfredus"). For other sales of clothing out of the drapers' shops, see Fil. Notti, fols. 33v, 43, 64v.

12. Fil. Notti, f. 41.

13. For sales of Florentine cloth, see Fil. Notti, fols. 1v, 18v, 24v, 25v, 17v, 29v, 30, 30v, 31v, 32, 35, 35v, 36, 37, 45v, 46v, 47, 59, 50v, 59v, 64v, 65, 65v, 68v, 73v.

14. For cloth of Verona, see Fil. Notti, fols. 2v, 3, 5v, 6v, 23v, 32v, 35, 37, 37v, 38, 38v, 39v, 40, 40v, 41, 47v, 48, 49v, 56, 60, 62, 62v, 64v, 73v. Pegolotti mentions a cloth known as *santelarezine* called *santelaxerio* in the Venetian sources. This was a specialty of the Veronese cloth industry: see A. Evans, ed., *Pegolotti, La Pratica della Mercatura* (Cambridge, Mass., 1936), p. 429; for the specifications of the manufacture of *santelari*, see L. Simioni, ed., *Gil antichi statuti delle arti veronesi secondo la revisione scaligera del 1319*, in *Monumenti storici pubblicati dalla R. Deputazione Veneta di Storia*, 2nd ser., *Statuti. (Venice, 1914)*, IV, pp. 7, 11, 15–18.

15. Fil. Notti, f. 18v.

16. Fil. Notti, f. 51 (April 26, 1246): Salamone quondam Sacchi de plebe S. Macharei (located three kilometers from Lucca on the lower Serchio) stipulated that he had in partnership with the two drapers for a period of five months one mule valued at 13 pounds. The drapers conferred into the partnership the sum of 34 sol. which entitled one or the other of them to use the animal two days of each month. For use of the mule beyond two days in any given month, the partners agreed to pay a per diem fee of 12 den. The terms of this arrangement imply that the partners did not envision employing the animal on extended journeys.

17. The importance of Lucca as a center of foreign commerce may be deduced from the number of brokers and money-changers operating in the city in the thirteenth and fourteenth centuries. See T. Bini, "Sui Lucchesi a Venezia; memorie dei secoli XIII e XIV," *Atti della R. Accademia lucchese di Scienze, Lettere ed Arti*, XV (1854), pp. 82, 86ff., and F. Edler, "The Silk Trade of Lucca during the Thirteenth and Fourteenth centuries," unpublished dissertation submitted to the Dept. of History, University of Chicago, Chicago, 1930, pp. 99–104 for the activities of Lucchese brokers and money-changers. I am currently collecting material relating to the money-changers of Lucca which I hope will result in a more detailed analysis of their activities.

18. R. S. Lopez, "L'attività economica di Genova nel Marzo 1253 secondo gli atti notarili del tempo," *Atti della Società Ligure di Storià Patria*, LXIV (1935), p. 195, has indicated the increasing importance of Lombard cloth in the Genoese market during the course of the thirteenth century.

19. For the close political and economic ties existing between Lucca and Genoa, see A. Schaube, *Storia del commercio dei popoli latini*, pp. 798–800, 805–806 and F. Edler, "The Silk Trade of Lucca," pp. 113–123. See also my unpublished Master's essay, "Lucchese Commercial Activities in Genoa, 1186–1226," submitted to the Dept. of History, University of Minnesota, Minneapolis, 1960. For the Lucchese at the fairs of Champagne, F. Bourquelot, *Études sur les foires de Champagne, sur la nature, l'etendue et les règles du commerce qui s'y faisait au XIIe, XIIIe et XIVe siècles*, (Paris, 1865), I. pp. 166–175; Schaube, pp. 420–423, and Edler, pp. 93–96.

20. See Fil. Notti, fols. 45, 45v, 57v, 58v, 59, for sales of *gliscelli, verdelli*, and *crentoni* of Arras and fols. 9, 45v for *sanguinei* and *rosei* of Ypres.

21. The term *baracanus* was apparently of Arabic origin referring to a camlet of mohair. However, a Florentine tariff of the fourteenth century lists *baraccani* among the wares of the *lanaiuoli*: see A. Evans, ed., *Pegolotti, La Pratica della Mercatura*, p. 414.

22. For sales of *baracani*, see Fil. Notti, fols. 5v, 7, 23, 28, 28v, 29v, 31, 32, 33, 33v, 34, 34v, 38v, 39v, 41, 46v, 56, 69, 70v, 71v, 74.

23. T. Bini, "Sui Lucchesi a Venezia," pp. 15–24 has argued that the thirteenth-century Lucchese woolen industry was more advanced than that of Florence. Bini's thesis has been refuted by S. Bongi, "Della mercatura dei Lucchesi nei secoli XIII e XIV," *Atti della R. Accademia lucchese di Scienza, Lettere ed Arti*, XXIII (1884), pp. 445–456. However, only a cursory glance through the notarial documents in the LL series of the Cathedral Archives of Lucca is sufficient to indicate the importance of wool to the economy of Lucca in the first half of the thirteenth century. One hopes that this material will soon form the basis for a full scale study of the Lucchese industry. By 1265 woolens from Lucca were mentioned in a Venetian tariff indicating that by that date the industry was organized for export commerce as well as for local needs: see H. Laurent, *Un grand commerce d'exportation*, pp. 76–77.

24. See T. Bini, "Sui Lucchesi a Venezia," p. 62 ff. for Lucchese weavers and the formation of a weavers' gild.

25. The statute of the Lucchese dyers guild of 1225 has been edited by P. Guerra, *Statuto dell'Arte dei Tintori di Lucca del 1255*, (Lucca, 1864). A more recent edition may be found as an appendix to Edler, "The Silk Industry of Lucca." This statute was a revision of an earlier document and hence we may date the dyers guild from before 1255. For the Lucchese guilds of the Middle Ages, see E. Lazzareschi, "Fonti di archivio per lo studio delle corporazioni artigiane di Lucca," *Bollettino Storico Lucchese*, IX (1937), 65–81, 141–158.

26. See above, note 16.

27. For these early cloth salesmen in Pisa, see Herlihy, *Pisa in the Early Renaissance*, pp. 157–158.

28. Professor Herlihy, *ibid*; pp. 156–157 has stressed the importance of the Valdarno, especially Calci, as the birthplace of the Pisan woolen industry. For Bonaccursus, see Fil. Notti, fols. 24, 26v, 27. On March 19 he sold 11 *cannae*, 3½ *brac. celestri facti de Luce* for 14 pounds 16 sol. and 12 *cannae* of the same blue cloth for 15 pounds. Two days later Bonaccursus also vended one piece Lucchese vermilion for 10 pounds and a piece of blue cloth at a price of 17 pounds.

29. For the sale of one piece *panni bladecti facti Luce* by Armannus quondam Lamberti de Capite burgi, see Fil. Notti, f. 27, and for the sale of four pieces *panni facti Luce ad III liccias* by Meliore quondam Beliocci, florentinus, f. 40v. Noteworthy for its absence from the Lucchese sources is cloth from the Garfagnana, the *carfagnini* noted by Professor Herlihy, *Pisa in the Early Renaissance*, p. 158, note 91. If cloth was carried to Lucca from the Garfagnana it probably lost its identity in the city and became subsumed under the general *panni facti Luce*.

# VII

THE FIRST CONSULS AT LUCCA: 10 JULY 1119

Thomas W. Blomquist - Duane J. Osheim

On 10 July 1119, « such a multitude of the Lucchese popolo gathered [in the episcopal palace] that they could barely fit
into the foresaid palace ». This gathering has long held the attention of historians because it included the three men who were at
that time the consuls of the Lucchese people—the first time
consuls were mentioned by name at Lucca. Athough the existence
of this document has been known since Pietro Guidi's edition
of Almerico Guerra's *Compendio di storia ecclesiastica lucchese*
which first appeared in 1914, there has continued to be some
confusion about just when consuls were first documented at
Lucca. Antonio Cianelli, citing Francesco Bendinelli and Bartolomeo Beverini, said that by 1075 there were consuls—namely
Consuls of the Treguana meeting in the church of San Sentio.
Citing Bartolomeo Mansi he said that in 1088 Lambertus, Rolandus and Gerardus were consuls in Lucca. But as Salvatore
Bongi observed, lacking extant documents, it would be wise to
disregard the assertions of sixteenth - and seventeenth - century
authors. Girolamo Tommasi and Domenico Bertini, misreading

1107 for 1173, said there were consuls by that early date ([1]). Given this confusion and the potential importance of the Lucchese example in the question of the rise of consuls, it would be of great value to reconsider this document and to clarify what is known about the earliest appearance of consuls at Lucca.

The document of 10 July is interesting because it contains the names of so many Lucchesi. It will offer the social historian an almost unexcelled opportunity to delve into the backgrounds and origins of the earliest consuls and their supporters ([2]). Nothing is as yet known about Uberto del fu Conetti, Salomone del fu Salomone and Giovanni—the three who were noted as being consuls at that time. But of others, some of whom were later consuls, there is some information available in already published Lucchese sources. Within this group it seems difficult to overestimate the role of the judges and notaries. Seventeen of the laymen noted as present were in some way connected with judges and notaries. These men were the ones who seem to have been in almost constant attendance when matters affecting the bishopric or chapter were taken up. Bernardo del fu Uberto

---

(1) Almerico Guerra and Pietro Guidi, *Compendio di storia ecclesiastica lucchese dalle origini a tutto il secolo XII* (Lucca, 1924), p. 182 n. 1; Antonio Cianelli, *Dissertazioni sopra la storia lucchese*, Memorie e documenti per servire alla storia di Lucca, I (Lucca, 1814), 189; Domenico Bertini, *Dissertazioni sopra la storia ecclesiastica lucchese*, Mem. e doc., IV, pt II (Lucca, 1836). Appendix p. 126; Girolamo Tommasi, *Sommario della Storia di Lucca* (Florence, 1847: reprinted with an introduction by Domenico Corsi, Lucca 1969), p. 156 n. 14 and appendix p. 5 doc. II; Salvatore Bongi, *Inventario del R. Archivio di Stato in Lucca*, 4 vols. (Lucca, 1872), II 293-94; Augusto Mancini, *Storia di Lucca* (Florence, 1950) p. 70; and Luigi Nanni, *La Parrocchia studiata nei documenti lucchesi dei secoli VIII-XIII*, Anacleta Gregoriana, 47 (Rome, 1948) p. 108. Most recently both Hansmartin Schwarzmaier, *Lucca und das Reich bis zum Ende des 11. Jahrhunderts* Bibliothek des Deutschen Historischen Instituts in Rom, 41 (Tübingen, 1972) p. 331 and Duane J. Osheim, *An Italian Lordship, the Bishopric of Lucca in the Late Middle Ages*, Publications of the Center for Medieval and Renaissance Studies, UCLA, 11 (Berkeley, 1977) pp. 72, 186 n. 8 cite the document of 1173 wtihout having corrected the date.

(2) See e. g., Schwarzmaier, *Lucca* and Hagen Keller, « Die Entstehung der italienischen Stadtkommunen als Problem der Sozialgeschichte », *Frühmittelalterliche Studien*, 10 (1976), 169-211.

is an example. His father had been a judge. His family had extensive holdings in Sorbano del Vescovo. Between 1112 and 1127 he appeared as a witness to six capitular transactions ([3]). These men often seem to have had considerable landed possessions. Bernardo himself had lands at Patrigne ([4]). Ferolfo del fu Bellone had lands along the Via mezzana ([5]). Gerardo and Ugo del fu Fralmo and their family had extensive holdings throughout the Lucchesia—some of which they contributed to the chapter ([6]). Whether these and other families took advantage of inflated prices for urban lands to build their fortunes, whether they represent rural aristocrats who moved into the city and whether they had feudal ties to the bishop and chapter are all questions that need to be settled in order to clarify the debate over communal origins. The answers to these questions await the analysis of this and other early twelfth - century documents by social historians.

When Fedor Schneider first published a partial transcription of the document of 1119, he found it to be significant for two reasons. It, of course, named the consuls. But more importantly, it was, he throught, an important example of the development of « *der städtischen Gerichtsbarkeit* » under episcopal protection ([7]). According to Schneider, the document records a court session presided over by the bishop. At the session two brothers,

---

(3) For Bernardo del fu Uberto see SCHWARZMAIER, *Lucca*, pp. 326, 327; DOMENICO BARSOCCHINI, *Dissertazioni intorno alla storia ecclesiastica* Mem. e doc., V, pt I-III (Lucca, 1837-44), III, no 1813; *Regesto del Capitolo di Lucca*, eds Pietro Guidi and Oreste Parenti, Regesta Chartarum Italiae, 6, 9, 18, 18bis (Rome, 1910-39), nos 612, 721, 806, 813, 820, 823, 836. Similarly, e. g. Guido del fu Rolando: SCHWARZMAIER, *Lucca*, p. 324; *Regesto del Capitolo*, nos 542, 789, 836.

(4) *Regesto del Capitolo* no. 612.

(5) *Ibid.*, no. 846.

(6) *Ibid.*, nos 518, 644, 669, 865, 1314, 1473. See also SCHWARZMAIER, *Lucca*, pp. 240f.

(7) FEDOR SCHNEIDER, « Nachlese in Toscana », *Quellen und Forschungen aus Italienischen Archiven und Bibliotheken*, 22 (1931), 31-86.

Martino and Baroncione del fu Stefano of Sorbano del Vescovo renounced their rights to lands in the area of Sorbano del Vescovo. They agreed that these lands would revert to the control of the bishopric. While there is an indication of prior episcopal claims, as well as a reference to earlier litigation between the two parties, if we consider the *repromissionis pagina* which Schneider left untranscribed, the document seems less judicial in character. It seems rather to be a purchase of possesions. Having received a *meritum* worth 700 Lucchese denari, the brothers gave up their rights over the lands. And as such, it is similar to other acquisions or repossessions of lands and jurisdictions by the bishopric in the early twelfth - century ([8]).

If the document of 1119 does not record a judicial gathering, we might ask what significance the presence of consuls had. In studying the formation of the commune of Parma and the basis of its authority, Reinhold Schumann noted the partecipation of *boni homines* in a transaction between the Sabbioneta family and the monastery of S. Prospero of Reggio. They were present, he argued, « to safeguard the interests of their city in the property of their respective ecclesiastical institutions. The listing in a special clause suggests that their presence was necessary for the validity of the action » ([9]). The Lucchese consuls almost certainly were not present under the rubric of *quod omnes tangit*. Among those listed as present we find seven cathedral canons, followed by three judges, four causidici, four notaries, and then the three consuls. And even then the notary Dario recorded 24 others by name and mentioned that there were others who could barely get into the place.

The almost casual mention of the consuls as present *inter alia* raises the question of just what function the consuls fulfilled. They were, obviously enough, important men, but they do not

---

(8) OSHEIM, *An Italian Lordship*, pp. 19-29, 131-36.

(9) REINHOLD SCHUMANN, *Authority and the Commune, Parma 833-1133*, Fonti e Studi, 2nd ser., 8 (Parma, 1973), p. 236.

seem to have had an official function in the action of 1119. They seem to be present because the occasion of the sale was politically important for the bishop. Thus there would have been a great propaganda value to the presence of a large number of Lucchese inhabitants.

This might become clearer if we look briefly at other early sources mentioning consuls. According to Bishop Rangerio's metrical *Vita Anselmi,* the pseudo - Bishop Pietro (who assumed the bishopric in 1081 when San Anselmo was forced to abandon the city) and a pro - reform canon Bardo debated the issue of reform at Lucca in 1088-89. Pietro called together the *urbis maiores* and they came along with a good number of the little people *(de populo pars magna minore).* Pietro seems to have intended to try to build up support for his position by making a public speech. He was anticipated and his attempt thwarted by one Tado del fu Villani *(subtilis ad omnia* Rangerio called him). Tado suggested that the decision should not be in the hands of the masses, but rather that the problem should be debated before the consuls *(Quare consulibus placet haec sententia nostris, / Quorum consilio stamus et auxilio, / Ut veniant et conveniant cum pace vocati, / De quibus haec hominum tanta procella fremit)* ([10]). Alfred Overmann is certain that this mention of consuls at Lucca refers to an already functioning government ([11]). It is significant, he suggests, that Rangerio mentioned the *urbis maiores,* a phrase that recalls the *consules maiores* of later documents. They represent « *die oberste Behörde der Stadt* ». Thus he seems to interpret Rangerio to say that Pietro called out the consuls *(urbis maiores)* and many of the inhabitants *(populo*

---

(10) *Vita metrica s. Anselmi Lucensis episcopi auctore Rangerio lucensi,* eds E. Sackur, G. Schwartz and B. Schmeidler, Monumenta Germaniae Historica, Scriptores, XXX, pt. 2 (Hannover, 1934) lines 5249-5314. The debate is dated by Bernhard Schmeidler, « Kleine Studien zu den Viten des Bischofs Anselm und zur Geschichte des Investiturstreits in Lucca », *Neues Archiv,* 43 (1920-22) 543-49.

(11) ALFRED OVERMANN, « Die Vita Anselmi Lucensis episcopi des Rangerius », *Neues Archiv,* 21 (1895) 434-35.

*minore).* Overmann's interpretation seems unlikely because the two phrases more probably refer to those two socio - economic groups regulary mentioned in late twelfth - and thirteenth - century documents.

Do Rangerio's remarks indicate that by the 1080s Lucca had consuls who were « the highest governmental authority? ». It seems unlikely. The consuls Tado appealed to were probably more like the Consuls of Treguana who were empowered to adjudicate matters between laymen and churchmen. The Consuls of the Treguana could only act if both parties agreed to litigate before them *(si coram eis litigare voluerint)* (12). Thus the eleventh - century consuls could be called upon to witness or arbitrate an issue, if necessary. They might look after the interests of the people, but it is doubtful that, as at Parma, their presence was required. If it were required, and if they did represent the highest authority of the city, why would Rangerio say of Tado's desire to appeal to consuls (especially since Pietro had already asked the *urbis maiores* to appear) « *ad hoc verbum metuens insurgere vulgus / Demulcet verbis anticipatque Petrum?* ». It seems more likely that Tado did fear the multitude and wished to have the issue decided before a smaller group of representatives. If that is the case, it is unlikely that the consuls already had been asked to attend *ex officio.*

Thus, while there is a mention of consuls at Lucca as early as 1087-1088, there is no indication that they represent an organized governmental body. And in extant documents of 1119 and 1121 the consuls still do not appear as authoritative representatives of the Lucchese people. On 11 July 1119, the consul Gottifredo del fu Giovanni did appear in episcopal court. Again he was listed after the judges Fralmo da Ottavo and Riccardo and just before other *fideles* of the bishop. In 1121, on 1 January, 20 January and 24 August, the consul Fulcerio del fu Rainerio was listed among the witnesses to episcopal actions. In

---

(12) BONGI, *Inventario*, II, 300.

these acts there is no clear indication that the presence of consuls, however desirable for political reasons, was in any sense
required ([13]).

The importance of the distinction is perhaps clearer if we
compare these early indications of consular activities to a document from the late 1130s. On 19 March 1138, the consul Baldic-
cione del fu Bello took possession of the jurisdiction of the
castle and territory of Montopoli. He did this, the document
records, « *ad partem, et utilitatem Ecclesie, et Episcopatus Sci.
Martini... et pro universo Populo Lucane Civitatis, et pro omnibus
hominibus, qui in predicta Civitate et eius Burgis nunc sunt,
vel in antea fuerint...* » ([14]). It is at this point that the interests,
preeminence and authority of the Lucchese consuls are clearly
evident.


# APPENDIX


Lucca, Archivio arcivescovile; †† P, no. 99, 10 July 1119

In nomine sancte et individue trinitatis, anno dominice incarnationis
millesimo centesimo nonodecimo, sexto idus iulii, indictione duodecima.

Dum Benedictus gratia dei venerabilis Lucanus episcopus in palatio quod
est prope ecclesiam episcopatus sancti Martini in civitate Luca resideret, assi-
dentibus Sigismundo vicedomino, Rainero primicerio, Huberto archipresbite-
ro, Mauro cantore presbitero, Alberto canonico et presbitero, nec non Scotto
diacono et Gregorio subdiacono canonicis atque Flayperto qui Donnadeu vo-
catur, Leo et Ricardo iudicibus, Hubaldo, Fralmo, Henrico, Lupicino causidi-
cis et Corrado, Hugo, Lanfranco, Riccomo notariis simulque Huberto quon-

-----

(13) SCHNEIDER, « Nachlese », 68; BERTINI, Mem e doc., IV, pt II, appendix
no. 99; BARSOCCHINI, Mem. e doc., V, pt III, nos. 1813, 1814.

(14) BERTINI, Mem. e doc. IV, pt II no. 122.

dam Conecti, Salomone item quondam Salomonis et Iohanne quondam [1]),
tunc Lucensis populi consulibus et Hugo et Gerardo germanis quondam
Fralmi, Malatasca quondam Adalmari, Bernardo quondam Huberti judicis,
Guilielmo quondam suprascripti Conecti, Gotefredo quondam Iohannis,
Fulcerio quondam Rainerii, Hildebrando quondam Amici notarii, Gotefredo
quondam Cenami, Bertelotto filio Falconis, Gerardo quondam Glandi, Benedicto quondam Rolandi, Vitali quondam Appollonii, Ferolfo quondam Bellonis, Huberto quondam Donnane, Bonacio quondam Rustichi, Rolando quon-
dam Signorecti, Rolando quondam Antonii iudicis, Guido quondam Rolandi
iudicis, Rolando et Inghefredo germanis quondam Sassi, Rolando quondam
Becti, Bernardino quondam Fantini et Iohanne quondam Bendii clerici omnibus his presentibus et preter hos tanta Lucensis populi multitudine congrega-
ta, que vix in predicto palatio consistere posset, Martinus et Baroncione germani quondam Stefani de loco Sorbano qui dicitur episcopi, omnium predictorum presentia, ambo insimul per fustem quem suis detinebant manibus
refutaverunt in manu prenominati Benedicti episcopi omnes terras, casas
et cassinas, prata et pascua, paludes et piscationes, buscari et omnia super
predictis terris vel in illis habentia quanta et qualia predicti germani aut
aliquis pro eis vel ab eis quocumque modo habebant vel detinebant, que
essent vel pertinerent de suprascripto episcopatu Lucensi sancti Martini.
Ut autem suprascripti germani predictam refutationem incorruptam invio-
lentamque servarent, hanc inferius descriptam repromissionem scribere
rogaverunt.

   In nomine domini nostri Ieshu christi Dei eterni, anno ab incarnatione
eius millesimo centesimo nonodecimo, sexto idus iulii, indictione duodecima. Manifesti sumus nos Martinus et Baroncione germani quondam Stefani
de loco Sorbano qui dicitur episcopi, quia tu Benedictus Lucane ecclesie
episcopus dedistis nobis meritum anulum aureum pro solidis septecentum
lucensium denariorum, propterea per hanc repromissionis paginam reprom-
mittimus tibi, ut amodo nunquam in aliquo tempore nos qui sunt germani
vel nostri heredes aut nostra submissa persona illo modo non habemus
agere vel causare aut requirire sive intentionare seu ullam litem movere vel
facere adversum episcopatum Lucensem sancti Martini vel adversus te predictum Benedictum episcopum, sive contra posteros successoresque tuos,
neque contra illos quibus vos dederistis, vel aliquo modo habere decreveri-
stis, de illis casis et cassinis, terris et rebus, pratis, pascuis, paludibus sive
depiscatonibus aut de aquis, de aquariis seu de arboribus vel buscariis nec
de ullis rebus quantas et quales ullo modo nos vel aliquis pro nobis aut
a nobis usque modo tenuimus, que sunt de suprascripto episcopatu sancti
Martini de quibus in vostra manu refutationem fecimus, que sunt in loco
et finibus Sorbano qui dicitur episcopi vel in Casaio et in loco et finibus ubi
dicitur Adsprangam et in loco et finibus ubi dicitur Sighine, sive in aliis
locis vel vocabulis, neque apparebit de illis ullum temporem datum vel
factum, neque pro illa blava quam vos de predictis terris recolligere fecistis,
neque pro ulla offensione pro illa lite quam usque modo nobiscum habui-
stis nobis facta ullo modo offendemus aut offendere faciemus tibi suprascripto Benedicto episcopo sive in rebus aut manentibus vel tenitoribus de
episcopatu predicti sancti Martini. Et omni tempori de predictis omnibus
rebus et causis tacta et contenta herimus nec ullam amplius de his remo-
tionem faciemus. Quod si hec omnia sicut superius leguntur non fecerimus

---

(1) Left blank by the scribe.

et non observaverimus prout supra promisimus per quemlibet ingenium pondemus nos qui sunt Martinus et Baroncione germani una cum nostris heredibus componeri tibi prenominato Benedicto Episcopo et tuis posteris ac successoribus aut illi homini qui hanc promissionem premanibus habuerit et eam nobis ostenderit penam argenti optimi libras centum et post penam solutam suprascriptam promissio nostram omni tempori obtineat firmitatem. Quia in tali ordine hanc promissionem Darium notarium donni regis scribere rogavimus.

Actum Luce in predicto palatio.

Signum manuum suprascriptorum Martini et Baroncionis germanorum qui hanc promissionem fieri rogaverunt.

Leo iudex donni Imperatoris subscripsi.

S. n. Flaipertus judex domni Imperatoris subscripsi.

S. n. Feralmus causidicus subscripsi.

S. n. Conradus notarius domni Imperatoris subscripsi.

S. n. Lanfrancus notarius donni regis subscripsi.

S. n. Hugo notarius donni regis subscripsi.

S. n. Richomo notarius donni Imperatoris subscripsi.

Signum manum [sup]radictorum Huberti et Salomonis et Iohannis consulum, et Gerardi quondam Glandi et Benedicti quondam Rolandi, Ferolfi quondam Bellonis et Fulcieri quondam Rainerii rogati testes.

Ego Darius notarius donni regis post traditam complevi atque dedi.

Gli studi condotti ai primi del nostro secolo hanno appurato l'esistenza a Lucca dei consoli a partire dal dodicesimo secolo. La testimonianza che si pubblica documenta la loro esistenza nel palazzo episcopale a partire dal 1119 e i loro nominativi. Non si può affermare, con sicurezza, che in detto periodo la loro presenza fosse legalmente necessaria, e sembra che il loro intervento abbia avuto rilevanza testimoniale, assieme ad altri cittadini. Verso il 1130 si chiarisce il loro ruolo istituzionale e la loro posizione ufficiale nei confronti del Comune e del Vescovato.

Les études faites au début de notre siècle ont confirmé l'existence de consuls à Lucques, à partir du douzième siècle. Le témoignage que nous publions assure leur existence dans le palais épiscopal à partir de 1119

ainsi que leurs noms. On ne peut affirmer avec certitude que, à ladite période, leur présence ait été légalement nécessaire et il semble que leur intervention ait eu une importance testimoniale, en même temps que celle d'autres habitants. Vers 1130, leur rôle institutionnel et leur position officielle envers la Commune et l'Evêché se précisent.

\*  
\* \*

Die am Anfang unseres Jahrhunderts durchgeführten Studien haben bewiesen, dass es ab des zwölften Jahrhunderts Konsuln in Lucca gab.

Der Beweis, der veröffentlicht wird, beurkundet ihre Existenz im Bischofspalast ab des Jähres. 1119 und ihre Namen.

Es kann nicht mit Sicherheit behauptet werden, dass ihre Gegenwart in dieser Periode gesetzlich nötig gewesen wâre, und es scheint, dass ihre Anwesenheit, mit anderen Bürgern zusammen, Bedeutung zur Beurkundung gehabt hätte.

Gegen das Jahr 1130 klärt sich ihre Institutionsrolle und ihre amtliche Stelle der Gemeinde und dem Bischofsitz gegenüber auf.

# Commercial Association in Thirteenth-Century Lucca[*]

❡ Professor Blomquist describes and analyzes various forms of business association in an important northern Italian city during the period of economic growth in the thirteenth century. These included two basic forms of partnerships, as well as an early version of limited liability association.

Economic historians of the Middle Ages are generally agreed that the thirteenth century was a period of economic growth. In all sectors — population, food production, industry, and commerce — the indicators point to a quantitative advance.[1] I should like in the following paper to look at some of the ways entrepreneurs in Lucca, one of the most important industrial and commercial centers of thirteenth-century Italy, responded to the opportunities afforded enterprise in a period of economic growth.[2] Particularly, I will examine how they marshalled their human and capital resources to exploit best the possibilities for profit. I would also like to suggest that — although a part of trends in Italy generally — Lucchese entrepreneurial activity and its attendant organizational innovations were key factors not only in sustaining but in stimulating growth.

The favored method of doing business in Lucca, as elsewhere in Italy, was through association: at all levels of business, capital

*Business History Review*, Vol. XLV, No. 2 (Summer, 1971). Copyright © The President and Fellows of Harvard College.

* A slightly altered version of this paper was presented to the section on economic history of the Fifth Biennial Western Michigan Medieval Conference, May 1970.

[1] For general economic conditions, the reader is referred to the *Cambridge Economic History*, Vols. I–III. On the theoretical level, see the recent article of D. C. North and R. P. Thomas, "An Economic Theory of the Growth of the Western World," *Economic History Review*, 2nd ser. XXIII (1970), 1–17.

[2] The literature on Lucchese economic and social history in the Middle Ages is sparse. See especially the unfortunately unpublished study by Florence Edler, "The Silk Trade of Lucca during the Thirteenth and Fourteenth Centuries," (Ph.D. dissertation, University of Chicago, Chicago, 1930). Also T. Blomquist, "Trade and Commerce in Thirteenth-Century Lucca," (Ph.D. dissertation, University of Minnesota, 1966). Cf. the earlier works of T. Bini, *I Lucchesi a Venezia: alcuni studi sopra i secoli XIII e XIV*, 2 vols. (Lucca, 1853–1856), and S. Bongi, "Della Mercatura dei lucchesi nei secoli XIII e XIV," *Atti della Reale Accademia Lucchese di Scienze, Lettere ed Arti*, XVIII (1868), 1–55. For Lucca in the Middle Ages, see G. Tommasi, *Sommario della storia di Lucca* published as *Archivio Storico Italiano*, X (1876) and the more general treatment of A. Mancini, *Storia di Lucca*, Firenze, 1950.

and/or labor were pooled in order to realize a maximum economic potential.[3] Although no merchant's account books have survived from thirteenth-century Lucca, we are nonetheless fortunate in possessing extensive runs of notarial contracts which can, in part at least, offset the lack of more explicit documentation about the Lucchese organization of enterprise.[4]

### MEDIEVAL BUSINESS ORGANIZATION

From the legal point of view, the most common form of association was regular partnership, — societas, compagnia or societas et compagnia — in the sources. Here, however, we must make a distinction, for regular partnerships differed widely in terms of composition, duration and purpose. It may be useful, therefore, to conceive of Lucchese partnership arrangements in hierarchical terms on the basis of the economic activity which they reflect. At the top would rank the large-scale organizations whose field of enterprise was primarily international commerce and finance. At the next level were those partnerships created to carry on activities which, although locally based, were still dependent upon international or at least inter-regional traffic. In this category would fall the associations formed for the manufacture and/or distribution of silk cloth, the partnerships of dyers of silk or woolens or the associations formed for the distribution of northern cloth.

Such activities required sizable capital investment, as well as commercial know-how, and thus may be distinguished from a third level of enterprise and its reflection in the kind of partnership which it produced. I am thinking here, by way of example, of the partnerships generated by two or more artisans combining their labor and capital, or of the partnerships which brought together a merchant and an artisan. These arrangements are distinguishable from the first two types by degree: they were short term, usually lasting a few months, involving only two or three individuals with modest capital resources, and they were strictly local in outlook and activity.

Economically, the most important commercial organizations

---

[3] A. Sapori, Le Marchand Italien (Paris, 1952), 15–21 provides an annotated bibliography on the subject of medieval partnership and business organization. L. Goldschmidt, Storia Universale del Diritto Commerciale (Torino, 1913), remains a classic in the field, while an excellent summary may be found in R. de Roover, "The Organization of Trade," Cambridge Economic History (Cambridge, 1963), III, 70–86.

[4] On the notarial archives of Lucca, see R. S. Lopez, "The Unexplored Wealth of the Notarial Archives of Pisa and Lucca," Mélanges d'histoire du moyen-âge dédiés à la mémoire de Louis Halphen (Paris, 1951), 417–433 and E. Lazzareschi, "L'Achivio dei Notari della Repubblica lucchese", Gli archivi italiani, II (1915), 175–210.

were those partnerships engaged in international commerce and finance — the mercantile-banking organizations. Perhaps the most famous such Lucchese structure was that of the Ricciardi family.[5] However, the partnerships identified with the Lucchese families of the Battosi, Bettori, Cardellini, Gentili, Guinigi, Onesti, Paganelli, Scorcialupi, Terizendi, Tignosini and others were equally represented among the Italian enterprises doing business in the international market places of late thirteenth-century Europe.[6]

Legally these associations were ordinary partnerships regulated by the principle of joint and unlimited liability.[7] However, in practice Lucchese businessmen, by the last quarter of the century, stimulated by the opportunities offered through the development of new markets in northern Europe—France, England, the Low Countries — and the possibilities resulting from their position as papal depositories, had expanded their organizations beyond the limiting confines of regular partnership.[8]

In Lucca towards the end of the thirteenth century, there were at least twenty-two large-scale partnerships operating in the international field. These organizations were seemingly recent creations, and if we were to seek a date, the decade of the 1250's would appear to have been critical — a period of "take-off" as it were. When, for example, we turn to the Genoese notarial materials relating to the traffic between Genoa and Northern Europe published by Renée Doehaerd, we find that Lucchese business in Genoa before the mid-century was carried on by merchants having no permanent associative ties beyond those of the family.[9] When these merchants did

---

[5] For the Ricciardi, see E. Re, "La compagnia dei Ricciardi in Inghilterra e il suo fallimento alla fine del secolo XIII," *Archivio della Reale Società Romana di storia patria,* XXXVII (1914), 87–138. Re's work is based essentially upon Vatican sources and consequently presents a rather one sided point of view.

[6] The partnerships in which the Gentili and Terizendi families seemingly predominate are not identified in the sources by a partnership style. However, the clear preponderance of members of these families within the partnerships seemed to justify appropriating their names for ease in identification. The above named organizations all functioned as papal depositories: see E. Jordan, *De Mercatoribus camerae apostolicae seculo XIII* (Rennes, 1909); W. E. Lunt, *Financial Relations of the Papacy with England to 1327* (Cambridge, Mass., 1939), 77–114; and G. Arias, *Studi e documenti di storia del diritto* (Florence, 1902), 77–114. For the names of the partners of the above organizations as well as other partnerships engaged in international finance as reconstructed from the Lucchese sources, see the accompanying Appendix.

[7] On the juridical status of Italian partnership and especially the problem of liability, see A. Sapori, "Le compagnie mercantili toscane del dugento e dei primi del trecento: la responsibilità dei compagni verso i terzi," *Studi di storia economica,* 3 vols., 3rd ed., (Florence, n.d.), II, 765–808.

[8] For Lucchese commercial penetration of northern Europe, see F. Edler, "The Silk Trade of Lucca during the Thirteenth and Fourteenth Centuries," and T. Blomquist, "Trade and Commerce in Thirteenth-Century Lucca," 56–81. See also R. de Roover, "The Organization of Trade," 70–76.

[9] R. Doehaerd, *Les relations commerciales entre Gênes, la Belgique et l'Outremont d'après les archives notariales génoises aux XIIIe et XIVe siècles,* 3 vols. (Bruxelles-Rome, 1941). Madame Doehaerd's collection of the Genoese notarial instruments dealing with Italian trade with the north are a mine of information about the Lucchese in Genoa and

cooperate it was usually on the basis of joint venture. The earliest reference to a Lucchese partnership in this body of material is dated 1253.[10] However, after this date the majority of Lucchese transactions in Genoa were effected by businessmen acting in the capacity of partner or agent for a partnership based in Lucca. Of the thirty-one Lucchese merchants mentioned in the abstracts of the notarial documents published by Ferretto for the period 1266–1280, all acted for partnerships based in Lucca.[11] This represents a significant shift in the organization of business and an important increase in the potential for generating new business.

The distinguishing feature of these new organizations was size. Whereas the typical partnership of the first half of the century consisted of father and son combinations, several brothers or merchants or artisans doing business together, the large mercantile-banking organizations such as the Ricciardi might number as many as nineteen partners. Although the apparent outgrowth from a familial nucleus, the large mercantile-banking structures were open, in the sense that in seeking fresh capital and/or business know-how, the founders welcomed as partners men from outside the immediate family circle. A case in point would be the evolution of the business organization put together in the 1270's by Castracane, the son of Rugerio Castracanis and the grandfather of Castruccio.[12] In the 1250's Castracane, his father and brother, were engaged in the art of money changing, a profession in which the family had apparently been interested for generations. In the 1270's, however, Castracane successfully expanded his business horizons and extended his operations into the field of international mercantile banking. The resulting partnership consisted of at least seven associates, five directly related either by blood or marriage to Castracane but with the inclusion of two outsiders, one of whom served the partnership as their representative in northern Europe at the Champagne fairs. Other large-scale organizations may well have followed a similar pattern of development and growth. The *societas filiorum Paganelli*, for instance, while dominated by the five sons of Paganello Dulcis also listed at least twelve non-family partners. The *societas Car-*

---

their business organizations. This material puts in a clear light the importance of Genoa as an international entrepot in the period of the "commercial revolution." For a discussion of Lucchese activities in Genoa, see T. Blomquist, "Trade and Commerce in Thirteenth Century Lucca," 37–49.

[10] R. Doehaerd, *Les relations commerciales*, no. 785.

[11] A. Ferretto, *Il codice diplomatico delle relazioni fra la Toscana e Lunigiana ai tempi di Dante* (1265–1321), 2 pts., *Atti della Società ligure di storia patria*, XXXI (1901–1903), *passim*.

[12] For the Castracani, see my forthcoming article in *Speculum*, "The Castracani Family of Thirteenth-Century Lucca."

*dellinorum* counted six members of the Cardellini family but also five non-family members in the partnership. We find a similar inclusion of non-family partners in the organizations dominated by the Bettori, Battosi, Onesti, Scorcialupi, and Ricciardi, among other Lucchese groups operating in the international sphere.[13] Thus, the open character of the Lucchese mercantile-banking partnerships allowed the influx of new expertise and capital, while also serving no doubt to broaden the sociological base upon which international business rested.

We have seen that in Genoa in the 1250's Lucchese businessmen were increasingly affiliated with partnerships based in Lucca. The establishment of representation in the Mediterranean seems well advanced by the 1260's and representatives of the Lucchese mercantile-banking partnerships were settled at the Papal Curia and somewhat later at the Angevin court as well as Nimes, Narbonne, and Marseilles in southern France.[14] In terms of new markets, however, the most significant advances at this time were in northern Europe.

The main point of contact between Lucca and the North, in the thirteenth century, was the fairs of Champagne.[15] Merchants of Lucca had been visiting the fairs at least since the middle of the twelfth century, and some Lucchese appear to have settled in Champagne by the latter half of the century.[16] For the thirteenth century our evidence for a community of Lucchese merchants there is conclusive. In 1250 merchants of Lucca were in possession of quarters in both Provins and Troyes; and when they renewed the lease of a stone house in the latter city in 1266, sixteen Lucchese

[13] For purposes of this study I have assumed that where no explicit evidence exists of relationship between the dominant family and those partners bearing another patronymic, the latter were outsiders. Continued research may well indicate collateral relationships in some cases, but it is doubtful that such discoveries would alter the above conclusions. On the evolution from the closed family partnership to the open structure, see A. Sapori, "Le compagnie mercantili del dugento e dei primi del trecento," 803–804 and R. de Roover, "The Organization of Trade," 74–75.

[14] T. Blomquist, "Trade and Commerce in Thirteenth-Century Lucca," 37–55 deals with Lucchese penetration of Italian markets. For Lucchese contacts with Nimes, Narbonne, and Marseilles, see *ibid.*, 62–66 and F. Edler, "The Silk Trade of Lucca," 96–99.

[15] For the Lucchese in the north, apart from the above indicated unpublished studies, see the work of F. Bouquelot, *Études sur les foires de Champagne*, 2 vols., published as *Mémoires présentées par divers savants a l'Académie des Inscriptions et Belles-Lettres* (Paris, 1865-1866); A. Schaube, *Storia del commercio dei popoli latini del Mediterraneo sino alla fine della crociate*, tr. P. Bonfante (Torino, 1915); and L. Mirot, *Études lucquoises* (Paris, 1930).

[16] A treaty of 1153 concluded between Lucca and Genoa spelled out among its other provisions the terms under which Lucchese merchants might traverse Genoese territory on their way to and from the northern fairs: for the treaty see, C. Imperiale, ed., *Codice diplomatico della Repubblica di Genova*, 3 vols. (Rome, 1936–1942), I, no. 238. Count Thibault VI of Champagne, in 1222 granted protection and exemption from military service to Lucchese in Champagne, suggesting that Lucchese were sufficiently numerous to warrant special consideration and that their stay was of a duration to make them liable for a military obligation: see F. Bourquelot, *Études sur les foires*, I, 175 and A. Schaube, *Storia del commercio*, 422.

signed the agreement.[17] Among these were two partners of the Ricciardi, two members of the Bettori organization and one each from the partnerships of the Gentili and the Guinigi. In 1284 the Lucchese operating in Champagne, on a more or less permanent basis, numbered at least forty.[18]

In the context of the 1280's, however, representation abroad should be understood not in the sense of permanent branches such as developed in the fourteenth and fifteenth centuries, but rather as the conduct of business through one or perhaps two partners located in the north.[19] The Lucchese sources do indicate that in addition to partners acting for their various organizations abroad, partnerships sent out employees, *factores*, to provide assistance and no doubt to gain valuable business experience.[20] But, despite these limited references to staff, we may infer from the sources that the Lucchese businessman abroad in the thirteenth century personally despatched whatever business came to hand and that he assumed a broad initiative in generating new business. These partners operating throughout northern Europe were the cutting edge, so to speak, of Italian economic penetration.

Although the fairs retained their importance for Lucchese commerce throughout the thirteenth century, late in the period merchants of Lucca were beginning to expand their operations beyond these emporia and to deal directly with the cloth producing centers of Flanders.[21] Traffic in both money and merchandise constituted sources of profit. In Flanders the Ricciardi, Paganelli, and Cardellini companies frequently extended credit to the city of Ypres.[22] In 1282 the Paganelli partnership acted as agents for Bruges in settling

---

[17] F. Bourquelot, *Etudes sur les foires*, I, 166, II, 15 and L. Mirot, *Études lucquoises*, 52, note 6.

[18] T. Blomquist, "Trade and Commerce in Thirteenth-Century Lucca," 57, note 7.

[19] R. de Roover, "The Organization of Trade," 70–88, has called attention to the significance of the establishment of permanent branch offices, as well as the structural innovations distinguishing the late thirteenth century from the fifteenth century mercantile-banking organization. For an example of the latter, see the same author's *The Rise and Decline of the Medici Bank* (New York, 1966).

[20] *Archivio di Stato in Lucca* (Hereafter cited as ASL), *Achivio dei Notari, registro* 1, m. 15, (Notaries Bartolomeo Fulcieri, Tegrimo Fulcieri, Fulciero Fulcieri), fol. 295 v, 19 May, 1284; fol. 427, 30 August, 1284 for payment effected in Champagne by *factores* of Alberto Callianelli and Rainerio Mariani respectively.

[21] Among the terms of the will of one Trasmundino Baldinocti Burlamacchi, a Lucchese silk merchant, was the provision for restitution of usury to the men of the towns *que vocantur Ramerru episcopatu Trasi et Argilliera episcopatus Cialone*. Troyes was a fair town while Châlons-sur-Marne was a cloth producing center. For Trasmundino's will, see ASL, *Archivio dei Notari, registro* 1, n. 5 (Notary Gherardetto da Chiatri), fol. 19. For a similar restitution to French communities *pro remedio anime sue et suorum peccatorum*, see the testament drawn up in 1284 by Giovanni Paganelli Dulcis: ASL, *Archivio dei Notari, registro* 1, n. 15 (notaries Bartolomeo Fulcieri, Tegrimo Fulcieri, Fulciero Fulcieri), fol. 494v.

[22] G. Bigwood, *Le régime juridique et économique du commerce de L'Argent dans la Belgique au Moyen-Âge*, 2 pts., published as *Mémoires de l'Academie Royale de Belgique, Classe des Lettres et des Sciences morales et politiques*, XIV (1921–1922), I, 180, 641.

a debt at Rome, while Lucchese merchants were also purveyors of luxury cloths to the Counts of Flanders and Hainault, as well as to the court of Champagne.[23] In the last quarter of the century, merchants of Lucca had begun to settle at Paris. The first Lucchese to take up residence there were from the same partnerships which had established themselves at the fairs. The register of the taille from the 1290's lists sixteen Lucchese representing the partnerships of the Guinigi, Ricciardi, Onesti, Corbollani, Moriconi, and Martini.[24]

It was in England, however, that Italian merchants in general, and the Lucchese in particular, found perhaps the most fertile field for their entrepreneurial skills.[25] Arriving in England shortly after the Piacenzans, Bolognese, Romans, and the first Tuscans (who were Sienese), the Lucchese appear in the 1240's as purveyors of silk cloth and dealers in stanforts.[26] The most important single Italian business enterprise in late-thirteenth century England was the partnership of the Ricciardi.[27] But the Ricciardi were only one — albeit the most potent — of a number of Italian partnerships carrying on business in England. Among the Lucchese, the Cardellini, Squarcialupi, Bettori, Paganelli, and Onesti were influential at court. They acted as papal depositories, engaged in the importation of silk cloth and the exportation of wool, as well as being active in finance.[28] The role of Italians and especially Lucchese was, in short, one critical to English economic development in the thirteenth century.

[23] Ibid., and L. Mirot, Études lucquoises, 53–54.

[24] L. Mirot, Études lucquoises, 56 and C. Piton, Les Lombards en France et à Paris: leurs marques, leurs poids-monnaies, leur sceaux de plomb, 2 vols. (Paris, 1892–1893), I, 125.

[25] For the Italian presence in England see A. Sapori, La compagnia dei Frescobaldi in Inghilterra (Florence, 1947); W. E. Rhodes, "The Italian Bankers and their Loans to Edward I and Edward II," Historical Essays by Members of the Owens College Manchester (London, 1902), 137–168; R. Whitwell, "Italian Bankers and the English Crown," Transactions of the Royal Historical Society, XVII (1903), 175–233 and "English Monasteries and the Wool Trade in the Thirteenth Century," Vierteljahrschrift für Sozial- und Wirtschaftsgeschichte, II (1904), 1–33. See also G. Bigwood, "Un marché des matières premières: laines d'Angleterre et marchands italiens vers la fin du XIIIe siècle," Annales d'histoire économique et sociale, I (1930), 193–211; W. E. Lunt, Financial Relations of the Papacy with England, and E. Re, "La compagnia dei Ricciardi," as well as F. Edler, "The Silk Trade of Lucca," 123–131 and T. Blomquist, "Trade and Commerce in Thirteenth-Century Lucca," 67–81.

[26] W. Lunt, Financial Relations, 598–599.

[27] A. Sapori, La compagnia dei Frescobaldi in Inghilterra, 3–4, has divided the history of the Italians in England into three periods, each dominated by one company: the first extending from the appearance of the Ricciardi until their fall about 1300, the second dominated by the Frescobaldi until their decline from royal favor around 1311, and the third, the period of the Bardi and Peruzzi of Florence lasting until 1338.

[28] T. Blomquist, "Trade and Commerce in Thirteenth-Century Lucca," 67–81. For references to partners of these organizations and their business see the volumes relevant to the reigns of Henry III and Edward I in Calendar of Patent Rolls Preserved in the Public Record Office, Calendar of Close Rolls Preserved in the Public Record Office and the documents published by E. A. Bond, "Extracts from the Liberate Rolls Relative to Loans Supplied by Italian Merchants to the Kings of England in the 13th and 14th Centuries," Archaelogia, XXVIII (1840), pt. 2, 207–326.

164

The foregoing summary of Lucchese penetration and exploitation of new markets is intended to suggest something of the complexity of business generated by these enlarged partnerships, as well as to underscore the European-wide influence of Italy in promoting economic growth. Yet, the degree of centralized control exercised from Lucca over these far-flung partners or agents should not be over exaggerated.[29] Indeed the failure of overall management control has been advanced as the most significant factor in the fall of the Sienese Bonsignori at the end of the century.[30] Still, the enlarged partnership, centrally, if imperfectly, controlled represents a remarkable advance in the technique of doing business.

As we have noted, these international mercantile-banking structures were becoming more than simple partnerships. They were in fact assuming the characteristics of a distinct legal entity. There is considerable evidence indicating that contemporaries considered them as something above the aggregate indentities of the partners. What is suggested here is best illustrated by the use of the company name — *societas Ricciardorum, societas filiorum Paganelli* — and so forth. By the last quarter of the thirteenth century, a formula appeared in the contracts through which agents acting for a partnership obligated not only associated partners but the partnership in its corporate sense as well. Thus, in 1296 in a document of procuration we find twelve members of the Ricciardi stipulating *pro se ipsis et pro dicta societate et gestorio nomine pro aliis eorum et dicta societate.*[31] Moreover, the use of a partnership seal further reinforced the concept of large-scale partnership as an entity.[32]

This apparent conception of the large-scale partnership as more than the aggregate of the individual partners was further reinforced by the longevity of the organization. For, although the departure or admission of new partners and changes in the partnership capital through the distribution of profits or recapitalization apparently necessitated the dissolution of the partnership and the formation of a new association. This new association carried over the company name, and presumably the good will, the debits, and the

---

[29] This point is discussed by R. de Roover, "The Organization of Trade," 87–89. See also the same author's *The Rise and Decline of the Medici Bank* for an analysis of the pitfalls besetting fifteenth century business managers.

[30] M. Chiaudano, "I Rothschild del Dugento, La Gran Tavola di Orlando Bonsignori," *Bullettino senese di storia patria*, n.s., VI (1935), 119–120.

[31] ASL, *Archivio dei Notari, registro 9*, m. 17 (Notary Alluminato Parensi, Bonifazio Parenti, Nicolao Passamonti), fol. 94.

[32] See the example cited by M. Chiaudano, "Le compangie bancarie senesi nel Dugento," *Studi e documenti per la storia del diritto commerciale italiano nel secolo XIII* (Torino, 1930), 38, in which a partner of the Ricciardi in England authenticated a document of procuration by affixing his seal and that of the partnership with the words: *E io Rainieri sopradito con la mia mano abo jscrito quie di soto e messo lo mio sugelo con quelo de la compagnia.*

credits of the old. As far as third parties were concerned, there was no interruption in the continuity of the institution. Third parties need only have been assured that they were dealing with a bona fide representative of the partnership bearing the company name at the time a particular transaction was carried out. The principle of joint and unlimited liability guaranteed the fulfillment of the obligation, regardless of alterations in the internal organization of the company.[33]

Unfortunately the Lucchese cartularies preserve no partnership agreements drawn up by the large-scale organizations. Those agreements which have survived record the associations formed between merchants and/or artisans for the conduct of business at a lower level of economic activity. These are fairly standard in terms of form.[34] The contracts of partnership always specified the type of activity to be undertaken: general trade (*de omni mercadantia de qua possent lucrari bona fide*); merchandising a specific commodity (*de arte sete et sendadorum et omnium aliarum merciarum et de omnibus que ad mercadantiam pertinent*); the exercise of a craft (*de arte tinctore sendadorum*), and so forth.

Flexibility was the rule with respect to the formation of the partnership capital. In the small associations of two, three, perhaps four partners, capital was frequently conferred equally by all participants. However, instances in which some associates brought lesser amounts of capital, or even none at all, and compensated thereby with their labor, are not rare in the Lucchese documents.[35] In brief, the way in which the partnership capital was organized depended upon particular circumstances.

The duration of the partnership was stated: it might be as short as a few months or last a number of years, and a clause was usually inserted allowing the extension of the agreement by common consent of the contracting parties. Provision sometimes was made for the withdrawal of one or another of the partners before the terminal date of the agreement, in which case the retiring partner was liable to his former associates for payment of damages.

Further, all contracts of partnership specified the method of distributing profits. At the level of business illustrated in the

[33] A. Sapori, "Storia interna della compagnia mercantile dei Peruzzi," *Studi di storia economica*, II, 665–669. R. de Roover, "The Organization of Trade," 76.

[34] There are numerous examples of partnership contracts in the Lucchese notarial documents. See the following as typical examples: *Archivio capitolare*, Lucca, *LL* 11, *Notaio Ciabatto*, fol. 176, 9 April 1238; ASL, *Archivio dei Notari, registro* 1, n. 15, (notaries Bartolomeo Fulcieri, Tegrimo Fulcieri, Fulciero Fulcieri), fol. 163v, 15 February 1284; *ibid.*, fol. 385, 31 July 1284; *ibid.*, fol. 473, 30 November 1284. See also the partnership agreements of the money-changers cited in T. Blomquist, "The Castracani Family of Thirteenth-Century Lucca."

[35] T. Blomquist, "Castracani Family," note 25. See the above cited *Archivio capitolare*, LL 11, *Notaio Ciabatto*, fol. 176 for an example of such an arrangement.

notarial cortularies, the profits were most always apportioned equally among partners even though there may have been a disparity in capital conferred. But, here again circumstances varied. In general, the large-scale companies, composed of many partners, each of whom contributed varying amounts of capital and each of whom participated to a varying degree in the activities of the company shared in the profits on a pro rated basis.[36]

Prior to the distribution of profits, or the dissolution of the partnership, a general accounting was held to determine each partner's share of the assets or liabilities.[37] If the purpose of the accounting was to liquidate, some or all of the partners were assigned responsibility for winding up particular segments of business outstanding.[38] The assets or liabilities thus involved were accordingly credited or debited to the partner's equity in the partnership. During the winding-up period, all participants were specifically forbidden to obligate the other partners in any way not directly connected with the liquidation. If the partners could not agree upon an equitable division of assets it was customary to resort to arbitration in order to resolve the difficulties.[39]

This then was regular partnership in thirteenth-century Lucca. Yet, within this institutional framework there was ample scope for entrepreneurial innovation. In Lucca, as elsewhere in Italy, new conditions and possibilities resulted in innovation. It would appear that Lucchese were experimenting in the thirteenth century with a type of business organization resembling the modern holding company, the kind of structure employed by the Medici Bank in the fifteenth century.[40]

We may cite one example of such an arrangement revealed in the notarial documents of 1284.[41] In that year three members of

---

[36] M. Chiaudano, "Le compagnie bancarie senesi nel Dugento," *Studi e documenti per la storia del diritto commerciale italiano nel secolo XIII* published as *Memorie dell'Istituto Giuridico, Reale Università di Torino*, VIII (1930), 30–31; A. Sapori, "Storia interna della Compagnia mercantile dei Peruzzi," 672–680; R. de Roover, "The Organization of Trade," 76–78. In the Lucchese contracts partners stipulating on behalf of their partnership did so *pro se ipsis et pro aliis sociis pro quibus de rata promiserunt.*

[37] See for example ASL, *Archivio dei Notari, registro* 1, n. 15 (Notaries Bartolomeo Fulcieri, Tegrimo Fulcieri, Fulciero Fulcieri), fol. 385, 31 July, 1284: *in capite dicti termini vel quando dicta societas seperabitur promisit* (the one partner to the other) . . . *et inde omni in capite dicti termini veram rationem et non perfuntoriam seu fictitiam facere.*

[38] As examples of contracts resulting from the dissolution of partnership, see ASL, *Archivio dei Notari, registro* 2. n. 18 [Notary Alluminato Parensi (1286, 1287, 1290)], fol. 14, 18 June 1287; fol. 40v, 11 December 1287: *registro* 1, n. 17 (Notary Alluminato Parensi (1299)).

[39] For the settlement of a disputed partnership dissolution, see the above cited cartulary of the notary Alluminato Parensi (1286, 1287, 1290), fol. 14.

[40] For the structure of the Medici enterprise, see R. de Roover, *The Rise and Decline of the Medici Bank*, especially 81–84.

[41] ASL, *Archivio dei Notari, registro* 1, n. 15 (Notaries Bartolomeo Fulcieri, Tegrimo Fulcieri, Fulciero Fulcieri), fol. 163v, 15 February 1284.

the Tignosini family, Bonagiunta and his two sons, Betto and Francesco, were active in a partnership engaged in commerce and banking which included at least one outsider, Gualtrotto Castagnacii. But in February the three Tignosini comprised one party to the formation of another partnership with the silk merchant Cinquarino Guidi Cinque for the express purpose of trading in silk and related merchandise. This partnership was capitalized at £ 2,000 Luchese, a considerable sum; the Tignosini contributing £ 1,300 and Cinquarino £ 700. Upon termination of the agreement after one year, the profits were to be divided equally between the two contracting parties despite the disparity in the capital sum contributed. The difference, of course, was represented by Cinquarino's labor. It is interesting to note further that Cinquarino was enjoined from participating in any other partnership during the duration of this agreement. How widespread this technique of forming subsidiary partnerships to achieve diversification was, the surviving contracts do not show. However, it may be said that in this instance Lucchese practice anticipated the developments of the fourteenth and fifteenth centuries.

While regular partnership was the basic juridical form for the organization of business in medieval Lucca, the joint venture was frequently employed as a means of achieving greater flexibility in organizing capital, diversifying activity and dividing risk. A joint venture brought two or more parties, either individuals or partnerships, together to carry out a single transaction or a series of transactions. The parties to a joint venture were, like general partners, liable without limit for all obligations properly negotiated.[42] Instruments of exchange and all manner of commodities were bought and sold by syndicates of individuals and/or partnerships. The importance of joint venture as a means of organizing enterprise may perhaps best be suggested by pointing out that in the Lucchese notarial contracts of the last half of the thirteenth century the solitary entrepreneur acting on his own behalf is indeed a rarity. The medieval Italian businessman of the commercial revolution preferred to act through the collectivities of partnership or joint venture syndicate.

### LIMITED LIABILITY ASSOCIATIONS

Regular partnership and joint venture, both characterized by the principle of joint and unlimited liability, were the most common

---

[42] In contracts in which two or more parties acted jointly they expressly stipulated their liability *omnes similiter et quilibet eorum principaliter et in solidum.*

means through which Lucchese merchants and artisans organized their capital and labor. However, economic conditions in Lucca resulted in the development of a third associative form, one seemingly suited to the attraction of capital from sources outside the business and commercial community. In order to meet the capital demands of an expanding economy there evolved a form of association in which the liability of some of the participants was limited to the amount of their investment.[43] *Societas ad partem Lucri, societas et ad partem lucri, compagnia et ad partem lucri, societas et compagnia ad partem lucri, accomadiscia ad partem lucri,* or simply *societas et compagnia,* as the Lucchese sources variously termed this institution, would appear to have performed the same economic function as deposit at fixed interest.[44] But the popularity of the former in late thirteenth-century Lucca, if we may judge from the frequency of its appearance among the notarial contracts, suggests that many investors were attracted by a possibility of gain greater than the normal 10 per cent earned from capital invested through deposit at interest.[45]

Through this institution, which for convenience we may term "association *ad partem lucri*," the investor placed his funds with an individual merchant or an existing partnership. Such a sum the active partner (or partners) was to employ equally with his own capital in the stated enterprise. As with regular partnership, the

[43] The problem of the origins of limited partnership in Italy has given rise to considerable debate and a correspondingly sizable literature. The most recent consideration of the problem of which I am aware, A. Sapori, "Le compagnie mercantili toscane del dugento e dei primi del trecento," concludes that in thirteenth-century Tuscany there were indeed more or less informal "variations of regular partnership" in which some participants enjoyed a limited liability. However, according to Professor Sapori, towards the end of the thirteenth century the governments and gilds of the various commercial centers began to take an interest in the internal structure of their cities' partnerships. Accordingly, communal authorities and gilds, in order to protect the good name of their merchants abroad, reaffirmed in public law and mercantile practice the norm of joint and unlimited liability. Our Lucchese associations *ad partem lucri* might well be termed "variations of regular partnership." However, whether they gave way in the fourteenth century to deposit at interest as the preferred form of raising capital, as Professor Sapori theorizes, remains a question yet to be investigated. Cf. the views of A. Arcangeli, "L' Origine ed i caratteri della società in accomandita semplice," and "Gli istituti del diritto commerciale nel Costituto senese del 1310," in his *Scritti di diritto commerciale ed agrario*, 3 vols. (Padua, 1935-1936), I, 54-148 and 159-244; Q. Senigalia, "Le compagnie bancarie senesi nei secoli XIII e XIV," *Studi senese nel Circolo Giuridico della R. Università*, XIV, XXV (1907, 1908), 149-217, 3-66; M. Chiaudano, "Le compagnie bancarie senesi nel dugento"; L. Goldschmidt, *Storia universale*, 227-228.

[44] For representative examples see ASL, *Archivio dei Notari, registro* 1, *n.* 12 (Notary Bartolomeo Tacchi di Gerardino), fol. 66, 7 March 1272; *registro* 1, *n.* 12 (Notary Paganello di Fiandrada), fol. 16v. 28 January 1273 and fol. 54, 26 June 1273; *registro* 1, *n.* 15 (Notaries Bartolomeo Fulcieri, Tegrimo Fulcieri, Fulciero Fulcieri), fol. 8, 5 January 1284.

[45] Although there are no surviving references to interest among the Lucchese documents, R.S. Lopez, *La prima crisi della banca de Genova (1250-1259)*, (Milan, 1956), 34-35 has indicated that the banks of the Genoese money-changers paid a 10 per cent return on deposits and M. Chiaudano, "Affari e contabilita dei banchieri fiorentini nel Dugento," *Studi e documenti*, 70-72 has shown that deposits with Florentine bankers earned the same rate.

contract of association *ad partem lucri* always indicated the term of the agreement – which might vary from a few months up to a year or even longer. Upon termination, the active partner was obligated to return the initial investment plus or minus whatever percentage of profit or loss he wished to assign to the investor. It is not improbable that in practice the percentage of profit on the investment was informally determined in advance by the active partner and the investor, and thus it might be argued that association *ad partem lucri* was in fact a form of deposit.[46] But the language of the contracts would clearly seem to indicate that we are indeed dealing with a juridical form distinct from deposit, however similar the two were in function.

The contracts expressly stated that the active partner has accepted the investment in partnership, *in societatem ad partem lucri*. Also the share of profit or loss returned to the investor by the active partner was apparently based upon the success of the enterprise as a whole. More important for the juridical classification of association *ad partem lucri*, however, was the fact that the investor could not in the case of failure of the enterprise appear as a creditor of the active partner as, of course, could a depositor. Contracts of association *ad partem lucri* explicitly limited the liability of the investor to the sum invested. And as the documents phrased it, the investor assumed the liability for his capital, but only for that capital, just as the active partner assumed the risk for his funds. If, however, the investor enjoyed a liability limited to his investment so also he implicitly renounced any future claim against the active partner for that sum.

The economic significance and function of the Lucchese association *ad partem lucri* should, however, take precedence over debate as to its precise juridical nature. Although a full tabulation and study of those contracts surviving in the Lucchese notarial cartularies remains to be done, the evidence at hand would indicate

---

[46] Q. Senigalia, "Le compagnie bancarie senesi nei secoli XIII e XIV," has, for example, suggested that the Florentine and Sienese institutions of *accomandigia* were the precursors of limited partnership because the depositor shared proportionally in the profits of the entire enterprise. These he has called "irregular deposit." R. de Roover, *The Rise and Decline of the Medici Bank*, 104 has argued that a contractual arrangement, similar to the association *ad partem lucri*, although reading as a partnership agreement "involving participation in profits or losses of a business venture" was instead a deposit certificate providing for the payment of interest. For the reasons set forth below I would maintain, however, that association *ad partem lucri* was considered by contemporaries to be a form of partnership and not a deposit. Deposits in the Lucchese sources were specifically termed *depositum* or *depositum seu accomandigia*: see T. Blomquist, "The Castracani Family of Thirteenth-Century Lucca." M. Lecce, "Mutui commerciali a Verona nel trecento," *Economia e Storia*, IX (1962), 213–219, refers to the investor participating in the fourteenth century Veronese *Instrumentum societatis sive mutui*, an institution similar in some respects to the Lucchese association *ad partem lucri*, as a "near partner", *quasi socio*.

that association *ad partem lucri* played an important role in marshalling capital for the expanding trade and commerce of thirteenth-century Lucca. Some examples will perhaps demonstrate more clearly the function of this institution.

The partnership of the sons of Orlando Bettori was one of the more important Lucchese organizations engaged in international commerce and finance. By 1272 the Bettori were represented in Genoa, where they dealt in raw silk and banking.[47] Their agents were among the first Lucchese in England where they were active in the wool trade, finance, and later as papal depositories.[48] But in spite of their apparent ability to draw upon considerable resources, the Bettori nevertheless accepted funds in association *ad partem lucri* from individuals who were themselves not actively engaged in business or commerce — from what might be designated non-commercial sources. In January 1273, for example, Lanfranco, Bonaccorso, and Jacobo, sons of the late Orlando Bettori, with their partner Stefano Pitotelli, received £ 380 *in societatem et compagniam* from two brothers, Jacobo and Niccolò, sons of the late Ugolino Ponci.[49] The Bettori accordingly promised to utilize the sum invested with the capital of their partnership and to return the original investment plus or minus whatever percentage of profit or loss they wished to assign to the investor. The liability of the two brothers was limited to the £ 380 invested. In September of the same year we again find the Bettori partnership accepting capital through association *ad partem lucri*; on this occasion £ 410 from the noble Guido Porcho.[50]

An interesting utilization of association *ad partem lucri* occurred in June 1273 when the partnership of the sons of the late Arrigo Sandonis placed £ 50 with one Bonaccorso Ubaldi Bianchi.[51] The

---

[47] A. Ferretto, *Il codice diplomatico*, I, no. 673: on 10 September 1272 the partnership's agent in Genoa, Rabito Ugolini Teste, procurator of the partners Bartolomeo and Lanfranco, sons of the late Orlando Bettori, Pietro Ugolinelli, Gottefredo Conetti Bonosti, Caccianemico Overardi, and Stefano Giovanni Pisanelli, received a sum Genoese from one Lanfranco Ceba which he promised to repay at the Fair of Troyes with £ 200 *provinois*. The partnership received sizable sums in deposit from the Genoese nephews of Pope Innocent IV. On 7 October 1273 Cardinal Ottobono Fieschi instructed "his friends Bartolomeo, Buongiorno and others of the Bettori of Lucca" to pay his brother, Nicolo Fieschi, £ 4,000 *tourois* from his account with them: see *ibid.*, no. 786. One week later the agent of Nicolaus de Flische, *palatini et lavanie comes*, one *magister* Phinus de Sancto Stefano, received the above sum from the Bettori in Lucca. The same contract also shows that the Cardinal had deposits of £ 4,000 Genoese with the Ricciardi, £ 6,000 Genoese with the Chiarrenti of Pistoia and 500 marks of silver with the Adamati, also of Pistoia. For the original of the above document see ASL, *Archivio dei Notari, registro 1, n. 12* (Notary Paganello di Fiandrada), fol. 80v.

[48] Pietro Ugolinelli was in England as early as 1255: *Calendar of Patent Rolls, Henry III (1247-1258)*, 404. During the 1270's the patent rolls indicate that the partnership was represented in England by Aldebrandino and Theobaldo Malagalye, Stefano Pitutelli, Niccolò Teste and Ugolino Ugolinelli.

[49] ASL, *Archivio dei Notari, registro 1, n. 12* (Notary Paganello di Fiandrada), fol. 16v.

[50] *Ibid.*, fol. 77.

[51] *Ibid.*, fol. 54.

term of the contract was six months, during which period Bonaccorso was to engage the invested capital, along with his own, in
trade within the city and district of Lucca. The Sandone were
successful silk and cloth merchants of the 1270's and in this instance
we may presume that the purpose of their investment was to secure
Bonaccorso's labor in merchandising cloth locally. By this arrangement the local merchant received financing while the brothers
shared in the rewards of his labor without assuming a risk greater
than their £ 50 invested.

Turning to a consideration of the sources of capital invested *ad
partem lucri*, our evidence indicates that funds placed in this way
typically came from individuals who were themselves not actively
involved in business or commerce. The £ 150 invested with two silk
merchants *ad partem lucri* in 1284 by *domina* Filioccia, wife of
*dominus* Aldebrandino of Porcari, like the sum mentioned above
invested by Guido Porcho, would fall into this category.[52] So also
the £ 150 belonging to Pagana, the daughter of a baker, placed with
the partnership of the Tignosini in 1279 apparently originated from
an artisanal patrimony.[53] Significantly, in the same year the
Tignosini also received £ 105 *ad partem lucri* from one Matthea,
daughter of *frater* Bonagiunta Somani, indicating that they, like
the Bettori, regularly accepted funds through this instrumentality.[54]

Thus association *ad partem lucri* provided a convenient means
for channeling investments into business and commerce in the late-
thirteenth century, a period of economic expansion and high
capital demand. As our examples show, this type of association
with limited liability was important in financing mercantile-banking
partnerships as well as lesser commercial undertakings and individual entrepreneurial enterprises. Our material further suggests
that the activities of Lucchese merchants were sustained by an
economic base of investments drawn from a wide cross section of
Lucchese society.

## Conclusion

We have seen in this brief consideration of commercial association in thirteenth-century Lucca some of the means by which
Lucchese organized and financed enterprise. Although I would
not wish to give the impression that the businessmen of Lucca

[52] *ASL, Archivio dei Notari, registro* 1, *n.* 15 (Notaries Bartolomeo Fulcieri, Tegrimo
Fulcieri, Fulcerio Fulcieri), fol. 8.
[53] *ASL, Archivio dei Notari, registro* 3, *n.* 13 (Notary Armanno di Armanno,
fol. 5.
[54] *Ibid.*, fol. 36.

were unique among their co-nationals, Italian medieval business-men — indeed in terms of business techniques northern Italy seem-ingly advanced as one in the Middle Ages, — I cannot fail to admire the boldness of their entrepreneurial response to the challenges and opportunities of economic change. They explored new forms of business organization which contributed to the economic growth of the thirteenth century.

APPENDIX

LUCCHESE PARTNERSHIPS, 1284

The following list of partnerships and partners is based upon the contracts contained in the cartulary *Bartolomeo Fulcieri, Tegrimo Fulcieri, Fulciero Fulcieri* of 1284. The clients of the Fulcieri were drawn almost exclusively from the upper ranks of the Lucchese mercantile community. Numbered among the individuals appear-ing in the contracts were representatives of the major mercantile-banking structures, as well as many merchants representing smaller partnerships but who were nonetheless engaged in international commerce.

The cartulary is chronologically complete for the entire year, suggesting that the contracts therein may well represent a major portion, if not all, of the production done by the Fulcieri on behalf of these clients in 1284. There is, however, nothing to indicate that these merchants brought their business only to the Fulcieri. Indeed, from the same year, 1284, there exists a series of contracts redacted by the notary Nicolao Alamanni relating to the business of foreign exchange conducted by Savarigio Pilii Castracanis, evidence that the Fulcieri did not possess a monopoly on this class of contract. Consequently it is impossible to estimate the percentage of the total business activity in the area of international finance and commerce that is represented by this material. Nonetheless, the emphasis upon international business, the fact that many of the large-scale Lucchese companies are mentioned and the lack of apparent *lacunae* make of this cartulary of the Fulcieri a unique source for the business history of Lucca in the late-thirteenth century.

The lists of partnerships and partners were assembled by collating all contracts relating to each merchant mentioned in the cartulary and noting each instance in which the term partner, *socius*, described the relationship of that merchant and other merchants associated with him in his various transactions. For example, the partners of Francesco Norradini Onesti were determined by observing that on October 18, 1284 he, Ghetto Norradini Onesti, and Gaddo Norradini Onesti received through an exchange contract a quantity of Lucchese money which they promised to repay in *provinois* in Champagne. The three were described as *socii et cives et mercatores Luce*. But Gaddo and Ghetto also acted in a similar transaction with Nicoluccio Brancasecche and these three were also characterized as *socii*; while in yet another contract Ghetto and Fatio Onesti were listed as partners. Thus, at least four merchants emerge as partners of the original Francesco. Furthermore, the returns of the papal depositories in England published by Professor Lunt provide the partnership style: *societas Ghecti Honesti*.

Since it was customary to include the names of only one, two, or perhaps three partners participating in a purchase-sale or exchange contract, indicating where applicable that they stipulated *pro aliis suis sociis*, the following lists in most cases can only be considered as partial. It cannot be known whether they represent the complete membership of a partnership or only a portion thereof. These lists should consequently be considered only a beginning towards the recovery of a full register of Lucchese merchant partnerships.

I.   *Societas filiorum Paganelli*

1. Guido Paganelli Dulcis
2. Jacobus Paganelli Dulcis
3. Johannes Paganelli Dulcis
4. Nicolaus Paganelli Dulcis
5. Orlandinus Paganelli Dulcis
6. Adrogadus Puliti
7. Ardicione Malisti

8. Arrigus Bocciale
9. Cecus Dentis Cangnoli
10. Fregioctus de Montechiaro
11. Lumbardus Gratiani
12. Martinus Manni
13. Petrus Gratiani
14. Riccardinus Maile
15. Thomazollus Domini Alcherii
16. Tosanus Cristofani
17. Ubaldus Loçarii Bernarduccii

II. *Societas Cardellinorum*

1. Albertinus Cardellini
2. Bendinellus Cardellini
3. Burnectus quondam Bonaccursi Cardellini
4. Dinus Cardellini
5. Ubaldus quondam Bonaccursi Cardellini
6. Ubertinus quondam Bonaccursi Cardellini
7. Arrigus filius Jacobi Cimacchi
8. Gerardus Cimacchi
9. Guido Guidocti de Tassignano
10. Guilielmus Cimacchi
11. Percivalleus filius Adversi Raffacanelli

III. *Societas Bectorum*

1. Bartholomeus quondam Orlandi Bectori
2. Bonaccursus Bectori
3. Jacobus Bectori
4. Lippus filius Bartholomei Bectori
5. Cecius filius Aldibrandini Faitinelli
6. Duccius Bonaccursi
7. Franciscus quondam Pieri Ugolinelli
8. Guilielmus quondam Aldibrandini Faitinelli
9. Naddorus Teste
10. Nectus Teste
11. Rabitus Teste

Merchants appearing as agents of the partnership

1. Bandinus Cistelle
2. Dinus Honesti
3. Gadduccius Spade

IV.

1. Balduccius filius Marsilii Macacciori
2. Bonaccursus filius Jacobi Cimacchi
3. Calvanus Macacciori
4. Fredus quondam Gentilis Guasconis
5. Jacobus Cimacchi
6. Lucterius quondam Gentilis Guasconis
7. Michele quondam Gentilis Guasconis
8. Nicholaus Guercii

9. Ubertus Fangi
10. Ubalduccius filius Marsilii Macacciori

V. *Societas Ricciardorum* \*
1. Guidiccione Guidiccionis
2. Paganuccius Guidi
3. Riccardus quondam Paganini Guidiccionis
4. Tomasinus Guidiccionis quondam Paganini Guidi

Merchants appearing as agents of the partnership
1. Bartaloctus quondam Bugianensis Bandini
2. Barchetta Barche
3. Vannes Rosciompeli
4. Riccardinus quondam Domini Bonfatti Gottori

VI. *Societas Battosorum*
1. Custore quondam Battosi
2. Johannes quondam Battosi
3. Orlandus quondam Battosi
4. Aldebrandinus Spiafame
5. Arrigus quondam Jacobi Spiafame
6. Rainerius quondam Jacobi Spiafame
7. Feduccius filius Rodulfini Diversi

Merchants appearing as agents of the partnership
1. Cecchorus filius Johannis Battosi
2. Duccius Calganecti
3. Nicholaus Dentis
4. Johannes Oddi

VII. *Societas Scorcialupi*
1. Cialupus quondam Jacobi Scorcialupi
2. Belluccius quondam Ugolini Belli
3. Cinus Ronthini
4. Landus Ronthini
5. Puccius Pagonelli

VIII. *Societas Ghecti Honesti*
1. Ghectus quondam Norradini Honesti
2. Fatius Honesti
3. Francischus quondam Norradini Honesti
4. Gaddus quondam Norradini Honesti
5. Nicoluccius Brancasecche

---

\* The partners of the company in 1286 are known through a contract confirming the power of attorney granted to Frederigus quondam Sarracini Incallocchiati and Nicoluccius quondam Bonacursi Mignosii. In all, there were nineteen partners: Frederigus and Nicoluccius, Dominus Andrea Parenti, Ricciardus Ricciardi, Philippus Ricciardi, Paganus Guidiccionis, Adiutus Rosciompile, Johannes Symonetti, Raynerius Bandini, Guidicciones Paganni, Thomazini Guidicionis, Vannes Rosciompeli, Abates Talgardi, Raynerius Maghiarii, Bendinus Peruchi, Philipucius Talgardi, Frederigus Venture, Saracenus Macchi, and Johannes Gambardi. For the complete document, see G. Arias, *Studi e documenti di storia del diritto*, 157; A. Sapori, "Le compagnie mercantili toscane del dugento e dei primi del trecento," 769.

Merchants appearing as agents of the partnership

1. Dinus Honesti
2. Gadduccius Spade
3. Baldus Roseli

IX.

1. Arriguccius Boccialle
2. Arrigus Arnolfini
3. Bendinus quondam Albertini de Tasse
4. Bonaiuncta quondam Riccomi Urbicciani
5. Duccius Calganecti
6. Petruccius Schiatisse
7. Tacus Arnolfini
8. Tedicius Lamberti de Porta
9. Ugolinus Jacobi Boccielle

Merchants appearing as agents of the partnership

1. Rainerius Mariani
2. Feduccius Diversi
3. Cecchorus Battosi
4. Arrigus Spiafame

X.

1. Allexius quondam Uberti Terizendi
2. Bectus quondam Aldibrandi Terizendi
3. Ghinus quondam Aldibrandini Terizendi
4. Nectus filius Becti Terizendi
5. Ugolinus quondam Aldibrandini Terizendi

XI. *Societas Tingnosini*

1. Betius filius Bonaiuncte Tingnosini
2. Bonaiuncta Tingnosini
3. Cecius filius Bonaiuncte Tingnosini
4. Gualtroctus Castagnaccii

Merchants appearing as agents of the partnership

1. Gerardinus Gualtrocti
2. Gaddus Talgardi

XII.

1. Arriguccius quondam Soffreduccii Bocchadivacche
2. Castracanne Rugerii
3. Coluccius quondam Castracannis Rugerii
4. Durassus quondam Durassi
5. Gerius filius Castracannis Rugerii
6. Neus filius Castracannis Rugerii

Merchants appearing as agents of the partnership

1. Buiamonte Turchii

XIII.

    1. Bectus quondam domini Uberti Diversi
    2. Chellus Morlani
    3. Johannes Alluccii
    4. Johannes Morlani
    5. Johannes Ramori
    6. Lucieptus filius Johanis Aluccii
    7. Rustichellus Aluccii

Merchants appearing as agents of the partnership

    1. Aldibrandinus Cistelle

XIV.   *Societas Guiniscii*

    1. Bartholomeus quondam Guiniscii Rustichi
    2. Bectus quondam Panfolie Guiniscii
    3. Bonifatius quondam Panfolie Guiniscii
    4. Conte quondam Albertini Guiniscii
    5. Filippus quondam Albertini Guiniscii
    6. Pinus Guiniscii
    7. Puccius quondam Albertini Guiniscii
    8. Filippus quondam Uguiccionis Brancoli
    9. Ubaldus quondam Uguiccionis Brancoli

XV.

    1. Boldorus quondam Ugolini Cispe
    2. Geraldus Posarelli quondam Federigi
    3. Marconaldus quondam Faitinelli Mordecastelli
    4. Pannochia quondam Faitinelli Mordecastelli
    5. Ranuccius quondam Faitinelli Mordecastelli

Merchants appearing as agents of the partnership

    1. Buiamonte Turchii

XVI.

    1. Albertinus Callianelli
    2. Aldebrandinus quondam Rugerii Ghiocti
    3. Fedinus quondam Cecii Callianelli
    4. Guiduccius quondam Aldibrandini de Partignano

Merchants appearing as agents

    1. Ubertus Antelmini

XVII.

    1. Cacciaguerra Gualfredi
    2. Gratuccius filius Federigi Callianelli
    3. Homodeus Fiadonis
    4. Jacobus Melanensis
    5. Salliente filius Jacobi Melanensis

XVIII.

1. Armannus Mattafelonis
2. Manninus Gerardini
3. Puccius filius Alamanni
4. Ubertus quondam Uberti Mangialmacchi

XIX.

1. Arrigus quondam Arrigi Moriconis
2. Guccius quondam Arrigi Martini
3. Johannes quondam Deodati Moriconis
4. Landus quondam Arrigi Moriconis
5. Nicoluccius quondam Arrigi Moriconis
6. Schiacta Bernardini

XX.

1. Bartholomeus quondam Venture Paravillani
2. Ghedus Buiamontis Rossi
3. Montuccius filius Bartholomei Paravillani
4. Paganellus quondam domini Deodati Cristofani
5. Paruccius filius Bartholomei Paravillani

XXI.

1. Arrigus quondam Tedeschi Porcelli
2. Coscius Divisi
3. Mingus quondam Bernardini Tenensis
4. Orlandellus quondam Bonaventure Porcelli

XXII.

1. Andruccius filius Benectonis Arnolfi
2. Pierus filius Benectonis Arnolfi
3. Simus filius Benectonis Arnolfi
4. Vannes filius Benectonis Arnolfi

# The Dawn of Banking in an Italian Commune: Thirteenth Century Lucca

THE TUSCAN CITY OF LUCCA, although overshadowed by her neighbor Florence in the later Middle Ages, was in the thirteenth century the chief center of the silk industry in the West and the hub of a network of mercantile banking partnerships which by 1300 extended to every major European financial and commercial center.[1] Locally, her money changers,

The archival research upon which this study is based was made possible by fellowship support from the American Council of Learned Societies and grants from the Penrose Fund, the American Philosophical Society, and The Dean's Fund, Northern Illinois University. To each I am deeply grateful.

1. Two excellent surveys of medieval Italian commercial and business history are Robert S. Lopez, "The Trade of Medieval Europe: The South," *Cambridge Economic History of Europe*, ed. Michael M. Postan et al. 2 (Cambridge 1952) 257–534, and Raymond de Roover, "The Organization of Trade," ibid. 3 (Cambridge 1963) 42–104. Robert S. Lopez, *The Commercial Revolution of the Middle Ages, 950–1350* (Englewood Cliffs, N.J. 1971) presents an analytical survey of the European economy in the High Middle Ages, while John K. Hyde, *Society and Politics in Medieval Italy: The Evolution of the Civil Life 1000–1350*

at first catering primarily to foreign visitors—pilgrims flocking along the Via Francigena to Rome and those pausing to venerate the local icon, *Il Volto Santo,* or merchants needing to exchange foreign currency brought from abroad—had moved beyond manual exchange and dealings in bullion into the area of deposit and transfer banking.[2] Both abroad and at home, men of Lucca were in the forefront of the Commercial Revolution of the thirteenth century as essential protagonists in the early history of European banking and credit.[3]

Fortunately, the state archive and the archiepiscopal and capitular archives of Lucca preserve a mass of notarial materials in which the development of banking techniques as well as the organization of the local capital market can be traced.[4] This essay summarizes my findings after extensive work with these documents; it will be followed by a more comprehensive account later.

In thirteenth century Lucca two groups of professional

---

(New York 1973), provides a recent synthesis of Italian urban history in the communal period. For Lucca, Thomas W. Blomquist, "Commercial Association in Thirteenth Century Lucca," *Business History Review* 45 (1971) 157–78.

2. Thomas W. Blomquist, "The Castracani Family of Thirteenth-Century Lucca," *Speculum* 46 (1971) 459–76, examines the history of a family of Lucchese changers.

3. On the concept of a "commercial revolution of the thirteenth century," see Raymond de Roover, "The Commercial Revolution of the Thirteenth Century," *Bulletin of the Business Historical Society* 16 (1942) 34–39.

4. For a description of the Lucchese notarial archives housed in the *Archivio di Stato di Lucca* (hereafter *ASL*) see Robert S. Lopez, "The Unexplored Wealth of the Notarial Archives of Pisa and Lucca," *Mélanges d'histoire du Moyen Age dédiés à la mémoire de Louis Halphen* (Paris 1951) 417–32. Eugenio Lazzareschi, "L'Archivio dei Notari della Repubblica lucchese," *Gli archivi italiani* 2 (1915) 175–210, catalogues the cartularies. On the archiepiscopal and chapter archives, see Sac. Giuseppe Ghilarducci, *Le biblioteche e gli archivi arcivescovili e capitolari della Diocesi di Lucca* (Lucca 1969) and Duane J. Osheim, "The Episcopal Archive of Lucca in the Middle Ages," *Manuscripta* 17 (1973) 131–46. The information regarding the money changers is derived primarily from the LL series in the chapter archive (hereafter LL).

bankers may be distinguished. The first, the money changers, had already flourished a long time before our sources allow anything like a detailed analysis of their business. The second, merchants engaged in long-range commerce, were perfecting the financial techniques and business organization upon which thirteenth century international commerce and finance were to rest. Although the process was by no means complete, the money changers were evolving into deposit and transfer bankers at the same time the international merchants increasingly generated commercial credit by routine dealings in foreign exchange. For Lucca, this was a formative period in which deposit and transfer banking was maturing side by side with international exchange banking.

The art of money changing was a venerable one in Lucca. In 1111 the oath required of all money changers (*campsores*) or spice dealers (*speciarii*) wishing to set up shop in the cathedral square was inscribed upon the façade of the cathedral of San Martino, where it can still be seen today.[5] The oath, in which the changers and dealers in spices swore to commit "no theft, nor trick nor falsification," was also visible to their customers, who thronged the cathedral square to change money or to buy exotic herbs and medicines at the portable tables and stalls set up there. No other twelfth century reference to money changers is to be found in the Lucchese sources; however, one can infer that the primary activity of campsores in this earlier period was manual exchange, which by its nature did not involve a contract and hence the intervention of a notary. Although manual exchange certainly continued as an essential service of the money changers, by the thirteenth century they were adding other functions to their repertory.

The cathedral square remained the center of the changers' activities throughout the Middle Ages. Outdoor business was

5. Eugenio Lazzareschi, "Fonti d'archivio per lo studio delle corporazioni artigiane di Lucca," *Bollettino storico lucchese* 9 (1937) 78. The inscription is translated in Robert S. Lopez and Irving W. Raymond, *Medieval Trade in the Mediterranean World* (New York and London 1955) 418–19.

conducted from a seat behind a portable table (*tavola* or *mensula*), probably covered by a canopy. The ground upon which the table stood was either owned or leased by the changer.[6] Whether all money changers maintained outdoor tables is problematical; I tend to doubt it. Much of the changers' business was conducted from shops, *apothece*, ranged in houses fronting upon the Court of San Martino, which also served as offices and supply depots for the various campsores and their associates.[7] Considerable business was conducted in a tower, also fronting on the square, which belonged to the Passavanti, a patrician family long associated with the money changers' profession.[8] In fact, the tower seems to have been an informal gathering place for the changers, and it was here in the *turre (Passavantis)*, as it was familiarly styled in the contracts, that the money changers guild held its meetings.[9]

Precisely when the changers organized themselves into a corporate body is not known. The oath of 1111 makes no men-

6. See *Archivio capitolare*, LL 5, fol. 81v, 14 Oct. 1230 for the one-year rental of a *locum campsorum* to Bonconsilius Genovensis at an annual rent of 40s. Lucchese; LL 23, fol. 73v, 23 April 1249 for the cathedral chapter's formal possession of the table bequeathed to it by Quiricus Sciagri, which was under the porch of the cathedral and in front of the table belonging to Rogerius Castracanis; LL 28, fol. 150v, 24 Oct. 1254 for Gerardus Arzuri's rental of a table, formerly belonging to Genovese Anticus, which was next to the door of the cathedral and "against the ground and table of the late Pilius Castracanis" ("qui est contra locum et tabulam quondam Pilii Castracanis iuxta portam S. Martini"). See also Blomquist, "Castracani" (n. 2 above) 463–64 for the purchase of a table and ground in 1252 by Rogerius and Luccerius Castracanis for £15 from Bonifatius Ubertelli Baiori.

7. LL 20, fol. 43v, 8 April 1245: "Actum Luce in apotheca ubi Vethus moratur ad cambium"; LL 36, fol. 33, 7 June 1271: "Actum Luce in apotheca cambii ipsius Castracanis."

8. Rolandus Passavantis owned ground and a table in 1172: LL 27, fol. 18v, 10 Nov. 1252. In 1245 the changer Albertinus Malagallie married the daughter of Orlandus Passavantis: LL 20, fol. 7v, 13 Jan. On 10 March 1251, Orlandus and his brother, Genovese, elected their third brother "captain or consul" of their clan (*domus*): LL 26, fol. 82.

9. Elections of the consuls of the changers guild were held in the tower: LL 11, fol. 4, 7 Feb. 1236, . . . *in turre Passavantis;* fol. 69v, 20 Jan. 1237, . . . *in turre;* fol. 160, 30 Jan. 1238, . . . *in turre Passavantis.*

tion of a corporate organization. A document dated 7 February 1236 refers to the assumption of office by Bonconsilius Genovensis and Ubertus Rodolosi, "the new consuls of the money changers of the Court of Saint Martin" *(novi consules campsorum curie Sancti Martini)*.[10] The guild itself, referred to simply as "the exchange of Saint Martin" *(cambium Sancti Martini)*, had its office in, or near, the cathedral proper.[11] The guild maintained a small treasury which was entrusted to the incumbent consuls and passed on to their successors. In 1236 Bonconsilius and Ubertus received £21 5s. Lucchese from their predecessors in office; a year later they handed over to Pilius *quondam* Castracanis and Galganectus *filius* Gulielmi Genovensis, the new consuls for 1237, the diminished sum of £11 19s., "since no more remained after the old consuls had paid all expenses" ("cum non essent plures qui remanissent suprascriptis veteris consulibus factis et solutis omnibus expensis ab eis").[12] But in the next year, 1238, Genovese *filius* Gulielmi and Ubertus Maghiari Cipoletta were entrusted with a treasury, probably swelled by dues, fines, or both, of £14 18s.[13]

Unfortunately it is impossible to give any exact figures for the size of the money changers guild. However, the cartulary of Ser Ciabatto, who plied his trade in the environs of Saint Martin and who numbered a host of changers among his clients, records the names of fifty known or presumed money changers for the period 1236–38.[14] Ciabatto's cartularies surviving from the decade of the thirties contain the names of sixty-eight individuals who, even if not explicitly styled *campsor*, nonetheless repeatedly engaged in activities connected with the art.[15] In the forty-one-year period 1230–71,

10. LL 11, fol. 4.
11. LL 11, fol. 67v, 10 Jan. 1236, "Actum Luce ante ecclesiam S. Martini apud cambium"; fol. 28v, 20 June 1236, "Actum Luce sub porticu cambii in Curia S. Martini"; LL 32, fol. 17, 8 Feb. 1259, "Actum Luce apud cambium S. Martini."
12. LL 11, fol. 69v.
13. LL 11, fol. 160.
14. LL 11, passim.
15. LL 5 through LL 11 inclusive.

the names of some 103 campsores turn up.[16] We may surmise that the number of changers working at any one time was slightly less than fifty.

Apparently common guild membership and professional interests were often reinforced by intermarriage between the families of changers. For example, Castracane *filius* Rugerii in 1250 married Diamante, daughter of Durassus Durassi campsor.[17] Felicita, daughter of the changer Gerardus Maghiari, was the widow of another money changer, Perfectus Schlacte.[18] Genovese Gulielmi, who had been consul of the money changers guild in 1238, was the nephew of the campsor Passavante Guidocti, while the latter's son, Genovese, married the daughter of the changer Genovese Lupardi.[19] The list is by no means exhaustive, but we may still cite one Jacobus *quondam* Gerardi. His half-sister Columba was the daughter of the changer Arrigus Rape and he, Jacobus, was the nephew of Gulielmus Genovensis, who apparently belonged to a veritable clan of money changers.[20]

While the organization of the money changers' business seems family oriented, individual changers occasionally pooled their resources in partnership. Such enterprises were also small, characteristically involving two or perhaps three changers. The earliest instance of partnership I have uncovered is dated 27 November 1230 and shows only three "partners of the table" (*socii tabule*).[21] The term of individual partnership arrangements was usually short, three months to a year. But once two changers came together they tended to stay

16. LL 2 through LL 36 inclusive.

17. LL 24, fol. 70.

18. LL 21, fol. 102, 21 Sept. 1246.

19. For Genovese and Passavante, see LL 5, fol. 84, 25 Oct. 1230.

20. Jacobus *quondam* Gerardi was the son of Berta, the widow of Arrigus Rape: LL 5, fol. 27v, 29 Jan. 1230. Arrigus Rape's daughter, Columba, was married to Orlandinus Guasconis: LL 5, fol. 27v and LL 6, fol. 6, fol. 37, 28 Aug. 1230. In LL 8, fol. 4, 11 Jan. 1231, Columba is described as Jacobus's *sorella* (sister). Jacobus, in turn, was Gulielmus Genovensis's nephew: LL 11, fol. 71v, 17 Feb. 1237.

21. LL 5, fol. 87v.

together for a considerable time by successively drawing up new partnership arrangements. Thus, Bertaloctus Painella was in partnership with Vethus *campsor quondam* Deotifeci in 1230,[22] and when the two dissolved a partnership in the year 1243 their relationship was described as being of long standing (*per longum tempus*).[23] Similarly, the changers Castracane Rugerii and Genovese Perfectuccii augmented their working capital through a series of short-term partnership arrangements which spanned the period 1256–71.[24]

If the number of partners jointly operating a *tabula* remained small throughout the thirteenth century, their capitalization tended to increase. In 1249 the brothers Guido and Genovese formed a *societatem de arte cambii* with a working capital of £200.[25] But when Guido entered into three successive partnerships with the brothers Castracane and Luccerius Castracanis in 1254, 1255, and 1256, the average capitalization amounted to £936 6s. 8d.[26] And in the last of the known associations formed by Genovese and Castracane in 1271, the capital conferred by the partners amounted to £3,800.[27] Yet even when partnerships had been contracted and considerable capital committed to them, the partners continued to act on their own behalf as well as in partnership affairs. The changers considered themselves essentially individual entrepreneurs, who combined with their confreres when opportunity and circumstances dictated, but they desired above all to maintain their freedom of economic action.

Archival materials tell us something of how the money changers' profession was organized as well as where and under what circumstances they worked. The changers' common non-banking involvements in urban and rural real estate, investment in livestock, and mining or mercantile enterprises must

22. LL 5, fol. 69v, 28 Aug. 1230; fol. 70, 3 Sept. 1230.
23. LL 17, fol. 86, 16 Sept. 1243.
24. Blomquist, "Castracani" (n. 2 above) 464–66.
25. LL 23, fol. 78, 5 May 1249.
26. Blomquist, "Castracani" (n. 2 above) 464–66.
27. Ibid.

have occupied a good deal of time.[28] What were their activities in the field of finance and credit, and what role did they play in the history of early banking?

We need not dwell upon the money changers' function as literal changers of money since there is no way to gauge the extent, and therefore the importance, of this activity; save to say that campsores, stationed at their tables, continued manually to exchange petty foreign coin into legal Lucchese tender. The contracts do, however, show changers occasionally lending sums in foreign coin to clients;[29] unfortunately, we do not know the purpose to which this capital was put before being repaid to the changer. At the same time, the money changers dealt extensively in gold and silver, either worked into leaves and thread or in bullion form.[30] In this commerce they cooperated closely with the gold-beaters, to whom they sold the refined metal and from whom they also secured for resale the finely worked thread and leaves used to enhance the more luxurious of Lucchese silk cloth.[31] Some changers were also

28. See ibid. for the "outside" business and investments of the Castracani. Their activities appear to have been typical.

29. See inter alia LL 5, fols. 46, 2 April 1230; 47v, 15 May 1230; 69v, 28 Aug. 1230; 85, 26 Oct. 1230; 87v, 27 Nov. 1230; LL 11, fols. 5, 29 Jan. 1236; 16, 26 Mar. 1236; 138, 20 Oct. 1237; 257v, 5 Nov. 1238; 235, 8 Aug. 1238; LL 17, fol. 22v, 19 Mar. 1243; LL 25, fols. 116, n.d., 1250; 125, 1 Dec. 1250; LL 27, fols. 43v, 3 Jan. 1256; 45, 5 Feb. 1256; 48, 17 Feb. 1256; 48v, 8 Mar. 1256; LL 33, fol. 136v, 31 Jan. 1269.

30. LL 11, fol. 165, 17 Feb. 1238; LL 20, fol. 35, 16 Mar. 1245 and 17 Mar. 1245; LL 21, fols. 24, 24 Feb. 1246; 28, 5 Mar. 1246; 39v, 28 Mar. 1246; 41, 28 Mar. 1246; 77v, 25 July 1246; 98v, 15 Sept. 1246; LL 23, fols. 55v, 3 Mar. 1249; 66v, 27 Mar. 1249; LL 24, fol. 95, 2 Sept. 1250; LL 25, fol. 116v, 28 Nov. 1250; LL 27, fols. 31, 13 May 1253; 34, 13 May 1253; 121v, 26 Sept. 1252; LL 28, fols. 3, 2 June 1254; 127, 31 Aug. 1254. Also see LL 20, fol. 74, 20 June 1245, in which Benectus Puliti rented out a silver smelter, *furnum argenti*.

31. In 1259, one Ugolinus Gulielmi *magister* agreed to work all the gold and silver which Castracane Rugerii supplied him. In 1266, Castracane, Genovese Perfectuccii, and Barocchus Barocchi, all three of whom were changers, formed a partnership with the gold-beater Rubertinus Bonaventure who was obliged to work into leaves, *folia*, all the gold and silver supplied him by the partnership: Blomquist, "Castracani" (n. 2 above) 466 n. 33. Also ibid. 467 n. 34, for the dealings of Luccerius Castracanis in wrought gold and silver.

involved in mining silver in the nearby mountains of Versilia.[32]

The evidence is tantalizingly vague regarding the changers' relationship to the mint and hence to the flow of specie. Although a technical knowledge of the minting process is suggested by the Lucchese changer Barocchus Barocchi's undertaking to make dies and strike coins in Arezzo and Perugia,[33] the fact remains that no evidence links the changers to the Lucchese mint. Indeed, the only direct evidence for the operation of the Lucchese mint, the 1308 Statute of the Commune of Lucca, states that the changers were to have nothing to do with the striking of coin;[34] monetary policy was to be defined in the Great Council of the Commune and carried out by the chief executive, the *Podestà*.[35] We must remember, however, that the statute of 1308 was produced by the Black faction which came to power in the wake of the popular rebellion of 1300.[36] Many of its provisions therefore must be interpreted as reactions against the policies of the defeated, merchant banker dominated, regime. Explicitly banning the money changers from the minting process could well have been the response to what the popular regime viewed as an untoward influence by the changers in the administration of the mint. At the same time, vesting the Great Council with the formulation of monetary policy has a populist ring to it, and this accords with the spirit of the document. For in addition to

32. Benectus Puliti possessed an *argenteria* in Versilia as well as a smelter for silver and iron: LL 24, fol. 70v, 25 Jan. 1250. For the Castracani involvement in silver mining, see Blomquist, "Castracani" (n. 2 above) 462–63, 466.

33. LL 33, fol. 66, 3 Oct. 1266, and LL 24, fol. 78, 2 April 1250.

34. Salvatore Bongi and Leone Del Prete, eds., *Statuto del Comune di Lucca dell'anno MCCCVIII* (Lucca 1867) 26: "et nullus campsor lucanus habere debeat in dicta moneta lucana aliquod officium."

35. Ibid. The Statute provides that "dictam monetam laborari faciam [the incoming *Podestà*] continue, exceptis diebus festivis et solepnibus, bona fide, sine fraude in loco Curte Regis, ubi consuetum est fieri, si a maiori parte Consilii et invitatorum fuerit iudicatum."

36. For a contemporary account of the events of 1300, see Bernhard Schmeidler, ed., *Tholomei lucensis annales*, Monumenta germaniae historica, Scriptores rerum germanicarum, n.s. 8 (Berlin 1930) 318–19.

the provisions regarding money, the Black faction brought the *Collegium mercatorum* under its scrutiny and sharply curtailed the political prerogatives of those adherents to the defeated White party—to which all the mercantile banking families belonged—who abjured exile and remained in Lucca.[37] In other words, it seems justifiable to conclude that the statute provisions of 1308 reflect conditions somewhat different regarding the mint—and the changers' relationship to it—than those existing in the thirteenth century. We should not, then, exclude on the basis of the statute the likelihood that the changers were suppliers of bullion to the mint. Certainly the very nature of the profession required that they retire worn or clipped coins, as well as some foreign issues, to the mint.[38] These responsibilities must have been spelled out in the lost guild statutes.

But, while the exact nature of the campsores' dealings with the mint and their role in determining the money supply remain obscure, their activities as bankers in the thirteenth century are relatively well documented. Our sources show them regularly accepting deposits from their clients. Deposits, just as today, took various forms. The changers augmented their working capital through time and demand deposits, with a variant on the latter resembling the continental *depôts à préavis*. The contracts of deposit varied in their terminology: *depositum seu accomandiscia, accomandiscia seu prestantia,* and *mutuum seu prestantia* were used indiscriminately to describe a deposit with a changer, and the exact character of

37. Bongi and Del Prete (n. 34 above) 153. The guild could meet only in the church of San Cristoforo or the *Curia mercatorum*. The merchants could not appear before the *Podestà* or in the Council of the Commune without the express permission of those authorities. Nor could the guild have a notary who was not a member of the popular militia organization, *societas armorum*. Also see ibid. 241-44 for a list of those families branded *casastici* and *potentes*.

38. Ibid. Changers were required, on pain of a £100 fine, to destroy false coins. Only coins equal to the Florentine *à piccioli* were allowed to circulate.

the deposit was spelled out in the details of the contract. The thirteen contracts of deposit that survive from the decade of the 1230s indicate that persons making deposits at the changers' tables came from the middle to upper range of the social strata. We find two judges and a successful merchant along with an artisan and a *magister scolarum* investing capital through the medium of deposit at a changer's bank.[39] And we also find the changers Arrigus Durassi and Gerardus Arzuri investing a portion of the estates of their respective wards at the banks of Genovese *anticus quondam* Aldibrandini and Talliabove and Marcoaldus Perfecti.[40] The total amount placed in this fashion came to £390, or an average per deposit of £32 10s. By contrast, the eighty contracts reflecting the changer's loans in the same period totaled £489 3s. 3d. and averaged £6 2s. 3d. for each loan. These figures conform to the general pattern of borrowing and lending established by the Castracani family in their exchange dealings between 1254 and 1274, with deposits averaging £96 6s. 6d. per individual deposit and loans amounting to £22 12s.[41] Although the ratio of loan size to deposit is somewhat lower in the case of the Castracani than for the earlier period, it is clear from these figures that the size of deposits consistently averaged about five times that of the loans made by the campsores. Moreover, deposits were held for a relatively long term. Time deposits varied in length from three months to a year, while the term of depôt à préavis and demand deposits depended on the needs and wishes of the depositors. In general, the changers accepted few demand deposits, preferring, it would seem, the more or less fixed terms to the unpredictable demand deposit. The time deposit allowed the changer to gauge his roll-over of capital and thus to maintain a lower fractional reserve than

39. LL 11, fol. 235v, 7 Aug. 1238: Aldibrandinus *judex quondam* Leonardi; fol. 230v, 27 July 1238: Aldebrandinus *judex* Malagallie; fol. 257v, 5 Nov. 1238: *Magister* Guido *quondam magistri* Bonaiuncte; fol. 44v, 7 Oct. 1236: Fiamingus *quondam* Orlandi Mosche; fol. 49, 13 Nov.; and fol. 251, 11 Sept. 1236: Benvenutus magister scolarum.
40. LL 11, fols. 262v, 30 Nov., and 168, 14 Feb. 1238.
41. Blomquist, "Castracani" (n. 2 above) 468.

would have been possible had his funds been subject to recall on demand.

As we have seen, the typical changer's loans were smaller in size but greater in frequency than were his deposit transactions. Loans were also consistently of shorter duration than deposit arrangements: the changers borrowed long and lent short. Contractually, these were straight loans, *mutua*; most were made to socially obscure persons from both city and country. Indeed, the peasantry constituted a favored target of the changers' lending. Loans to the peasantry were relatively safe since they involved the peasants' crops as security—and crops could not disappear. The peasant borrowed cash at the *tavola*, small sums to tide him over or to purchase seed or tools, but obligated himself to repay in kind—either grain or wine—at harvest or vintage time. Such loans were not only safe, they were profitable. Although in the absence of price lists for grain and wine we cannot be sure of the profit on these agricultural loans, the price fixed at the time of the loan was likely to be pegged lower than that expected at harvest.[42] In the Florentine *contado* such lending returned a profit of 30%.[43] This was clearly exploitative and may in part explain the money changers' extensive holdings of rural land.[44] Only one instance survives of a changer foreclosing on a peasant, but we may surmise that some, if not most, of the changers' rural holdings were acquired by seizure for debt or bought on favorable terms from a vulnerable peasantry.[45] But

42. On 20 Nov. 1234, one Albertinus Orsecti appealed to the archdeacon, claiming that he had been usuriously victimized by Biancone Overardi, who may have been a changer, in the sale of grain made to Biancone ("de dando ei granum quod ei vendidit et que venditio facta fuit in fraudem usurarum"). Interestingly, although no details are given, Albertinus's plea was denied and he was ordered to pay £6 and one *modium* of grain to Biancone within four months. See LL 9, fol. 12.

43. David Herlihy, "Santa Maria Impruneta: A Rural Commune in the Late Middle Ages," *Florentine Studies,* ed. Nicolai Rubinstein (Evanston, Ill. 1968) 262.

44. On the rural holdings of the Castracani, see Blomquist, "Castracani" (n. 2 above) 462–63.

45. LL 11, fol. 50v, 18 Nov. 1236.

the impact of urban credit and credit mechanisms upon the structure of the Lucchese countryside is all too seldom visible in our sources.

The occupations of the campsores' debtors in the city are difficult to define since many borrowers appear in the documents only once and are otherwise unidentifiable. Yet their very anonymity suggests that they belonged on the lower rungs of the social ladder. In the city as in the country most loans were straight loans, mutua. But not infrequently the changers accepted articles of clothing, utensils, or even horses in pledge against a loan.[46] To be sure, we are witnessing in these "consumption" loans, credit transfer at a very modest level, yet this aspect of the changers' business must have been, in the aggregate, of considerable economic and social consequence.

On the other hand, the evidence suggests that changers were active in supplying capital, around mid-century, to the nascent mercantile banking organizations. At least some merchants in international commerce used such services.[47] These larger advances to the commercial community reveal the money changers channeling the savings of the non-business sector into the economically productive one of industry and trade. Although no absolute quantitative conclusions can be drawn, I think some examples make the case. On two occasions in 1245, Panfollia and Albertinus *quondam* Rustici Guinigi, founders of the Guinigi family fortunes and the mercantile banking partnership bearing their family name, borrowed £100 and £50 respectively from the money changer Gerardus Arzuri.[48] Similarly, in the same year, Perfectus Ricciardi *quondam* Gratiani, the founder of what at the end of the century would be one of the most powerful merchant banking partnerships in Europe, the *Societas Ricciardorum*, received

46. For loans with a pledge, see inter alia LL 8, fols. 18v, 13 Mar. 1231; 73, 4 April 1231; LL 11, fols. 16v, 4 April 1236; 59v, 3 Jan. 1237; LL 18, fols. 30v, 15 March 1244; 81, 3 Sept. 1244; LL 21, fol. 69v, 28 June 1246; LL 23, fol. 14, 13 Nov. 1249; LL 33, fol. 31v, 10 Dec. 1265.

47. Cf. Blomquist, "Commercial Association" (n. 1 above) for a discussion of the large-scale Lucchese partnerships.

48. LL 20, fols. 74v, 21 June 1245, and 146v, 12 Dec. 1245.

on 27 January and 4 March loans of £100 and £200.[49] Also on 27 January, Perfectus borrowed £150 from the changers Soldanus, Gerardus, and Uguiccione Maghiari.[50] Given the woefully fragmentary nature of our sources, these instances— not in themselves particularly imposing—may be only a small fraction of similar but now lost transactions.

Enough scattered evidence from Lucca exists for us to conclude that the changers paid interest on deposits.[51] The rate is hard to ascertain, since medieval lenders were extremely chary of stating in contractual form the return to be gained from a loan. But one surviving contract shows the money changer Gerardus Arzuri accepting a deposit of £50 on 17 March 1230 from the guardians of the minor heirs of Ubertus *quondam* Bugianese and promising to pay £6, or 12%, annually in interest.[52]

Transfer banking, in retrospect perhaps the most significant of the money changers' activities, is the hardest to detect in the Lucchese sources. My reading of the sources indicates that the money changers did, to a limited degree, clear their clients' obligations by transferring debts on their books. Compared to

49. LL 20, fol. 57.

50. LL 20, fols. 13 and 25v. On the Ricciardi in England, see Emilio Re, "La compagnia dei Ricciardi in Inghilterra e il suo fallimento alla fine del secolo XIII," *Archivio della Società Romana di Storia Patria* 37 (1914), and, more recently, Richard W. Kaeuper, *Bankers to the Crown: The Riccardi of Lucca and Edward I* (Princeton 1973). Cf. Thomas W. Blomquist, "Administration of a Thirteenth-Century Mercantile Banking Partnership: An Episode in the History of the Ricciardi of Lucca," *Revue internationale d'histoire de la banque* 7 (1973) 1–9.

51. See my remarks on usury in "De Roover on Business, Banking and Economic Thought," *Journal of Economic History* 35 (1975) 825–26.

52. LL 5, fol. 57. Volume 1 of the *Inventario del Reale Archivio di Stato in Lucca*, ed. Salvatore Bongi (4 vols. Lucca 1872), held by the Newberry Library of Chicago, contains on p. 210 a marginal note, written in a nineteenth century Italian hand, citing a parchment document of 1304 to the effect that 12% was recognized by statute as a legal return ("interesse o benefecio") on a loan: "Da pergamena 5 Dic. 1304 della Certosa si cava che, per lo Statuto vigente allora l'interesse o beneficio del denaro era stabilito al 12% l'anno."

Genoa, however, where as early as 1200 a client could order a banker to settle a debt by merely crediting the amount owed to his creditor's account in bank,[53] in Lucca this clearing function did not become routinized during the thirteenth century. In Lucca such transactions required recourse to a notary rather than simple entry in the banker's books. On 14 October 1245, for example, the changer Albertinus *quondam* Aldebrandini Malagallie acknowledged that he had received from the campsor Genovese Anticus the sum of £15 Lucchese from those £44 which Goldus and Bonagiunta *quondam* Bonaccursi Ronthi owed to him, Albertinus, and his brother.[54] In other words, Albertinus was being reimbursed from the account maintained with Genovese by Goldus and Bonagiunta, which would in this case accordingly be debited in the amount of £15. On 23 January 1245, the changer Soldanus Gerardi paid £50 owed to the cathedral chapter by another changer, Gerardus Maghiari.[55] In neither case was the changer acting explicitly as an agent for his client. This business indicates that the changers kept drawing accounts with one another in order to facilitate settlement of debts through bank transfer.

The conclusion that settlement by transfer was becoming increasingly common is supported by evidence that the changers posted credits to clients' accounts from payments by third parties at the changers' banks. In 1256 Castracane Rugerii, mentioned earlier, stipulated in a notarial contract to Savariscius Ubaldi Rainerii that he, Castracane, had received on behalf of the notary £84 from the *sindicus* of Controne, £30 from the Commune of Lucca, £21 from one Bonaccorsus de Batone, and £30 as partial payment due from Custor Battosi; and that he, Castracane, was as a result in the debt of

---

53. Robert S. Lopez, *La prima crisi della banca di Genova (1250–1259)* (Milan 1956) 28–29, and R. L. Reynolds, "A Business Affair in Genoa in the Year 1200; Banking, Bookkeeping, a Broker and a Lawsuit," *Studi di storia e diritto in onore di Enrico Besta* (4 vols. Milan 1939) 2.7–19.

54. LL 20, fol. 116v.

55. LL 20, fol. 12.

Savariscius for £165, the total of these sums.[56] Although nothing directly indicates that the campsores routinely allowed overdrafts to their clients, given the existence of transfer it would be logical for a changer to permit such credit extension by merely posting an entry to the client's debit column. In fact, some of the notarial contracts recording the existence of debt to a changer may have arisen from a prior overdraft. In any case, the activities of the Lucchese changers—acceptance of deposits, supplying "consumer" and commercial credit, facilitating debt clearance through transfer, and (possibly) creating credit by allowing overdrafts—clearly served to rationalize the distribution of credit and to focus purchasing power where it was needed.

The field of the money changers, as they provided credit services to the populace at large, was essentially local. Some campsores, however, such as Gerardus Arzuri or Aldebrandinus Malagallie, did leave their native city for extended sojourns north of the Alps to engage in petty moneylending and pawnbroking among the cash-poor inhabitants of the smaller rural towns and settlements, principally in the county of Champagne.[57] But Italian international commerce in the course of the thirteenth century was becoming ever more concentrated in the hands of "big business"—that is, the large-scale, centrally directed mercantile banking partnerships that were making their appearance in all the major towns of north and central Italy around the mid-thirteenth century. Lucca was no exception in the willingness of her merchants to explore new ways to respond to the challenges of economic opportunity. By 1284 there were twenty-two identifiable large-scale partnerships engaging in international trade and commerce through partners or agents representing them in foreign markets.[58] Eleven of these organizations were designated by the papacy as depositories of papal funds collected abroad and

56. Blomquist, "Castracani" (n. 2 above) 468.
57. LL 30, fol. 94v, 2 Dec. 1245, and LL 31, fol. 164, 4 Dec. 1258.
58. See Blomquist, "Commercial Association" (n. 1 above) for these partnerships.

as such were among the wealthiest and most powerful business organizations operating in the West.[59]

Here we can deal only with the banking and credit functions of these large-scale partnerships, putting aside the more detailed study of their complex business with the reminder that in the unspecialized Middle Ages commerce and finance went hand in hand. Among the fragmentary and scattered references to international exchange banking in the surviving notarial materials, one piece of evidence stands out. In 1284 the notary Bartolomeus Fulcieri and his two sons Tegrimus and Fulcierus were active among a clientele drawn almost exclusively from the ranks of international merchants and financiers of Lucca.[60] The cartulary which they produced, chronologically complete for the year, numbers among its 506 folio pages and thousands of individual agreements some 205 rough drafts of contracts, *instrumenta ex causa cambii*, reflecting foreign exchange dealings of Lucchese merchant bankers in the great cycle of Champagne fairs. Representing only a fraction of the total banking business between Lucca and Champagne, these documents provide the fullest, most concentrated, and earliest evidence for the workings of an international banking place.

International banking developed in tandem with international money markets and the techniques of foreign exchange. Lucchese merchants as early as 1200 had developed considerable skill in financing commerce by recourse to foreign exchange. As an industrial center, Lucca was particularly dependent upon Genoa as port of entry for raw silk and dye stuffs to feed her burgeoning silk industry.[61] In order to ex-

---

59. Ibid. 159.

60. On the Fulcieri, see ibid. 172–73.

61. For the Lucchese in Genoa: Florence M. Edler, "The Silk Trade of Lucca during the Thirteenth and Fourteenth Centuries" (Ph.D. diss. University of Chicago 1930) 116–23; Domenico Gioffrè, "L'attività economica dei Lucchesi a Genova fra il 1190 e il 1280," *Lucca archivistica, storica, economica: relazioni e comunicazioni al XV Congresso Nazionale Archivistico, Lucca, Ottobre 1969* (Rome 1973) 94–111; and M. Baldovini, "Santa Croce di Sarzano ed i mercanti lucchesi a Genova (sec. XIII–XIV)," *Atti della Società Ligure di Storia Patria* n.s. 2 (1962) 76–96.

pedite this traffic, a group of Lucchese resident in Genoa began to advance Genoese funds to their conationals visiting the Ligurian port to secure silk, dyes, and other wares for export to their city. In return, the visiting merchant would hand over a notarial instrument in which he promised repayment in Lucca to the lender's agent or partner, usually within two or three weeks, of a sum in Lucchese coin equivalent to that received in Genoa.[62]

The other major terminus of Lucchese trade and finance was the entrepôt centered upon the annual cycle of six great fairs held in the county of Champagne at the towns of Troyes, Provins, Bar-sur-Aube, and Lagny.[63] The Lucchese were the first Tuscan merchants, and among the first Italians, to be in regular contact with ultramontane Europe. As early as 1153, Genoa granted to the merchants of Lucca the privilege of traversing Genoese territory on their way to and from the "northern fairs."[64] We may assume a traffic already in existence, perhaps of long standing, in which Lucchese silks constituted the bulk of wares moving north, with cloth of northern manufacture the dominant commodity on the return journey. In this early commerce, the merchant customarily accompanied his wares and was able to supervise their sale and the reinvestment of the proceeds for export to Italy. But by the late twelfth century, merchants were beginning to rely upon partners or agents to handle their affairs abroad. In the following century these practices were institutionalized by the emergence of the large-scale international mercantile banking partnership which maintained permanent foreign representation through partners or employees, termed *factors* in the Lucchese sources, stationed abroad.[65]

Accompanying the expansion of international commerce between Lucca and northern Europe was the development in Lucca of an organized money market based upon the fairs of

62. Blomquist, "Castracani" (n. 2 above) 471–72.
63. Gioffrè (n. 61 above) 95–96.
64. The treaty is published in Cesare Imperiale, ed., *Il Codice diplomatico della Repubblica di Genova* 1 (Rome 1936) no. 238.
65. De Roover, "Organization" (n. 1 above) 70–76.

Champagne. It should be emphasized, perhaps, that Lucchese merchants dealing in Lucca with northern Europe did so exclusively through the fairs. Exchange transactions drawing upon other places are extremely rare in the Lucchese material. Furthermore, the Lucchese international money market served the needs of the Lucchese mercantile community and, unlike Genoa, did not attract many foreign merchant bankers.

Although the primary function of exchange was the transfer of funds from one place to another, medieval dealings in foreign exchange were also by their very nature credit transactions, and they were to become the principal means by which international merchant bankers secured short-term funds and invested capital. In other words, as Raymond de Roover so effectively demonstrated, international mercantile banking rested squarely upon negotiating short-term exchange transactions.[66] The buyer, or giver, of exchange delivered funds in Lucca and received from the seller, the taker, a notarial instrument promising repayment at one of the Champagne fairs in an equivalent amount of money of Provins.[67] But repayment at one or another of the fairs inevitably meant repayment at some time in the future and hence the buyer was in effect a lender, the seller a borrower, with interest on the buyer's capital built into the fluctuating rates of exchange.

Our contracts reveal that in 1284 Lucchese merchant bankers negotiating among themselves purchased through 205 contracts a total of £44,941 *provinois* payable at one or another

66. De Roover made this point repeatedly in discussing early banking history, but for convenience I will cite only *The Bruges Money Market Around 1400*, with a Statistical Supplement by Hyman Sardy (Brussels 1968) 21–30, and *The Rise and Decline of the Medici Bank, 1397–1494* (New York 1966) 9–14. For a full bibliography of de Roover's work and reprints of ten of his articles (an eleventh, "Gerard de Malynes as an Economic Writer: From Scholasticism to Mercantilism," was published posthumously), see Raymond de Roover, *Business, Banking, and Economic Thought in Late Medieval and Early Modern Europe: Selected Studies of Raymond de Roover*, ed. Julius Kirshner (Chicago and London 1974).

67. Raymond de Roover, *L'évolution de la lettre de change (XIVᵉ– XVIIIᵉ siècles)* (Paris 1953), and *Money, Banking, and Credit in Mediaeval Bruges* (Cambridge, Mass. 1948) 52–55.

of the fairs, with £171,244 Lucchese disbursed in Lucca.[68] These truly impressive figures represent only a fraction of the total exchange business conducted in Lucca. Although no comparable data survive from other banking places for the year 1284, Pierre Racine, using Genoese notarial materials, has shown that in 1288 the sum of recorded exchange transactions concluded in Genoa drawing upon the fairs amounted to at least £60,190 provinois, or a volume roughly one third greater than that recorded for Lucca in 1284.[69] Of course, Genoa as an entrepôt drew representatives of mercantile banking houses from the whole of north Italy. The same material reveals that in 1291 the Lucchese mercantile bankers were the most active in Genoa in dealing on the fair money market, with total transactions of £40,737 3s. 4d. provinois, or 36.30% of the volume in that year.[70] And the Lucchese maintained their leadership in the years 1293–94 with 34% of the market for provinois in Genoa.[71] Thus the £44,941 provinois traded in Lucca in 1284 are likely to have been considerably augmented by the dealings with the fairs of Lucchese bankers situated in Genoa.

The exchange transaction encouraged international commerce by facilitating international payments without requiring large movements of specie. Indeed, the greatest of the Lucchese partnerships—the Bettori, Paganelli, Cardellini, Tignosini, and Honesti—regularly drew upon their assets at the fairs in an obvious effort to repatriate their northern profits. Lucchese importers of northern cloth, too, could avail themselves of the international banker's services and secure capital to pay for cloth purchased in the north. But the exchange transaction was also a credit instrument, and the bankers profited as they bought and sold northern credits for delivery

68. *ASL, Archivio dei notari*, no. 15 (notaries Bartholomeo Fulcieri, Tegrimo Fulcieri, Fulciero Fulcieri), passim.

69. Pierre Racine, "I banchieri piacentini ed i campi sulle Fiere di Champagne alla fine del Duecento," *Studi storici in onore di Emilio Nasalli Rocca* (Piacenza 1971) 481.

70. Ibid. 483.

71. Ibid. 483–84.

at the fair. The bankers' profit derived from interest built into the rate of exchange rather than from discounting.

The movement of the exchange rates on the Lucchese money market confirms for our period what de Roover showed was the case in the fifteenth century: the shorter the term of the transaction the lower the interest charges as expressed in the rates.[72] This may be seen in the movement of exchange rates in contracts drawing upon the May fair of Provins, expressed in so many Lucchese *denarii* to one *solidus* of Provins. The May fair opened, in 1284, on 16 May and closed either 30 June or 6 July.[73] Trading in provinois payable at the May fair began in March and continued into June.[74] If we average the rates for each month, a clear rising pattern of Lucchese against provinois emerges: the seven transactions negotiated in March show an average of 43.43d. Lucchese for one *solidus provinois*; seventeen documents from April indicate a rate of

72. De Roover, *The Bruges Money Market* (n. 66 above) 32–37.

73. The May fair of Provins, according to the texts published by Paul Huvelin, *Essai historique sur le droit des marchés et des foires* (Paris 1897) 600–03, began on the Tuesday before Ascension Day, or 16 May. For the opening dates of the fairs, see Félix Bourquelot, *Études sur les Foires de Champagne* (Paris 1865) part 1, 80–83; Charles Alengry, *Les Foires de Champagne: Étude d'histoire économique* (Paris 1915) 96–98; Levin Goldschmidt, "Die Geschäftsoperationen auf den Messen der Champagne," *Zeitschrift für das gesamte Handelsrecht* 40 (1892) 8–10. According to Goldschmidt, p. 9, the May fair of Provins lasted 46 days. Elisabeth Bassermann, *Die Champagnermessen. Ein Beitrag zur Geschichte des Kredits* (Tübingen and Leipzig 1911) 13–15, and Elizabeth Chapin, *Les villes de Foires de Champagne des origines au début du XIVᵉ siècle* (Paris 1937) 107 n. 9, concur; whereas Richard Face, "Techniques of Business in the Trade between the Fairs of Champagne and the South of Europe in the Twelfth and Thirteenth Centuries," *Economic History Review* 10 (1958) 427 n. 2, and "The Vectuarii in the Overland Commerce between Champagne and Southern Europe," *Economic History Review* 12 (1959) 240 n. 8, following Bourquelot, argues a 52-day cycle. A 46-day duration would have closed the May fair, in 1284, on 30 June, and a 52-day cycle on 6 July. The fair of St. John at Troyes, following Huvelin's texts, opened the first Tuesday a fortnight after St. John's Day, or 11 July.

74. *ASL, Archivio dei notari*, no. 15, fols. 205v, 15 March 1284, and 324v, 6 June 1284.

43.86d.; eleven from May give a rate of 45.95d.; and in June, seven documents yield an average rate of 46.59d. As the rates rose, the seller, that is the borrower, received more in Lucca for a promise to pay a given amount of provinois at the May fair.

Thus, if a merchant sold one solidus of Provins in March for delivery at the May fair, he received, on the average, 43.43d. Lucchese from the buyer, that is, the lender. In June the same merchant received 46.59d. Or, to put it another way, the borrower taking funds in Lucca in June was able, due to the shorter term of the transaction, to borrow 7% more for the same price. Of course, as de Roover also pointed out, other factors besides interest moved the rates of exchange, but given the evidence of Lucca from the year 1284, it seems clear that interest was indeed a powerful element in determining the international rates of exchange.[75] Barring wild fluctuations, the merchant banker could be certain of a profit on his exchange dealings; and the decade of the 1280s does not seem to have been one of turmoil in the monetary relations between Lucca and Champagne.

The evidence for years other than 1284 is sparse indeed, but from what has survived the rates appear remarkably steady. In 1279 the rate was 40.87 denarii Lucchese per shilling of Provins—only slightly below the range of rates for 1284.[76] Only one contract survives from 1294, but it provides a rate of 45.5 denarii per shilling, well within the range of the 1284 figures.[77] The information appended by the notary in the margin of his cartulary, indicating the circumstances under which each obligation was satisfied and rendering the contract void, demonstrates that these transactions were, for the most part, fulfilled in Champagne. In other words, the contracts are genuine and do not represent efforts to avoid the taint of

75. De Roover, *The Bruges Money Market* (n. 66 above) 31–50.
76. *ASL, Archivio dei notari*, no. 13, reg. 1 (notary Armanno di Armanno), fol. 9v, 31 Jan. 1279.
77. *ASL, Archivio dei notari*, no. 29, reg. 1 (notary Gregorio Paganelli), fol. 21v, 11 Feb. 1294.

usury by disguising straight loans as legitimate—in the eyes of the canonists—exchange transactions.

Of the 205 instrumenta ex causa cambii, the cancellations reveal that 111 were actually fulfilled in accordance with the contractual terms, another 34 were cancelled with no information as to where the contract was settled, 35 were not cancelled at all, and 25 were settled in Lucca. I suspect these last were concluded in Lucca as a convenience to the contracting parties and not because of any predetermined agreement on their part. In short, I do not believe that they were set up as fictitious exchanges in order to avoid a nearly unenforceable usury prohibition. But if evasion were intended, the notary would hardly be expected to state in the cancellation that the debt had been liquidated in Lucca. Rather, he would have simply ignored the place of cancellation and the suggestion of a fictitious exchange.

What, then, were the economic consequences of this traffic in foreign exchange? Perhaps the most obvious is the expediting of foreign balances of payment without recourse to large movements of specie. But the existence of an institutionalized money market such as Lucca's, sustained international commerce by giving merchants access to capital in the north as well as a routine means of returning their profits from abroad. Similarly, the exchange market allowed merchant bankers to raise commercial capital at home, which stimulated industry and so animated the entire economy of thirteenth century Lucca.

# X

# The Early History of European Banking: Merchants, Bankers and Lombards of Thirteenth-Century Lucca in the County of Champagne

The late Professor Raymond de Roover in his magisterial studies of the development and structure of banking in the Middle Ages argued vigorously against what he believed was a serious confusion on the part of other historians regarding the use and meaning of the term "lombard" as it appeared in contemporary texts. For de Roover, this confusion led in turn to larger and more important errors of interpretation in the history of early European banking.[1] He

\* I wish to express my thinks to the Graduate School, Northern Illinois University for a summer grant which made possible the archival research necessary for the completion of this paper. I am also grateful to Professor Theodore Evergates of Western Maryland College for his identification of the locations in the County of Champagne cited in notes 33, 39 and 43 below, and for his helpful comments on the text. And I would like to thank Professors Duane J. Osheim of the University of Virginia and my colleague William Beik for their constructive criticisms as the paper passed through various stages to completion.

[1] RAYMOND DE ROOVER, *Money, Banking and Credit in Mediaeval Bruges. Italian Merchant-Bankers, Lombards and Money-Changers: A Study in the Origins of Banking* (Cambridge, Mass., 1948), 36: "One of the causes of the prevailing confusion on medieval banking is apparently the failure of modern scholars to see that the word "lombard" in mediaeval sources has two meanings." See also de Roover's "New Interpretations of the History of Banking," *Journal of World History*, 2 (1954), 38-78; reprinted in R. DE ROOVER, *Business, Banking and Economic Thought in Late Medieval and Early Modern Europe*, ed., Julius Kirshner (Chicago-London, 1974), 200-238 with a full bibliography of de Roover's writings.

was especially critical of Georges Bigwood and Josef Kulischer for their failure to distinguish between the term "Lombard" used in a geographical sense to denote anyone hailing from Lombardy and "lombard" employed as a technical term to mean a person engaged in pawnbroking and petty money-lending. On the basis of these oversights, claimed de Roover, Bigwood, Kulischer and others confounded the representatives of the large Italian mercantile-banking houses, whose business was commerce and foreign exchange, with the small operator engaged in the rather odious business of pawnbroking.[2]

Drawing upon sources from fourteenth and fifteenth century Bruges, De Roover insisted that these financial activities were discrete, a petty lender and pawn-broker, i.e., a lombard, would never deal in foreign exchange transactions while by the same token no merchant-banker would engage in pawnbroking and petty money-lending. In de Roover's reconstruction of the evolution of banking technique, three categories of financial activity existed in the Middle Ages: merchant-banking which evolved into exchange banking; money-changing which evolved into deposit and transfer banking; and pawnbroking which led nowhere insofar as banking history is concerned since the services that the pawnbroker provided to impecunious borrowers were for the most part taken over by charitable public institutions in the sixteenth century.[3]

DeRoover was, of course, quite right in drawing technical distinctions between mercantile banking, money-changing and pawnbroking. It goes without saying that negotiating instruments of exchange involved different techniques and different fiduciary purposes from pawnbroking. The deposit and transfer banking engaged in by the money-changers similarly may be distinguished in terms of technique from mercantile-banking and to some extent from pawnbroking. But were the social boundaries between these classes of financier as tightly drawn as de Roover suggested?

On the basis of evidence from the State and Capitular Archives of Tuscan Lucca, I will argue in the following essay that the kind of professional segrega-

---

[2] GEORGES BIGWOOD, *Le régime juridique et économique du commerce de l'argent dans la Belgique du moyen âge: Mémoires de l'Académie royale de Belgique, Classe des lettres et des scéances morales et politiques*, 2nd series, XIV, 2 parts (Brussels, 1921-1922) and Josef Kulisher, "Warenhändler und Geldausleiher im Mittelalter," *Zeitechrift für Volkswirtschaft*, Sozialpolitik und Verwaltung, XVII (1908), 29-71, 201-254. De Roover, *Money, Banking and Credit*, 345-347, 355 note 1 chided Bigwood for including the Italians "Pierre Cape le Lombard" and "Pieter Scandalioenne le Lombard" among the pawnbrokers when they should have been identified as merchant-bankers. "Lombard" thus, according to de Roover, should have been understood in these instances in its geographical sense to mean a person from Lombardy. Furthermore Kulischer, among other things, writes de Roover, badly confused the Italian merchant-bankers with pawnbrokers and also claimed that there was little difference between the money-changers' operations and those of the pawnshops.

[3] R. DE ROOVER, "New Interpretations of the History of Banking," *passim* and *Money, Banking and Credit*, especially 345-357.

tion apparently existing in the Italian community of late-medieval Bruges was not necessarily typical of conditions in the formative stage of European banking.[4] The thirteenth-century Lucchese material shows money-changers engaging in commerce, merchants trafficking in petty money-lending and merchant-bankers involved in pawnbroking as men of Lucca exploited the early market for capital and credit in northern Europe. The historical picture that emerges from the thirteenth century is one of a more fluid social and professional situation than de Roover found existing among the Italians in the later Middle Ages.

\* \* \*

Merchants of Lucca were among the first Italians to extend their commercial operations to Northern Europe. The earliest reference to a continuing commercial link between Italy and the North derives from a treaty, ratified 10 July, 1153, between Lucca and her close ally Genoa.[5] Among other terms of the treaty, Genoa undertook to protect the person and goods of Lucchese merchants passing through Genoese territory on their way to the "northern fairs" (*ad ferias ultramontanas*) with the proviso that their merchandise would not compe-

---

[4] *Archivio di Stato in Lucca*, hereafter *ASL* and, *Archivio Capitolare*, hereafter *AC*. On the archives of Lucca, see ROBERT S. LOPEZ "The Unexplored Wealth of the Notarial Archives of Pisa and Lucca", *Mélanges d'histoire de moyen âge dédiés à la mémoire du Louis Halphen* (Paris, 1951), 417-432; EUGENIO LAZZARESCHI, "L'Archivio dei Notari della Repubblica lucchese, *"Gli archivi italiani*, II (1915), 175-210; ROBERT H. BAUTIER, "Notes sur les sources de l'histoire économique médiévale dans les archives italiennes", *Mélanges d'archéologie et d'histoire"*, LVIII (1941-1946), 299-300; SAC. GIUSEPPE GHIRLARDUCCI, *Le biblioteche e gli archivi arcivescovile e capitolari* (Lucca, 1969) and Duane Osheim, "The Episcopal Archive of Lucca in the Middle Ages", *Manuscripta*, XVII (1973), 131-146. Survey histories of thirteenth-century Lucca are GIROLAMO TOMMASI, *Sommario della storia di Lucca*, published as *Archivio storico italiano*, X (1876) and Augusto Macini, *Storia di Lucca* (Florence, 1950).

[5] The document is published in CESARE IMPERIALE DI SANT'ANGELO, ed., *Il codice diplomatico della Repubblica di Genova*, I (Rome, 1936), no. 238. ROBERT H. BAUTIER, "Les foires de Champagne", *La foire: Recueils de la Société Jean Bodin*, V (1953), 105, note 2, attempting to deny the presence of Italian merchants at the Champagne fairs before the turn of the twelfth century, erroneously dates the treaty to 1258. However the names of the Genoese consuls in the document published by Imperiale are identical with those given by the Genoese annalist Caffaro for the year 1153 and thus confirms the accuracy of the 1153 date: cf. LUIGI TOMMASO BELGRANO and CESARE IMPERIALE DI SANT'ANGELO, eds., *Annali genovesi di Caffaro e de' suoi continuatori dal MXCIX al MCCXCIII* in *Fonti per la storia di Italia*, XI (Rome, 1890), 37. For the evolution of the Champagne fairs, in addition to the studies cited below in notes 8 and 11, cf. MICHEL BUR, *La formation du Comté de Champagne v. 950-v. 1150*, in *Mémoires des Annales de l'Est*, no. 54 (Nancy, 1977), 282-307.

te directly with that of Genoa (*exceptis illis rebus, que sint contraria nostris mercibus*). Similarly, the Lucchese were permitted to carry back through Genoa cloth of northern provenance (...*reducere ex illis feriis in nostram civitatem pannos albos et blavos et aspersatos*) upon which a toll of 5s. Genoese per *torsello* was levied. We may presume that this compact reflected a regular traffic already in existence if one not already old.

Unfortunately the archives of Lucca provide no direct evidence for the Lucchese commercial penetration into Northern Europe before the decade of the 1230's. However, published French sources show a continuous Lucchese presence in the region in the early thirteenth century.

In 1209 merchants of Lucca were named, along with their compatriots from Florence, Pistoia, Milan, Genoa and Venice, as recipients of royal protection granted by Philip II guaranteeing their safety while in transit to and from the Fairs of Champagne.[6] Relations between the comital court of Champagne and the Lucchese were especially cordial in this early period. In 1218 one Lamberto of Lucca was listed as a creditor of the Countess Blanche.[7] And four years later, the new Count, Thibault IV, took the merchants of Lucca and Siena residing in the County under his protection and granted them the privilege of engaging in all types of financial transactions, except short-term loans of weekly duration, as well as exempting them from military service.[8] In 1232 Lucca and money-lending were again linked in Champagne when Thibault engaged a Lucchese dyer for his wife, and conferred upon him license to traffic in money.[9] Such inducements held out to the Lucchese and other Italians suggest the need within the County for the ready cash the lenders could inject into the local economy. Throughout the thirteenth century Champagne remained the focal point of Luchese commercial and financial operations in northern Europe.

In 1250 merchants of Lucca were in possession of permanent quarters in the two fair towns of Provins and Troyes.[10] When in 1266 they renewed the lease on a stone house, complete with cellars for storage, sleeping area and stables, in the

---

[6] W. Heyd, *Histoire du commerce du Levant au moyen-âge*, 2 vols. (Leipzig, 1923), II, 714. Florence Edler, "The Silk Trade of Lucca during the Thirteenth and Fourteenth centuries", (Ph.D. dissertation, University of Chicago, Chicago, 1930), 94.

[7] Félix Bourquelot, "Fragments de comptes du XIIIᴱ siele," *Bibliothèque de l'école des chartes*, XXIV (1863), 58. F. Edler, *loc. cit.*

[8] Félix Bourquelot, *Études sur les foires de Champagne*, 2 parts, published as *Mémoires présentées par divers savants à l'Académie des Inscriptions et Belles-Lettres* (Paris, 1865-1866), I, 175. Adolphe Schaube, *Storia del commercio dei popoli latini del Mediterraneo sino alla fine delle crociate*, tr. P. Bonfante (Torino, 1915), 422. F. Edler, *loc. cit.*

[9] F. Bourquelot, *Études sur les foires*, I, 261. F. Edler, *loc. cit.*

[10] F. Bourquelot, *Études sur les foires*, I, 166. F. Edler, *loc. cit.*

X

latter city, sixteen merchants signed the agreement.[11] Among the lessees were
members of six Lucchese families which either were, or would become, influential in four of the mercantile-banking partnerships taking shape in Lucca around
this time. These were "Berthelon Bandini" and "Richardo Guidechonis" (Bartholomeus Bandini and Ricciardus Guidiccioni) of the Ricciardi partnership,
"Guillelemo Fantinelli" and "Colinus Teste" (Gullielmus Faitinelli and Ugolinus Teste) of the Bettori company, "Locherio Gentili" (Lotarius Gentili) of the
Gentili partnership and "Lazario Denis" (Lazarius Guinigi) of the G  nigi.[12]

In addition, one "J. Morlain" of the original document may well have been
Johannes Morlani who was a partner of a Lucchese mercantile-banking company in 1284.[13] "Bartholomeo Thoringuelli" can be placed within the Toringhelli
family which furnished at least one partner to the Ricciardi company.[14] "Renau-
dot dou Bart" is the same Rainaldus de Barcha whom we shall encounter below
in connection with the operation of a pawnshop in Champagne.[15] "Tebaldino
Massiamac" and "Brunetto de Garbe" were members of two prominant Lucchese merchant families, the Mangialmacchi and De Garbo.[16] These men provided the nucleus of permanent representation for their Lucchese compatriots in
the North. From the house in Troyes in which "solent morari ... tam extra
nundinas quam in nundinas" they could look after the affairs of their respective
partnerships at the Champagne fairs, act as agents for independent Lucchese
merchants and extend the lines of their operations into neighboring rural
villages.

Just how many Lucchese were active in Northern Europe around the
mid-thirteenth century cannot be known. However, it seems certain that their
numbers were growing throughout the latter part of the century. For example,
in 1268 they apparently were sufficiently numerous, and geographically dispersed, to warrant the appelation *universis mercatoribus de Luca commorantibus in
Francia ac aliis regionibus convincinis* in a letter sent by Charles of Anjou's vicar

[11] F. BOURQUELOT, *loc. cit.* LEON MIROT, "Études lucquoises: la colonie lucquoise à
Paris du XIIIᵉ au XVᵉ siècle, *"Bibliotheque de l'École des Chartes*, LXXXVIII (1927), 52,
note 6. Elizabeth Chapin, *Les villes des foires de Champagne des origines au début du
XIVᵉ siècle* (Paris, 1937), 110, note 18. F. EDLER, "The Silk Trade of Lucca, » 95.

[12] For a list of the partners of the Lucchese mercantile-banking companies in 1284, see
THOMAS W. BLOMQUIST, "Commercial Association in Thirteenth-Century Lucca," *The
Business History Review*, XLV (1971), 172-178.

[13] IBID., 177. No company style is given for the partnership to which Johannes
belonged.

[14] RICHARD W. KAEUPER, *Bankers to the Crown: The Ricciardi of Lucca and Edward
I* (Princeton, 1973), 57: Bacciomeo Toringhelli was in England on behalf of the Ricciardi
in 1297.

[15] See below, 10.

[16] F. EDLER, "The Silk Trade of Lucca". On the merchant Uguiccione Mangialmacchi and his affairs in Northern Europe, see below, 10.

in Lucca announcing the capture of the port of Motrone in Versilia by Charles' forces.[17] In 1277 the northern based Lucchese elected two of their confreres, Nicolaus Mordecastelli and Enricus De Castri, to represent their interests in the *Societas mercatorum tuscanorum et lombardorum*,[18] the corporation of Italian merchants doing business at the Champagne fairs. For the year 1284, the notarial contracts redacted in Lucca reflecting foreign exchange transactions drawing upon the Fairs provide the names of forty-six Lucchese representing the major mercantile-banking partnerships of Lucca in Champagne.[19] But representatives of the large-scale partnerships that emerged in Lucca in the second half of the thirteenth century were by no means the only Lucchese active in the region.[20]

The earliest emphasis of Lucchese *ultramontaine* activities, judging by the Lucca-Genoa treaty of 1153, was upon commerce, specifically the distribution of finished Lucchese silks in the North with returns made in the form of northern cloth.[21] This pattern of trade remained an important element of Lucchese mercantile operations throughout the Middle Ages but money-lending and credit dealings, as we have seen, soon attracted the northern based Lucchese who found a ready outlet for their venture capital in the cash-shy economy of the North. The fields of money-lending and pawnbroking drew merchant-bankers, professional money-changers and petty entrepreneurs alike.

The oldest surviving Lucchese archival references to northern Europe reveal a commerce in the hands of travelling merchants unencumbered by associative ties: only from the 1250's do we find evidence of large-scale Lucchese mercantile-banking organizations operating in the North.[22] Typical perhaps of these relatively independent entrepreneurs was Gentile *quondam* Lamberti Guassosi — possibly the father, certainly the kin of Lotarius Gentili one of the lessees of the house in Troyes in 1266 — who on 7 September 1242 declared to the Consuls of the New Court of Justice in Lucca that he wished to go to France ("dicens se velle ire in Francia") and that he had appointed one Lambertus *medicus quondam* Martini his procurator for the period of his absence.[23] Three years later Gentile was in Troyes where he witnessed payment of 214 *provinois* to his fellow

---

[17] *ASL, Archivio dei notari*, no. 6 (notary Giovanni Gigli), f. 255.

[18] F. BOURQUELOT, *Étude sur les foires*, I, 170.

[19] *ASL, Archivio dei notari*, no. 15 (notaries Bartolomeo Fulcieri, Tegrimo Fulciero, Fulciero Fulcieri), *passim*.

[20] On Lucchese mercantile-banking companies, see T. Blomquist, "Commercial Association," 158-165 and the relevant discussion in T. Blomquist, "Lineage, Land and Business in the Thirteenth Century: the Guidiccioni Family of Lucca," *Actum Luce*, IX (1980), 7-29.

[21] For the distribution of Lucchese silk cloths, see F. Edler, "The Silk Trade of Lucca."

[22] T. BLOMQUIST, "Commercial Association," 159, note 9.

[23] *ASL, S. Maria Corteolandini*, 7 September 1242.

[24] *Ibid.*, 6 December 1245.

Lucchese, Aldebrandinus Guidiccionis, partner in the fledgling Ricciardi company.[25] There is nothing in the evidence, however, to suggest that Gentile was allied through partnership with any other merchant. His career was probably a solitary one, although the particulars of his activities in the North remain an unknown quantity.

Similarly independent in his journey *ultramontanas* was the money-changer Menabue Passavantis who in 1245 engaged one Gerardinus *quondam* Sordi to accompany him for one year in the North ("stare cum eo et ire cum eo ad ultramontanas partes et alibi vero sibi placuerit...") at a salary of 100s *lucchese* plus room and board.[25] Again, the details of Menabue's business elude us, but given his profession in Lucca, it may be assumed that he continued to ply his trade while abroad. He and the other Lucchese *campsores* who followed him across the Alps probably found employment as bankers at the fairs of Champagne where their skills as deposit and transfer bankers were in considerable demand. But Lucchese changers, in addition to clearing their clients' obligation by in-bank transfers from one account to another or by inter-bank clearance, engaged as well in pettylending activities and dabbled in commerce.

On 2 April 1250 Francescus Boniorni hired Gerardus, son of the money-changer Perfectus Schlacte, to remain with him and assist him in the shop which he planned to open in France ("...stare et morari cum eo et servire eidem Francesco pro apotheca et apothece in Francia in quacumque parte Francie eam haberet bona fide...").[26] The duration of the projected stay abroad, like that of Menabue, was only a year. The intended location of the *apotheca* was probably in or near one of the fair towns of Champagne since Francescus stipulated that in addition to room, board and a stipend of L 6 *provinois* Gerardus was to be reimbursed for any expenses he should incur whether at a fair or not ("Verumtamen, si dictus Gerardus acquireret in fera vel extra feram aliquid seu de suo expenderet pro utilitate apothece ipsius Francesci idem Francescus conservare debet eumdem Gerardum inde indempni."). Furthermore, Gerardus had the option of investing directly in the shop. If he put L 60 *provinois* into the operation he would receive 20% of the profits in addition to a reduced salary of L 3 *provinois* for his labour ("Item, si dictus Gerardus mitteret in dicta apotheca de suo usque in libras sexaginta provenesinorum dictus Francescus assignat ei et dare teneatur et debeat libras XX provenesinorum ad rationem centenarii sicut venerit per rationem pro suo lucro et guadagno et /——/ libras III provenesinorum pro suo servitio et faciendo apothece...").

The nature of the business that took place in the shop is a matter of conjecture. No direct connection between Francescus and the money-changer's profession survives, but Gerardus was the son of Perfectus, a campsor in Lucca, and it was usual in Lucca for the son of a changer to follow in his father's

---

[25] *AC, LL* 20, f. 19: 4 February 1245.
[26] *AC, LL* 25, f. 58.

footsteps.[27] At the very least, some of Perfectus Schlacte's expertise as a changer must have rubbed off on the son. Also the contract establishing the relationship between Francescus and Gerardus was drawn up in the "tower of Passavante" where the gild of the Lucchese changers habitually held its meetings and where a good deal of the collective business of the changers was conducted: to come together in the *turre Passavantis* presumes some link to money-changing.[28] Furthermore the term *apotheca* was used in Lucca consistently to designate the working area of a *campsor*, the place where he stored his working capital, his ledgers, the scales and instruments of the trade and where he also met his clientele. Finally, an ultramontane trip of short duration fits a pattern of professional behaviour not untypical of Lucchese money-changers.

The easy coming and going of Lucchese money-changers between Lucca and the North is illustrated by the movements of the *campsor* Aldebrandinus *quondam* Malagallie. Sometime before 1252 he and a fellow changer, Lambertus Rofredi, had been in France where they engaged one Johannes of Lyon to accompany them on their return trip to Lucca. On 28 November 1252 Johannes acknowledged full payment of the monies owed him by the two *campsores* for the journey and for services subsequently rendered in Lucca.[29] But in December 1258 Aldebrandinus was preparing for yet another journey to France. Before his departure he met with the Franciscan monk, Brother Augustinus, to whom in rather dramatic fashion ("promisit et convenit in manibus dicti fratris") he vowed that while on his impending sojourn in France he would return L 50 *tournois* gouged usuriously from former clients.[30] Whether this restitution was due solely to Aldebrandinus' sense of remorse over shady lending practices, to the insistent prodding of the good Brother Augustinus, or to a combination of the two is, of course, a moot question. However, Aldebrandinus' action informs us that a part — and probably a good part — of the Lucchese money-changer's activities abroad centred upon petty money-lending to a local clientele.

However, money-lending was not the exclusive preserve of the professional changer nor were the changers limited in the North solely to petty lending. In December 1255 yet another *campsor*, Gerardus Arzuri, in the course of ordering his business before departing for France appointed his son procurator of his affairs.[31] In the notarial document of procuration Gerardus expressly stated that

---

[27] Thomas W. Blomquist, "The Dawn of Banking in an Italian Commune: Thirteenth Century Lucca," Center for Medieval and Renaissance Studies, Univesity of California, Los Angeles, *The Dawn of Modern Banking* (New Haven-London, 1979), 53-68.

[28] *Ibid.*, 56.

[29] AC, LL 27, f. 71.

[30] AC, LL 31, f. 164: 4 December 1258.

[31] AC, LL 30, f. 94v: 2 December 1255.

he intended to engage in commerce or "other business" ("...in Francigenis partibus et ibidem marcadantiam exerceret aut aliam negotationem quacumque faceret..."). It may be assumed that a professional changer such as Gerardus would not forswear his art in an area where that trade must have been highly lucrative. He probably envisaged combining lending with some form of commerce.

Two documents from the year 1262 provide somewhat clearer examples of the blurring of occupational lines between merchant and petty money-lender. On 13 August 1262 Trasmondinus *quondam* Baldinocti Burlamacchi, a successful silk merchant, drew up his last will and testament.[32] Among numerous provisions and bequests, Trasmondinus instructed the executors to make restitution, following his death, of usurious profits in the considerable sum of L 400 *tournois* to the men of the towns *que vocantur Ramerru episcopatus Trasi et Argilliera episcopatus Cialone*.[33] Troyes was one of the fair towns and Chalons was the centre of an important cloth industry. Evidently, Trasmondinus, the silk merchant, had branched out into petty money-lending in the smaller communities of the Champenois.

The second document of 1262 indicates a similar move into the domain of the lombard by Trasmondinus' partner in the silk business, Uguiccione Mangialmacchi.[34] In that year Uguiccione saw fit to divide a portion of his estate between his two sons, Francescus and Ubertus. Among his assets Uguiccione listed all rights *adversus et contra omnes debitores de Francia qui dare tenentur ab annis V tam de parva summa quam magna*. The distinction between "small" and "great" sums was probably as much qualitative as quantitative. The lombards habitually made small loans secured by pledges to the economically disadvantaged element of the northern population; but they, as did the merchant-bankers, also committed larger amounts to municipal authorities, ecclesiastiques, territorial lords and the minor nobility.[35] The fact that Uguiccione made "large" as well as "small" loans suggests that he covered the entire range of the lombards' traditional clientele. And this from a man whose principal occupation was the silk trade.

---

[32] *ASL, Archivio dei notari*, no. 5 (notary Gherardetto da Chiatri), f. 19.

[33] *Ramerru* of the Italian text may be Ramerupt, a town on the river Aube: see Theodore Evergates, *Feudal Society in the Baillage of Troyes under the Counts of Champagne, 1152-1284* (Baltimore-London, 1975), 5. *Argilliera* is probably Argilliere, c. St. Menehould.

[34] *ASL, Archivio dei notari*, no. 5 (notary Gherardetto da Chiatri), f. 25: Transmondinus had L 600 *lucchese* invested *in societate cum Uguiccione Mangialmacchi* of which the partnership still owed him L 150 *lucchese* as *in libris dicte societatis continetur*.

[35] G. BIGWOOD, *Le régime juridique, passim*. R. DE ROOVER, *Money, Banking and Credit*, 118-119.

The evidence set forth up to this point presents a somewhat less precise view of Lucchese activities in the North than we might wish. Yet, it does indicate the money-lending operations engaged in both by merchants and money-changers; and, in the case of Gerardus Arzuri, shows a professional changer mixing trade with lending. Additional Lucchese documentation from the latter half of the thirteenth century reveals Lucchese merchant-bankers also entering into money-lending and pawnbroking.

\* \* \*

The origins of the large-scale Lucchese mercantile-banking companies are shrouded in obscurity. By 1250, however, the trend to larger partnerships, centrally managed from a home office (*apotheca*) and represented permanently abroad by partners or employees (*factores*) was in full force. The Ricciardi partnership, perhaps the most powerful Italian thirteenth-century mercantile-banking organization, first appears in the Lucchese sources as the *Societas Ricciardorum* in 1247 when the organization consisted of at least thirteen partners.[36] In the Genoese notarial materials relating to the commercial traffic between Genoa and northern Europe published by Professor Renée Doehaerd, the earliest reference to a Lucchese partnership is dated 1253.[37] After that date the majority of Lucchese business transactions in Genoa dealing with the North were effected by merchants acting in their capacities as partner or agent for a mercantile-banking company based in Lucca. By the last quarter of the thirteenth century, twenty-two partnerships engaged in international trade and finance existed in Lucca.[38]

The representatives of these companies, asserted de Roover, occupied themselves primarily in negotiating bills of exchange and large-scale commercial traffic and thus were not to be confused with their lowly brethren; the moneylending, pawnbroking, lombards. However, Lucchese evidence from the year 1260 reveals merchant-bankers investing directly in a pawnshop in Champagne, while a second document of the year 1265 suggests a close affinity between the activities of the money-changers and those of pawnbrokers.

On 2 August 1260 Rainaldus de Barcha, who also acted for Orlandus Jordani and Bonaccursus Johannis; Lucius de Lucha; and Orlandus Paganelli, stipulating for himself and his brother, Johannes; came together in Troyes to form a

---

[36] *Biblioteca governativa*, Lucca; Can. GIUSEPPE VINCENZO BARONI, *Notizie geneologiche delle famiglie lucchesi*, ms. no. 1115: year 1247. I am assuming Baroni's "Compagnia dei Ricciardi" to be the Italian rendering of *Societas Riciardorum* in the original latin text.

[37] RENÉE DOEHAERD, *Les relations commerciales entre Gênes, la Belgique et l'Outremont d'après les archives notariales génoises aux XIIIᵉ et XIVᵉ siècles*, 3 vols. (Bruxelles-Rome, 1941), II, no. 785.

[38] T. BLOMQUIST, "Commercial Association," 172-178.

partnership for the operation of a pawnshop in the neighbouring town of
Poigny situated in the lordship of one Guido de Labersotto ("...in quadam
cassana sive butecha in loco ubi dicitur Pugni iusitia et terra Guidonis de
Labersotto").[39] Two of the principals were actively engaged in international
finance and commerce around the time of the agreement. Lucius de Lucha was
the same Lucasius Natale who was operating in England on behalf of the
Ricciardi company in 1240 where he remained the leading partner of the firm
until the mid-1270's.[40] Orlandus Paganelli, with his brother Johannes for whom
he acted in this undertaking, was a founder of the *Societas filiorum Paganelli*,
one of Lucca's most important mercantile-banking organizations.[41]

The partnership was to last for six years and was capitalized at L 800
*tournois*. Rainaldus conferred L 400 on his own behalf and for Orlandus and
Bonaccursus. Lucius committed L 200 and the brothers Paganelli also conferred
L 200. The profits were to be distributed pro rata to the three contracting parties
on the basis of capital placed in the venture.

The remaining clauses of the articles of partnership deal with the workings of
the shop and are interesting for what they reveal about the milieu of the
pawnbroker operating in foreign climes. It was stated that at least one of the
partners must be on the premises at all times. And while there, extra-curricular
activities with females were strictly forbidden. It seems, perhaps, a bit quaint to
include clauses in a formal legal document forbidding the resident partner, or
partners, to sleep with a female domestic servant ("Item statuerunt quod ille qui
moratur sive morabuntur in dicta butecha non possint iacere cum servienta eius
famulla (sic) que maneat secum tam de die quam de notte. Et hoc teneatur per
iuramentum facere.") or to bring a woman into the shop for carnal purposes
("Item ordinaverunt quod nullus non debeat facere venire aliquam mulierem
occasione iacendi secum de notte..."). However, these injunctions were perhaps
motivated as much by practical as by moral concerns. It was further stated that if
anyone indeed should introduce a woman into the premises and if any harm
should come as a consequence, the partner guilty of the transgression was liable
for any damages ("Et quod si aliquis duxerit eam in dicta domo et aliquid
dampnum venisse seu veniet pro predicta occasione totum dampnum vel grava-
mine fiat super illum qui duxerit eam vel super illum qui possuerit eam in dicta
cassana."). Evidently, these stipulations arose out of the desire to maintain an
orderly house. Given the inevitable resentment of denizens against foreign
lenders, it is hardly surprising that the pawnbrokers wanted to avoid the
additional opprobrium that carrying on with local women could engender.
There was also concern, no doubt, over the potential damage to internal har-

---

[39] *ASL, S. Maria Corteorlandini*, 2 August 1260. "Pugni" of the Italian document
may be Poigny, c. Provins. The lord Guy remains unidentifiable.
[40] R. KAEUPER, *Bankers to the Crown*, 5-6, 12, 77.
[41] T. BLOMQUIST, "Commercial Association," 173-174. See below, 19.

mony among partners that might result from such activities. Under the circumstances, these contractual prohibitions were consonant with good business practice. Yet the very fact that they were included in the partnership agreement testifies to a continuing problem for men removed from hearth and home.

The business of the partnership was narrowly defined. It was pawnbroking and only pawnbroking. The partners were forbidden by the terms of the contract from trafficking in merchandise either in the shop or in town ("Item statuerunt quod nullus non faciat facere nullam mercatantiam nec permitat facere in dictam domum nec extra in dicto loco."). If the resident partner accepted goods in pawn that were worth less than three-quarters the amount of the loan, or in the case of objects of gold or silver four-fifths the value of the loan; and the shop should lose money, the partner who had accepted the pledge had to make good on the loss ("... et si quis qui prestaverit super pignoram que non valeat den. tres quattuor vel super pignorem auri vel argenti que non valeat den. quattuor quinque ut predictum est quod ille... et aliquid dampnum sit super illum qui possuerit eum in dicta butecha vel super suam partem."). The partner or partners on the scene were responsible for keeping the books and the accounts were routinely to be audited three times a year in the presence of at least two partners. Unfortunately, the involvement of the respective partners in the day-to-day operation of the shop is not spelled out, but for present purposes it is the direct participation of Lucasius Natale and the Paganelli brothers, merchant-bankers, that is significant.

The second Lucchese document dealing with the operation of a pawnshop was drawn up in Troyes on 25 August 1265.[42] It, in fact, records two separate transactions. In the first of these two parts, two Lucchese citizens, Guido Chiarelli and his brother Nicolaus, sold one-half of the monopoly over money-lending (*ius presti*) which they held in the Castle and Vill of "Salynay" from one noble knight John to the Lucchese merchants Lotarius Gentili, whom we have encountered as a lessee of the stone house in Troyes, and his partner in the mercantile-banking enterprise of the Gentili, Ricciardinus *filius* Michaelis Mayre.[43] The sale was in all likelihood prompted by cash-flow problems in the seller's operation which the influx of fresh capital could alleviate. At the time of the transaction Guido and Nicolaus had a total of L. 970 *tournois* in outstanding credits and the value of pledges in their possession. In effect Lotarius and Ricciardinus were buying half the assets of the partnership of Guido and Nicolaus for the sale price of L. 485 *tournois*. Apparently the Lord John did not

---

[42] *ASL, S. Maria Corteorlandini*, 25 August 1265.

[43] See SERGIO TERLIZZI, *Documenti delle relazioni tra Carlo I d'Angio e la Toscana*, in *Documenti di storia italiana*, XII (Florence, 1950), 35, no. 51: "Lotterius Gentilis, Michael frater eius, Mazzacanus Marsilii, Bonaccursus Cimachi, Ollandinus Paganelli, Coscius Cangke et Ricardus Demaire" are described as partners and granted immunity from tolls within the *Regno* by Charles of Anjou. "Salynay" would appear to be Savigny, c. Provins.

exact a licence fee from his Lucchese lombards in exchange for the right to establish a pawnshop within his territories, a fact arguing that such an undertaking was viewed at this time in the North, at least among the feudal rulers, as economically necessary to satisfy the short-term and periodic needs of the rural populace for cash.

The buyers paid the cash equivalent of one-half the capital value of the money-lending operation in Savigny, but they also gained the right to live in the Castle and Vill of "Salynay"; to deal in loans, with or without pledges ("... possint... pecuniam suam mutuo tradere super pignoribus et sine pignoribus..."); to invest in trade ("mercatare et de eorum pecunia lucrari"); and to change money ("cambiri"). The *ius presti*, then, in Savigny embraced pawnbroking, trade and money-changing. There is no reason to assume our Lucchese did not exploit all of these opportunities for profit. And it should be noted that Lotarius was described in the document as *civis et mercator lucanus*, the traditional appelation in the Lucchese sources for the merchant-banker whom we would not expect to find associated with a pawnshop.

In the second transaction, redacted on the same parchment as the first, the same contracting parties, Guido and Nicolaus on the one hand, Lotarius and Ricciardinus on the other, formed a partnership, *societate de prestu*, to exploit the right of money-lending and its concomitant privileges in the Castle and Vill of Savigny. The partnership was to last six years, or longer if all partners were in agreement. It was capitalized at L. 600 *tournois*, slightly less than the other Lucchese shop, with each party contributing the equal amount of L. 300. A general accounting was to be held once a year, although profits might be distributed at any time by unanimous agreement of the partners.

Apparently individual associates, at least two of whom were required to reside in Savigny at any given time, had a greater measure of individual discretion in the conduct of business than their Lucchese counterparts in Poigny. For eample, the articles of association imply that one of the resident partners might independently carry on partnership business, the only caveat being that he must duly turn over any resulting profit to the shop ("Et totum lucrum quod fecerint seu unius eorum fecerit ipsa occasione mittere et reducere in comunem ipsius societatis..."). Similarly, if any partner borrowed money in the name of the partnership he was held to record the transaction on the same day or the day following in the shop's book, thus obligating all partners and their heirs for satisfaction of the debt ("Item quod si aliquis ipsorum sociorum pro ipsa societate aliquos denarios mutuo acquireret debeat et teneatur ipsos denarios scribere seu scribi facere in libro comune ipsius societatis ea die vel sequenti in qua ipsi denarii fuerunt mutuo acquisiti... et omnes ipsi socii et societas eorum et heredes eorum et bona ad reddendum ipsos denarios mutuo acquisitos eo modo sic teneretur ille qui eos mutuo acceperit."). This clause indicates that the partners envisaged doing business, unfortunately to an extent impossible to gauge, with the capital of others. In fact, de Roover found the pawnbrokers of Bruges doing the same thing but pointed out that the acceptance of what amounted to time deposits did not involve book transfers from one client's account to another. The reception of funds from third parties, therefore, according to de Roover, does not mean that the lombards were encroaching upon the transfer-banking camp of the money-changers.[44] This I am inclined to think was generally so, that the lombards probably did not routinely engage in transfer banking. However, if these Lucchese lombards accepted third-party funds through the *mutuum* there was nothing to have prevented them from clearing accounts among their creditors by simple book transfer. They did accept capital from outsiders and the contract of association envisaged them engaging in exchange (*cambiri*), a primary function of the money-changers. To be sure, we are dealing here with matters of degree and emphasis, but it would appear that Lucchese pawnshops located in small villages indeed assumed some of the characteristics of a money-changer's *tavola*.

Additional clauses of the articles of association precluded one resident partner from lending money without a pawn to either John, Lord of Savigny, John's wife or his bailiff without the approval of the other resident ("Item quod aliquis eorum non possit nec debeat muturare alicui aliquem denarium sine gagio nec dicto Domino Johanni, Domino dicti Castri, et eius uxori et eorum balino unius sine consensu alterius.") — a wise precaution in view of the later history of disastrous Italian loans to fickle princes. No partner could give, *donare*, from the partnership capital or property more than the amount of 12d. *tournois* to any person without the consent of the residents. Nor could one resident engage in trade without the approval of the other ("Item quod non possit facere aliquam mercatantiam sine voluntate socii sui qui cum eo steterit in dicta casana."). But if a partner was absent on his own business, he was required to underwrite his own expenses while keeping the partnership free of any involvement in case of loss ("Item quod si aliquis sociorum pro suo facto et non societatis iret extra dictam villam debeat omnes expensas de suo facere et si dampnum habuerit sustinere et non de bonis dicte societatis."). Since only two partners were on the spot in Savigny at any given time, the other two were presumably free to pursue other interests. This provision was no doubt intended to protect the partnership from any detrimental involvement in the affairs of individual associates. As was the case with the preceding partnership contract, it is unclear as to how the labour was to be divided; just which of the partners were expected to man the shop at what time and for how long. But it appears that all the partners expected to take part, to one degree or another, in the management of the business.

Finally, the partnership contract betrays the same concern for the associates' private behaviour while on the job as did the earlier articles of association. The residents were prohibited from bringing a female into the shop for carnal purposes and from going abroad in the village seeking feminine companionship

---

[44] R. DE ROOVER, *Money, Banking and Credit*, 118, 348.

("Item quod aliquis ipsorum sociorum non possit nec debeat de notte in domo in qua morabuntur in dicta villa retinere aliquam feminam tam cognoscendi carnaliter nec debeat morari de notte extra dictam domum in tota ipsa villa et iurisdictione ipsius ville tam morandi cum aliqua femina."). In the same vein, no partner could play games at which it was possible to lose money or property ("Item quod non possit aliquis sociorum nec debeat ludere com aliquo in quo ludo sive ad quem ludem perdat pecuniam nec alias res."). The necessity for these injunctions probably came from experience and again remind us of the situation in which these aliens abroad found themselves.

Lacking as we do the books of the Lucchese pawn shops, there is no way to get at the levels of profit generated through these operations. De Roover, comparing data from fourteenth-century Pistoia in Tuscany with that of Nivelles and Tournai, has concluded that profit margins of pawnshops on invested capital were relatively small.[45] Overheads in the form of licensing fees, shop rental and the cost of borrowed money kept pawnbroker's interest rates high and their profits low. However, the fact that Guido and Nicolaus experienced a cash shortage that apparently led them to sell half their monopoly suggests that their loan services were in inconsiderable demand. In these circumstances, unless some limit to interest charges had been set by the Lord John, and no such restrictions were alluded to in the purchase-sale contract, the partners could have adjusted their charges to accord with demand. Furthermore, the last will and testament of Johannes Paganelli, whom we have encountered as a partner in the 1260 venture at Poigny drawn up in 1284 suggests that whatever the profit levels, the aggregate sums involved could nonetheless be significant.

By the year 1284 Johannes had returned to Lucca where he was a senior partner in one of the largest and most important Lucchese mercantile-banking organizations. The *Societas filiorum Paganelli* numbered at least seventeen partners among its ranks.[46] The firm trafficked in raw silk, in foreign exchange and was a papal depository in the provinces of Mayence and Treves as well as in England.[47] While thus engaged as a merchant-banker, Johannes, judging from the terms of his will, continued his activities as a lombard in northern Europe. In his last testament Johannes set aside *pro remedio anime sue et suorum peccatorum* the sizeable sum of L 800 *lucchese* for restitution after his death to the men of the territories of *Alaforte della lopiere que est in Francia, Senante Furtolo unius*

---

[45] *Ibid.*, 120-129.

[46] T. BLOMQUIST, "Commercial Association,' 173-174.

[47] On the Paganelli and other Lucchese mercantile-banking organizations as papal depositories in England, see WILLIAM E. LUNT, *Financial Relations of the Papacy with England to 1327* (Cambridge, Mass., 1939), 77-114. For contracts of procuration in which partners of the Paganelli were appointed to receive papal revenues in Mayence and Treves respectively, *ASL, Archivio dei notari*, no. 15 (notaries Bartolomeo Fulcieri, Tegrimo Fulcieri, Fulciero Fulcieri), f. 224.

*alie Francie* and to the inhabitants of other French lands ("aliarum terrarum Francie") called *Intracastilione et Apugni et Salinai et Lagi Locastello et Serugieri in Otta*.[48] Although I have not been able to place "Intracastillione", "Lagi Locastello" and "Serugieri" on the map, Poigny and Savigny, as we have seen, were in Champagne and these other villages were probably not far distant. In any case, Johannes, most likely in partnership with his brothers, was involved in petty-lending in at least several villages. He, the esteemed merchant-banker, if anyone, surely qualified to be tarred with the twin epithets lombard and usurer.

\* \* \*

This then is the evidence for the Lucchese advance into Northern France, principally into the County of Champagne. It remains to ask if these examples of professional diversity were typical of Lucchese merchants and bankers in general. A good deal more evidence would be required to provide a definitive answer, yet we may add here Richard Kaepuper's material on the Ricciardi Company's operations in England during the reign of Edward I. As Kaeuper observes these "Bankers to the Crown" — merchant-bankers par excellence — were also"... money lenders to great and lesser men on a considerable scale."[49]

A pattern — or perhaps better, the lack of a pattern — of Italian behaviour does nonetheless emerge from the available documentation. Money-changers routinely journeyed to Northern Europe where they engaged in trade as well as their primary profession. Merchants residing in the North for any length of time also crossed professional boundaries to traffic in money-lending. Partners of the mercantile-banking companies occupied themselves with pawnbroking. And pawnbrokers dealt in trade and deposit banking. These activities should caution against viewing the classes of early bankers in rigid hierarchical terms. The formative period of European banking would appear to have been more loosely structured professionally and socially than de Roover's later evidence from Bruges might lead us to believe. In this context, and in conclusion, I would suggest that the pejorative epithet "lombard" was a blanket term used by northerners to describe any Italian dealing in money. How, after all, could the borrowers have drawn a clear line between merchant-banker, money-changer and pawnbroker?

---

[48] *Ibid.*, f. 494v.
[49] R. KAEUPER, *Bankers to the Crown*, 31.

# Some Observations on Early Foreign Exchange Banking Based Upon New Evidence from Thirteenth-Century Lucca

Historians of medieval Italian foreign exchange banking are, due to the distribution and nature of the sources, inevitably much better informed about conditions prevailing in the Later MiddleAges than they are about the preceding period. The survival of account books, mint records, merchant correspondence, merchant manuals and other types of documentation has allowed the economic historian to construct up to this point a relatively — the work goes on — clear picture of the operations of contemporary mercantile-banking companies and the workings of the international money markets in the fourteenth and fifteenth centuries.[1] Not that we are wholly without do-

* Research for this paper was carried out in the Lucchese archives under grants from the American Council of Learned Societies, The American Philosophical Society and the Graduate School, Northern Illinois University: to each I am grateful. An earlier version was presented at the annual meeting of the American Historical Association in San Francisco, December, 1983 and I would like to thank my colleagues on the panel, Professors Mavis Mate, Harry Miskimin, Louise B. Robbert and Peter Spufford for their helpful comments. I also wish to express my gratitude to Dr. Alan Stahl, Curator of Medieval Coins at the American Numismatic Society, New York, for his aid, council and hospitality while I was probing monetary problems relating to the rates of exchange as a guest at the Society during the summer of 1983.

[1] In the interests of brevity, for the vast literature on finance and commerce in Late Medieval Italy the reader is referred here only to the bibliographies in FREDERICK C. LANE and REINHOLD C. MUELLER, *Money and Banking in Medieval and Renaissance Venice*, I, *Coins and Moneys of Account* (Baltimore-London, 1985), ARMANDO SAPORI, *Studi di Storia economica, secoli XIII-XIV-XV*, 3 vols. (Florence, 1955-1967) and the same author's *Le marchand italien* (Paris, 1952). Two still excellent surveys of medieval Italian commercial and business history are ROBERT S. LOPEZ, "The Trade of Medieval Europe": The South, MICHAEL M. POSTAN et al.,

cumentary access to the business history of the thirteenth century.[2] This latter period has, however, bequeathed a comparatively limited and scattered harvest of sources that can illuminate the dynamic of organizational and technical advances in the field of international trade, commerce and finance which collectively have inspired the tag, "The Commercial Revolution of the Thirteenth Century.[3] In the following essay I would like to set out some new data bearing upon the long and short-term movements of foreign exchange rates on the money market of thirteenth-century Lucca and to make some qualified remarks about the structure of the Lucchese money market and the way in which foreign exchange banking functioned in the thirteenth century.

The rates of exchange that I propose to examine are commercial rates reflected in instruments of exchange (*instrumenta ex causa cambii*) negotiated in Lucca and drawn upon one or another of the Fairs of Champagne. The rates are taken from contracts scattered about in the cartularies of several Lucchese notaries and a handful of surviving parchments spanning the years 1240-1302.[4] I propose to look first at the long-run movement of the rates

---

eds., *Cambridge Economic History of Europe*, II (Cambridge, 1952), 257-334, and RAYMOND DE ROOVER, The Organization of Trade," *ibidem* III, (Cambridge, 1963), 42-104, also now PETER SPUFFORD, *Money and Medieval Europe* (Cambridge, 1988).

[2] On the sources and literature dealing with thirteenth-century Italian commercial and business history, see especially the works of MARIO CHIAUDANO, general editors, *Documenti e studi per la storia del commercio e del diritto commerciale italiano*, I, II, XI, XII, XIII, XV, XVI, XVII, XVIII (Turin, 1935-1940) which provides the surviving minutes of five Genoese notaries, 1154-1211; DINA BIZZARRI, ed., *Liber imbreviaturarum Appuliesis notarii Communis Senarum, 1221-1223* (Turin, 1934) and *Liber imbreviaturarum Ildibrandini notarii, 1227-1229* (Turin, 1938): the surviving materials of the notary Amalric (1248-1249) of Marseilles are in LOUIS BLANCARD, *Documents inédits sur le commerce de Marseille au moyen âé*, 2 vols. (Marseille, 1884). In addition, RENE DOEHAERD, *Les relations commerciales entre Gênes, la Belgique et l'Outremont d'après les archives notariales génois aux XIIIe et XIVe siècles*, 3 vols. (Brussels-Rome, 1941) has calendared the Genoese notarial instruments relating to Italian commercial and financial relations with Northern Europe. PETER SPUFFORD and WENDY WILKENSON, *Interim Listing of the Exchange Rates of Medieval Europe* (Keele, 1977) is a massive compilation of data. Professor Spufford promises a final edition shortly.

[3] The concept of a "Commercial Revolution of the Thirteenth Century" was envisaged by RAYMOND DE ROOVER, "The Commercial Revolution of the Thirteenth Century," *Bulletin of the Business Historical Society*, XVI (1942), 34-39. See also PETER SPUFFORD, "Le rôle de la monnaie dans la révolution commerciale du XIII siècle," JOHN DAY, ed., *Etudes, d'histoire monetaire* (Lille, 1984), 356-395.

[4] For a description of the Lucchese notarial materials housed in the *Archivio di Stato in Lucca*, see ROBERT S. LOPEZ, "The Unexplored Wealth of the Notarial Archives of Pisa and Lucca," *Mélanges d'histoire du Moyen Âge dédiés à la mémoire de Louis Halphen* (Paris, 1951), 417-432; ROBERT-HENRI BAUTIER, "Notes sur les sources de l'histoire économique médiévale dans les archives italiennes," *Mélanges d'archéolo-*

over this sixty-year period and then to narrow the focus down to one year, 1284, from which survive an exceptionally concentrated run of rates. This later series is taken from the cartulary compiled in 1284 by the notarial team of Bartolomeo Fulcieri and his two sons Tegrimo and Fulciero.[5] The cartulary is important for our purposes in two respects. First, among their clientele, the Fulcieri numbered numerous partners of the some twenty-two mercantile-banking companies operating on the Lucchese exchange market in 1284.[6] Second, the cartulary contains an almost continuous string of *instrumenta ex causa cambii* since it is chronologically complete for the year — there appear to be no gaps — and I assume that it represents the total number of contracts redacted by the Fulcieri for this particular constituency. In sum, the Fulcieri instruments of exchange permit the construction of the most compact homogeneous run of thirteenth-century rates compiled to date.[7]

Taken together, these two series — the long and the short run — can provide us with valuable insights into how exchange banking functioned before the fourteenth-century development of the informal holographic letter of exchange and before the emergence of a relatively large number of banking places scattered throughout northern Europe replaced the Fairs of Champagne as the more or less single point of financial contact with the Mediterranean. But, it must be noted that any conclusions drawn from the data must be regarded with all due caution, for it must be kept in mind that we are dealing essentially with a one-sided equations since no comparable data survives from Champagne.[8]

---

*gie et d'histoire*, LVIII (1941-1946), 299-300; "Eugenio Lazzareschi, "L'Archivio dei Notari della Repubblica lucchese," *Gli archivi italiani*, II (1915), 175-210; MARTINO GIUSTI, "Lucca archivistica," offprint from *Archivi e cultura*, V (1971); Sac. GIUSEPPE GHILARDUCCI, *Le biblioteche e gli archivi arcivescovile e capitolari della Diocesi di Lucca* (Lucca, 1969); DUANE J. OSHEIM, "The Episcopal Archive of Lucca in the Middle Ages," *Manuscripta*, XVII (1973), 131-46.

[5] *Archivio di Stato in Lucca, Archivio dei notari*, no. 15 (notaries Bartolomeo Fulcieri, Tegrino Fulcieri, Fulciero Fulcieri). A description of the cartulary may be found in THOMAS W. BLOMQUIST, "Commercial Association in Thirteenth-Century Lucca," *Business History Review*, XLV (1971), 172-73.

[6] BLOMQUIST, "Commercial Association," 172-78, for the partial rosters of these companies.

[7] Among the contracts calendared by R. Doehaerd, *Les relations commerciales*, vols. II and III, are numerous *instrumenta ex causa cambii* drawn upon the Fairs of Champagne. The Genoese, however, were unfortunately circumspect in wording their contracts, usually omitting the amount Genoese disbursed (*tot genoinos*) in Genoa to acquire a stated amount of *provinois* at the Fairs. It is thus impossible to establish the rates of exchange between Genoa and the Fairs on the basis of this otherwise rich data. The *instrumenta ex causa cambii* so far published from Siena and Marseilles are too thin in number to permit the construction of short term runs similar to those included in this essay.

[8] The only surviving production of a fair notary is dated 1296 and according to its

\* \* \*

Champagne gave its currency to Lucca; that is to say that the rates in the Lucchese instruments of exchange drawing upon the Fairs were quoted in a varying number of Lucchese *denarii* of account to the fixed *solidus provinois* of the city of Provins which constituted the principal currency of account at the Fairs. Only in the 1290's does the money of Tours appear as the expression of value between Lucca and Champagne but since the *tournois* and the *provinois* were equivalent and since the method of quotation the same — so many *denarii* Lucchese to the *solidus tournois* — I have not distinguished in the accompanying graphs between the two currencies.[9] The method of expressing the rates in the Lucchese contracts of exchange meant that a decline in the rates favoured Lucca while a rise was correspondingly unfavourable. Also it needs to be noted that the delivery dates of all contracts drawing upon Champagne in Lucca were fixed to the period of payment of one or another of the Fairs.[10] It was not, therefore, a customary and regular period of usance

discoverer, ROBERT-HENRI BAUTIER, "Les registres des foires de Champagne: à propos d'un feuillet récemment découvert," *Bulletin philologique et historique du Comité des Travaux Historiques et Scientifiques du Ministère de l'Education Nationale, 1942-1943* (Paris, 1945), 157-88, contains a number of exchange contracts among a total of some fifty transactions. These are, however, among the exemplars published by the author, no exchange rates. Adolf Schaube, "Ein italienischer Coursbericht von der Messe von Troyes aus dem 13. Jahrhundert," *Zeitschrift fur Sozial-und Wirstschaftsgeschichte*, V (1897), 248-308 provides references to a number of exchange transactions but no exchange rates. CESARE PAOLI and ENEA PICCOLOMINI (eds.), *Lettere volgari del secolo XIII scritte da Senesi* (Bologna, 1871 – reprint Bologna, 1968), have published four letters written by Sienese merchants doing business at the Fairs. The few references to exchange and the accompanying rates quote the price of *provinois* in Siena in 1260 at 33d. and 31d. Sienese on the St. John Fair: see *ibid.*, 20. The first rate is given in the text as 33 *solidi* per *solidus (la doçina)*, of Provins, but since the Sienese penny was equal to the Lucchese such a rate is patently wrong and *denarius* should be understood. It should be noted that the 31d. and 33d. rates accord perfectly with those of Lucca from the same time.
    [9] On the parity between the *tournois* and the *provinois* from ca. 1210 or 1224, see J.-Adrien Blanchet and Adolphe Dieudonné, *Manual de numismatique francaise*, 4 vols. (Paris, 1912-1936), IV, 132-33.
    [10] The precise internal organization as well as the opening and closing dates of the Fairs present a number of problems. I will use here the dates given by ABBOTT PAYSON USHER, *The Early History of Deposit Banking in Mediterranean Europe* (Cambridge, Mass., 1943), 118: Lagny, 2 Januaray- 22 February; Bar-sur-Aube, 24 February - 30 March — 15 April - 20 May; May Fair (Provins), 28 April - 1 June — 13 June - 16 July; St. John (Troyes), 9 July - 15 July — 29 August - 4 September; St. Ayoul (Provins), 14 September - 1 November; St. Remi (Troyes), 2 November - 23 December.
    For the opening dates of the Fairs, see the texts published by PAUL HUVELIN, *Essai historique sur le droit des marchés et des foires* (Paris, 1897), 600-603. The fundamental

between two banking places that established the duration between the taking up of funds in one place and repayment in another. This fact marks an important difference in the means of conducting exchange banking between the thirteenth and later centuries when new banking places had arisen in northern Europe to replace the declining Fairs and when the letter of exchange was displacing the formal notarial *instrumentum ex causa cambii*.[11] The significance of this difference will be taken up more fully below.

* * *

The long term behaviour of the Lucca-Champagne rates of exchange are displayed in Graph I. The time line shows four fairly distinct periods in terms of the levels of the exchange points: the years 1240-1253 during which the rates hovered around 28 *denarii* Lucchese per *solidus* of Provins with a slight upturn towards the end of the period; the years 1253-1273/1279 when they stood at about 33.3; the era post 1279 to 1295 when the rates averaged out at 44.32 *denarii*; and, lastly 1295-1302, when the Lucchese showed renewed strength against the *provinois, tournois*. What external variables might be adduced to explain the alterations in the otherwise fairly tranquil levels of the rates?

The first significant jump in the rates — unfavourable, as we have noted, to Lucca — took place in the early 1250's. The event that stands out clearly at this point in Tuscan monetary history is the return to gold with the issuance of the Florentine gold florin late in 1252.[12] By my reckoning, the gold/silver

study of the Fairs remains Felix Bourquelot, *Etudes sur les foires de Champagne* (Paris, 1865); for the opening dates, see part I, 80-83. See also Charles Alengry, *Les foires de Champagne: étude d'histoire économique* (Paris, 1915); LEVIN GOLD-SCHMIDT, "Die Geschäftsoperationen auf den Messen der Champagne," *Zeitschrift für das gesamte Handelsrecht*, XL (1892), 8-10; ELISABETH BASSERMANN, *Die Champagnermessen. Ein Beitrag zur Geschichte des Kredits* (Tubingen-Leipzig, 1911), 13-15; ELIZABETH CHAPIN, *Les villes de Foires de Champagne des origines au début du XIV^e siècle* (Paris, 1937), 107, note 9 and Robert-Henri Bautier, "Les foires de Champagne: Recherches sur une évolution historique," *La foire* (Brussels, 1953), 97-147.

The standard wording of the Lucchese contracts called for payment within eight days of the public summons to payment: *infra VIII proximos dies ex quo preconizatum fuerit ara ara ad pagamentum tabule et ab ydonea tabula ut est usus in fera.*

[11] For these points, see the studies of Raymond de Roover cited below in note 29.

[12] On the issuance of gold coinages in Genoa and Florence, see ROBERT S. LOPEZ, "Settecento anni fa: il ritorno all'oro nell'occidentale duecentesco," *Rivista storica italiana*, LXV (1953), 19-55, 161-198; re-issued under the same title as *Quaderni della Rivista Storica Italiana*, 4 (Naples, 1955) and the author's abbreviated English version "Back to Gold, 1252," *The Economic History Review*, 2nd series, IX (1956-57), 219-240. For the Florentine florin see, MARIO BERNOCCHI, *Le monete della repubblica fiorentina*, 4 vols. (Florence, 1974-1978), III, 58 ff. On the role of the florin as the dominant coin in international commerce until the end of the fifteenth century, see

ratio stood in Lucca in 1245 at the remarkably low rate of about 1:8;[13] reflecting to some degree the shortage of silver created by the expanded outputs of the Tuscan mints in the wake of the striking of the Tuscan groat during the previous three decades.[14] The issuance of the florin and the accompanying increase in the demand for gold seems, despite new inflows into Italy, to have brought an end to the era of cheap gold.[15] Mario Bernocchi gives a gold/silver ratio of 1:8.99 in 1250;[16] Robert Lopez similarly offers a rate under 1:9 in the years immediately preceding the issuance of the florin;[17] while Carlo Cipolla provides a ratio of 1:10.7 in 1252.[18] Thus, Tuscan silver lost 12.3% against the primary metal between 1245 and 1250; another 19% between 1250 and 1252; and 33.7% overall between 1245 and the time of the appearance of gold coinage. The proximity of this decline in the relative value of Tuscan silver to the 16% drop in Lucchese money against the *provinois* on the foreign exchange market seems to me to be more than fortuitous. The realignments in the gold/silver ratio in central Italy must have been a primary causal factor in the adjustment of the exchange points as reflected in our series.

The second realignment in the Lucca-Champagne rates took place at sometime between 1273 and 1279 — no intermediate data survives in Lucca from this period — when the Lucchese lost nearly another 25% against the money of Provins. The 1270's were a period of especial turmoil — apparently

CARLO M. CIPOLLA, *Money, Prices and Civilization in the Mediterranean World* (Princeton, 1956), 20-21) the same author's *The Monetary Policy of Fourteenth-Century Florence* (Berkeley, 1982), XI-XIV, and THOMAS WALKER, "The Italian Gold Revolution of 1252: Shifting Currents in the Pan-Mediterranean Flow of Gold," JOHN F. RICHARDS, ed., *Precious Metals in the Later Medieval and Modern Worlds* (Durham, NC, 1983), 29-52.

[13] Lucca, *Archivio capitolare*, LL 20, f. 43v: 10 ounces *argenti battuti* sold for Ł 9 Lucchese or 18s. per ounce while LL 20, f. 120 records that on 24 October 1245 1 ounce *auri* and 5 ounces *argenti* sold for Ł 11 14s. Lucchese. Using these figures, we arrive at the 1:8 ratio gold/silver. In reality, however, the ratio was no doubt somewhat higher since the *argenti battuti* was worked, while the 5 ounces of silver were presumably fine.

[14] On the striking of the full weight Tuscan *grosso of 12 denarii*, see DAVID HERLIHY, "Pisan Coinage and the Monetary History of Tuscany, 1150-1250," *Le zecche minore toscane fino al XIV secolo (Atti del III Convegno Internazionale di Studi di Storia e d'Arte)*, (Pistoia, 1967), 169-192: this is an expanded version of an article which appeared under the same title in *The American Numismatic Society Museum Notes* (New York, 1954).

[15] LOPEZ, "Settecento anni fa," and "Back to Gold:" WALKER, "The Italian Gold Revolution of 1252."

[16] BERNOCCHI, *Le monete*, III, 142.

[17] LOPEZ, "Back to Gold", 232-35.

[18] CARLO M. CIPOLLA, *Studi di storia della moneta*, I, *I movimenti dei cambi in Italia dal secolo XIII al XV* (Pavia, 1948), 129.

caused by a severe shortage of silver — in Tuscan and Lucchese monetary history.[19] The decade was also preceded by debasement of the Lucchese silver *denarius* in late 1267 or 1268. The first mention in the sources of a debased silver Lucchese penny is dated 31 March 1268 with the reference to a *denarius novus* valued at 16.6% less than the traditional *Decenarius parvus*[20] Just why this debasement took some three to four years to register on the exchange market is difficult to fathom but the best hypothesis would seem that for purposes of exchange the merchant-bankers retained the traditional lira of account, equaling a nominal 31.68 grams silver, that had obtained in Lucca since a monetary reform in 1181.[21] Apparently, only some years later was the debasement of 1268 expressed in a new pound of account value. In fact the jump in the rates between 1273 and 1279 show an increase for the *provinois* of 20%, about what we might have anticipated given the appearance of a new Lucchese penny debased by close to that figure.

As to the rejuvenation of the money of Lucca on the Lucchese foreign exchange market in the 1290's, we probably need look no further than the policies of debasement in the royal coinage implemented by Philip the Fair to explain the gains of Lucchese silver against a progressively weakened *tournois*[22].

\* \* \*

It goes without saying that the movement of the Lucca-Champagne rates of exchange was a more complex matter than our scattered data can reveal. Within the long-term secular pattern, the medieval merchant unquestionably had to contend with short-run fluctuations in the points. In the somewhat busy Graph II, I have charted the total volume of exchange traded in Lucca, averaged per month, for the year 1284; the rates of exchange, also averaged per month; and the monthly volume of silk imports from Genoa into Lucca,

---

[19] Bernocchi, *Le monete*, III, 144-45.

[20] Lucca, *Archivio capitolare*, LL 33, f. 107: On 31 March 1268 the money-changer, Castracane *quondam* Rugerii, sold 144 "good new pennies" for the price of 120 *denariorum lucensium*. The stated exchange was 24 new *denarii* to 20 of the old or a debasement of 16.6%.

[21] This pound value is based upon a *denarius* of an intrinsic worth of 132 grams silver: see my article "Alle origini del 'grosso' toscano: la testimonianza delle fonti lucchesi del XIIIᵉ secolo", forthcoming in *Archivio storico italiano*.

[22] On Philip's monetary policies and their consequences, see Jean La Faurie, "Le gros tournois en France", *Numismatický Sborník*, XII (1972), 49-61; Joseph Strayer, "Italian Bankers and Philip the Fair", *Explorations in Economic History*, VII (1969), 113-121; Armand Grunzweig, "Les incidences internationales des mutations monétaires de Philipe le Bel", *Moyen Âge*, LIX (1953), 117-173; Adolphe Dieudonné, "Changes et monnaies au Moyen Âge", *Revue des deux mondes*, I, (1927), 24-37; A. Landry, *Essai économique sur les mutations des monnaies dans l'ancienne France, de Philippe le Bel à Charles VIII* (Paris, 1910).

as revealed in the contracts of the Fulcieri. A quick visual scan shows large volume trading in April, May, June, October and November with a peak of over L. 7,000 Lucchese in August. The lowest trading volumes were in February, September and December. Sharp upward swings occurred between March and April, July and August, September and October, with equally dramatic downturns taking place between June and July, August and September, and November-December. Turning now to the rates as expressed in the graph, there appears a positive correlation between the volume of pounds traded in a given month and the behaviour of the rates. As might be expected, the rise in volume pushed the value of the *provinois* upward in Lucca while a decrease lowered its worth on the Lucchese market.[23] The law of supply and demand is clearly at work here. But what generated demand?

The third element factored into the equation of Graph II is the volume of raw silk imported from Genoa and traded in Lucca in 1284. I have included these figures, taken from the pages of the Fulcieri cartulary, because of the critical signifiance of raw silk needed to feed Lucca's primary industry, the manufacture of fine silk clothes.[24] The volume of raw silk traded in Lucca at any given time ought to have been a key indicator of the city's overall economic vitality. The most striking feature of this data is the zero level of imports in August, attributable unquestionably to the epic naval battle of Meloria, waged off the Pisan coast on 6 August 1284 between Pisan and Genoese forces.[25] The diversion of Genoese energies toward this confrontation evi-

---

[23] For an analysis of the effects of supply and demand for specie and its effects upon the exchange market between Florence and Venice, see REINHOLD C. MUELLER, "Chome l'uccielo di passagio: la domande saisonnière des espèces et la marché des changes à Venise au Moyen Age", Day, ed., *Etudes d'histoire monétaire*, 195-219.

[24] For the Lucchese silk industry, see FLORENCE EDLER, "The Silk Trade of Lucca during the Thirteenth and Fourteenth Centuries", doctoral dissertation, Department of History, University of Chicago (Chicago, 1930); EUGENIO LAZZARESCHI and FRANCESO PARDI, *Lucca nella storia, nell'arte, e nell'industria* (Pescia, 1941); TELESFORO BINI, *I Lucchesi a Venezia: alcuni studi sopra i secoli XIII e XIV*, 2 Vols. (Lucca, 1853) and SALVATORE BONGI, "Della mercatura dei Lucchesi nei secoli XIII e XIV", *Atti della Reale Accademia Lucchese di Scienze, Lettere ed Arti*, XVIII (1868). For the Lucchese in Genoa, see especially Edler, "The Silk Trade"; DOMENICO GIOFFRÉ, "L'attività economica dei Lucchesi a Genova fra il 1190 e il 1280", *Lucca archivistica, storica, economica* in *Fonti e studi del corpus membranarum italicarum*, X (Rome, 1973), 94-111; PIERRE RACINE, "I banchieri piacentini ed i campi sulle fiere di Champagne alla fine del Duecento", *Studi storici in onore di Emilio Nasalli Rocca* (Piacenza, 1971) and *ibidem*, "Le marché génoise de la soie en 1288", *Revue des études sud-est européennes*, VIII (1970): also see the documents published by DOEHAERD, *Les relations*, and ARTURO FERRETTO, *Il codice diplomatico delle relazioni fra la Toscana e Lunigiana ai tempi di Dante*, 2 parts, *Atti della Società Ligure di Storia Patria*, XXXI (1901-1903).

[25] For chronicle accounts of the battle, see LUIGI T. BELGRANO and CESARE IMPERIALE DI SANT ANGELO, eds., *Annali genovesi di Caffaro e de' suoi continuatori dal*

debtially choked off normal commercial activity in the Ligurian port and temporarily halted the flow of raw silk into Lucca. The volume of trading in foreign exchange in Lucca peaked in the month of August precisely when little, if any, raw silk was available in the market place. Conversely, when in December the pound value of imported silk soared, the amount of exchange dealings with the North plummeted. The data, then, indicate that sharp alternations in the configuration of trade had effect upon the rates of exchange by increasing or lowering demand for credit in Lucca, which in turn, as we have already observed, had a direct impact upon the behaviour of the exchange points.

Yet another related and measurable factor that needs examination is the possibility that some Fairs traditionally attracted more business than others. Here, however, the relationship seems negative: each year appears to have had its own variations in the relative volume of business conducted at each of the Fairs. For example, turning to Graph III which depicts the volume of exchange transactions drawn on each Fair in 1284, we find the St. John Fair of Troyes in the lead, the May Fair of Provins second, followed by the Troyes Fair of St. Remi, St. Ayoul of Provins with Lagny and the Fair held at Bar-sur-Aube bringing up the rear. Drawing upon similar data complied from Genoa by Pierre Racine (Graph IV), the Troyes Fair of St. Remi is number one with Lagny second, followed by Bar, St. John, St. Ayoul and the May Fair in that order.[26] Furthermore, the figures published by Abbot Payson Usher showing the annual revenues from the six Fairs for the years 1275, 1276, 1317, 1326 and 1341 show the same flip-flopping in the yearly rank order of the volume of business conducted at each of the Fairs.[27] Apparently seasonality, insofar as it affected financial dealings between Lucca and the Fairs, was random and fluctuated according to the yearly exigencies of international and domestic trade, commerce and finance.[28]

*MXCIX al MCCXCII*, 5 vols. published as vols. 11-14:2 of *Fonti per la storia d'Italia: scrittori secolo XIII* (Rome, 1890-1929), V, 55-57 and BERNHARD SCHMEIDLER, ed., *Tholomei lucensis annales* in *Monumenta germaniae historica*: Scriptores rerum germanicorum, n.e. VIII (Berlin, 1930), 203. For an evaluation of the impact of the battle upon Pisan society, see DAVID HERLIHY, *Pisa in the Early Renaissance: A Study in Urban Growth* (New Haven, 1958).

   [26] RACINE, "I banchieri piacentini", 481-82.
   [27] USHER, *Deposit Banking*, 118.
   [28] MUELLER, "Chome l'uccielo di passagio", 197-198 has observed that Florence "loin de la mer" lacked an annual pattern of seasonality. Lucca, however, was tied to the sea by her dependence upon Genoa as a source of raw silk and in other years her exchange market may well have showed a closer relationship to the rhythm of Genoese trade than in 1284.

\* \* \*

No analysis of medieval foreign exchange banking would be complete without reference to built-in interest charges as a motor driving the rates --an issue so vigorously set forth by the late Professor Raymond de Roover in his many works dealing with medieval banking. De Roover's views are well known and I will here give only a brief résumé of his position regarding interest, foreign exchange and early banking.[29] De Roover emphasized that the *cambium* contract was a credit as well as an exchange operation; involving credit because the deliverer, or lender in his words, advanced funds in one place payable at home time in the future. The bankers did not, however, forego interest owing on the time factor but instead of charging up front--which would have brought them into conflict with the Church's usury ban--they "cleverly concealed" interest within the rates of exchange "by either adding or subtracting something from the rate or price of exchange." To be complete, according to de Roover's analysis, an exchange transaction involved at least two contracts: in the first the delivering banker acquired a balance abroad in a foreign currency; in the second he, or his agent, delivered this balance to a taker, or his agent, who promised repayment in an equivalent sum in the currency of the first contract at the original place. Only when the exchange operation had been fulfilled through remittance by re-exchange a was the banker able to know his profit or loss. Although De Roover admitted that the bankers could lose dealing in exchange, he nonetheless insisted that the deck was stacked, due to concealed interest, in their favour and losses were consequently rare. Furthermore, argued De Roover, since canon law defined any certain profit on a loan (*mutuum*) as usury, bankers had to find other ways of lending at a profit. The favoured method was by means of the *cambium* which the civil and canon lawyers considered a licit contract because of the uncertain return due to the vagaries of the exchange rates: therefore large-scale banking became virtually synonymus with foreign banking until the

[29] *Inter alia*, see "What is Dry Exchange? A Contribution to the Study of English Mercantilism", *Journal of Political Economy*, LII (1944), 250-266 (reprinted in JULIUS KIRSHNER, ed., *Business, Banking and Economic Thought in Late Medieval and Early Modern Europe: Selected Studies of Raymond de Roover* (Chicago-London, 1974), 183-199); *La lettre du change, XIVᵉ-XVIIIᵉ siècles* (Paris, 1953); "New Interpretations of the History of Banking", *Journal of World History*, II (1954), 28-76 (reprinted in KIRSHNER, *Business, Banking and Economic Thought*, 200-238); "Cambium ad Venetias: Contribution to the History of Foreign Exchange", *Studi in onore di Armando Sapori*, 2 vols. (Milan, 1957), 631-638 (reprinted in KIRSHNER, *Business, Banking and Economic Thought*, 239-259); *The Rise and Decline of the Medici Bank, 1397-1494* (Cambridge, Mass., 1963). (Italian edition, Il Banco Medici dalle origini al declino, 1397-1494). *The Bruges Money Market around 1400 with a Statistical Supplement by Hyman Sardy* (Brussels, 1968). For a complete bibliography of de Roover's work, see KIRSHNER, *Business, Banking and Economic Thought*.

eighteenth century. Although our evidence is taken from an earlier period than deRoover, his views are still relevant to the 1284 data.

The cartulary of the Fulcieri numbers among its 513 folio pages and thousands of individual agreements some 202 rough drafts of *instrumenta ex causa cambii* reflecting an unknown fraction of the total exchange dealings of Lucchese merchant-bankers in 1284 with the Fairs of Champagne. The total volume exchanged through these contracts comes to £ 44,941 *provinois*, payable at one or another of the fairs, purchased with £ 171,244 Lucchese disbursed in Lucca. Furthermore, the information appended by the notary in the margin of his cartulary, indicating the circumstances under which each obligation was satisfied and rendering the contract void, demonstrates that these transactions were, for the most part, fulfilled in Champagne. In other words, the contracts are genuine and do not represent efforts to avoid the taint of usury by disguising straight loans as legitimate--in the eyes of the canonists--exchange transactons. Of the 202 *instrumenta* negotiated in Lucca, 114 were actually fulfilled in accordance with the contractual terms, 27 were cancelled with no comment, 32 were not cancelled at all and 29 were settled in Lucca.[30] Since the information regarding the circumstances of the settlement in the North had to have come from the original deliverer who had no compelling motive to register the cancellation in the notary's cartulary--for his purposes entry of the payment in his own books was sufficient--my sense is that in 27 cases the deliverer gave only a bare bones oral acknowledgment that he had been paid while in the other 32 instances he simply neglected to do so. Similarly, from the taker's perspective, the cancellation was superfluous since he would have had his northern agent's evidence of settlement in Champagne in the event of a later challenge. In short, it seems reasonable to assume that most, if not all, of these 59 transaction were indeed fulfilled at the Fairs. Regarding the 29 contracts settled in Lucca, I suspect that they were concluded there as a convenience to the contracting parties and not because of any pretermined agreement to avoid a nearly unenforceable usury prohibition. If this reasoning is sound, then 86% of the exchange agreements contracted in Lucca were actually settled in the North.

But was interest an element in setting the exchange points? The Lucchese material suggests that--in a manner not envisaioned by deRoover--it was. But again I must remind the reader that we are dealing only with the view from Lucca and in the absence of contemporaneous data from the Fairs it is unpossible to verify the profit or loss sustained by the bankers had they chosen in fact to repatriate their funds through re-exchange; that is, by delivering a se-

---

[30] The notary cancelled the entries in his cartulary by drawing crossed diagonal lines across the face of each. He then added in the margin or beneath the text the information relevant to the satisfaction of the terms of the contract. Thus is appended the information that the agent of a given deliverer received payment in Champagne through the agent of the taker on such and such a date.

cond contract at the Fairs payable in Lucca. It should be noted, moreover, that I have found no evidence whatever in the archives that Lucchese merchant-bankers operating in the North engaged in direct re-exchange with Lucca. There were other means by which the Lucchese bankers brought their capital home.

Let us examine first the dealings on the May Fair of Provins illustrated in Graph V. Here the data show that the shorter the term of the contract, the lower the supposed interest charges as expressed in the rates. The May Fair opened in 1284 on 16 May and closed on either 30 June or 6 July.[31] Trading in *provinois* in Lucca payable at the May Fair began in March and continued into June. If we average the rates for each month, a clear rising pattern of the Lucchese against the *provinois* emerges: the seven transactions negotiated in March show an average of 43.43 *denarii* Lucchese to one *solidus* of provins; seventeen documents from April indicate a rate of 43.86 *denarii;* eleven from May give an average of 46.59 *denarii.* A rising rate favored the taker who consequently received more in Lucca for his promise to pay a fixed sum at the May Fair as the value date drew closer. If, for example, the taker traded one *solidus provinois* in March for delivery at the May Fair he received in Lucca on average 43.43 *denarii* Lucchese from the giver. In June a taker would have received 46.59 *denarii* for the same amount of *provinois* payable at the Fair. Looking at the data from the other fairs, the same configuration more or less obtained at the Troyes Fair of St. Remi (Graph VI) where the spread between the opening and closing of trading was a sizeable 11%; on the Fair of Lagny (Graph VII) the difference was ultimately 3% but the months of November, December and January show no movement at all; St. John and Bar-sur-Aube (Graph VIII and IX) show modest rises of 2.5 and 2.2 respectively: finally the Fair of St.Ayoul (Graph X) registered only a sight gain of .05%. The rising tendency of the exchange points favored the taker, as we have noted, and must have reflected an interest factor since the only constant within the rate series for each Fair is the decreasing time element between the negotiation of the *cambium* contract and the value date. By deli-

---

[31] The May Fair of Provins, according to the texts published by Huvelin, *Essai historique,* 600-603, began on the Tuesday before Ascension Day, or 16 May. According to GOLDSCHMIDT, *Die Geschaftsoperationen,* 9, the May Fair lasted 46 days: BASSERMANN, *Die Champagnermessen,* 13-15 and CHAPIN, *Les villes de Foires,* 107, note 9, concur. RICHARD FACE, "Techniques of Business in the Trade between the Fairs of Champagne and the South of Europe in the Twelfth and Thirteenth Centuries", *Economic History Review,* X (1958), 427, note 2 and "The Vectuarii in the Overland Commerce between Champagne and Southern Europe", *Economic History Review,* XII (1959), 240, note 8, following Bourquelot, argues a 52-day cycle. A 46-day duration would have closed the Fair, in 1284, on 30 June; a 52-day cycle on 6 July. The Fair of St. John, following Huvelin's texts, opened the first Tuesday a fortnight after St. John's Day, or 11 July.

vering funds at a low rate and taking high, bankers could turn a nice to moderate profit on the Lucchese exchange market.

As an example of how this could work, we may turn to the fourteen *cambia* contracts negotiated by Arrigus Arnolfini and Tedicius Lamberti *de Porta*, acting for themselves and their partners, between 21 March and 5 April.[32] In the eight of the fourteen deals, Arrigus and Tedicius were deliverers, distributing a total of £ 8,802 ls. 8d. Lucchese at an average rate of £ 44.03 *denarii* per *solidus provinois* and receiving promises of £ 2,400 *provinois* payable in seven instances at the May Fair of Provins, with one contract due at Bar-sur-Aube. In the remaining six transactions, the partners took up £ 7,856 5s. Lucchese at an average rate of £ 44.83 *denarii* Lucchese per *solidus* of Provins promising to repay five loans at Bar-sur-Aube and one at the May Fair with a total of £ 2,100 *provinois*. The results of this trading left Arrigus, Tedicius and partners with a balance of 300 *provinois* in the North which they had secured at an effective rate of 37.833 *denarii* per *solidus provinois*, a rate well below those prevailing on the Lucchese market in 1284. Such a process of trading could continue indefinitely. As long as there existed in Lucca an effective supply and demand for short-term loans on the one hand and credit balances in the North on the other, profits were to be had working the market.

As for those who delivered at high rates, i.e., at relatively low interest, it may be presumed that their commercial interests dictated that they shift capital to the North where it could profitably be invested. If a merchant-banker chose, in fact, to collect his balances at the Fairs, how did he make his returns and thus complete the transaction in Lucca? Two phenomena must be considered more fully in this context. First, there is no evidence from Lucca, as we have seen, indicating that funds were repatriated from the North by reexchange. Second, is the fact that Italian capital did not remain idle in northern Europe.

Lucchese merchant-bankers intensively engaged in trade, commerce and money lending in the North in addition to their dealings at the Fairs.[33] Some forty-six partners of Lucchese merchant-banking companies represented their respective organizations in Champagne in the 1280's.[34] They transacted their

---

[32] This material is summarized in the Appendix.

[33] In Flanders the Ricciardi, Paganelli and Cardellini companies of Lucca frequently extended credit to the city of Ypres; in 1282 the Paganelli company acted for the city of Bruges in settling a debt in Rome while Lucchese merchants were also purveyors of luxury cloths to the Counts of Flanders and Hainault as well as the court of Champagne: see GEORGES BIGWOOD, *Le régime juridique et économique du commerce de l'argent dans la Belgique au moyen-âge*, 2 parts, published as *Mémoires de l'Academie Royale de Belgique, classe des lettres et des sciences morales et politiques*, XIV (1921-1922), I, 180, 641; LEON MIROT, *Etudes lucquoises* (Paris, 1930), 53-56; and CHARLES PITON, *Les Lombards en France et à Paris: leurs marques, leurs poids-monnaies, leur sceau de plomb*, 2 vols. (Paris, 1892-1893), I, 125.

[34] BLOMQUIST, "Commercial Association", 162.

companies business at the Fairs--acting as payers and payees in exchange dealings, buying and selling merchandise and lending money to a varied northern constituency. Other Lucchese operated pawn shops in the County of Champagne, while still others, money-changers and lesser merchants, engaged in petty trade and money lending with the denizens of the smaller towns and villages of the Champenois.[35] In short, profitable outlets for capital could not only have kept Lucchese balances in the North for long periods of time but also could have acted as a magnet drawing ever fresh stocks northward.

If quick returns were the objective, however, there existed in Lucca a lively market for northern cloths and the merchant-bankers were thus presented with the prospect of investing their balances by buying fine woollen cloths for export to Lucca and other Tuscan markets.[36] It is reasonable to assume that a not inconsiderable portion of the credits transferred to the North via exchange banking was invested in cloth intended for re-sale in Lucca and other Tuscan markets. Indeed, the bankers may have shifted their capital to the Fairs expressly for the purpose of making such investments.

The evidence also points to a complementary, if more complicated, method of repatriating northern balances. Pierre Racine has shown that in the last decades of the thirteenth century Lucchese mercantile-banking companies — the same that were working the Fairs — were the most active dealers in Genoa in exchange operations with the Fairs.[37] These were the same companies that dominated the Lucchese exchange in 1284. Domenico Gioffrè has further noted that the Lucchese operating in Genoa were primarily takers; i.e., they were accepting funds in Genoa and promising payment from balances built up at the Fairs.[38] Simultaneously, these and other Lucchese were the most prominent buyers of raw silk in Genoa in the last two decades of the thirteenth century. [39]In addition, then, to the bi-lateral Lucca-Champagne configuration of trade, commerce and finance, there existed a regular trilateral pattern involving Lucca-Champagne, Champagne-Genoa and Genoa-Lucca in the movement of Lucchese goods and credits. In the latter cycle,

---

[35] THOMAS W. BLOMQUIST, "The Early History of European Banking: Merchants, Bankers and Lombards of Thirteenth-Century Lucca in the County of Champagne", *The Journal of European Economic History*, 14 (1985), 521-536.

[36] On the northern organization of the cloth industry, see HENRI LAURENT, *Un grand commerce d'exportation au moyen-âge: la draperie des pays-bas en France et dans les pays méditerranéens XII-XV siècles* (Paris, 1935). Numerous contracts for the sale of northern cloth survive in the cartularies of late thirteenth-century Lucca. This material has not as yet been tabulated and I therefore cannot give precise figures. For the circulation of northern cloth in the Lucchese *contado* in 1249, see THOMAS W. BLOMQUIST, "The Drapers of Lucca and the Distribution of Cloth in the Mid-Thirteenth Century", VII (1969), 65-73.

[37] RACINE, "I banchieri piacentini", 481.

[38] GIOFFRÉ, "L'attività economica dei lucchesi a Genova", 108.

[39] RACINE, "Le marché génoise de la soie en 1288, 409.

Lucchese northern balances were shifted to Genoa by taking up funds there through *cambia* contracts drawing upon the Fairs, with this capital ultimately invested in raw silk destined for export to Lucca. It would seem that in order to return their capital to Lucca, Lucchese bankers did not employ the device of re-exchange but rather chose to invest in the northern economy, to buy northern merchandise, or to draw in Lucca — or Genoa — upon their credits at the Fairs.

* * *

If, indeed, the silence of the sources regarding re-exchange as a means of repatriating balances from abroad is a reliable indicator of the thirteenth century international merchant-banker's operations, we must seek an explanation as to why. Re-exchange was, after all, a regular feature of banking behaviour in the Late Middle Ages.[40] The solution lies, I would argue, in the way in which the linkage of the duration of the thirteenth-century *cambium* contract to the immovable period of *pagamentum* at the Fairs, conditioned exchange banking in this period.

The lag between the time a *cambium* was drawn and the fixed due date determined the duration of the contract. This in practice made for far greater variations in the length of individual contracts than was necessarily so in the following centuries when the value dates were fixed by a customary usance between two banking places. A glance at Graph V-X shows, for example, terms for contracts drawn on a specific Fair varying from a few weeks to over three months. All *cambia* drawn on a given Fair were, however, nominally due on the same date regardless of when the contract had been executed. But in deRoover's analysis of fifteenth - century foreign exchange banking, the banker's profit stemmed from a market in equilibrium — that is, between two banking places the rate had always to be higher in that place which gave its currency to the other. Between Champagne and Lucca, the former gave its currency to the latter, in the sense that the rates were quoted in the both places on the basis of the *solidus* of Provin and a variable amount of *denarii* Lucchese: for the market to have been in equilibrium, the rates would have to have been higher at any given time in Champagne than in Lucca.[41]Such a market situation, while perhaps existing from time to time, would have been im-

---

[40] MUELLER, "Chome l'ucciello di passagio", 199-200, stresses the importance of regular usance in keeping the Florence-Venice, Venice-Florence exchange in equilibrium and thus making possible a regular flow of credit between the two places via exchange and re-exchange. For further examples of these types of dealings, see DEROOVER, "Cambium ad Venetas", and GIULIO MANDICH, "Per una ricostruzione delle operazioni mercantili e bancarie della Compagnia dei Covoni", in ARMANDO SAPORI, ed., *Libro Giallo della Compagnia dei Covoni* (Milan, 1970), chapter VII.

[41] In the absence of comparable rate data from Champagne, such a situation is impossible to verify.

possible to sustain consistently — given the absence of time rates — by merely adding or subtracting at one end or the other something from the price of
exchange.

To make the point clearer, we may refer again by way of example to the
data reflecting dealings on the May Fair of Provins where the spread between
the opening and closing of trading amounted to 7% and ranged between
43.43 and 46.59 *denarii* Lucchese respectively. [42]In all, forty-three separate
*cambium* contracts were negotiated within this time span, yet all were payable on the same date. How could the northern exchange market have acco-
modated to the variation in the rates at which these contracts were concluded
and yet have retained the relationship between the points in Lucca and
Champagne demanded by deRoover's model of equilibrium? Apparently it
could not. The consequent lack of correlation between the prices of exchange
in Lucca and Champagne led to conditions that made re-exchange too uncertain a means of regularly repatriating capital to Lucca. Also in Genoa, it
should be emphasized, capital was transferred there by drawing upon balances at the Fairs instead of drawing in Champagne upon the Ligurian port.

＊ ＊ ＊

In sum, the Lucchese data shows that over the long run of some sixty
years the foreign exchange market in Lucca, based upon the Fairs of Champagne, was characterized by lengthy periods of relatve stability. Sharp read-
justments in the comparative prices of the money of Lucca and Champagne
were results essentially of monetary dislocations — the introduction of the
gold florin and the attendant decline in the value of Tuscan silver, and the
subsequent debasements of the silver coinage first in Tuscany and then in
France. The short-term run of rates from the years 1284 indicates that the volume of raw silk coming into Lucca at any given time had an important impact upon the exchange market. Large quantities of imported silk created a
correspondingly large demand for short-terms credits to settle purchases: the
resulting tight money market forced the price of the *provinois* upward while
low volumes of imports freed capital for investments in foreign exchange and
the loose money market resulted in the fall of the price of *provinois*. Seasonality in the sense that any particular Fair or Fairs generated regularly year after
year more business than others does not seem to have been a factor moving
the price of exchange. Any predictability in the behaviour of the rates derived
from the interest factor built into the points as they were quoted on given
Fairs. Bankers dealing on the Lucchese exchange could, indeed, turn specula-
tive profits but they were forced to return their capital home by drawing on
Champagne.

---

[42] See Graph V.

*Some Observations on Early Foreign Exchange Banking Based Upon New Evidence*

\* \* \*

This preliminary excursion into the Lucchese evidence bearing upon thirteenth-century exchange banking has only touched upon the surface. The general outline of the behaviour of the exchange rates over the long run needs to be refined by additional data from other places. A synthesis of Italian patterns of investments in northen Europe needs to be done. Further analysis of the short-term run of rates from 1284 [43] probing the investment strategies of the individual Lucchese merchant-banking companies has to be accomplished. Finally, an overall picture of the inter-action between Italian exchange banking and the European-wide economy of the thirteenth century must be drawn.

In the meantime, it may be hoped that this brief introduction will serve to re-open a discussion of the structures, methods and economic importance of exchange banking in the era of "The Commercial Revolution of the Thirteenth Century."

[43] The comprehensive data regarding exchange rates soon to be published by Peter Spufford should aid enormously in this task. (Now available as *Handbook of Medieval Exchange* (London, 1986).

## Graph I
### THIRTEENTH CENTURY RATES OF EXCHANGE, LUCCA-CAMPAGNE, EXPRESSED IN DENARII LUCCHESE PER SOLIDUS PROVINOIS/TOURNOIS

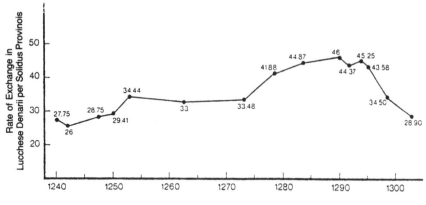

## Graph II

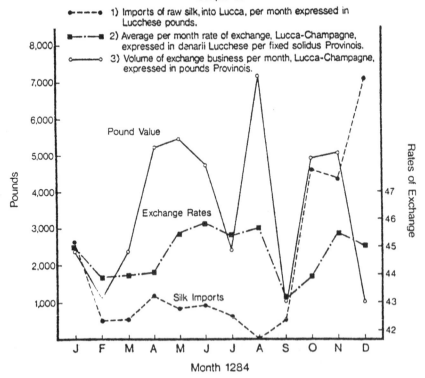

1) Imports of raw silk, into Lucca, per month expressed in Lucchese pounds.
2) Average per month rate of exchange, Lucca-Champagne, expressed in denarii Lucchese per fixed solidus Provinois.
3) Volume of exchange business per month, Lucca-Champagne, expressed in pounds Provinois.

Pound Value

Exchange Rates

Silk Imports

Month 1284

Graph III

VALUE OF EXCHANGE TRANSACTIONS IN LUCCA DRAWING
ON THE CHAMPAGNE FAIRS IN 1284 EXPRESSED IN 1000
PROVINOIS POUND UNITS

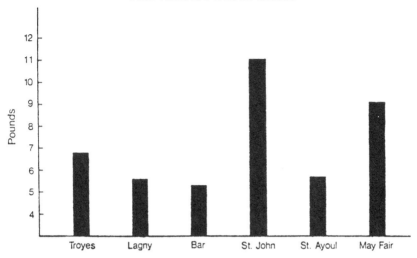

Graph IV

VALUE OF EXCHANGE TRANSACTIONS IN GENOA DRAWING
ON THE CHAMPAGNE FAIRS IN 1288 EXPRESSED IN 1000
PROVINOIS POUND UNITS. *

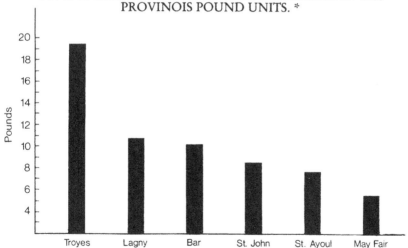

* Pierre Racine, ' I banchieri piacentini ed i campi sulle fiere di Champagne alla fine del Duecento,'
*Studi storici in onore di Emilio Nasalli Rocca,* (Piacenza, 1971), 481

*371*

## Graph V
## PROVINS-MAY FAIR (42 DOCS.)

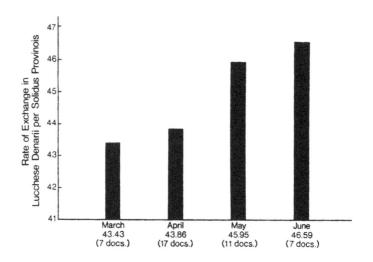

|  | March 43.43 (7 docs.) | April 43.86 (17 docs.) | May 45.95 (11 docs.) | June 46.59 (7 docs.) |

## Graph VI
## ST. REMI (30 DOCS)

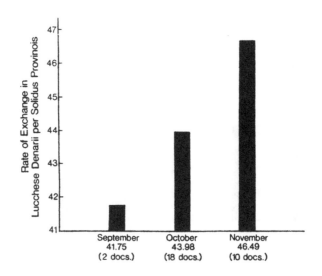

|  | September 41.75 (2 docs.) | October 43.98 (18 docs.) | November 46.49 (10 docs.) |

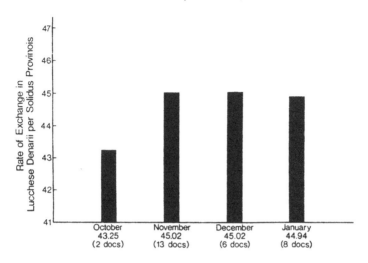

Graph VII
LAGNY (29 DOCS.)

Rate of Exchange in Lucchese Denarii per Solidus Provinois

| October 43.25 (2 docs) | November 45.02 (13 docs) | December 45.02 (6 docs) | January 44.94 (8 docs) |

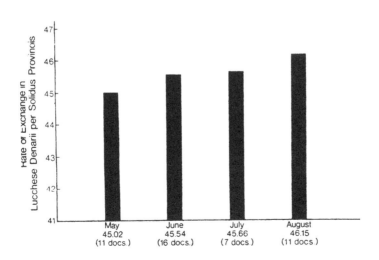

Graph VIII
ST. JOHN (45 DOCS.)

Rate of Exchange in Lucchese Denarii per Solidus Provinois

| May 45.02 (11 docs.) | June 45.54 (16 docs.) | July 45.66 (7 docs.) | August 46.15 (11 docs.) |

Graph IX
BAR (30 DOCS.)

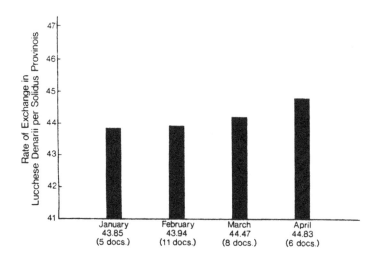

Graph X
ST. AYOUL (26 DOCS.)

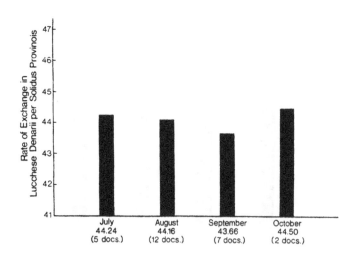

APPENDIX

The dealing of Arrigus Arnolfini, Tedicius Lamberti *de Porta* and partners between 21 March and 5 April 1284 are taken from folios 214v-244 of *Archivio di Stato in Lucca*, no. 15 (notaries Bartolomeo Fulcieri, Tegrimo Fulcieri, Fulciero Fulcieri). Under the heading "Rate" below are listed the numbers of *denarii* Lucchese per *solidus* Provinois. For analysis, see p. 365 above.

DELIVER CR

| Date | Folio | Amount Lucchese | | Amount Provinois | Fair | Rate |
|------|-------|-----------------|-----|------------------|------|------|
| 21/3 | 214 | £1,100 | 0s. 2d. | £300 | May | 44.75 |
| 1/4 | 234 | 1,833 | 6s. 8d. | 500 | May | 44 |
| 4/4 | 237v | 364 | 11s. 8d. | 100 | May | 43.75 |
| 4/4 | 239v | 1,100 | 0s. 0d. | 300 | May | 44 |
| 4/4 | 240 | 1,833 | 6s. 8d. | 500 | May | 44 |
| 5/4 | 242v | 364 | 11s. 8d. | 100 | May | 43.75 |
| 5/4 | 243 | 1,833 | 6s. 8d. | 500 | May | 44 |
| 5/4 | 244 | 372 | 18s. 4d. | 100 | Bar | 44 |
| | | £8,802 total | 1s. 8d. | £2,400 total | | 44.03 average |

TAKE R

| Date | Folio | Amount Lucchese | Amount Provinois | Fair | Rate |
|------|-------|-----------------|------------------|------|------|
| 21/3 | 214v | 1,125 | 300 | Bar-sur-Aube | 45 |
| 4/4 | 239v | 1,131 | 300 | Bar-sur-Aube | 45.5 |
| 4/4 | 240 | 1,875 | 500 | Bar-sur-Aube | 45 |
| 4/4 | 240 | 1,125 | 300 | Bar-sur-Aube | 45 |
| 5/4 | 243v | 1,875 | 500 | Bar-sur-Aube | 45 |
| 5/4 | 243v | 725 | 200 | May Fair | 43.5 |
| Totals | | 7,856 | 2,100 | average | 44,83 |

*375*

# XII

ADMINISTRATION OF A THIRTEENTH-CENTURY
MERCANTILE-BANKING PARTNERSHIP:
AN EPISODE IN THE HISTORY OF THE RICCIARDI OF LUCCA

A great deal has been written about the organization and conduct of medieval business and the recent publication of medieval account books, business letters and notarial contracts has revealed much about the organization and conduct of medieval enterprise [1]. Yet, the nature of our sources inevitably leaves some important aspects of medieval business shrouded in obscurity. One such dim area involves the administration of the thirteenth-century mercantile-banking organization which developed in Northern and Central Italy. What were the decision making processes? How were these partnerships managed? We know precious little about the internal dynamism of large-scale thirteenth-century business and each piece of information, however slight, which casts light upon the administrative side of *Duecento* practice is most welcome.

It is within this context that the appended document is of interest, for it deals with the election of executive officers of the Ricciardi partnership of Lucca, one of the most important mercantile-banking organizations of thirteenth-century Europe [2]. Our document survives as an entry in the cartulary of the notary Alluminato Parensi under the date 1 August 1296 and specifically records the choice of Conte Guidiccionis as director (*capud, gubernator, magister*) and Matteo Gottori as secretary-treasurer (*in claviam scriptorem et rationatorem librorum et denariorum*) of the Ricciardi [3]. But apart from the interest attaching to the history of this partnership, the implications of such an election

---

[1] R. DE ROOVER, "The Organization of Trade", *The Cambridge Economic History*, vol. III, Cambridge, 1963, pp. 42-118 is a brief yet excellent introduction to subject of medieval business. A. SAPORI, *Le marchand italien*, Paris, 1952, pp. 6-14 provides a bibliography of published sources relating to business history. For more recent bibliography, see the same author's *Studi di storia economica, secoli XIII-XIV-XV*, vol. II, 3rd ed., Florence, 1955, and vol. III, Florence, n.d.

[2] The only study of the Ricciardi is E. RE, "La compagnia dei Ricciardi in Inghilterra e il suo fallimento alla fine del secolo XIII ", *Archivio della Società Romana di Storia Patria*, XXXVII, 1914, pp. 87-138.

[3] ARCHIVIO DI STATO DI LUCCA, *Archivio dei Notari*, no. 24 (notary Alluminato Parensi), fol. 95. The document is cited in T. BINI, "Sui Lucchesi a Venezia: memorie dei secoli XIII e XIV ", *Atti della Reale Accademia Lucchese di Scienze, Lettere ed Arti*, XV, 1854-55, p. 129 and F. EDLER, "The Silk Trade of Lucca during the Thirteenth and Fourteenth Centuries " (Ph. D. dissertation, University of Chicago, 1930), pp. 126-128.

serve not only to illuminate medieval business practice but to suggest as well new possibilities for inquiry into the commercial and financial economy of the late-thirteenth century.

The Ricciardi organization belonged to what we may term the first generation of international mercantile-banking partnership [4]. Although many of these enterprises ended in failure in the last decade of the thirteenth and early years of the fourteenth centuries, they nonetheless mark a critical stage in the development of business organization and technique [5]. Italian merchants of the last half of the Duecento pioneered large-scale and geographically widespread enterprise centrally directed from a " home office " (described as *apotheca* in the Lucchese sources). The distinguishing feature of these new business organizations was size. Whereas the typical partnership of the first half of the century consisted of father and son combinations, several brothers, or two or three merchants combined for commercial or industrial purposes, the mercantile-banking partnerships such as the Ricciardi numbered at least nineteen partners and the Bonsignori of Siena twenty-three [6]. The apparent outgrowth of a familial nucleus, the large-scale partnerships by the late thirteenth century were open: open in the sense that in seeking fresh capital and business skills the founders welcomed as partners men from outside the immediate family circle. Of the twenty-three known partners of the Bonsignori, for example, seventeen were outsiders. The open character of the mercantile-banking partnership allowed the influx of new expertise and capital and also served to broaden the sociological base upon which international business rested.

---

[4] By " first generation mercantile-banking partnership " is here intended those enterprises having their origins in international finance and commerce in the decades of the 1260's or 1270's and obtaining the height of their development in the 1290's. Granted that the phrase is imprecise, there would yet seem to be a rhythm to the history of the Italian mercantile-banking partnership punctuated by the failures of the late-thirteenth and early-fourteenth centuries. Given this conceptualization, the Ricciardi, and Bonsignori, the Ammanati and Chiarenti of Pistoia, the Cerchi of Florence and the Scotti of Piacenza to name but a few pertain to the first generation: the Bardi and Peruzzi of Florence to the second, i.e. those partnerships which flourished in the first half of the fourteenth century.

[5] R. DE ROOVER, " The Commercial Revolution of the 13th Century ", in F. LANE and S. RIEMERSA, eds., *Enterprise and Secular Change*, London, 1953, pp. 80-82 discusses the evolution of large-scale enterprise within the broader context of a " revolution " in business technique. For the early mercantile-banking partnerships in Lucca, see T. BLOMQUIST, " Commercial Association in Thirteenth-Century Lucca ", *Business History Review*, XLV, 1971, pp. 157-177 and expecially pp. 173-177 for a register of twenty-two Lucchese partnerships engaged in international trade and commerce in the year 1284.

[6] For the Ricciardi, *ibidem*, p. 175 and for the Bonsignori, M. CHIAUDANO, " Note e documenti sulla compagnia dei Bonsignori ", in M. CHIAUDANO, *Studi e documenti per la storia del diritto commerciale italiano nel secolo XIII*, Torino, 1930, pp. 121-122.

But if the large-scale mercantile-banking partnership was better able as an institution to exploit profit opportunities on a broad geographical front, its very size gave rise to managerial and administrative problems of a corresponding magnitude. Partners, factors and agents situated abroad had to be instructed and their myriad activities coordinated. So also fundamental decisions such as when to hold a general accounting, the method of distributing profits and whether or not to extend, reorganize or liquidate the partnership had to be made.

Professor Armando Sapori, marshalling evidence primarily from the history of the Sienese Bonsignori and the Florentine Peruzzi partnerships, has argued that the day to day managerial responsibility was vested in the hands of a director who usually was a member of the family giving its name to the partnership or one of the more prominant investors [7]. In administering the affairs of the partnership the director would normally draw upon the advice and counsel of other partners resident at the home office [8]. But the central point of Professor Sapori's position is that the partners located at the home office did not constitute *conditio iuris* a distinct directorate but instead all partners had an equal right to a voice in partnership affairs [9]. Similarly, the director was responsible to his fellow partners and as long as his performance was deemed satisfactory he continued in office. But, a failure in the director's management, as measured in the balance sheet or his inability to maintain internal harmony (financial success and internal dissatisfaction were obviously conjoined) could, and indeed did in the case of the Bonsignori, result in his removal from office or at least in the circumscription of his freedom of action [10].

In light of this view what can our document tell us about the administration of the thirteenth century mercantile banking partnership? The evidence indicates the *de jure* participation of all partners in the formal election of officers. Clearly, partners stationed abroad could not take part directly in the deliberations leading up to the final choice,

---

[7] A. SAPORI, " Storia interna della compagnia mercantile dei Peruzzi ", *Studi di storia economica*, cit., vol. III, pp. 680-683.

[8] A. SAPORI, " Le compagnie mercantili toscane del Dugento e dei primi del Trecento: la responsabilità dei compagni verso i terzi ", *Studi di storia economica*, cit., vol. III, pp. 784-786.

[9] *Ibidem* and A. SAPORI, " Storia interna della compagnia mercantile dei Peruzzi ", cit., p. 660, note 1. This point turns on the larger question, which is beyond the scope of this article, of the existence in the thirteenth century of limited partnerships. For a summary of the argument see Professor Sapori's article " Le compagnie mercantili toscane " cited above. For an example of an institution which would seem to have involved limited liability, see T. BLOMQUIST, " Commercial Association ", cit., pp. 167-172.

[10] A. SAPORI, " Le compagnie mercantili toscane ", cit., pp. 786-788.

yet it is equally plain that the election was held in the name of all partners wheter physically present or no. The language of the document is straight-forward enough: the associates present in Lucca and voting did so *pro se ipsis et dicta societate et gestorio nomine pro aliis omnibus et singulis eorum sociis dicte societatis...* The voting partners therefore thought of themselves as voting not only *pro se ipsis* but — *gestorio nomine* — for their absent peers as well. Since by *gestorio nomine* we may under-stand a concept whereby a *gestor*, in this case a voting partner, per-formed an action on his own initiative without a specific mandate from a principal, in this instance the absent partner; which action the latter could subsequently modify or set aside as he saw fit[11]. There is in this no suggestion of a transference by mandate of the right to a voice in partnership decisions to the absent partner's colleagues situated in Lucca. On the contrary, the absent partner's right would seem to be specifically reinforced by the particular turn of phrase employed in the document[12].

The evidence thus weighs against the argument that those members of mercantile-banking partnership resident at the parent city constituted a quasi-juridical directorate of the partnership[13]. It is, of course, quite reasonable to assume that partners who pertained to the founding family, partners who had accumulated years of valuable business ex-perience or partners who conferred inordinately large capital sums (none of these categories are mutually exclusive) were correspondingly in-

---

[11] *Gestorio nomine* would clearly seem to be related to the classical Roman concept of *negotiorum gestor*. The essence of which was the absence of a specific mandate. *Negotiorum gestor* arose when a person acted in the interest of another during the later's absence in order to defend the absent party's rights. If the absent party specifically gave his consent or, negatively, failed to protest the action of the *gestor* after he had knowledge of the action, the legal situation was considered a mandate. See *Digest*, 3.5; and *Code*, 2.18. For a discussion of *negotiorum gestor*, see PAULY-WISSOWA, *Realenzyklopädie classischen Altertumswissenschaft, Supple-menband*, VII, Stuttgart, 1940, pp. 551-559. A brief analysis may be found in A. BERGER, *Encyclopedic Dictionary of Roman Law*, in *Transactions of the Ameri-can Philosophical Society*, n.s. vol. 43, pt. 2, Philadelphia, 1953, pp. 593-594.

[12] Common notarial form in Lucca juxtaposed the concepts of *gestor* and *procurator* to express the relationship between an absent principal and agent, who might be the principal's partner or near relative, acting on his behalf. To take the most frequent instance: when an agent entered into a contract binding himself and his principal, the usual phrase indicated that he did so *gestorio et procuratorio nomine*. It would appear significant in the present case that *procuratorio* is omitted from the formula. Procuration, of course, involved a mandate and the ability of the agent to bind the principal.

[13] M. CHIAUDANO, "Le compagnie bancarie senesi del Duecento", *Studi e do-cumenti*, cit., p. 37: "Nelle compagnie senesi si distinguono i compagni che restano in Siena, da quelli che vanno all'estero per trattare affari". See also Q. SENIGALIA, "Le compagnie bancarie senesi nei secoli XIII e XIV", *Studi senesi nel Circolo giuridico della R. Università*, XXIV, 1907, p. 306 and A. ARCANGELI, "Gli istituti del diritto commerciale nel costituto senese del 1310", in A. ARCANGELI, *Scritti di diritto commerciale ed agrario*, 3 vols., Padova, 1935-1936, I, p. 205.

fluential within the partnership [14]. The essential point, however, remains: such influence did not preclude the participation of all partners in partnership affairs.

Moreover, as Professor Sapori has pointed out, the group at the home office was hardly stable [15]. It was general managerial policy to shift personnel from post to post with some frequency. Indeed, it is noteworthy that at the time of his elevation to the post of director Conte himself was stationed in France on partnership business. Such mobility certainly militated against the emergeance of a juridically discrete directorate based upon location at the home office.

Conte's absence at the time of the election obviously did not constitute a barrier to his entrance into the highest executive office of the partnership. But, as one of the Guidiccione family, members of which had long been active in the Ricciardi enterprise, we may assume that he had a solid base of support in Lucca during the deliberations leading to the formal election [16]. And, parenthetically, it is worth suggesting that Conte's very absence may have in fact been an advantage to his candidacy since it kept him above the battle, as it were, and these were embattled times for the Ricciardi [17].

The term of office was indefinite but it is obvious that what the partners could confer the partners could also take away. The managing-partner's responsibility to his peers seems evident enough.

How was the outcome of the election determined? On this point our document is unclear although it would seem that an attempt was made to preserve at least the fiction of unanimity among those partners present in Lucca [18]. Despite the adherence of twelve partners to the ratification of the election and despite the fact that these twelve spoke *pro aliis omnibus et singulis eorum sociis* there seems to have been the desire to gain maximum, and probably unanimous, coherence of the resident partners.

---

[14] A. SAPORI, " Le compagnie mercantili toscane ", cit., p. 784 the same author's " Storia interna della compagnia mercantile dei Peruzzi ", cit., pp. 653-694 and A. SAYOUS, " Dans l'Italie à l'intérieur des terres: Sienne de 1221 à 1229 ", *Annales d'histoire économique et sociale*, III, 1931, p. 199.

[15] A. SAPORI, " Le compagnie mercantili toscane ", cit., pp. 776-777 and " Il personale delle compagnie mercantili del medioevo ", *Studi di storia economica*, vol. II, p. 700, note 2.

[16] In 1284 there were at least four of the Guidiccione active in the Ricciardi partnership; Guidiccione Guidiccionis, Paganaccius Guidi(iccionis), Riccardus quondam Pagannini Guidiccionis and Tomasinus Guidiccionis quondam Paganini Guidi(iccionis): see T. BLOMQUIST, " Commercial Association ", cit., p. 175.

[17] See below p. 7, note 22.

[18] As Professor Chiaudano, " Le compagnie bancarie senesi del Duecento ", p. 32, points out there is evidence for decision making either on the basis of a majority or by unanimous adherence in addition to one instance of the power of decision lodged in the hands of three partners. On this latter example compare the views of A. SAPORI, " Le compagnie mercantili toscane ", cit., pp. 784-786.

Giovanni Sexmundi and Guidiccione Guidiccionis were sought out in their respective homes in order that they record two codicils added to the principal document in the form of their formal agreement to the proceedings.

The choice of secretary-treasurer is intriguing. The office was an important one since the holder was charged with keeping the various sets of books generated by the typical mercantile-banking partnerships. The secretary-treasurer inevitably had his finger to the pulse of the partnership and the position certainly carried a good deal of authority [19]. We would expect then to find the encumbent a full-fledged partner. However, the Ricciardi turned to the level of factor rather than partner in filling this crucial post when they appointed Matteo Gottori secretary-treasurer for a term of office of a year and a half. Matteo was not without support within the partnership, however, as his brother Ricciardinus had long been actively associated with the Ricciardi [20]. Yet, the appointment of a non-partner and the short term are somewhat surprising in view of what we know of the policies of the Florentine Peruzzi [21].

It remains to inquire into the circumstances surrounding the election of 1296; were these procedings typical or atypical of Ricciardi administrative practice? On 1 August, the date on which the election was formalized by a notarial instrument, the two offices in question were apparently vacant. Conte's term as director became effective upon his return from France while in the meantime Ricciardinus Gottori was to serve as interim manager. Had this been a routine election to choose a successor to a retiring encumbent we would expect that the latter would continue in office until the newly elected were able to assume his duties. But this was not the case. Nor is there a reference to the former secretary-treasurer which suggests that that office was likewise vacant. Unless, of course, death had simultaneously carried off the previous director and secretary-treasurer, a highly unlikely turn of events, it would seem that both former incumbents had stepped-down concurrently and in such circumstances as precluded either from continuing in office, even on a care-taker basis, until Conte's return.

The partnership in the 1290's had experienced mounting difficulties which by 1296 had led to the appointment of arbiters who were to try in

---

[19] A. SAPORI, " Il personale delle compagnie mercantili del medioevo ", cit., pp. 698-699 describes the *scrivani e segretari* as ranking in authority just under *il capo e direttore.*

[20] Ricciardinus was a partner of the Ricciardi in 1284 (T. BLOMQUIST, " Commercial Association ", cit., p. 175).

[21] A. SAPORI, " Storia interna della compagnia mercantile dei Peruzzi ", cit., pp. 684-685.

vain to bring order to the Ricciardi's tangled affairs [22]. Given this crisis, it is reasonable to argue that the former holders of these executive offices had resigned probably under pressure, and that the choice of Conte and Matteo represents the wresting of power from an old, and patently unsuccessful, directorate.

It seems doubtful then that we should construe this elections as routine administrative procedure, for evidently it took place in the context of internal discord connected with the failing fortunes of the partnership. However, such a conclusion does not obviate the important facts of administrative responsibility to the partners as well as the right of partners to a voice in partership affairs. In short, our document explicitly confirms Professor Sapori's interpretation of the managerial structure of the thirteenth-century mercantile-banking partnership while throwing light upon the procedural mechanism, a formal election, which animated that structure.

By way of conclusion, however, our document and the issues to which it gives rise may be placed in a somewhat wider historical context. Despite Re's works, for example, there is still much to be learned about the later years of the Ricciardi partnership. The details of the mounting crisis, the response to that crisis and the events of the ultimate demise of the partnership are all important objects of future research.

Moreover, these questions in turn suggest broader lines of inquiry. What were the inter-relationships between the failures of the Ricciardi, the Bonsignori and the other first-generation mercantile-banking partnerships? Is the evidence sufficient to warrant postulating an Italian-wide banking crisis? Were these failures symptomatic of the levelling off of medieval prosperity; or, on the other hand, were they simply isolated instances of over-extension of resources and internal disorganization coupled with simultaneous financial and political pressures from the kings of France, and England as well as the papacy? Another suggestive avenue of investigation involves the connections between the banking failures of the late-thirteenth century and the wave of internal social upheaval which erupted concurrently, at least in Tuscany, in the form of Black-White factionalism. For Lucca at least the relationship between

---

[22] E. RE, "La compagnia dei Ricciardi in Inghilterra", cit., pp. 104-123 discusses the problems of the Ricciardi in Northern Europe and attributes their difficulties to the outbreak of hostilities between Edward I and Philip IV both of whom were clients of the partnership. From 1294 onward the situation of the Ricciardi operating in England and France became increasingly precarious and by 1295 had led to internal strife among the partners in Lucca. For the appointment of four arbiters charged a *rivedere et sentensiare li chointi de li chompagni perche ci ae a rimettere lo faccia* (*Ibidem*, pp. 120-121).

the social disorder erupting in 1300 and the crisis afflicting her major
mercantile-banking organization certainly warrants attention [23].

## APPENDIX

Labor condam Ghirarducci Volpelli
Adiutus condam Guilielmi Rosciompeli
Bertaloctus condam Bugianensis Bandini
Dinus condam Domini Soffredi Tadolini
Arrigus condam Tegrimi de Podio
Riccardu condam Paganini Guidiccionis
Bendinus Panichi
Saracinus condam Albertini Macchi
Raynerius condam Ghirardi Maghiari
Vante condam (condam repeated) Curradi Honesti
Ricciardinus condam Domini Bonifatti Gottori
Vannes filius dicti Adiuti                                  qui omnes
sunt socii societatis apothece Ricciardorum de Luca, pro se ipsis et dicta societate
et gestorio nomine pro aliis omnibus et singulis eorum sociis dicte societatis, quod
hec omnia singula infrascripta ratificabunt et approbunt et firma et rata habebunt
per omnia fecerunt et constituerunt et firmaverunt ut dictum est in eorum et
cuiusque eorum et dicte societatis capud gubernatorem et magistrum Contem condam Alderini Guidiccionis eorum et dicte societatis consocium absentem in partibus
Francie tamquam presentem in omnibus et singulis negotiis et aliis rebus que modo
pertinent vel in antea pertinebunt ad dictos socios et ipsam societatem apothece
Ricciardorum et in omnibus et singulis aliis que spectare videbuntur et spectabunt
ad dictum Contem ratione dicti officii cuius officium esse intelligantur et incipiat
a die sue reversionis ad civitatem Lucanam in antea.

Item simili modo dicti socii pro se ipsis et dicta societate et ut dictum est
fecerunt et constituerunt eorum et dicte societatis in magistrum et capud et gubernatorem Riccardum predictum presentem et suscipientem in omnibus et singulis
in quibus fecerunt et constituerunt dictum Contem per omnia cuius officium du-
raret debeat et duret et durare intelligatur ab hodie usque ad reversionem dicti
Contis ad civitatem Lucanam et non ultra.

Item dicti socii pro se ipsis et aliis eorum sociis et dicta societate ut dictum
est et dictus Ricciardus tamquam capud gubernator et magister dicte societatis et
sociorum apotheca Ricciardorum simili modo et ut dictum est hoc presenti scripto

---

[23] For the events of the Black-White split in Lucca, see the contemporary
account of Tolomey of Lucca in B. SHMEIDLER, ed., *Tholomei lucensis annales*,
in *Monumenta germaniae historica, Scriptores rerum germanicorum*, n.s. VIII,
Berlin, 1930, pp. 318-319. It should also be noted that in the split between the
Blacks and Whites in Lucca virtually all Lucchese international mercantile-bankers
adhered to the conservative White faction: compare the list of those branded
*casastici et potentes* in S. BONGI - L. DEL PRETE, eds., *Statuto del Comune di Lucca
dell'anno MCCCVIII*, Lucca, 1867, pp. 241-244 with the list of partners of the
various Lucchese mercantile-banking partnerships in T. BLOMQUIST, " Commercial
Association ", cit., pp. 157-177.

fecerunt et constituerunt et elegerunt in eorum et cuiusque sociorum et dicte societatis Ricciardorum Matheum condam Bonifatii Gottori factorem dicte societatis et
sociorum in clavanum scriptorem et ratiotinatorem librorum et denariorum dicte
societatis et sociorum Ricciardorum hinc ad kalendas januarii futuras et ab inde
ad unum annum prosimum subsequentem duraturum.

Actum Luce in domo Domini Andree condam Domini Parenti Ricciardi et
Dominorum Filippi et Ricciardi condam Domini Ranerii Ricciardi ubi dicti socii
detenent eorum apothecam. Coram Salembene condam Guidi notarii et Matheo
condam Orlandi Trentacoste et Guido condam Orlandi civibus lucanis testibus
ad hiis rogatis A.N.D. MCCLXXXXVI indictione VIIII die primo mensis Augusti,
ante tertiam.

Post hoc, suprascriptis anno indictione et die, Luce in domo Johannis Symonetti condam Bonifatii Sexmundi, coram dictis testibus. Johannes consocius predictorum Labri et altrorum et dicte societatis, auditis et intellectis plenane omnibus
et singulis suprascriptis, eis omnibus et singulis consentiet et ea omnia et singula
ratificavit et approbavit et fecit per omnia ut supra alii eius consocii fecerunt
et constituerunt.

Post hoc, suprascriptis anno indictione et die, in domo Guidiccionis condam
Paganini Guidiccionis posita extra et iusta fossam lucani comunis socii predictorum
sociorum et dicte societatis, coram predictis Matheo et Guido. Suprascriptus
Guidiccione auditis et intellectis omnibus suprascriptis ea omnia et singula ratificavit et approbavit et firma habuit et similiter fecit.

Ego Alluminatus Jacobi notarius hoc scripsi.

# XIII

## De Roover on Business, Banking, and Economic Thought

The untimely death of Raymond de Roover in March 1972 removed one of the major figures from the field of medieval economic history. Now there has appeared a collection of eleven of de Roover's articles, one of them not previously published, to remind us of the magisterial quality of their author's contributions to our knowledge of medieval business and banking techniques and the milieu in which the medieval man of business operated.[1] The volume was edited by Professor Julius Kirshner of the University of Chicago and is prefaced by two incisive and informed introductory essays: one by the editor, entitled "Raymond de Roover on Scholastic Economic Thought" and the other by Professor Richard Goldthwaite of Johns Hopkins, "Raymond de Roover on Late Medieval and Early Modern Economic History." The articles, which de Roover himself helped select, are grouped under three headings: "Business History and History of Accounting," "History of Banking and Foreign Exchange," and "History of Economic Thought." The first rubric offers "The Story of the Alberti Company of Florence: 1302-1348, as Revealed in Its Account Books" (1958), "A Florentine Firm of Cloth Manufacturers" (1941), and "The Development of Accounting prior to Luca Pacioli according to the Account Books of Medieval Merchants" (1956). The second category contains "What is Dry Exchange? A Contribution to the Study of English Mercantilism" (1944), "New Interpretations of the History of Banking" (1954), "Cambium ad Venetias: Contribution to the History of Foreign Exchange" (1957), and "The Antecedents of the Medici Bank: The Banking House of Messer Vieri di Cambio de' Medici" (1965). The last grouping consists of "Monopoly Theory prior to Adam Smith: A Revision" (1951), "Scholastic Economics: Survival and Lasting Influence from the Sixteenth Century to Adam Smith" (1955), "The Scholastic Attitude toward Trade and Entrepreneurship" (1963), and the posthumous "Gerard de Malynes as an Economic Writer: From Scholasticism to Mercantilism." The volume concludes with a chronologically organized bibliography of de Roover's publications. Taken as a whole the selections provide an excellent introduction to their author's work as well as a point of departure for comment upon his role as an economic historian.

Raymond de Roover brought a rare combination of background and

---

[1] Raymond de Roover, *Business, Banking and Economic Thought in Late Medieval and Early Modern Europe: Selected Studies of Raymond de Roover.* Edited by Julius Kirshner (Chicago and London: The University of Chicago Press, 1974. Pp. viii, 383). Hereafter cited as *Business, Banking and Economic Thought.*

training to his studies of medieval business.[2] Born in Antwerp in 1904 where his father was a successful industrialist, he studied business administration and accountancy before coming to the United States and the Harvard Graduate School of Business in 1936. His formal education was augmented by practical experience in a bank and as head of the accounting department of a shipping firm. Although thus engaged in a business career, de Roover utilized his spare moments to pursue in the Antwerp archives his interest in the history of accounting. This interest eventually led him to Bruges in search of account books older than those of the sixteenth century available in his native city. These part-time researches resulted in the mastery of the technical problems of dealing with medieval account books, and he was able to publish in this period a number of articles dealing with accounting techniques, money-changing, and business organization.[3]

In 1936, just before leaving Europe, Raymond de Roover married the American scholar Florence Edler. By the time of her marriage Dr. Edler had written her dissertation on the silk industry of Lucca and had published the still standard *Glossary of Mediaeval Terms of Business*.[4] Her training in history was to aid and complement her husband's knowledge and experience of the technical side of business. In effect the two formed a team, and de Roover was frequent and frank in acknowledging the debt to his wife.

Although de Roover's arrival at Harvard was hardly fortuitous—Mrs. de Roover returned to a position in Cambridge as a Resident Associate of the Mediaeval Academy of America—it was nonetheless a case of the right man in the right place at the right time. N. S. B. Gras had successfully pushed the cause of business history within the Business School while Abbott Payson Usher had already published on the early history of deposit banking in the Mediterranean.[5] Both men were to nourish and influence the interests of the thirty-two year old Belgian. As de Roover later acknowledged it was Gras who stimulated "the emphasis on mana-

[2] The biographical material that follows is taken from the prefaces to de Roover's *The Rise and Decline of the Medici Bank, 1397-1494* and *Money, Banking, and Credit in Mediaeval Bruges*, both cited in full below; from David Herlihy, "Raymond de Roover, Historian of Mercantile Capitalism," *The Journal of European Economic History*, I (1972), 755-762; from Richard Goldthwaite's prefatory article and de Roover's biographical entry in *American Men of Science: Social and Behavioral Sciences*, (11th ed.; New York and London, 1968).

[3] L. A. Carmen, "Researches of Raymond de Roover in Flemish Accounting of the Fourteenth Century," *The Journal of Accountancy*, LX (1935), 111-122.

[4] Florence Edler, *Glossary of Mediaeval Terms of Business, Italian Series 1200-1600* (Cambridge, Mass., 1934).

[5] A. P. Usher, "The Origins of Banking: The Primitive Bank of Deposit, 1200-1600," *The Economic History Review*, IV (1934), 399-428; and the later, *The Early History of Deposit Banking in Mediterranean Europe* (Cambridge, Mass., 1943).

gerial problems, on business policy, and on administration."[6] In particular, his views on the stages of the growth of capitalism were to influence directly de Roover's formulation of his concept of the "commercial revolution of the thirteenth century."[7] Usher's work on early banking, again in de Roover's own words, "provided the starting point from which I have gone on to develop the theory of interest in exchange and to find the solution to other puzzling problems concerning the mechanism of the medieval money market."[8]

After taking his M.B.A. in 1938, de Roover moved to his wife's alma mater, the University of Chicago, where he continued his work in economics under John U. Nef and received a Ph.D. in 1943. It is ironic that although much of de Roover's training and teaching (until 1961) took place in departments of economics,[9] he adopted a rather skeptical attitude toward social science methodology, the new economic history, and especially toward what he clearly viewed as a naive fascination with mathematics and the computer. In particular, he chided economists for believing that the history of economic thought began with Adam Smith and for remaining steadfastly ignorant of the contributions of the scholastics to their discipline.[10] De Roover was also wary of the economists' theoretical models, but it seems to me that he was somewhat ambivalent about the relationship of economic theory to economic history. Although he insisted that historical research must be guided by theory, I believe that by theory he really meant a working hypothesis rather than theory in the social scientific sense of the term. De Roover was above all an empiricist whose method was, in the words of Robert Lopez, "first gather the facts, explain the smaller problems that each of them involves, and finally see what general theory, if any, can be built upon them."[11] De Roover did indeed evolve a guiding theory but it was one set firmly upon the foundation of empirical data.

The unifying theme of de Roover's work was the concept of "The Commercial Revolution of the Thirteenth Century."[12] By this he meant literally a revolution, "a drastic change in the methods of doing business

[6] R. de Roover, *Money, Banking, and Credit in Mediaeval Bruges: Italian Merchant-Bankers, Lombards, and Money-Changers* (Cambridge, Mass., 1948), p. viii.
[7] Gras' views were stated fully in his *Business and Capitalism: An Introduction to Business History* (New York, 1939).
[8] De Roover, *Bruges*, p. viii.
[9] De Roover taught at Wells College and Boston College. Not until moving to Brooklyn College in 1961 did he have a full-time appointment in history.
[10] See his remarks in *La pensée économique des scholastiques: doctrines et méthodes* (Montreal and Paris: Institute d' Etudes Medievales, 1971), pp. 9-18.
[11] Robert S. Lopez, "Italian Leadership in the Medieval Business World," THE JOURNAL OF ECONOMIC HISTORY, VII (1948), 63.
[12] R. de Roover, "The Commercial Revolution of the Thirteenth Century," *Bulletin of the Business Historical Society*, XVI (1942), 34-39, reprinted in F. Lane and J. Riemersma, eds., *Enterprise and Secular Change* (Homewood, Ill., 1953), pp. 80-85.

or in the organization of business enterprises," occuring in Italy and dividing the Middle Ages into two distinct periods of business and commercial history. The period of "petty capitalism," extending to about the middle of the thirteenth century, was dominated by the travelling merchant who accompanied his goods to foreign markets. The succeeding period, which endured until the industrial revolution, marked the stage of mercantile or commercial capitalism, and was differentiated from the first by the figure of the sedentary merchant. Thus, prior to that time international commerce was based upon the Fairs of Champagne where travelling merchants from Italy and Provence met their Northern counterparts and exchanged the luxury wares of the south for Flemish cloth. Around the beginning of the fourteenth century, however, the Italians began to by-pass the fairs and to deal directly with the cloth producing centers of the Low Countries where they established permanent branches managed from the counting house located in the home city of the firm. In consequence, Italian business organization became more complex, centering upon the large-scale mercantile-banking partnership formed for a longer duration than the single-venture associations of travelling merchants. Bookkeeping developed from the crude personal accounts suitable to the needs of the travelling merchant into more complex methods, first the bi-lateral form and eventually double entry. Financial techniques also developed with the same chronological rhythm: the letter of exchange evolved out of the thirteenth-century promise to pay, and exchange dealings came to dominate international banking. De Roover's interpretation of these developments, which he believed resulted in an Italian commercial and financial hegemony over Western Europe, were spelled out most fully in an excellent summary article, "The Organization of Trade" in Volume III of *The Cambridge Economic History*.[13] Whether writing the history of a particular medieval enterprise, explicating the workings of the medieval money market or the techniques of bookkeeping, or analyzing scholastic economic thought, each of de Roover's studies was firmly linked to the intellectual construct of the commercial revolution, and despite his fondness for repeating old arguments, each piece added new clarity to the picture.

In *Money, Banking, and Credit in Mediaeval Bruges*, which won the Charles Homer Haskins medal of the Mediaeval Academy of America, de Roover expanded upon his earlier work with fourteenth-century account books to examine the financial institutions and credit techniques of that city. In fourteenth- and fifteenth-century Bruges he found three distinct types of credit activity and three classes of money-dealers: the Italian mercantile-bankers; the Lombards, that is, Italian money-lenders and pawnbrokers; and the money-changers who also occupied themselves with local deposit and transfer banking. These distinctions were critical to de Roover's interpretation of the early history of banking and became

---

[13] R. de Roover, "The Organization of Trade," in M. M. Postan, E. Rich, and E. Miller, eds., *The Cambridge Economic History of Europe*, III (Cambridge, 1963), 42-118.

intimately related conceptually to the ecclesiastical doctrine of usury and the evolution and practical application of the foreign exchange transaction.

De Roover's central tenet in explaining the origins of banking was that it developed out of exchange, both manual and foreign, and not out of credit extension, as André Sayous held. The money-changers graduated into the field of deposit and transfer banking while the Italian merchant-bankers, after establishing themselves in the major markets of Western Europe around 1300, turned to the negotiation of foreign bills. The latter were forced into this channel by the Church's prohibition against the taking of interest on loans (*mutuum*). The foreign exchange contract, however, was considered licit by the jurists and moralists primarily because it was not a loan and because risk was involved. Thus, as de Roover pointed out in his magisterial *L'évolution de la lettre de change (XIVᵉ-XVIIIᵉ siècles)*,[14] and in the articles "New Interpretations of the History of Banking" and "Early Banking before 1500 and the Development of Capitalism"[15] as well as in other works, religion indeed affected the development of capitalism, but not in the way that Max Weber believed. Catholicism, according to de Roover, did not retard capitalism but changed the course of its evolution by precluding the discounting of foreign bills and retarding the development of negotiability. Consequently medieval and early modern practice differed from modern techniques in that prior to 1800 banking was synonymous with the buying and selling of bills of exchange rather than with the discounting of commercial paper.

De Roover explored further the workings of foreign exchange in a later book, *The Bruges Money Market around 1400*, which included a statistical supplement by Hyman Sardy. The result was a mathematical confirmation of de Roover's analysis of the role of interest upon the rates of exchange as well as additional support for his postulate of a negative balance of trade of the North with Italy.[16] In other words, as de Roover proclaimed, perhaps somewhat smugly, the computer and statistical analysis had merely confirmed what had been determined by traditional historical methodology.

In agreement with de Roover, I would regard the matter of interest built into rates of foreign exchange as settled. I find, however, the relationship between the Church's usury doctrine and the techniques of medieval banking difficult to accept in the form he sets out. In the first

[14] Paris, 1953.
[15] De Roover, "New Interpretations of the History of Banking," *Journal of World History*, II (1954), 38-76; *Business, Banking, and Economic Thought*, pp. 200-238; and "Early Banking before 1500 and the Development of Capitalism," *Revue internationale d'histoire de la banque*, IV (1971), 1-16.
[16] *The Bruges Money Market around 1400, with a Statistical Supplement* by Hyman Sardy, Verhandelingen van de Koninklijke Vlaamse Academie voor Wetenschappen, Letteren en Schone Kunsten van Belgie (Brussels, 1968); also R. de Roover, "La balance commerciale entre Pays-Bas et l'Italie au quinzième siècle," *Revue belge de philologie et d'histoire*, XXXVII (1959), 374-386.

826

place, what can really be known about the practical consequences of the usury prohibition on the conduct of business and on the form of business institutions?[17] From the work of Benjamin Nelson and John Noonan,[18] among others, we know a good deal about what individual jurists and moralists thought on the subject of usury, but is this really sufficient to support the weight of de Roover's theory? Secondly, the cartularies of medieval notaries do reveal after all an economic world in which seemingly everyone was lending to everyone else through the contractual medium of the *mutuum*, or straight loan.[19] The practice appears so widespread that in San Gimignano as early as 1228 the communal statutes expressly permitted the taking of up to 20 percent interest on loans.[20] Professor Lopez has indicated that twenty percent was also considered a legitimate return on loans in Genoa, and Frederic C. Lane has pointed out that in Venice a kind of businessmen's standard of usury was enacted, different from the strict ecclesiastical definition, and also admitting 20 percent as a legitimate return.[21] Lane further states that in seeking to explain every medieval departure from modern business practice the tendency has been to ascribe the difference to the effect of the usury laws even when the older forms can be satisfactorily explained by their suitability to the economic conditions of the times.[22] Without entering further into the thicket of the controversy over the medieval usury doctrine, I would simply suggest that banking and dealings in exchange took the forms they did because they were suitable to contemporary economic requirements and were perhaps more closely linked to the needs of the medieval international merchant-banker to transfer credit from place to place than de Roover thought. It may be, however, that we are only dealing here with a problem of emphasis since I would not want to deny the long-run influence of the scholastic position on usury upon business attitudes. In any case, whatever the impact of the moralists, de Roover has definitely described for us the techniques of the medieval banker.

De Roover was ultimately interested in the problems of management, organization, and function of business, and was at his finest as a scholar when writing about individual firms. Although he contributed a number

[17] An interesting, if not conclusive attempt to evaluate the impact of the usury doctrine is B. N. Nelson, "The Usurer and the Merchant Prince: Italian Businessmen and the Ecclesiastical Law of Restitution, 1100-1550," THE JOURNAL OF ECONOMIC HISTORY (Supplement), VII (1947), 104-122.

[18] B. N. Nelson, *The Idea of Usury* (Princeton, 1949) and J. T. Noonan, *The Scholastic Analysis of Usury* (Cambridge, Mass., 1957).

[19] This statement is based upon my own reading in the mass of thirteenth-century notarial contracts preserved in the Tuscan city of Lucca.

[20] E. Fiumi, *Storia economica e sociale di San Gimignano* (Florence, 1961), p. 87, n. 286.

[21] R. S. Lopez, *La prima crisi della banca di Genova (1250-1259)* (Genoa, 1956), pp. 34-35, and F. C. Lane, "Investment and Usury," in F. C. Lane, *Venice and History: The Collected Papers of Frederic C. Lane* (Baltimore, 1966), p. 64.

[22] *Ibid.*, pp. 60-61.

of essays on the history of accounting, he viewed bookkeeping not as a kind of mystical science but rather as a functional part of management.[23] His intimate understanding of accounting permitted him to peer over the shoulders of the medieval man of business, to perceive his mistakes and to sympathize with his problems, as few other scholars could or would. While still at Harvard de Roover wrote the prize-winning essay, "A Florentine Firm of Cloth Manufacturers: Management and Organization of a Sixteenth-Century Business," based upon the Medici materials in the Selfridge Collection at the Baker Library.[24] By an exhaustive examination of the account books of two partnerships formed for the manufacture of woolen cloth by members of a sixteenth-century branch of the Medici family, de Roover was able to offer a generalized picture of the organization of the Florentine woolen industry considerably at variance with the older views of Alfred Doren. In his study of the industry Doren had relied primarily upon fourteenth-century gild statutes which afford virtually no insights into the day to day operations of individual enterprises. As a result he depicted an industry based upon large manufacturies which he insisted were essentially capitalist in scale and organization.[25] De Roover, on the other hand, working with the records of a single firm which he assumed to be more or less typical, revealed an industry based upon relatively small shops of modest capitalization and only an indirect control over labor. He concluded this early study with an appeal for greater scholarly appreciation of the administrative problems faced by sixteenth-century businessmen. The owner of a Florentine wool shop, he argued, was an entrepreneur operating in a highly competitive and complex industry, not even a merchant and hardly a great capitalist in Doren's mold.

By the early 1940's de Roover had shown what an assiduous reading of account books could reveal and in subsequent years he continued his research in the Medici papers at Harvard, focusing upon the enterprise controlled by the fifteenth-century ruling family. In 1948 he published a monograph on the Medici Bank,[26] but in the following two years Mrs. de Roover discovered much new material in the Florentine Archivio di Stato, including the secret account books (*libri segreti*) in a mislabeled bundle which she urged her husband to use in an expansion of his earlier

---

[23] See especially "The Development of Accounting Prior to Luca Paccioli according to the Account-books of Medieval Merchants," in A. C. Littleton and B. S. Yamey, eds., *Studies in the History of Accounting* (Homewood, Ill., 1956), pp. 114-174; also *Business, Banking, and Economic Thought*, pp. 119-180.

[24] R. de Roover, "A Florentine Firm of Cloth Manufacturers: Management and Organization of a Sixteenth-Century Business," *Speculum*, XVI (1941), 3-33 and *Business, Banking, and Economic Thought*, pp. 85-118.

[25] A. Doren, *Studien aus der Florentiner Wirtschaftsgeschichte*, Vol. I, *Die Florentiner Wollentuchindustrie vom 14. bis zum 16. Jahrhundert* (Stuttgart, 1901) and *Storia economica dell'Italia nel Medio Evo*, trans. Gino Luzzatto (Bologna, 1936), pp. 485-495.

[26] R. de Roover, *The Medici Bank* (New York, 1948).

828

study. These form the backbone of de Roover's classic of business history, *The Rise and Decline of the Medici Bank, 1397-1494.*[27]

The last years of de Roover's life were increasingly occupied with the study of economic thought as developed by the scholastic Doctors from the thirteenth through the seventeenth centuries and with the influence of the schoolmen upon mercantilist and liberal economics.[28] In this area as in his reconstruction of business practice and institutions de Roover insisted upon the legacy that the medieval world bequeathed to modern capitalist society. He postulated a clear thread of economic theory running from Thomas Aquinas through the late scholastics to Gresham, Malynes, Misselden, Mun and the mercantilists on the one hand, and through the seventeenth-century moral philosophers Grotius and Pufendorf to Frances Hutchinson and his pupil Adam Smith on the other.[29] De Roover's arguments in favor of the medieval scholastics and his effort to reincorporate their doctrines into the mainstream of the history of economic thought received considerable impetus from the posthumous appearance in 1954 of Joseph Schumpeter's monumental, prestigious, and —among economists—controversial *History of Economic Analysis.*[30] Schumpeter's death left de Roover to defend the field and to carry the battle to the doubters.[31]

He proved more than adequate to the task of refining and providing the historical underpinning to Schumpeter's theoretical edifice. The last major work to appear before de Roover's death, *La pensée économique scholastique: doctrines et méthodes* marshalled the evidence and the arguments put forth in his earlier articles in order to answer the question

[27] Cambridge, Mass., 1963; paper edition, New York, 1966; Italian translation, *Il Banco Medici dalle origini al declino, 1397-1494* (Florence, 1970).

[28] See "Monopoly Theory prior to Adam Smith," *Quarterly Journal of Economics,* LXV (1951), 492-524; *Business, Banking and Economic Thought,* pp. 273-305; reprinted in R. E. Mulcahy, *Readings in Economics* (Westminster, Md., 1959), pp. 168-190; "Scholastic Economics: Survival and Lasting Influence from the Sixteenth Century to Adam Smith," *Quarterly Journal of Economics,* LXVIII (1955), 161-190; *Business, Banking and Economic Thought,* pp. 306-335; "Joseph A. Schumpeter and Scholastic Economics," *Kyklos,* X (1957), 115-146; "The Concept of the Just Price: Theory and Economic Policy," THE JOURNAL OF ECONOMIC HISTORY, XVIII (1958), 418-434; reprinted in James A. Gherity, ed., *Economic Thought: A Historical Anthology* (New York, 1965), pp. 23-41 and I. H. Rima, ed., *Readings in the History of Economic Theory* (New York, 1970), pp. 9-21; "The Scholastic Attitude toward Trade and Entrepreneurship," *Explorations in Entrepreneurial History,* 2nd. ser., I (1963), 76-87; *Business, Banking and Economic Thought,* pp. 336-345; reprinted in M. J. Kitch, ed., *Capitalism and the Reformation* (London, 1967), pp. 95-103; and *La pensée économique des scholastiques.*

[29] De Roover considered the economics of the mercantilists inferior to both the Schoolmen and the liberal economists. In addition to the works cited above, see R. de Roover, *Thomas Gresham on Foreign Exchange* (Cambridge, Mass., 1949), pp. 278-287, and the posthumous article "Gerard de Malynes as an Economic Writer," in *Business, Banking and Economic Thought,* pp. 346-366.

[30] Joseph A. Schumpeter, *A History of Economic Analysis,* ed. Elizabeth Boody Schumpeter (New York, 1954).

[31] See the remarks of Guy Fourquin, "Raymond de Roover, historien de la pensée économique," *Revue historique,* DVII (1973), 19-34.

*De Roover*

"if and to what degree was Schumpeter right or wrong" in asserting that the skeleton of Adam Smith's thought derived from the scholastics and the moral philosophers.[32] He considered Schumpeter's synthesis "a rapid and incomplete glance" at the economic doctrines of the scholastics and clearly felt that more work needed to be done before the history of economic analysis could be set straight. With de Roover's death it remains to be seen whether these lines of inquiry will be pursued.

But there was another, more practical, side to de Roover's interest in scholastic economic attitudes, for he insisted that the schoolmen's thought, although based on first principles, did not develop in isolation from the real world nor did it fail to affect the realm of everyday business affairs. The two fourteenth-century Tuscan saints, Bernardino and Antonino, whom de Roover regarded as "the two great economic thinkers of the Middle Ages" were men familiar with the market place and whose pronouncements from the pulpit fell upon attentive ears.[33] Thus the scholastic formulation of the usury doctrine altered the form of medieval banking while scholastic thought influenced the legislation enacted into public law by the ruling business class.[34]

In a singular article, "Labour Conditions in Florence around 1400: Theory, Policy, and Reality,"[35] de Roover set out to demonstrate the interaction between the theories expounded by the moralists on monopoly, price, and value and the behavior and attitudes of the ruling class in Florence at the time of the Ciompi rebellion in 1378. He harked back to his earlier analysis of the fragmented character of the Florentine woolen industry in which the relatively small shop owners had no control either over prices of raw materials or of their finished product, both of which were determined by conditions in distant markets. In these circumstances labor proved the only cost which the owners could effectively control, and they were ruthless in their practical efforts to contain the demands of the working man and particularly to put down any attempts by the workers to form collectives. The posture of the owners, however, was in perfect harmony with scholastic economic doctrine which viewed as anathema any interference—except on the part of the state—with the workings of the free market in establishing the "just price." Since the moralists considered labor a commodity, its value like that of any other good was to be determined through the mechanism of the free market—in which, of course, the owners held the trump cards. Furthermore, de Roover argued that the scholastic view of monopolies, which in theory condemned gilds as well as brotherhoods of wage-earners, was incorpo-

---

[32] De Roover, *La pensée économique scholastique*, n. 9.

[33] *San Bernardino of Siena and Sant'Antonino of Florence: The Two Great Economic Thinkers of the Middle Ages* (Boston, 1967).

[34] R. de Roover, "La doctrine scholastique en matière de monopole et son application à la politique économique des communes italiennes," in *Studi in onore di Amintore Fanfani*, I (Milan, 1962), 151-179, and "The Scholastics, Usury and Foreign Exchange," *Business History Review*, XLI (1967), 257-271.

[35] N. Rubinstein, ed., *Florentine Studies: Politics and Society in Renaissance Florence* (Evanston, Ill., 1968), pp. 277-313.

830

rated into public law, at least with respect to gilds of workers. In short, the Florentine ruling class in its suppression of labor organizations was acting in perfect tune with prevailing economic teachings and traditional policy. Here as in his other works de Roover's affinity with the man of business is manifest. It should be pointed out, however, that few if any scholars would have formulated the probem in the terms de Roover did, and by so doing he has provided us with an additional dimension to the economic reality of the Middle Ages.

Raymond de Roover worked at a time when the theories of Sombart and Weber on the sixteenth-century origins of capitalism still colored the scholarly vision of the economic structure of the Middle Ages. As recently as 1948 in the pages of this journal Carl Stephenson, lamenting *vox clamantis in deserto* the influence of Sombart and Weber upon interpretations of medieval commercial development, was constrained to plead "Will some reader of this journal, a better economist than I can ever be, please try to advance the argument from here on?"[36] No one responded with greater skill and energy to the need articulated in Stephenson's appeal than Raymond de Roover. It is to him and to others of his generation, Lopez, Lane, and Reynolds in this country, and Luzzatto, Renouard, Sapori, and Melis on the continent, to name a few, that we owe the dispersal of the idealist mist which not so long ago enshrouded the landscape of the medieval economy.

[36] C. Stephenson, "In Praise of Medieval Thinkers," THE JOURNAL OF ECONOMIC HISTORY, VIII (1948), 29.

[37] For a discussion of recent trends in medieval economic history, see the bibliographical essay by David Herlihy, "The Economy of Traditional Europe," THE JOURNAL OF ECONOMIC HISTORY, XXXI (March 1971), 153-163.

# Alle origini del «Grosso» toscano: la testimonianza delle fonti del XIII secolo*

L'introduzione delle monete auree locali nel sistema monetario europeo occidentale nel 1252 segna la conclusione logica di una serie di riforme attuate da varie città del Nord Italia durante i cent'anni precedenti.[1] Sebbene Genova avesse preceduto Firenze nella coniazione d'una moneta d'oro, fu il « fiorino d'oro » che dominò i mercati monetari per il successivo secolo e mezzo.[2] Considerando l'introduzione dell'oro dal punto

---

* Devo esprimere un ringraziamento particolare al Professor Emilio Cristiani che ha letto sia la versione inglese sia quella italiana di questo saggio. Vorrei anche ringraziare il Dottor Alan M. Stahl, Curator of Medieval Coins, The American Numismatic Society, New York, e la Professoressa Cristine Meek, Trinity College Dublin, per le loro critiche e commenti. E inoltre ringrazio mia moglie, Clelia Palmerio Blomquist, che mi ha aiutato nella traduzione dall'inglese in italiano. La responsabilità per le interpretazioni e per il linguaggio è, senz'altro, mia.

[1] Per la battitura delle monete «grossi» sia nell'Europa ultramontana che in Italia: P. GRIERSON, *The Origins of the Grosso and of Gold Coinage in Italy*, « Numismatichý Sbornik », XII, 1971-72, pp. 33-48. Sulla coniazione dei grossi di Genova e di Venezia in anticipo su quelli toscani: R. LOPEZ, *Prima del ritorno all'oro nell'Occidente duecentesco,* « Rivista storica italiana », LXXIX, 1967, pp. 174-181; L. ROBBERT, *Reorganization of the Venetian Coinage by Doge Enrico Dandolo,* « Speculum », XIL, 1974, pp. 48-60. Per la storia monetaria di Lucca in questa epoca: D. MASSAGLI, *Introduzione alla storia della zecca e della moneta lucchesi,* Lucca, Giusti 1870 (« Memorie e documenti per servire alla storia di Lucca », XI, 2ª parte).

[2] Per i retroscena dell'emissione delle monete d'oro a Genova e Firenze: R. LOPEZ, *Settecento anni fa: il ritorno all'oro nell'Occidente duecentesca,* « Rivista storica italiana », LXV, 1953, pp. 19-55, 161-198; ID., *Back to Gold, 1952,* « The Economic History Review », s. II, vol. IX,

di vista della storia della Toscana, si può dire che l'emissione del fiorino rese attuale il sistema di contare i valori monetari in « libre », « solidi » e « denarii » ereditato dal mondo carolingio. In questo sistema tradizionale, il denaro era la sola moneta battuta: il soldo equivaleva a 12 « denarii » e la « libra » era equivalente rispettivamente a 20 « solidi » e 240 « denarii ». Poiché sia la lira sia il soldo erano in effetti multipli astratti del denaro, Carlo Cipolla li nominò « monete fantasma ».[3] In Toscana, tuttavia, fra gli ultimi anni del decennio 1220 e il 1252 questi fantasmi divennero realtà; prima di tutto con l'emissione di una moneta d'argento più grande, detta « grossus », del valore di 12 denari, e poi con la materializzazione della lira nella forma del fiorino d'oro che apparve equivalente a 20 soldi oppure 240 denari.

Quantunque questo sistema simmetrico, che unisce le denominazioni di moneta di conto con i valori delle monete reali, non fosse permanente (a lungo andare la volubilità dei prezzi del mercato dell'oro e dell'argento e lo svilimento dei denari d'argento resero impossibile il mantenimento di stabili rapporti fra il fiorino d'oro e le monete frazionarie),[4] gli sforzi delle città toscane di produrre una moneta più grande e sta-

---

1956-57, pp. 219-240; M. BERNOCCHI, Le monete della Repubblica fiorentina, III, Firenze, Olschki 1976, p. 58 sgg. Sull'importanza del fiorino d'oro nel commercio internazionale: C. CIPOLLA, Moneta e civiltà mediterranea, Venezia, N. Pozza 1957, p. 33 (in inglese con titolo, Money Prices and Civilization in the Mediterranean World, Princeton, Princeton U. P. 1956); ID., The Monetary Policy of Fourteenth Century Florence, Berkeley, U. of California Press 1982, pp. XI-XIV (Non ho potuto servirmi del testo originale italiano, Il fiorino e il quattrino: la politica monetaria a Firenze nel Trecento, Bologna, Il Mulino 1982); T. WALKER, The Italian Gold Revolution of 1252: Shifting Currents in the Pan-Mediterranean Flow of Gold, in Precious Metals in the Later Medieval and Early Modern Worlds, a cura di J. RICHARDS, Durham, Carolina Academic Press 1983, pp. 29-52.

[3] C. CIPOLLA, Moneta e civiltà cit., p. 47.

[4] C. CIPOLLA, Moneta e civiltà cit., pp. 40-46; ID., The Monetary Policy cit., passim; ID., Le avventure della lira, Bologna, Il Mulino 1975, pp. 52-54. Il rapporto stabile fra il fiorino d'oro e le monete d'argento frazionarie era finito almeno dagli anni 1260: cfr. più avanti alla nota n. 53.

bile, conveniente ai fabbisogni di una popolazione in sviluppo e di un'economia commerciale in espansione, ebbero nondimeno un effetto notevole per la storia economica e monetaria dell'Occidente. Nel presente saggio vorrei ripercorrere a ritroso tale processo evolutivo fino agli inizi della tendenza toscana verso una stabilità monetaria, e specificamente vorrei prendere in considerazione gli eventi che condussero all'apparizione del «solidus» di conto mediante la coniazione del grosso toscano.

Prima di procedere bisogna comunque premettere un'avvertenza metodologica. Nel corso delle analisi seguenti sarà mio intento la ricostruzione dei valori intrinseci di vari tipi di monete.[5] Nel fare così, mi baserò sui dati raccolti, per la maggior parte dei casi, nei documenti privati che esprimono generalmente valori in termini di monete di conto piuttosto che in termini di denominazioni monetarie specifiche. Certamente si sarebbe avuto un aiuto molto maggiore se i registri delle zecche o altri tipi di documenti ufficiali fossero stati conservati per indicare le denominazioni e le caratteristiche delle monete toscane esistenti fra il dodicesimo e il tredicesimo secolo. Purtroppo, salvo qualche eccezione, documenti del genere non esistono e dobbiamo adoperare il materiale a nostra disposizione nel miglior modo possibile.

Il tema che mi propongo di esaminare in questa sede è stato acutamente indagato da David Herlihy, Carlo Cipolla, Mario Bernocchi e da Maria Luisa Ceccarelli Lemut.[6] Benché i

---

[5] Per qualche difficoltà e problema nello stabilire i valori intrinseci: F. LANE-R. MUELLER, *Money and Banking in Medieval and Renaissance Venice*, I, *Coins and Moneys of Account*, Baltimora-London, J. Hopkins U. P. 1985, pp. 44-64 e più avanti, nota n. 7.

[6] D. HERLIHY, *Pisan Coinage and the Monetary History of Tuscany, 1150-1250*, in *Le zecche minori toscane fino al XIV secolo*, Rastignano, Editografica s. d. (*Atti del 3° Convegno Internazionale di Studi: Centro Italiano di Studi di Storia e Storia dell'Arte*, Pistoia 1967), pp. 169-192 (Una prima versione inglese è comparsa sotto lo stesso titolo in «The American Numismatic Society Museum Notes», VI, 1954, pp. 143-168: tutte le citazioni seguenti vengono date seguendo la versione in *Le zecche minori*); C. CIPOLLA, *Le avventure della lira* cit., pp. 32-37 e note

risultati di questi studiosi siano ben fondati, rimangono comunque alcune contradizioni fra di loro che, mi pare, debbono essere chiarite. Particolarmente, mi interessa la identificazione del « denaro » locale sulla cui base si precisò il valore del grosso toscano. I calcoli teorici degli studiosi suddetti relativi al contenuto d'argento dei denari di Pisa e Siena – le monete su cui essi presumono che il valore del grosso fosse basato – non corrispondono alle già note caratteristiche del grosso stesso.[7]

Non più tardi dell'anno 1240, le cinque zecche maggiori di Toscana battevano un esemplare di grosso. Ognuno di questi grossi era uguale a 12 denari locali;[8] e ogni grosso ebbe

---

nn. 46-48; C. Bernocchi, *Le monete* cit., pp. 125-134; M. L. Ceccarelli Lemut, *L'uso della moneta nei documenti pisani dei secoli XI e XII*, in G. Garzella, M. L. Ceccarelli Lemut, B. Casini, *Studi sugli strumenti di scambio a Pisa nel Medioevo*, Pisa, Pacini 1979, pp. 49-127.

[7] D. Herlihy, *Pisan Coinage* cit., pp. 180-181 dà un peso di 0,7 grammi per i denari pisani e senesi intorno al 1190 mentre C. Cipolla, *Le avventure della lira* cit., p. 46 e nota n. 48, ipotizza una perdita a causa del logorio di peso di 0,8 grammi. Poiché la cifra di Herlihy è fondata sul dato documentario che i denari pisani e senesi erano battuti ad un tasso di quaranta per oncia di lega – tasso che torna per la cifra di 0,7 grammi e anche dà un peso teorico che si conforma a quello attuale dei denari pervenutici – ho accettato questa norma come base dei successivi calcoli. Dobbiamo, comunque, tenere conto che questi calcoli sono « teorici ».

Per quanto riguarda il problema dei valori intrinseci, D. Herlihy, *Pisan Coinage* cit., pp. 184-185, osservando le caratteristiche della zecca senese, arriva ad un contenuto teorico d'argento del 25 %, ovvero 0,175 grammi, per i denari rinforzati di Pisa e Siena verso l'anno 1190. C. Cipolla, *Le avventure della lira* cit., p. 26, note nn. 35 e 46, basando i suoi calcoli sul cambio fra il marco di Colonia e il denaro pisano dà un intrinseco per quest'ultimo di 0,19 grammi d'argento intorno al 1200. C. Bernocchi, *Le monete* cit., p. 131, similmente sulla base del cambio fra il marco di Colonia e il denaro pisano arriva ad una lega per questo ultimo di 0,1948 grammi nell'anno 1200. Inoltre, M. L. Ceccarelli Lemut, *L'uso della moneta* cit., p. 70, stabilisce un denaro pisano dell'anno 1179 di 0,19 grammi d'argento. Si veda più avanti alla nota n. 36.

[8] C. Bernocchi, *Le monete* cit., pp. 137-138, indica cinque documenti datati dall'11 marzo 1250 fino all'11 maggio 1252 che dimostrano che i grossi di Arezzo, Firenze, Lucca, Pisa e Siena circolavano ad un cambio di 1:12 con i denari di Pisa. Il denaro pisano, a sua volta, era equivalente a quello senese: cfr. D. Herlihy, *Pisan Coinage* cit., 183-184. Firenze non ha battuto un « denarius » fino all'anno 1258: cfr. C. Bernocchi, *Le monete*, p. 143. Il denaro lucchese equivaleva a quelli di Pisa e Siena. Per quanto riguarda Lucca e il cambio fra un grosso e il denaro, vedi *inter alia*: Lucca, Archivio Capitolare, LL 11, f. 116, 29 maggio

un valore intrinseco uguale, nonostante le differenze icono-grafiche. Dal fatto che i grossi erano dello stesso valore in-trinseco e dal fatto che ogni grosso era emesso ad un cambio di dodici denari consegue che un denaro toscano di valore co-mune era inferiore di qualche punto rispetto al grosso.[9] Ma quando, e come, la Toscana arrivò ad un « denarius » comune? E quale delle città toscane – Pisa, Siena o Lucca – decretò un intrinseco per la moneta sul cui tipo il grosso si sarebbe ba-sato?

I decenni che si iniziarono col 1180 e il 1190 furono anni nei quali i comuni toscani tendevano alla ricerca di unità monetaria regionale, benché si dovrebbe aggiungere che tale processo era apparentemente intervallato da alcune esitazioni. Lucca, per esem-pio, nel 1181 si accordò con Pisa, precisando, fra le altre cose, la divisione a metà dei profitti delle operazioni delle proprie zec-che e la circolazione libera delle monete da ciascun Comune nel territorio dell'altro.[10] Nononstante queste convenzioni, nel 1184 Lucca fu persino d'accordo di condividere anche con Firenze i profitti – dopo aver dedotto la metà dovuta ai Pisani – deri-vanti dalla coniazione dell'argento portato dai Fiorentini alla zecca lucchese.[11] Si presumerebbe che gli stessi Fiorentini ritor-nassero a casa con le monete lucchesi che, malgrado il dominio del denaro pisano sul mercato fiorentino, continuarono a cir-

---

1237; solidos XXV « bonorum denariorum lucensium parvorum vel dena-rios XXV grossorum lucensium »: LL 17, f. 111*v*, 4 dicembre 1243 in cui il cambiavalute, Vethus « quondam » Deotifeci, ha dato in prestito £ 3 « denariorum lucensium ». oppure 60 « denarios grossos de argento ».

[9] Sul fatto che si poteva intercambiare i grossi delle zecche maggiori toscane vedi: D. HERLIHY, *Pisan Coinage* cit., pp. 189-190 e C. BERNOC-CHI, *Le monete*, pp. 137-138. Per Lucca, vedi *inter alia*: LUCCA, Archivio Capitolare, LL 11, f. 16, 26 marzo 1236; « tot denarios grossos pisanos et lucenses »: LL 17, f. 16, 28 febbraio 1243; « solidos XLI denariorum lucensium grossorum argenti florentine, aretine et senensis »: LL 17, f. 42*v*, 23 maggio 1243; « scilicet tot grossos lucenses florentinos et are-tinos.

[10] Cfr. oltre alle pagine 250 sgg.

[11] *Documenti dell'antica costituzione del comune di Firenze*, a cura di P. SANTINI, I, Firenze, G. P. Vieusseux 1895 («Documenti di storia italiana», X), p. 20, doc. n. 14.

colare nelle città dell'Arno.[12] Inoltre, Pisa e Siena verso il 1181 emisero « denarii » uguali in peso e in lega.[13] In questo modo le strutture monetarie dei comuni toscani principali si erano interconnesse, e con l'emissione del grosso comune degli anni quaranta del secolo XIII – forse il risultato di una lega monetaria – la marcia verso l'unità monetaria si sarebbe completata.[14]

In pratica, la Toscana per secoli aveva costituito una singola area monetaria. Dal periodo tardo-carolingio fino alla

---

[12] C. Bernocchi, *Le monete* cit., pp. 129-131 documenta l'uso continuo della moneta lucchese in Firenze, nonostante l'uso crescente di quella pisana. Cfr. oltre alla nota n. 17.

[13] D. Herlihy, *Pisan Coinage* cit., p. 183, indica che Siena ha incominciato a coniare moneta nei primi anni del decennio 1190. Il *Regestum senense: Regesten der urkunden von Siena*, a c. di F. Schneider, Roma, Loescher 1911 («Regesta chartarum Italiae», VIII), pp. 118-119, doc. n. 307 riferisce «C lib. den. sen» e cfr. *Il cartulario della Berardenga*, a c. di E. Casanova, Siena, Lazzari 1914, doc. 183, che anche riporta questa prima menzione documentaria delle monete di Siena. M. L. Ceccarelli Lemut, *L'uso della moneta* cit., 66, nota n. 57, afferma che Siena non avrebbe potuto aprire la sua zecca prima del giugno 1181.

[14] Sulla congettura di una lega monetaria toscana che abbia stabilito l'emissione del grosso, cfr.: D. Herlihy, *Pisan Coinage* cit., pp. 189-190; R. Lopez, *Back to Gold* cit., p. 238; Id., *Settecento anni fa* cit., p. 46, nota n. 46; D. Promis, *Monete della Repubblica di Siena*, Torino, Stamperia Reale 1868 (estratto dalle «Memorie della Reale Accademia delle Scienze di Torino», s. II, vol. XXIV), p. 22, avanza l'opinione dell'esistenza di una lega monetaria toscana. M. Chiaudano, *Le compagnie bancarie senesi nel Duecento*, in *Studi e documenti per la storia del diritto commerciale italiano nel secolo XIII*, Torino, Istituto Giuridico della R. Università 1930 («Memorie dell'Istituto Giuridico», s. II, vol. VIII), pp. 1-152; a p. 24, nota n. 3, suppone pure l'esistenza d'una lega e a questo proposito cita le deliberazioni del Consiglio Generale di Siena: il 3 gennaio 1244 era deliberato «quod cudatur moneta grossa secundum modum et ordinamentum quod nunc et de moneta parva nichil fiat salvo quod si alie civitates Tuscie mutarent eorum monetas»; nell'agosto 1255 ambasciatori fiorentini e lucchesi comparirono di fronte al Consiglio e pregarono «tam de moneta senense et fiorentina et lucana fienda et cudenda unius ponderis et unius valoris»; il 5 gennaio 1256 era discusso «quod moneta grossa et minuta cudatur et fiat secundum modum et pondus monete florentine et pisane et aliarum monetarum Tuscie». Mi sembra comunque che queste testimonianze indichino che Siena unilateralmente, e qualche volta a malincuore, abbia mantenuto la sua moneta alla pari con quella delle altre città toscane. Dunque, invece di una lega formale che dirigesse la politica monetaria toscana in quest'anni, mi pare di vedere l'esistenza di una serie di accordi *ad hoc* come quelli stipulati negli anni 1180 fra Lucca-Firenze, Lucca-Pisa e Pisa-Siena che ebbero, come risultato quello di creare, in pratica, un'unione monetaria.

metà del dodicesimo secolo Lucca aveva operato come sola
zecca nella regione e le sue monete fornirono un unico esemplare monetario per tutta la Toscana.[15] Pisa fu la prima dei
comuni toscani a battere una moneta in competizione con il
denaro lucchese. Il più antico documento che si riferisce alla
moneta pisana è datato 1149; e questi «denarii» di Pisa co-
stituiscono una sfida notevole all'egemonia monetaria lucchese.[16]
Dal 1200 la moneta pisana, benché non avesse destituito com-
pletamente di importanza la moneta lucchese, sembra che fosse
la moneta più apprezzata in Toscana al di fuori della stessa
città di Lucca.[17]

Il primo «denarius» pisano nacque come imitazione ap-
prossimativa del denaro di Lucca contemporaneo. Sebbene nes-
sun esemplare della prima moneta sia rimasto né alcun esemplare possa essere identificato,[18] le accuse di contraffazione lan-

---

[15] F. PANVINI ROSATI, *La monetazione delle zecche minori toscane
nel periodo comunale*, in *Le zecche minori* cit., pp. 131-144; ID., *Note di
numismatica pisana*, «Rivista italiana di numismatica e scienze affini», s.
VI, vol. LXXVIII, 1976, pp. 209-219: p. 213; C. CIPOLLA, *Le avventure
della lira*, p. 20 sgg.

[16] M. L. CECCARELLI LEMUT, *L'uso della moneta* cit., p. 56, fornisce la data del 1149. D. HERLIHY, *Pisan Coinage* cit., p. 179, dà l'anno
1151 come primo riferimento documentario di una moneta pisana. L.
LENZI, *Zecche e monete di Pisa prima e dopo la Meloria*, in *1284: L'anno
della Meloria*, Pisa, ETS Editrice (s. d.), pp. 131-166; a p. 148, cita una
notizia messa in luce dalla CECCARELLI LEMUT, *L'uso della moneta* cit.,
pp. 56-57 relativa per l'anno 1131 si riferisce a «argenti optimi soldos mille,
probate monete pisane». Il Lenzi crede che questa indichi che Pisa abbia
battuto moneta da quella data. Ma mi pare molto improbabile che Pisa
avesse coniato moneta fra il 1131 e il 1149 senza lasciare indicazioni nei
documenti.

[17] Cfr.: D. HERLIHY, *Pisan Coinage* cit., p. 181 per il crescente uso
della moneta pisana in tutta la Toscana dopo l'anno 1181 a scapito di
quella già dominante di Lucca; C. BERNOCCHI, *Le monete* cit., p. 130, sot-
tolineando l'importanza della moneta di Pisa in Firenze nota, comunque,
che nel 1208 Firenze usa ancora ufficialmente la moneta di Lucca e di
altre città.

[18] Il *Corpus nummorum italicorum*, XI, *Toscana (zecche minori)*, Roma, Cecchini 1929, pp. 69-71, data i denari tipo «H» di Lucca agli anni
1039-1125 e (pp. 71-72) assegna denari lucchesi tipo «F», per Federico
I, agli anni 1152-1190. O. MURARI, *Sui denari di Pisa e di Lucca dell'imperatore Federico I*, «Rivista italiana di numismatica e scienze affini»,
LXXX, 1978, pp. 143-148, ha suggerito che i denari tipo «F» attribuiti

ciate dai Lucchesi verso i Pisani suggeriscono la presenza di notevole affinità numismatica fra le due monete.[19] Quindi, si può dedurre che il « denarius » pisano, come la sua controparte lucchese, portò al rovescio il monogramma dell'Imperatore Enrico III ed era simile, se non proprio uguale, al peso e alla lega del denaro lucchese. Invero, le due monete sono quasi invariabilmente collegate nelle fonti con la formula di pagamento specificata in « libras denariorum pisanorum vel lucensium », o con espressioni simili.[20] Inoltre, ambedue i sistemi monetari seguirono un parallelo processo di svilimento, approssimativamente, per i tre decenni seguenti.

David Herlihy ha osservato che fra il 1164 e il 1179 la moneta lucchese-pisana subì un declino della sua lega di quasi metà, crollando da 0,35 grammi circa a 0,19 grammi d'argento puro.[21] A questo punto, vorrei comunque proporre l'ipotesi che verso il 1181 lo svilimento delle due monete sia stato ancora più forte di questo presunto declino del 50 %. Consideriamo le testimonianze.

---

dal C.N.I. (*Corpus Nummorum Italicorum*) a Lucca in effetti erano battuti da Pisa; il C.N.I., p. 287, cita cinque primi denari tipo « F » che attribuisce a Pisa ma che si presentano « di rozza struttura e con leggende confuse ».

[19] D. HERLIHY, *Pisan Coinage* cit., pp. 180-181. O. BANTI, *A proposito della questione della moneta lucchese nel secolo XII e di un accordo monetario fra Pisa e Lucca del 1319*, « Quaderni ticinesi: numismatica e antichità classica », VII, 1978, pp. 291-304; F. PANVINI ROSATI, *Note di numismatica pisana*, « Rivista italiana di numismatica e scienze affini », LXXVIII, 1976, pp. 209-219: pp. 217-218; ID., *La monetazione* cit., p. 134, hanno ritenuto che il denaro pisano fosse un'imitazione di quello lucchese in peso e lega ma non nelle caratteristiche iconografiche.

Per le accuse contemporanee di falsificazione pisana, cfr. *Tholomei lucensis annales*, a c. di B. SCHMEIDLER, Berlin, Weidmannsche Buchandlung 1930 (« Monumenta Germaniae historica, Scriptores rerum germanicarum », n. s. vol. VIII), pp. 49, 62, 65, 72-73 e *Annali genovesi di Caffaro e dei suoi continuatori dal MXCIX al MCCXCIII*, a cura di L. T. BELGRANO-C. IMPERIALE DI SANT'ANGELO, II, Genova, R. Istituto Sordo-Muti 1901 (« Fonti per la storia di Italia », XII), p. 9.

[20] Per l'uguaglianza delle due monete in questo periodo, cfr. D. HERLIHY, *Pisan Coinage* cit., pp. 179-183 e M. L. CECCARELLI LEMUT, *L'uso della moneta* cit., p. 70; C. CIPOLLA, *Le avventure della lira* cit., p. 42.

[21] Cfr. D. HERLIHY, *Pisan Coinage* cit.

Nel 1181 le due città, Pisa e Lucca, come abbiamo visto, conclusero un accordo che forse costituì la più antica convenzione monetaria conosciuta in Europa.[22] Oltre all'accordo di dividere i profitti delle loro zecche, le due città stabilivano che la moneta pisana doveva essere chiaramente differenziata da quella lucchese con l'uso del monogramma « F » per l'Imperatore Federico, oppure « C » per Corrado, da un lato; mentre i Lucchesi avrebbero continuato ad adoperare la tradizionale « H », e si sarebbero messi i monogrammi di Lucca e di Pisa rispettivamente sui lati opposti. I consoli pisani che giurarono di mantenere le condizioni dei patti promisero anche di cominciare a battere queste monete nuove entro un mese e di smettere di contraffare le monete lucchesi.

Per quanto riguarda i pesi delle due monete c'è qualche incertezza. Nel testo dei giuramenti conclusi dai consoli pisani e lucchesi pubblicato da Carli-Rubbi, la parte pisana afferma che la moneta di Pisa doveva essere più larga di quella di Lucca.[23] Lo storico pisano Raffaello Roncioni, scrivendo nel 1606, diceva che la moneta pisana doveva essere più grande, « facendosi maggiore quella dei Pisani » di quella lucchese.[24] Ancora, la nuova edizione dei documenti che riguardano gli stessi patti, curata da Maria Luisa Ceccarelli Lemut, ripete che le monete pisane emesse secondo le condizioni della convenzione dovevano essere più grandi di quelle di Lucca.[25] D'altra parte, il cronista pisano Maragone e lo storico secentesco Paolo Tronci

---

[22] Il patto consiste di due giuramenti; l'uno fatto dai consoli pisani e l'altro fatto dai consoli lucchesi. I testi erano pubblicati da G. R. CARLI-RUBBI, *Delle monete e dell'istituzione delle zecche d'Italia*, II, Pisa, Giovanelli 1757, pp. 150-170. M. L. CECCARELLI LEMUT, *L'uso della moneta* cit., pp. 92-120, ha messo insieme una serie di documenti riguardanti l'accordo che include un nuovo testo dei due patti pubblicati dal Carli-Rubbi.

[23] G. R. CARLI-RUBBI, *Delle monete* cit., p. 155: « et quod ipsa Moneta Pisana debeat maior esse Lucana Moneta in magnitudine amplitudinis et rotunditatis ».

[24] R. RONCIONI, *Delle istorie pisane libri XVI*, a c. di F. BONAINI, I, Firenze, G. P. Viesseux 1844, p. 401. Cfr. M. L. CECCARELLI LEMUT, *L'uso della moneta* cit., pp. 95-97.

[25] M. L. CECCARELLI LEMUT, *L'uso della moneta* cit., p. 103.

affermarono che le monete di Pisa e di Lucca dovevano essere dello stesso peso.[26] Il professor Herlihy comunque ha pensato che l'affermazione relativa alle monete più pesanti di Pisa, che si trova nella redazione di Carli-Rubbi, fu in realtà una aggiunta più tarda,[27] ma gli avvenimenti, come vedremo, confermano che poco dopo la convenzione del 1181 Pisa emise una nuova moneta, « novus denarius »; mentre nello stesso tempo Lucca emetteva una moneta svilita, nominata nei documenti come « denarii lucenses novi et bruni ».

Il primo accenno all'esistenza di un « novus denarius » di Pisa è databile al 20 settembre 1182, quando la frase « veteres monete », cioè « monete vecchie », fu usata in un documento pisano.[28] La definizione di « moneta vecchia » presuppone l'esistenza di una nuova moneta; un documento del 1192 attesta che dodici « novi denarii » pisani valevano quattordici dei vecchi denari.[29] Questo rapporto rappresenta una rivalutazione del 16 % in confronto alla vecchia moneta. Benché nessuna di queste nuove monete pisane sia pervenuta – oppure almeno non possa essere individuata – è possibile, paragonandola ai denari di Siena comparsi circa allo stesso tempo, stabilire le sue caratteristiche.[30] La frase « denariorum senensium vel no-

---

[26] B. Marangone, *Annales pisani*, a c. di M. Lupo Gentile, Bologna, Zanichelli 1936 (« Rerum italicarum scriptores », VI, 2), pp. 72-73: « et la moneta del colore et medesimo peso ». Cfr. anche la versione emendata di questo passo in M. L. Ceccarelli Lemut, *L'uso della moneta* cit., pp. 95-97, e pp. 97-98 per il testo di Tronci che dice « che i Pisani dovessero batter le monete del medesimo peso e valore di quelle di Lucca ».

[27] D. Herlihy, *Pisan Coinage* cit., p. 181, nota n. 30.

[28] M. L. Ceccarelli Lemut, *L'uso della moneta* cit., p. 62. La prima notizia trovata da D. Herlihy, *Pisan Coinage* cit., p. 182, è datata 1° ottobre 1190.

[29] M. L. Ceccarelli Lemut, *L'uso della moneta* cit., data il primo cenno documentario di un « novus denarius » al 23 gennaio 1191. La prima indicazione di tale moneta trovata da D. Herlihy, *Pisan Coinage* cit., p. 182, è del 17 marzo 1192. Per il rapporto di 12:14, cfr. R. Davidsohn, *Storia di Firenze*, tr. G. B. Klein, I, Firenze, Sansoni 1956, p. 1195.

[30] O. Murari, *Sui denari di Pisa e di Lucca* cit., pp. 143-148, conclude che la moneta pisana tipo « F » sia stata battuta subito dopo l'accordo fra Lucca e Pisa del 1181.

vorum pisanorum » appare in un documento redatto a Travale
nel 1215 e pertanto sembra che il denaro di Siena, per primo
emesso nel 1181, fosse fondato sulle norme della moneta nuova
e rinforzata di Pisa.[31] Inoltre, dagli ordinamenti della zecca
senese sappiamo che questo denaro pesava 0,7 grammi ed aveva
il 25 %, ossia 0,175 grammi, d'argento puro.[32] Questi calcoli
presentano comunque incertezze e difficoltà.

Abbiamo osservato che intorno al 1180 si apprende che il
denaro di Pisa e di Lucca ·era stato dimezzato di valore durante
i precedenti cinquant'anni risultando un denaro pisano-lucchese
con un valore intrinseco all'incirca di grammi 0,19.[33] Questo
calcolo, però, non concorderebbe con il regolamento della zecca
senese che indicò un nuovo denaro senese-pisano di 0,175 grammi d'argento.[34] La notizia dell'emissione di una nuova moneta
pisana di un valore del 16 % in più del suo precedente segne-
rebbe un valore intrinseco della vecchia moneta di circa 0,15
grammi piuttosto che di 0,19.[35] Questo conteggio di 0,15 grammi, suggerirebbe inoltre, un deterioramento della moneta toscana verso il 1181 più forte di quanto i documenti sopravis-
suti vorrebbero farci credere. Più importante, tuttavia, per i

---

[31] F. SCHNEIDER, *Regestum senese* cit., pp. 236-238, doc. n. 535. M.
L. CECCARELLI LEMUT, *L'uso della moneta* cit., p. 66; D. HERLIHY, *Pisan Coinage* cit., p. 183. Cfr. sopra, nota n. 13.

[32] D. PROMIS, *Monete della Repubblica di Siena* cit., p. 77, doc.
n. 1, per le caratteristiche del denaro senese nell'anno 1250: « et monetam
senensem tenebo [il podestà] et teneri faciam rectam et legalem in pon-
dere et argento, videlicet de XL per unciam et de tribus unceis argenti
per libram ponderatam ad pondus senese et consolatam in bulgano ».
Però se Siena avesse avuto in vigore lo standard di 25 % (tre oncie
su dodici), cioè 0,175 grammi d'argento, nei primi anni del 1250, signi-
ficherebbe che, per quanto riguardava le altre città toscane, i Senesi
avevano già scelto la via monetaria unilaterale. Infatti, abbiamo visto sopra (nota n. 14) che nell'anno 1244 il Consiglio Generale di Siena di-
chiarò di non fare niente per quello che riguardava il coniare denaro
fino a che le altre città toscane non avessero alterato la lega dei loro
denari. Anche cfr. sopra, nota n. 7.

[33] Cfr. sopra, nota n. 21.

[34] Cfr. sopra, nota n. 32.

[35] 0,15 grammi x 16 % = 0,024 grammi: 0,024 grammi + 0,15
grammi = 0,175 grammi.

nostri fini deve essere il fatto che il calcolo di un denaro rinforzato a 0,175 grammi (oppure a 0,19) d'argento non si accorda con le norme conosciute della moneta di grossi coniata dalle zecche di Pisa, Siena e Lucca fra il 1220 e il 1230. Poiché il grosso fu battuto ad un peso di 1,7-1,8 grammi, 90-96 % puro (che doveva sempre riferirsi ai dodici denari locali), è evidente che la Toscana ha conosciuto una prima emissione di un denaro il cui peso era costantemente di 0,7 grammi, che conteneva, però, qualcosa come 0,135 grammi invece di 0,175 (oppure 0,19) grammi d'argento.[36]

Se Pisa e Siena, come ho riferito più sopra, rivalutarono il loro denaro del 16 per cento, passando da 0,15 a 0,175 grammi d'argento nel 1181, sembrerebbe che Lucca nello stesso

---

[36] D. HERLIHY, *Pisan Coinage* cit., p. 189, indica un valore intrinseco di « approximately » 96 % d'argento puro e C. BERNOCCHI, *Le monete* cit., p. 142, di 93,4 % per la lega del grosso che doveva pesare 1,7-1,8 grammi. Grazie all'impegno di Dottor Alan Stahl e *The American Numismatic Society*, sedici grossi toscani furono sottoposti ad una prova di « neutron activation ». Il saggio è piccolo e fortuito; però dimostra che il grosso era un pezzo abbastanza forte. I sedici campioni passano da 99,6 % a 77,8 % d'argento puro e contengono una lega d'argento media per volume di 88,13 %. Riflettendo su questi dati, mi sembra opportuno ipotizzare un grosso teoricamente 90-96 % fine, sebbene il contenuto d'argento tipico sia probabilmente più vicino alla percentuale più bassa che a quella più alta. Utilizzando queste cifre, possiamo stabilire i parametri dei valori intrinseci sia dei grossi sia dei denari (dei quali il grosso era un multiplo). Per il grosso i parametri sono: dal lato alto, 1,8 grammi × 96 % = 1,72 grammi e dal lato basso, 1,7 grammi × 90 % = 1,53 grammi. Dunque, la lega fine del denaro comune toscano all'epoca del grosso doveva restare fra 0,144 grammi (1,72 grammi ÷ 12 = 0,144) e 0,127 grammi (1,53 ÷ 12 = 0,127) di argento. Il BERNOCCHI, *Le monete* cit., p. 131, come abbiamo visto, ha calcolato un denaro pisano del valore intrinseco di 0,1948 grammi; poi descrive un grosso fiorentino dell'anno 1237 che conteneva 2,3908 grammi di argento e che pesava 2,4954 grammi. Anche il CIPOLLA, *Le avventure della lira* cit., p. 36, scrive che il grosso delle zecche toscane doveva contenere circa 2,3 grammi d'argento fino e valeva 12 denari pisani o lucchesi del tempo. P. GRIERSON (riportato dal BERNOCCHI, p. 138, nota 1), « è del parere che il valore del grosso, indicato nei documenti pari a 1/100 del marco di Colonia, sia dovuto ad un prezzo politico e che in realtà Firenze abbia battuto, nel secolo XIII, un unico grosso, corrispondente agli esemplari che conosciamo ». Né Herlihy né Ceccarelli Lemut si occupano del rapporto fra i calcoli del valore del denaro pisano e quelli del grosso.

arco di tempo abbia deprezzato il suo denaro approssimativamente del 10 %. In un documento datato 7 novembre 1183 nel Registro del Monastero di Camaldoli si allude a questo denaro svilito come a « denarii lucenses novi et bruni » – « denari lucchesi nuovi e scuri » – che non possono significare altro che una moneta recente svilita.[37] Ancora una volta, nell'anno 1185, le fonti citano i « denarii minuti lucenses » – « denari piccoli », che pure indicherebbero lo svilimento della moneta lucchese nel periodo immediatamente seguente al patto del 1181 con Pisa.[38] Se presumiamo che la svalutazione del denaro lucchese sia stata circa del 10 % della moneta di 0,15 grammi d'argento puro, arriviamo ad un pezzo con un intrinseco di 0,136 grammi. E questa cifra, quando è moltiplicata per dodici (il grosso era uguale ai dodici denari) risulterebbe di un peso d'argento di 1,62 grammi, un peso che cade proprio tra i parametri della lega teorica del grosso.[39]

A questo punto due documenti nuovi, provenienti da Lucca, ci permettono di passare da un livello di calcoli piuttosto astratto ad un terreno più solido riguardante la lega del « denarius minutus » lucchese. Il 16 marzo 1245 il cambiavalute Vethus « campsor » vendé due libbre d'argento ad un certo Luparellus quondam Ugolini per il prezzo di £ 21 12s.[40] Se noi adoperiamo il peso della libbra della zecca fiorentina di 339,542 grammi, il prezzo dell'argento in questo affare dimostrerebbe che il denaro lucchese sarebbe uguale all'incirca a 0,131 grammi d'argento sottile.[41] Il giorno seguente ancora

---

[37] *Regesto di Camaldoli*, a cura di L. SCHIAPARELLI-F. BALDASSERONI, Roma, Loescher 1922 (« Regesta chartarum Italiae », V), p. 261, doc. n. 1225.

[38] Citato da G. A. ZANETTI, *Nuova raccolta delle monete e zecche d'Italia*, III, Bologna, Della Volpe 1775, p. 367.

[39] Cfr. sopra, nota n. 36: i parametri della lega del grosso erano da 1,72 grammi da un lato e 1,53 grammi d'argento dall'altro.

[40] LUCCA, Archivio Capitolare, LL 20, f. 35.

[41] C. BERNOCCHI, *Le monete* cit., p. 133, fornisce il peso della libbra della zecca fiorentina. Per arrivare alla suddetta cifra: £ 21 12s = 5184d; 2 × 339,542 grammi = 679,084; 679,084 ÷ 5184 = 0,131 grammi.

Vethus vendé una quantità d'argento;[42] in questa occasione, il
compratore, Rainerius Amadore, comprò 5 once d'argento con
£ 4 8s 4d. Di nuovo, usando il peso della zecca fiorentina, cal-
coliamo un denaro lucchese equivalente a 0,1334 grammi d'argento.[43] Questi valori, mostrati sul mercato, sono abbastanza
vicini al nostro conteggio precedente – basato su una presunta
svalutazione del 10 % del denaro lucchese – per poter confermare quest'ultimo assunto. Insomma, tutte le indicazioni possono convergere nella conclusione che il « denarius minutus »
di Lucca, quello « nuovo e scuro » emesso per primo poco dopo
l'accordo monetario del 1181 ad un intrinseco di circa 0,134
grammi d'argento puro, fu il pezzo sul quale si basò il grosso
toscano.

Dobbiamo adesso affrontare la questione del valore del denaro contemporaneo di Pisa e Siena. Poiché è stato stabilito che
i grossi delle cinque zecche principali toscane erano uguali fra
loro, e poiché ogni grosso era un multiplo dei dodici denari locali, dovrebbe risultare che le città toscane hanno avuto anche
dei denari di valore uguale. Questa conclusione, però, come
abbiamo visto, è contraria alle caratteristiche della lega dei
denari pisani e senesi riconosciute dagli studiosi sopracitati.[44]
Nondimeno, queste contradizioni apparenti possono essere ri-
solte dalla lettura di un documento lucchese del 20 giugno 1231,
il quale dimostra che Pisa, e persino Siena, hanno seguito
l'esempio di Lucca nel coniare un denaro ribassato nella lega
ad un valore simile al denaro « nuovo e scuro » della città di
Lucca.

Nella data in questione, Opithus, canonico della cattedrale
lucchese, e Ranuccio de Podio pubblicarono una decisione in
un arbitrato fra Leulus quondam Bonaiuncte Accati, da una
parte, e i fratelli Vicedominus, Rainerius e Gaitanus filii quon-

---

[42] LUCCA, Archivio Capitolare, LL 20, f. 35.
[43] £ 4 8s 4d = 1060: 1 oncia = 28,2951 grammi × 5 = 141,4755
grammi: 141,4755 ÷ 1060 = 0,1334 grammi.
[44] Cfr. sopra, nota n. 36.

dam Turchii, dall'altra.[45] La disputa verteva sul reclamo di
Leulus che i fratelli avevano mancato di consegnare £ 84 di
denari genovesi in Sardegna, per i quali egli, Leulus, aveva
pagato, presumibilmente a Pisa, £ 140 «denariorum novorum
pisanorum in grossis et etiam in aliis denariis». Egli, conseguentemente, stava chiedendo ai fratelli il pagamento di £ 182
«denariorum novorum pisanorum minutorum», l'equivalente
del prezzo della compera originale, più ancora £ 182 di multa
(la «pena dupli») e £ 45 per le spese compiute. Questo è un
caso molto interessante. Comunque, i suoi dettagli sono troppo
complessi per trattarli in questo contesto, salvo dire che i
fratelli si erano difesi, con scarsi risultati, col pretesto che
l'affare fosse fin dall'inizio usurario e che Leulus fosse «un
ben conosciuto usuraio pubblico e manifesto». Gli arbitri
decisero che Leulus doveva essere ricompensato con £ 170
«denariorum novorum pisanorum minutorum», pagabili in
tre rate di £ 50, £ 60 e di £ 60 con l'ultima scadenza al 1° giugno 1232. La somma ridotta, che i giudici, assegnarono a Leulus, fu forse dovuta all'accoglimento della protesta dei fratelli
che il valore iniziale del cambio fra i denari di Pisa e di Genova era in parte manipolato, se non usurario.

Due punti d'informazione di molto interesse per l'argomento
che stiamo trattando emergono da questa transazione. Per
prima cosa la notizia di una moneta grossa pisana costituisce il
più antico dato specifico su questo pezzo che fino adesso è
venuto alla luce.[46] Questa indicazione, dunque, ci permette di
arrivare con una certa sicurezza alla data del conio dei grossi
pisani negli ultimi anni del decennio 1220, e perciò possiamo
affermare che Pisa fu il primo dei comuni toscani a battere

---

[45] LUCCA, Archivio Capitolare, LL 7, f. 22.
[46] M. L. CECCARELLI LEMUT, *L'uso della moneta* cit., p. 63, cita una
notizia di «pisanorum minutorum monete» datata il 30 gennaio 1229;
una indicazione di moneta minuta presume l'esistenza di una moneta più
grande, cioè il grosso. Lo HERLIHY, *Pisan Coinage*, p. 190, ha trovato un
riferimento dell'anno 1235 a «denarii minuti» pisani.

una tale moneta.[47] In secondo luogo i dettagli finanziari di questa operazione di cambio contenuti nel documento tendono a confermare il valore intrinseco dei denari pisani, senesi e lucchesi.

Leulus, secondo la sua versione della vertenza, valutò £ 140 « denariorum novorum pisanorum » con £ 182 « denariorum novorum pisanorum minutorum ». Ancora una volta qualche calcolo: accettando questo cambio di un denaro nuovo per 1,3 denari nuovi minuti, noi arriviamo ad una moneta piccola pisana svilita approssimativamente del 23 % del valore intrinseco delle monete nuove. Adoperando un valore intrinseco di 0,175 grammi, cioè la cifra calcolata da Herlihy, abbiamo un contenuto d'argento per il nuovo denaro minuto pisano all'incirca di 0,134 grammi, una cifra quasi identica al valore calcolato più sopra per il « denarius minutus » lucchese.

Per di più, un documento datato 11 novembre 1197 riferisce di 20 soldi « denariorum lucensium vel pisanorum vel senensium ».[48] E questa uguaglianza dei valori monetari lucchesi, pisani e senesi continuava fino agli anni 1240 quando Siena rinforzò il suo denaro.[49] Per esempio, in un contratto di prestito del 28 dicembre 1229, un certo Ugolinus de Selvalunga riceve 5s 8d da Jacobus de Verona quondam Raimondini a cui promette di restituirli con 5s 8d « bonorum denariorum

---

[47] D. HERLIHY, *Pisan Coinage* cit., data il grosso senese a « not long before 1231 » sulla base di una menzione di « denarii minores » di Siena. La prima moneta fiorentina era il grosso, il fiorino d'argento comparve nell'anno 1237: cfr. R. DAVIDSOHN, *Forschungen zur Geschichte von Florenz*, II, Berlin, Siegfried 1900, pp. 27-28; D. HERLIHY, *Pisan Coinage* cit. e C. BERNOCCHI, *Le monete* cit., p. 134. Il cenno più antico che ho trovato al grosso lucchese è « solidos XXXII videlicet tot denarios grossos pisanos vel lucanos »: LUCCA, Archivio Capitolare, LL 11 f. 16, 26 marzo 1236. La prima menzione di un grosso di Arezzo si trova in LUCCA, Archivio Capitolare, LL 17, f. 13, 27 gennaio 1243.

[48] *Documenti dell'antica costituzione* cit., p. 36, doc. n. 21, 11 novembre 1197: « XX solidis denariorum lucensium vel pisanorum vel senensium ».

[49] Cfr. sopra, nota n. 32.

lucensium vel pisanorum».[50] Inoltre, le notizie sull'uguaglianza monetaria dei denari pisani e senesi aumentano nei documenti dello stesso decennio.[51]

Infine, che cosa possiamo concludere della testimonianza lucchese sulle origini del grosso toscano? In primo luogo c'è l'indicazione che Pisa – seguita nell'ordine da Siena, Lucca, Firenze e Arezzo – fu la prima città toscana a coniare una moneta grossa.[52] In secondo luogo, benché Lucca avesse scisso l'unione monetaria con Pisa e Siena poco dopo il 1181, è chiaro che le ultime due città furono pronte ad emettere un « denarius » modellato su quello « nuovo e scuro » di Lucca, cioè il « denarius minutus » lucchese, che a turno fu adottato come la base intrinseca della moneta grossa toscana. In terzo luogo è evidente che il valore del denaro minuto lucchese di circa 0,134 grammi d'argento divenne la base per la lira di

---

50 LUCCA, Archivio Capitolare, LL 5, f. 16.

51 D. HERLIHY, *Pisan Coinage* cit., pp. 183-184.

52 D. HERLIHY, *Pisan Coinage* cit., p. 190, è dell'opinione che Siena, seguita da Pisa, sia stata la prima città toscana a coniare un grosso. Questa conclusione è fondata sull'esame della tipologia delle prime monete grosse di queste città, che l'Herlihy chiama « transitional grossi », e che stavano fra il denaro pisano-senese rinforzato e il grosso « puro » degli anni 1240. Per Pisa la distinzione fra il grosso tipo « F » e quello più tardo, tipo « Vergine » è chiara sia per la fattura che per il cambiamento del tipo. Inoltre, il *C.N.I.* cit., p. 287, nn. 5-8, cita nove grossi pisani tipo « F » che pesavano nel rango di 1,30-1,40 grammi, tanto meno quanto quelli tipo « Vergine ». Per quanto riguarda i « transitional grossi » di Siena, la distinzione fra i tipi più vecchi e quelli più recenti è meno ovvia. I primi grossi senesi, elencati nel *C.N.I.*, pp. 350-353, nn. 11-21, definiti come « Anteriori al 1250 », si distinguono dai grossi indicati come « Di poco posteriori ai precedenti » (*C.N.I.*, p. 352, nn. 22-28) dal fatto che la « S » in SIENA giace sullo suo dorso e che la « E » in SENA VETUS è arrotondata. Questi primi, presunti « transitional », grossi comunque pesavano fra 1,83-1,61 grammi, cioè lo stesso che i grossi senesi « posteriori » e grossi « puri » toscani degli anni 1240.

F. PANVINI ROSATI, *La monetazione delle zecche minori* cit., pp. 136-137, scrive che Lucca batté un grosso « subito dopo il 1209, cioè dopo la concessione di Ottone IV ». Mi sembra però che questa data sia troppo alta per la coniazione del grosso lucchese che, come abbiamo visto, non ha lasciato nessuna traccia nei documenti fino all'anno 1236. Per questo lungo silenzio riguardante i documenti su detta moneta, penso che sia opportuno datare il grosso lucchese ai primi anni del decennio 1230 e dopo la coniazione dei grossi pisani e senesi.

conto toscano che conseguentemente equivaleva all'incirca a 32,16 grammi d'argento. E questo valore servì alle città di Lucca, Pisa e Firenze fino alla nuova ondata di deprezzamento che colpì la moneta piccola di Toscana negli anni 1260.[53]

---

[53] Quando Firenze battè per la prima volta un denaro d'argento, nel 1258, fu coniato ad un contenuto d'argento di 0,132 grammi, cioè praticamente lo stesso intrinseco del denaro lucchese-pisano-senese del 1181 circa: cfr. C. BERNOCCHI, *Le monete* cit., p. 143. Lo stesso studioso (pp. 140-141) reca un « denarius » pisano dell'anno 1250 di 0,136 grammi, e dell'anno 1252 di 0,132 grammi; afferma, però, che quest'ultimo conteggio rappresenta uno svilimento dai 0,1948 grammi d'argento del denaro pisano del 1202 invece di riconoscere che questo è stato il valore costante dei denari toscani fin dagli anni 1180.

A Firenze il denaro piccolo, comparso nel 1258, mantiene la propria posizione verso il fiorino d'oro durante i primi anni del decennio 1260; però nel 1271 il fiorino d'oro equivaleva 30s « a piccioli »: cfr. C. BERNOCCHI, *Le monete* cit., p. 78. A Pisa il denaro piccolo mantenne similmente il suo valore fino agli anni 1260; comunque nel 1268 il denaro valeva £ 1 4s 6d rispetto al fiorino d'oro: cfr. B. CASINI, *Il corso dei cambi tra il fiorino e la moneta di piccioli a Pisa dal 1252 al 1500*, in G. GARZELLA, M. L. CECCARELLI LEMUT, B. CASINI, *Studi sugli strumenti di scambio* cit., pp. 131-169: pp. 147-148; C. BERNOCCHI, *Le monete* cit., p. 99 e D. HERLIHY, *Pisa in the Early Renaissance*, New Haven, Yale U. P. 1958, p. 196 (trad. it. con titolo *Pisa nel Duecento*, Pisa, Nistri-Lischi 1973), per il cambio tra il fiorino d'oro e il denaro pisano. La serie del BERNOCCHI, *Le monete* cit., p. 92 per il denaro senese e il fiorino non comincia fino al 1302. Lucca nel 1268, o poco prima, battè un nuovo denaro svilito del 20 % rispetto al precedente: cfr. LUCCA, Archivio Capitolare, LL 33, f. 107; il 31 marzo 1268 il cambiavalute, Castracane « quondam » Rugerii, vendè £ 144 « bonorum novorum denariorum lucensium » per il prezzo di £ 120 « denariorum lucensium ». Il cambio era dichiarato espressamente di 24 denari nuovi per 20 dei denari vecchi. Per varie parità fra le monete toscane nel tredicesimo secolo, cfr. R. DAVIDSHON, *Forschungen* cit., IV, Berlin, Siegfried 1908, pp. 316-322, però questi cambi sono più o meno quelli che Philip Grierson (cfr. sopra, nota n. 36) ha chiamato « prezzi politici » e devono essere utilizzati con cautela.

# XV

# The second issuance of a Tuscan gold coin: the gold groat of Lucca, 1256

*In 1252 Genoa and Florence embarked upon the issuance of gold coins. Although Genoa's effort ultimately failed due to an internal economic crisis, the Florentine florin dominated the international money markets of western Europe and beyond for the next two and a half centuries. Lucca, Florence's Tuscan neighbor, likewise ventured into the issuance of a gold coin at least by 1256. However, Lucca's gold issue was apparently of a modest scale and never mounted a challenge to the florin. This article establishes the date* ante quem *at which Lucca made her return to gold and attempts to explain why the Lucchese gold groat did not become a significant factor in Europe's earliest experiment with bimetallism.\**

Robert Lopez (1956–57:219) has remarked in commemorating the event that the striking of gold coinages by Genoa and Florence in the year 1252 "set off one of the greatest chain reactions in monetary history."[1] Although the *genoino d'oro* was doomed by internal economic dislocations in Genua to play a relatively modest role in the return to bimetallism in Western Europe (Lopez 1956–57:219–40 and Lopez 1953), the Florentine *fiorino d'oro* became the most widely sought and most valued coin in the money

markets of the West and beyond for the next two and a half centuries.[2] Indeed, if imitation is the highest form of flattery, the alacrity of the kings of England, Spain, France and Hungary as well as some forty-eight cities to venture into the issuance of gold bears witness to the prestige of the noble metal and to the timeliness of the issuance of a viable gold coin.[3]

In this rush to gold, Lucca, Florence's neighbor, was the third European and the second Tuscan city to assay the striking of a gold piece. Toward the end of the year 1256, if not before, Lucca issued a gold coin, the *grosso d'oro*.[4] The groat of Lucca appeared at the same weight and nominal value as its Florentine counterpart and thus was equal to 240 silver *denarii* and 20 silver *grossi* (*solidi* in money of account terms) respectively (Davidsohn 1956:571, n. 4). Lucca's gold coinage was, however, from all indications executed at a much more modest level than the Florentine program and the Lucchese piece enjoyed only a regional circulation, never achieving the international status of the florin. In this essay, I would like first to establish the date *ante quem* of the issuance of a Lucchese gold coin and then to seek an explanation as to why Lucca's gold groat failed to challenge the *fiorino d'oro* in the international market place.

Only five exemplars of the Lucchese gold groat are known to exist today.[5] Giovanni Sercambi, the Lucchese *novellista* and historian, recorded in an entry of his fourteenth-century chronicle under the year 1269 (Bongi 1892:39) that *E quine bacteò Lucca lo fiorino che vè lo Lucchese armato a chavallo* (and then Lucca struck the florin which is the Lucchese armed and on horseback).[6] Sercambi was wrong, however, in his dating and he was also evidently confusing the thirteenth-century Lucchese gold groat with the fourteenth-century Lucchese gold piece that bore on the reverse the image of Saint Martin mounted on horseback.[7] The first published documentary reference to a Lucchese gold coin is dated 1273 and records a pay-

ment made in Lucca to Charles of Anjou's treasurer for Tuscany by the sindic of Pistoia in *florinis et lucensibus de auro* (Davidsohn 1956:571, n. 4). Lucchese evidence, however, allows us to push back the date of the appearance of Lucchese gold at least to the year 1256.

On 19 January 1257 Gottefredus *quondam* Conetti Bonostri and Bartholomeus *quondam* Orlandi Bettori received in partnership *ad partem lucri* from Master Benencasa, canon of the Lucchese cathedral, £ 200 *denariorum lucensium in denariis grossis de auro et argento tante valentie ad parvos denarios*.[8] This, to my knowledge, constitutes the earliest mention in the sources of a Lucchese gold piece. Since the coin was in circulation slightly three weeks after the new year (Lucchese style), it seems more than probable that the

Figure 1. The gold groat of Lucca. (*Left*) Reverse: The Volto Santo. (*Right*) Obverse: monogram of Emperor Otto IV.

piece was struck no later than some time in the preceding year.

It might be objected at this juncture that a reference to an anonymous *grossus de auro* could refer to the Florentine florin rather than to a local gold coin. Sercambi, after all, from his fourteenth-century perspective, called the first Lucchese gold piece *lo fiorino*. Also, the Florentine chronicler Giovanni Villani (Drago Manni 1844:2839) informs us that in 1256 the Florentine host that had defeated a Pisan force on the banks of the Serchio river not far from Lucca and then driven into Pisan territory to *Chiesa San Jacopo in Poggio* paused there and cut down a great pine tree upon whose stump they struck *fiorini d'oro* (*tagliarono unde grande pino, e battere in sul ceppo del detto pino i fiorini d'oro*).[9] Villani then goes on to state that the coins thus minted had as a distinguishing commemorative mark a small tree of a shape resembling a shamrock between the feet of the figure of Saint John and that in his own day it was still possible to see a goodly number of these pieces (*e per ricordanza, quegli che in quello luogo furono coniati, ebbono per contrassegno tra'piedi di san Giovanni quasi come un trefoglio, a guisa d'uno piccolo alboro; e de'nostri dì ne vedremmo noi assai di quelli fiorini.*)[10] No doubt a number of these florins found their way into the Lucchese market place but it is highly unlikely that they would have passed anonymously into circulation without being identified as foreign coins.

In support of this conclusion is the fact that in Lucchese contracts, when money of account sums based upon the small silver

penny and its multiples the *solidus* and *libra* were transacted in coins of other denominations, the generic type and provenance of the pieces involved were frequently detailed. For example, after the appearance in Tuscany of silver groats of a common weight and value, issued first by Pisa in the 1220s and then in order in the 1230s by Siena, Lucca, Florence and Arezzo, it was customary, when *grossi d'argento* were employed in whole or in part as the means of payment, to specify the city or cities of their origin.[11] Instances of this usage are legion in the Lucchese documents but for the sake of illustration we may cite the following: 26 March 1236, payment in *tot denarios grossos pisanos et lucanos*; 28 February 1243 payment of 41s. *denariorum lucensium grossorum argenti florentie aretine et senensis*; 23 May 1243, payment in *tot grossos lucenses florentinos et aretinos*.[12] Viewed in this context, the language of the first mention of the Lucchese gold groat implies an indigenous coin. The money of account sum of £200 *denariorum lucensium ad parvos* indicated in our document was actually settled in otherwise unidentified groats of gold and silver. But given the above tendency to indicate what types of coins were used as the means of payment, it is reasonable to assume that a gold coin of foreign origin would not have gone unnoticed in the contract. Numismatic evidence, moreover, confirms the fact that we are dealing with a Lucchese gold coin and not the Florentine *fiorino d'oro*.

Panvini Rosati (1974:137–8) has observed that the Lucchese *grossus d'oro*, bearing on the obverse the portrait of St Martin in half profile and on the reverse the traditional monogram of the Emperor Otto IV, is closely related iconographically and stylistically to the Lucchese silver *grossi* circulating around the mid-thirteenth century.[13] He thus dates the gold groat to the decade following the issuance of the Florentine florin. This conclusion meshes perfectly with the Lucchese documentary evidence.

Furthermore, when the city of Perugia determined in 1259 to follow the path of gold, her authorities looked to two Lucchese money-changers, Barocchus Barocchi and Buonaguida Gherardini, to superintend the effort.[14] Although the Perugian flirtation with the issuance of gold came to naught, it is instructive that the Umbrian city turned to the Lucchese to oversee their experiments with the noble metal. We may speculate that they did so because of the recent experience of the Lucchese in launching a new gold currency.

The Lucchese gold groat seems to have played only a tangential and occasional role in the economic life of Lucca. In all, between January 1257 and 28 May 1268, I have found but twelve instances – with one stray reference from 1279 – when the gold coin was actually used as a means of effecting private payments. In four of these cases, money-changers accepted investments *ad partem lucri* from third parties in gold and silver groats and in petty silver deniers.[15] The transaction of 1279 is also an investment *ad partem lucri* but it is with the merchant-banking organization of the Tignosini.[16] The remaining eight surviving examples of the circulation of the gold groat in the Lucchese economy also involve money-changers, either as lenders or as recipients of deposits in gold coins.[17] The gold groat may well have circulated outside the ambience of the money-changers, leaving no traces in the sources, but judging from the meager indications of its presence in the hundreds of documents relating to the money-changers' business surviving from this period, it would seem that gold was little used at this time in the local economy.[18] Nor, as we have noted above, was the Lucchese *grossus d'oro* a factor in international commercial and financial circles. Lucchese merchant-bankers made their contracts for purchases of raw silk imported from Genoa and negotiated their foreign exchange dealings in silver coin.[19]

In monetary history arguments from silence can be most telling, and judging from the silence of the sources it is evident that Lucca's thirteenth-century issuance of a gold coinage was modest indeed. Bimetallism did not arrive in Lucca until the 1280s, nearly a quarter of a century after the appearance of the *grossus d'oro*, and when it did it came from abroad through the adoption of the Florentine florin as the standard gold piece.[20]

Why did the Lucchese gold coin fail to give the florin a run for its money in international monetary circles? Why were the Lucchese so apparently sparing in the volume of their gold issue? The answer may appear almost banal in its simplicity but I would argue that the *grossus d'oro* did not mount a challenge to the florin because it was never intended by the Lucchese merchant class that it do so. The argument that economic weakness or an economic slowdown hampered the ability of certain gold issues to succeed in the international market place, while appropriate in some cases, hardly seems applicable to Lucca.[21]

From all indications the 1250s were years of prosperity and expansion for Lucca, and the latter half of the thirteenth century a period of continued economic growth. The deposit banks of the money-changers were multiplying and flourishing in the decades of the 1250s and 1260s (Blomquist 1971a:459–76; 1979:55–68). More significantly, from around the mid-point of the thirteenth century, Lucchese merchants began to form partnerships for international commerce and finance on a much larger scale than hitherto known (Blomquist 1971b:158–67). The resulting mercantile-banking companies, centrally managed from Lucca, operated through an international network of partners or agents more or less permanently stationed in all the major industrial and financial centers of western Europe. Toward the end of the thirteenth century, there were at least twenty-two large-scale companies dealing in commerce and foreign exchange banking operating in international markets (Blomquist 1971b:172–7). Additionally, the Lucchese silk industry which at the time apparently enjoyed a virtual monopoly in medieval western Europe seems to have experienced a continued growth (Edler 1930; Gioffrè 1973). In short, on the basis of evidence in hand, there is no reason to assume that Lucca's economic strength was significantly less than neighboring Florence in the years during which the florin was conquering the money markets of the West and while the *grossus d'oro* was languishing, at best, as a regional coin.

To put the situation in better perspective, it should be noted that Tuscan monetary history in the thirteenth century was characterized by a considerable degree of cooperation between the otherwise normally contentiuous communes.[22] When Pisa, for example, issued an enlarged silver coin, the *grossus d'argento*, in the last years of the 1220s, her initiative was rapidly followed by Siena, Lucca, Florence and Arezzo and through the 1250s into the 1260s, the five major communes continued a close deliberation on monetary affairs.[23]

On 9 August 1255, shortly after the appearance of the florin, Florentine and Lucchese ambassadors appeared before the General Council of Siena to plead that "Sienese, Florentine and Lucchese money be of one weight and one value".[24] This would appear to have been a general request and it may be assumed that the ambassadors were referring to the standards of the small silver *denarius*, and its multiples, the silver groat and the gold florin. In other words, they were appealing that Siena join in establishing and maintaining a monetary system in which money of account denominations, namely the pound (*libra*) and shilling (*solidus*), were represented by actual circulating coins in the following relationship: 1 florin = 20 silver groats = 240 denarii and 12 denarii = 1 groat. The joint appearance of Florentine and Lucchese ambassadors indicates prior consultation on monetary policy between the two communes and it is not at all unlikely that such discussions took place regarding the cooperative issuance of the first Tuscan gold coins. The thrust of my argument – perhaps better, my hypothesis – is that Florence and Lucca had agreed to strike gold coins at about the same time, with Lucca undertaking, as a matter of monetary policy, a secondary role by issuing only a limited number of *grossi d'oro*. That there were perceived economic risks involved in adventuring into the striking of

gold is clear from the refusal of Siena, Pisa and Arezzo to listen to the petitions of the Florentines and Lucchese to follow their lead on such a monetary course.[25] In the event, the Lucchese were only slightly less circumspect than their three Tuscan neighbors. It seems to me hardly coincidental that the earliest previous documentary reference to the Lucchese gold groat occurs within the context of a public payment to the government of Charles of Anjou. In other words, it would appear that the *grossus d'oro* was conceived largely as a political, or ceremonial, symbol of the status of Lucca rather than as a coin to be widely and competitively diffused in the course of Lucca's international trade and commerce.

Much has been made of the advantage that the acceptance of the florin as the principal international standard of value gave to the Florentines in European commerce and finance.[26] While this ultimately may well have been so, it remains true that the Lucchese merchant-bankers of the thirteenth century hardly seem to have been disadvantaged. As pointed out above, the years post 1252 were ones of unrivaled prosperity in Lucca – her "golden age" without gold – as it were. Lucca's fourteenth-century economic decline was the result not so much of an eclipse by Florence as it was the consequence of internal turmoil that sent legions of skilled silk workers into exile and wrecked the unity of the merchant-banking class.[27]

## Notes

* I wish to express my thanks to Dr Alan Stahl of the American Numismatic Society, New York, and Professor John F. McGovern, University of Wiscon-

sin, Milwaukee, for their helpful comments on an earlier version of this paper.

[1] See also the seminal article of Bloch (1933) for a discussion of gold in medieval monetary history.

[2] On the importance of the florin in international commerce, see Cipolla 1956:20–1; 1982:XI–XIV. The success of the florin in the Levant is also underscored by Walker (1983). For the issuance of the florin and Florentine monetary history in general, see Bernocchi 1976:58ff.

[3] On the striking of gold coins in imitation of the florin, see Davidsohn 1956:571, Homan 1922:116–17, and Lopez 1953:167–8. Bernocchi 1985:487 states that from the end of the thirteenth to the fifteenth century sixty-one European mints struck coins similar to the florin. For a catalogue of the European imitations of the florin, see Gamberini di Scarfea 1956:233–76.

[4] The dating of the Lucchese gold groat will be discussed shortly. Lenzi (1978:77, no. 38) dates the exemplar of the Lucchese *grossus d'oro* in a Pisan hoard of 1925 *anteriore al fiorino d'oro fiorentino*. Such a chronological priority of the Lucchese over the Florentine gold piece seems, however, highly unlikely. But a strong case can be made suggesting that the florin and Lucchese gold groat were struck at about the same time as the result of a monetary accord between the two communes.

[5] According to Panvini Rosati (1974:137), these are, or were, in: (1) the royal collection of Victor Emanuel, (2) the *Museo Nazionale Romano*, (3) sold at auction in Milan some years ago, (4) one cited by Massagli as being in the *Museo di Lucca* but now apparently lost, and (5) the exemplar from the Pisan hoard. The Lucchese *grossi d'oro* discussed by Panvini Rosati (1974:137–8, figure no. 4) weigh, according to the author, about 3.60 grams. The exemplar found in the Pisan hoard and discussed by Lenzi 1978:77, no. 138 weighs 3.48 grams.

On the Lucchese gold groat, see also the *Corpus nummorum italicorum* (1929:74, plate 5, nos. 1 and 2), the compilors of which were unable to locate an exemplar of the Lucchese groat – the acquisition by Victor Emanuel was apparently made after publication of Volume 11 – and were forced to use the drawing in Massagli 1870, plate 8, nos. 2 and 3. See below, note no. 13.

[6] For the *novelle* of Sercambi, Sercambi 1972, Rossi 1974, and Cherubini 1974:3–49.

[7] For the fourteenth-century Lucchese gold piece, see Panvini Rosati 1974:138–9 and figure no 5; *Corpus numm. italicorum* 77; Massagli 1870, plate 8, nos. 4, 5 and 7.

[8] Lucca, *Archivio Capitolare*, (hereafter AC) LL30, f. 112v. *Societas et compagnia ad partem lucri* was a form of partnership in which the investors liability was limited to the sum invested: see Blomquist 1971b:167–71.

[9] See also Lenzi (1978:12).

[10] For these coins see Lenzi 1978:99–102, nos. 217–29.

[11] On the Tuscan *grossi*, see below note no. 23.

[12] AC LL11, f.16; LL17, f.16; LL17, f. 42v respectively.

[13] Panvini Rosati's photograph of the Lucchese *grossus d'oro* was apparently made from the one exemplar found among 229 pieces in a hoard discovered in 1925 beneath the *loggie dei Banchi* in Pisa. The hoard has been reported by Galeotti 1930 and Castellani 1937:476–84. See Lenzi 1978 for an evaluation of the hoard and Abulafia 1983:247.

[14] The details are provided in Lopez (1953:168–9): Perugia's contemplated coinage was to consist of silver *denarii* and *grossi* modelled on those of Siena and a gold coin *ad modum ponderis et legem comunis florentini*. Apparently the Perugian authorities failed to supply the Lucchese with the necessary means to launch the gold issue and Lopez ascribes this failure to the fact that Perugia was politically ambitious but economically weak. See also Lopez 1951:427, no. 6 for a transcription of the document (AC 8, LL32, f.44) recording the hiring of Bonifatius f. Cantonis by Barocchus and Bonaguida to cut dies for *grossi, piccoli* and gold coins to be struck in Perugia.

[15] AC LL30, f. 112v: 19 January 1257; LL32, f. 18: 17 March 1259; LL32, f. 23v: 28 March 1259; LL32, f. 53v: 31 July 1259. The investors were a canon of the Lucchese cathedral, a money-changer, a merchant-banker and another money-changer respectively.

[16] Lucca, AS *Archivio dei notari*, no. 13 (notary Armanno di Armanno), f. 5; 20 January 1279. The *Societas Tingnosini* was one of twenty-two large-scale Lucchese companies operating in international commerce and finance in the year 1284: Blomquist 1971b:172–8.

[17] AC "33, f. 63: 6 September 1266, changer Savariscius *quondam* Pilii Castracanis lends £ 7 12s. to Uphetinus *quondam* Saxhini de Vertiano; LL33, f. 65v: 22 September 1266, Savariscius lends £ 10 8s. to Cillianus de Plebe Sancti Pauli *quondam* Luccerii, to Guido, his brother, and to Guilielmus and Bonaiutus, brothers, *quondam* Simionis from the same place; LL33, f. 94v: 5 October 1267, changer Castruccio *quondam* Rugerii Castracanis lends £ 200 to Guigottus *quondam* Boccuci, Nardorus *quondam* Jacobini and

Bandinus, a cotton worker, *filius* Uguiccionis, all from the urban contrada of *Sancta Maria in palatio*.

LL33, f. 86: 2 May 1267, changer Castracane *quondam* Rugerii Castracanis receives a loan (*mutuum*) of £100 from Lupus *filius* Reialis *de Staffore*; LL33,, f.97v: 27 October 1267, Castracane receives a deposit of £208 from an unknown (the name is crossed out) canon of the Lucchese cathedral; LL33, f.109: 28 May 126, changer Savariscius quondam Pilii Castracanis receives *in accomandiscia* £42 from Gerarduccio *quondam* Benuti who now lives in *Contrate Sancti Martini* but who originally came from the Garfagnana; LL33, f.120: 5 October 1268, Castracane receives a loan of £100 from the same Lupus *quondam* Reialis as above. The fifth document, LL33, f.108v: 22 March 1268, involves a loan to one Guido Meluine of £70 denariorum lucensium in denariis grossis de auro et argento et minutis in which savariscius acts as a guarantor.

[18] For the sources bearing upon the banking activities of the Lucchese changers, Blomquist 1979:54.

[19] For the importation of raw silk from Genoa, see Florence Edler 1930:116–23; Gioffrè 1973:94–111. On the Lucchese as foreign exchange bankers, Racine 1970 and 1974 and Blomquist 1979:70–5.

[20] Massagli (1870:54) cites a Lucchese reference to the florin dated 1265. I have found only one other mention of the florin in Lucca between 1265 and 1286: see Lucca, AS *Archivio dei notari*, no. 12 (notary Paganello di Fiandrada), f. 16v. The 1286 reference is Lucca, AS *Archivio dei notari*, no. 16 (notary Ugolino Cincini), f.16v; 6 March 1286. Around this date there emerged in Lucca two novel money of account systems based upon the florin. In the one, *ad bonam monetam*, the Lucchese silver *denarius* was fixed for accounting purposes at 38s. 6d. per florin: in the second, *ad parvam monetam*, the silver penny was pegged at about 43s. per florin. For these two systems, see Lucca, AS *Archivio dei notari*, *passim*. For the difficulties in attempting to maintain a stable ratio between silver and gold coinages in a given monetary system, see Cipolla 1982 and Lane and Mueller 1985:257–415.

[21] Lopez (1953:197–8) points out that Genoa's gold issue did not take off because Genoa became caught up in a banking crisis and depression and thus had no need of a gold coin; while the Florentines, who launched the florin largely as a matter of pride, were fortunate enough to ride the crest of economic expansion. For the case of Perugia's failure to initiate a successful gold coinage, see above n. 14. Panvini Rosati (1974:138–9) has observed that "evidently the times were not 'mature' for the Lucchese gold piece

as they were not for the other cities of Tuscany."

[22] The identical weight and intrinsic value of the silver groats issued by the mints of Pisa, Siena, Lucca, Florence and Arezzo in the 1240s have led scholars to speculate on the existance of a formal Tuscan monetary league: see Herlihy 1967:189–90; Lopez 1956:57–238; 1953:46; Promis 1868:22. Chiaudano (1930:24) not only postulates the existence of a league but argues that it was destroyed by the issuance of the florin and the failure of the Sienese to cooperate in issuing a gold coin.

[23] Herlihy (1967:190) argues that Siena followed by Pisa were the first to strike silver groats in the early 1230s. Panvini Rosati (1974:136–7) suggests, however, that Pisa was the first to issue such a coin: see my forthcoming article, "Alle origini del 'grosso' toscano: la testimonianza Lucchese duecentesca," in Archivio storico italiano (1986), which supports the latter contention.

[24] Chiaudano 1930:24: *Cum intellexeritis ea que vobis in presenti consilio per ambasciatores florentini et ambasciatores lucani fuerunt diligenter exposita tam de moneta senense et florentina et lucana fienda et cudenda unius ponderis et unius valoris.*

[25] Following the appeal to the Sienese, two merchants were sent to Arezzo and Pisa to seek their respective adherence to a similar agreement but apparently to no avail: Promis 1868:238. In 1266 Florence again implored the Sienese to issue a gold coin and again they were refused: Chiaudano 1930:24. On the resistance to the striking of gold coins in England, France and other jurisdictions in the thirteenth and fourteenth centuries, see Bloch 1933:25–7.

[26] Among others, see Davidsohn 1956:570–1.

[27] For the Lucchese economy in the fourteenth century see Meek 1968 and Green 1981.

## Literature

Abulafia, D. 1983. Maometto e Carlo Magno: le due aree monetarie italiane dell'oro e dell'argento. In: Romano, R. and Vivente, C. (eds.), Storia d'Italia: Annali 6. Economia naturale, economia monetaria. Torino.

Bernocchi, M. 1976. Le monete della repubblica fiorentina, 3. Documentazione. Firenze.

Bernocchi, M. 1985. Le imitazione del fiorino d'oro dei secc. XIV e XVI. In: Aspetti della vita economica medievale: Atti del Convegno di Studi nel X Anniversario della Morte di Federigo Melis, Firenze-Pisa-Prato, 10–14 marzo 1984, 486–90. Firenze.

Bloch, M. 1933. Le problème de l'or au Moyen Age. Annales d'histoire économique et sociale 5:1–34.

Blomquist, T. W. 1971a. The Castracani family of thirteenth-century Lucca. Speculum 46:459–76.

Blomquist, T. W. 1971b. Commercial association in thirteenth-century Lucca. Business history review 41:157–78.

Blomquist, T. W. 1979. The dawn of banking in a medieval commune: thirteenth-century Lucca. In: The dawn of modern banking, Center for Medieval and Renaissance Studies, University of California, Los Angeles: 53–75. New Haven.

Bongi, S. (ed.) 1892. Croniche di Giovanni Sercambi, 1. Published as Fonti per la storia d'Italia 19. Roma.

Castellani, G. 1937. Il ripostiglio di Pisa. Bollettino d'arte 30:476–84.

Cherubini, G. 1974. Vita trecentesca nelle novelle di Giovanni Sercambi. In: Cherubini G., Signori, contadini, borghesi: ricerche sulla società italiana del Basso Medievo, 3–49. Firenze.

Chiaudano, M. 1930. Le compagnie bancarie senesi nel Duecento. In: Chiaudano, M. Studi e documenti per la storia del diritto commerciale italiano nel secolo XIII, 1–52. Torino.

Cipolla, C. M. 1956. Money, prices and civilization in the Mediterranean world. Princeton, NJ.

Cipolla, C. M. 1982. The monetary policy of fourteenth-century Florence. Berkeley, CA.

Corpus nummorum italicorum. 1929. 11, Toscana: zecche minori. Roma.

Davidsohn, R. 1956. Storia di Firenze, 2. Firenze.

Drago Manni, F. G. (ed.) 1844. Cronica di Giovanni Villani. Firenze.

Edler, F. 1930. The silk trade of Lucca during the thirteenth and fourteenth centuries. Ph.D. dissertation, University of Chicago. Chicago.

Galeotti, A. 1930. Il ripostiglio di Pisa. Rassegna numismatica 27.

Gamberini di Scarfea, C. 1956. Le imitazioni e le contraffazioni monetarie nel mondo: primo tentativo di uno studio generale e practico ad use dei numismatici, 1. Bologna.

Gioffrè, D. 1973. L'attività economica dei lucchesi à Genova fra il 1190 e il 1280. In: Lucca economica, storica, economica: relazioni e communicazioni al XV Congresso Nazionale Archivistico, Lucca, ottobre 1969, 94–111. Roma.

Green, L. 1981. Il commercio lucchese ai tempi di Castruccio Castracani. In: Atti del Primo Convegno di Studi Castrucciani: Coreglia Antelminelli, 21 maggio 1978, 5–19. Lucca.

Homan, H. 1922. La circolazione delle monete d'oro in Ungheria dal X al XIV secolo e la crisi europea dell'oro nel secolo XIV. Rivista italiana di numismatica e scienze affini 35:109–56.

Herlihy, D. 1967. Pisan coinage and the monetary history of Tuscany, 1150–1250. In: Le zecche minori toscane fino al XIV secolo: Atti del 3° Convegno Internazionale del Centro di Studi di Storia dell-Arte, Pistoia, 169–92. 1967. Rastignano.

Lane, F. C. and Mueller, R. C. 1985. Money and banking in medieval and renaissance Venice, 1. Coins and moneys of account. Baltimore.

Lenzi, L. 1978. Il ripostiglio di monete auree scoperto in Pisa sotto le loggie dei banchi: saggio numismatico con prefazione di Emilio Cristiani. Pisa.

Lopez, R. S. 1951. The unexplored wealth of the notarial archives of Pisa and Lucca. In: Mélanges d'histoire de moyen-âge dédiès à la mémoire de Louis Halphen, 417–32. Paris.

Lopez, R. S. 1953. Settecento anni fa: il ritorno all'oro nell'Occidente duecentesca 65:19–55, 161–98.

Lopez, R. S. 1956–57. Back to Gold, 1252. The economic history review. series 2, 9:219–40.

Massagli, D. 1870. Introduzione alla storia della zecca e della moneta lucchesi. Published as Memorie e documenti per servire alla storia di Lucca, 11, part 2. Lucca.

Meek, C. 1968. The trade and industry of Lucca in the fourteenth century. Historical studies 6:39–58.

Panvini Rosati, F. 1974. La monetazione delle zecche minori toscane nel periodo comunale. In: Le zecche minori toscane fino al XIV secolo: Atti del 3° Convegno Internazionale del Centro di Studi di Storia dell-Arte, Pistoia, 1967, 131–44. Rastignano.

Promis, D. 1868. Monete della Reale Accademia delle Scienze di Torino. series 2, 24. Torino.

Racine, P. 1970. Le marché génoise de la soie en 1288. Revue des études sud-est européenes 8.

Racine, P. 1974. I banchieri piacentini ed i campi sulle fiere di Champagne alla fine del Duecento. In: Studi storici in onore di Emilio Nasalli Rocca. Piacenza.

Rossi, L. 1974. Giovanni Sercambi, il novelliere. Roma.

Sercambi, G. 1972. Novelle. Sinicropi G. (ed.). Bari.

Walker, T. 1983. The italian gold revolution of 1252: shifting currents in the pan-Mediterranean flow of gold. In: J. F. Richards (ed.). Precious metals in the later medieval and early modern worlds, 29–52. Durham, NC.

# Alien coins and foreign exchange banking in a medieval commune: Thirteenth-century Lucca[*]

## Abstract

The tithing returns sent to Rome in 1296 from the dioceses of Tuscany reveal a variety of coins, foreign to each particular episcopate, included in the mix. This article deals with the presence, and presumably prior circulation, of coins of foreign provenence in thirteenth-century Lucca as indicated in the Lucchese notarial materials of the period. The results are analyzed and then compared with the representation of the types of coins included in Lucca's 1296 tithe, and explanations set forth as to why certain coins, e.g. the *gros tournois*, should be conspicuously under-represented in comparison with other Tuscan dioceses while the Venetian groat was over-represented. It is further argued that the determining factor for the lack or abundance of certain alien coins in Lucca turns on the availability or absence of routine mechanisms for the transfer of obligations abroad through foreign exchange banking which obviated the need for significant shipments of physical specie or bullion.

Professor John Day has observed that in medieval monetary history the chronic shortage of ready money guaranteed that all good specie would circulate freely within a given monetary region.[1] Day was writing with regard to the situation in Tuscany in 1296 on the basis of the returns paid from Tuscan bishoprics to the papacy as compiled in 1942 by Monsignori Guidi and Giusti.[2] His analysis of this material graphically demonstrates the accumulation of foreign coin – and pre-

THOMAS BLOMQUIST is Professor of History at Northern Illinois University. He has published numerous articles on the economy and society of medieval Lucca which have appeared in *Speculum*, *The Journal of Economic History*, *The Journal of European Economic History*, *The Journal of Medieval History*, *Archivio storico Italiano*, and other journals.

[*] An earlier version of this paper was presented at the *23rd International Congress on Medieval Studies*, May 1988. I am grateful to Professor Louise B. Robbert for including me in the symposium honoring Hilmar Krueger and to Dr. Alan Stahl for his helpful comments on the text.

[1] John Day, 'La circulation monétarie en Toscane en 1296,' *Annales E.S.C.*, 23 (1968), 1054–66. Now in translation in John Day, *The Medieval Market Economy* (Oxford, 1987), 129–40.

[2] P. Guidi and M. Giusti, *Rationes decimarum Italiae nei secoli XIII e XIV: Tuscia*, II (*Studi e Testi*, no. 98) (Città del Vaticano, 1942).

sumably its prior circulation – within the various dioceses of late thirteenth-century Tuscany. While it is not my intent here to dwell upon Day's figures for the whole of Tuscany, it is worth noting, by way of introduction to an examination of the circulation of alien coins in thirteenth-century Lucca, two of his findings from Tuscany as a whole. First, is the preponderance – with the exception of Lucca – throughout Tuscany of payment in a high percentage of Florentine florins. Second, and again excepting Lucca from the Tuscan-wide pattern, is the fact that the *gros tournois* was the dominant piece among the various silver groats that made up a combined 50.7% of the total disbursement to the papal camera.[3]

What then of Lucca? What do the data from 1296 tell us about this Tuscan city? Lucca, as we have just seen, presents a somewhat eccentric picture when the percentages of various specie making up her diocese's disbursement are compared with the pattern from the rest of Tuscany. The most notable difference is the low volume – only 9.5% of the total – of florins, which stands in contrast to the 50% from Florence, 31.9% from Pisa, 30.7% from Siena and 65.5% from Arezzo. A second unique characteristic of the Lucchese payment in 1296 is the low number of *gros tournois* and silver groats of other Tuscan mints: these two coins constituted but a combined 15% of Lucca's return compared to a total of 47.1% from Florence, 64.3% from Pisa, and 27.9% from Siena. Only Arezzo, with 65.5% of her payment in florins, matched Lucca in the niggardly amount of *gros tournois* and Tuscan groats, with an aggregate of 11.5%. Overwhelmingly, Lucca paid the papacy in silver groats of Venice and aquilins of Pisa, with totals of 30.4% and 42.6%, respectively. The remainder of the assessed amount was made up of the above-mentioned 9.5% in florins, 0.3% Neapolitan carlings and 1.1% petty billon deniers. This last figure, incidentally, corresponds generally to the small amount of pennies included in the overall Tuscan payment. As Day notes,

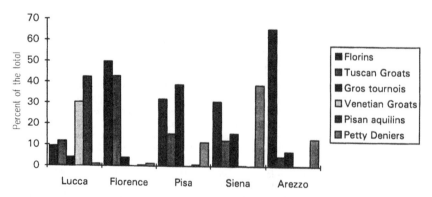

Fig. 1. Principal monies paid to Papal Collectors from Tuscany in 1296. Source: John Day, "la circulation monétaire en Toscane en 1296", Annales ECS, 23 (1968), 1057.

[3] For this and the following calculations, see the accompanying graph.

92% of the total Tuscan shipment of specie to Rome consisted of strong coins: i.e. florins and silver groats of various provenance. In light of these clear deviations in Lucca from the general norms exhibited by the rest of Tuscany in 1296, it seems to me that it might be useful to attempt to carry the inquiry a bit further by searching out in the Lucchese private documents indications of the presence of foreign coin within the city, and to offer an explanatory hypothesis for the skewed shape of Lucca's tithing returns. To those ends, I have turned to the Lucchese notarial materials in an effort to track down such information and to correlate the results with Day's findings.[4] There is, however, a serious limitation to this approach that should be spelled out before going forward. I refer here to the random way in which notarial chartularies in general have survived. The extant Lucchese chartularies constitute an unknown percentage of an equally unknown total of notarial contracts redacted in the thirteenth century, and spread unevenly chronologically over the period. Consequently, individual references to foreign coins in the remaining contracts may or may not accurately mirror the overall importance of these currencies within the Lucchese economy. Having said this, however, it nontheless remains true that references culled from the notarial documents to foreign coins circulating in Lucca, although not lending themselves to precise statistical analysis, can perhaps serve as a gauge to the types of alien monies attracted into the city.

The evidence that I have examined reveals a variety of foreign pieces circulating occasionally within Lucca. However, because of the conspicuous scarcity of the florin from the Lucchese tithe of 1296, let us begin with a look at gold. Lucca was the third European city – trailing Florence and Genoa by a few years – to issue a gold coin.[5] Like the *genoino d'oro*, however, the Lucchese *grossus d'oro* never achieved the international status of the Florentine piece and rather languished as a strictly local phenomenon. The reticence of Lucchese gold was not, I would maintain, due to the weakness of the city's economy, as Professor Lopez has argued was so for Genoa, but rather was due to the reluctance of the Lucchese merchant class to commit the Commune to a large-

---

[4] On the Lucchese notarial materials, see Robert S. Lopez, 'The unexplored wealth of the notarial archives of Lucca,' *Mélanges d'histoire du moyen âge dédiés à mémoire du Louis Halphen* (Paris, 1951) 417–32; Eugenio Lazzareschi, 'L'Archivio dei Notari della Repubblica lucchese, '*Gli archivi italiani*, 2 (1915) 175–210; Robert H. Bautier, 'Notes sur les sources de l'histoire économique médiévale dans les archives italiennes,' *Mélanges d'archéologie et d'histoire*, 58 (1941–46) 299–300; Mons. Giuseppe Ghirlarducci, *Le biblioteche e gli archivi arcivescovile e capitolari* (Lucca, 1969) and Duane Osheim, 'The episcopal archive of Lucca in the middle ages,' *Manuscripta*, 17 (1973) 131–46.

[5] Thomas Blomquist, 'The second issuance of a Tuscan gold coin: The gold groat of Lucca, 1256,' *Journal of Medieval History*, 13 (1987) 317–25. For an excellent discussion of medieval monetary history, see Peter Spufford, *Money and its use in medieval Europe* (Cambridge, Eng., 1988).

scale issuance of the noble metal.[6] Indeed, neither the Lucchese gold groat nor the Florentine florin appear to have played much of a role in the day-to-day workings of the Lucchese economy.

Apart from the earliest reference to a Lucchese gold groat dated 19 January 1257, I have located only twelve other indications of the *grossus d'oro* in the documents. These citations are bunched from the years 1267–68, 1270–71, 1273 and 1284,[7] and all reflect the business of local money-chargers or merchant-bankers. References to transactions made with the Florentine florin are equally rare in the Lucchese notarial materials. Between 1270 and 1299, I have found only nineteen documents specifically mentioning the florin.[8] Such lack of documentary evidence for the circulation of the Florentine gold pieces within Lucca may, of course, be due in part to the bias of the sources, but it does nonetheless confirm the low percentage of *fiorini d'oro* in the tithing returns of 1296. The trend seems clear and consistent, but it is difficult to explain.

Lucca entertained a number of Florentine merchant-banking companies engaged in buying silk and dealing in foreign exchange on a large and fairly regular scale. The Florentine society of Lapus Chiari, Michus, Arecchus and Cione Delcappone, along with Nerus Manni,[9] and that of Arrigus Bonrami, Ciericus Delpasso, Giani Della Bella, Rotinus Boninsegne *et aliis eorum sociis apothece*,[10] operating in Lucca in the 1290s, must have arrived there bearing florins. The question then arises as to why the florin – so prominent in other Tuscan cities – played such a minor role in the conduct of Lucchese business? Day suggests that the 50% of florins in the Florentine payment of 1296 indicates that the Arno city was a debtor, forced to export her own florins to offset expenditures for raw

[6] Robert S. Lopez, 'Settecento anni fa: il ritorno all 'oro nell' Occidente duecentesca,' *Rivista storica italiana*, 65 (1953) 197–98. Lucca's economy in the latter thirteenth century would appear to have been flourishing: on this matter see the discussion in Blomquist, 'The second issuance of a Tuscan gold coin,' 321–22.

[7] These citations may be found in 'The second issuance of a Tuscan gold coin,' notes nos 15, 16, and 17.

[8] Lucca, *Archivio capitolare* (hereafter AC), LL 36, f. 15, 21 October 1270; f. 27, 17 February 1271; *Archivio di Stato in Lucca, Archivio dei notari* (hereafter AN), notary Bartolomeo Lupardi, f. 42, 10 May 1286; AN, notary Giovanni Spiafame, f. 26v; 1 February 1287; Lucca, *Archivio arcivescovile* (hereafter AA), A.G., no. 19, 2 August 1288; AN, notary Giovanni Spiafame, f. 8, 18 January 1290; f. 10, 18 January 1290; f. 78v, 25 August 1290; f. 79, 25 August 1290; f. 83v, 27 August 1290; f. 3, 28 August 1290; f. 84v, 2 September 1290; AN, notary Filippo Risichi, f. 55, 27 December 1270; AN, notary Gregorio Paganello, f. 44, 21 August 1294; f. 62, 9 December 1294; AN, notary Filippo Risichi. 8 August 1299.

[9] For Lapus Chiari and his dealings as agent for his partners, the brothers Michus, Arecchus and Cione Delcappone and Nerus Manni, see AN, notary Gregorio Paganello, f. 29, 30 April 1294; f. 47v, 13 September 1294; f. 62, 9 December 1294; f. 90v, 23 February 1295; f. 111v, 1 July 1295; f. 117, 28 July 1295; f. 117v, 29 July 1295; f. 121, 11 August 1295; f. 121v, 18 August 1295; f. 138, 20 December 1295.

[10] For Arrigus Bonrami acting as agent in Lucca for his partners, see AN, notary Gregario Paganello, f. 51v, 16 November 1294.

materials and consumption goods.[11] I have reservations about this analysis, but if we were to accept it at face value, would not more of these florins have turned up in Lucca as they apparently did in other Tuscan cities? And if they were there, where did they go? The only Italian commune with which Lucca may have had a passive trade balance was Genoa, from whence came the bulk of the raw silk to feed Lucca's burgeoning silk industry,[12] but such payments were primarily effected by transferring to Genoa, through foreign exchange banking, credits that Lucchese merchant-bankers had accumulated in Northern Europe.[13] We are, in short, left with the apparent fact that Lucca did not assimilate a significant number of florins into her late thirteenth-century monetary structure.[14] However, looking at the volume of aquilins in the Lucchese tithe payment, it is conceivable that florins were drawn off to Pisa in exchange for these silver pieces. If so, this phenomenon would account for the high level of aquilins as well as the paucity of Florentine gold circulating in Lucca.

The coins, other than the penny, by which obligations were most frequently settled in Lucca were the silver groats of Lucca and the other four major Tuscan mints of Pisa, Siena, Florence and Arezzo. These heavy silver pieces, first struck at Pisa in the late 1220s, were circulating by the late 1230s at a common intrinsic worth equalling twelve local pennies – that is, they made tangible the *solidus* of account just as the florin or the Lucchese *grossus d'oro* made corporal the *libra* of account when they were issued at a nominal rate of 240 denarii and 20 solidi (or groats) respectively.[15]

These silver coins were used extensively as the means of payment in Lucca from about the mid-1230s through the 1260s, with a sharp decline in their appearances in the sources after 1269. Indeed, of the 187 indications of silver groats in the documents from 1236 through 1273, only three occur during the 1270s and none thereafter.[16] This, of course, does not mean that Tuscan *grossi* simply vanished from circulation in the last quarter of the thirteenth century. They do, after all, represent 11.8% of Lucca's 1296 remuneration to Rome. The absence of silver

[11] Day, 'La circulation,' p. 1065.

[12] For Lucchese trade with Genoa, see Domenico Gioffrè, 'L'attività economica dei lucchesi a Genova fra il 1190 e il 1280,' in: *Lucca archivistica storica economica: relazioni e communicazioni al XV Congresso Nazionale Archivistico (Lucca, Ottobre 1969)* (Rome, 1973) 94–111.

[13] Domenico Gioffrè, 'L'attività economica dei lucchesi a Genova, 105–6.

[14] Blomquist, 'The second issuance of a Tuscan gold coin,' note 20.

[15] Thomas Blomquist, 'Alle origini del'grosso toscano: la testimonianza delle fonti del XII secolo,' *Archivio storico italiano* 144 (1986) 243–60.

[16] The earliest reference to the Lucchese groat is AC, LL 11, f. 16, 26 March 1236. Those of the 1270s are LL 36, fols. 1 and 4.

groats from the sources and their low representation in the tithing amount do, however, present a puzzle to which a number of solutions – or combinations thereof – present themselves. There is the possibility that the heavy coins, groats and florins, were, as Carlo Cipolla has suggested, channelled into international commerce and trade, leaving the small *denarii* the coins of necessity in local dealings.[17] I find this possibility, at least for Lucca, less than compelling. Lucca's foreign trade balances were settled for the most part by offsetting through foreign exchange banking, thus precluding the shipment of specie over long distances. In other words, I do not see Lucca exporting – to borrow Day's wording – at least on any significant scale, her own coins to redress negative trade accounts.

In fact, my sense is that Lucca had a favorable balance with all of her trading partners save Genoa. If, on the other hand, clearance of international accounts by resort to inter-bank offsetting mitigates the argument of Lucchese coins draining into foreign markets, the same practice of international clearance most likely explains the dearth in Lucca of the *gros tournois* and the total absence of money of Provins in the list of 1296 and in the Lucchese notarial contracts. Likewise, no Genoese coins appear – and Genoa was Lucca's largest Italian trading partner – in the Lucchese sources except in *instrumenta ex causa cambii*, and here again foreign exchange banking negated the need for the physical transfer of specie in any significant volume. Returning to the original problem, however, how do we explain the apparent low volume of Lucchese and other Tuscan groats in the market place?

Obviously one has to face the recurring possibility that our sources are simply skewed and do not include records of transactions conducted in these coins. In the same vein, it may be that the linking of the silver currency to the florin simply obviated the need for the notary and participants to spell out in further detail the precise monies involved in any given deal. Under-reporting or over-reporting to one degree or another is always a likelihood, but assuming that both the tithe data and the notarial materials indicate at least a trend, could it not be that Lucca faced a shortage of indigenous silver to supply her mint and keep levels of production up to demand?

True enough, at the end of the century, silver mines were still operating in the Val d'Lima, but these veins had been exploited for at least some six decades, and no doubt longer, by this time.[18] The only references to bullion in the notarial contracts occur in connection with purchases of refined silver by gold and silver beaters, who obviously transformed the metal into leaves and thread to adorn Lucca's fine silk cloths.[19] The impact of the silver-working industry upon the

---

[17] Carolo M. Cipolla, *Money, prices and civilization in the Mediterranean world*, (Princeton, NJ, 1956).

[18] For Lucchese money-changers operating silver mines in the Val d'Lima, see AC, LL32, f. 78, 26 December 1259.

[19] Blomquist, 'The Castracani family of thirteenth-century Lucca', *Speculum* 46 (1971) 459–76.

available stock is impossible to fix, but it may very well have deflected bullion away from the mint in sufficient quantity to curtail the volume of production of good silver groats. Also, in 1268, Lucca struck a new and debased silver penny which was issued at a nominal face value 20% less than the old *denarius*.[20] Depending upon the volume of coins minted, these debased pieces could easily have driven the good groats into hoards or to the mint for re-coining, at a profit, into *denarii* with an official value above their intrinsic worth. Here again, however, we enter the realm of pure speculation.

If, as seems likely, Lucca faced a crisis with respect to her *grossi*, Pisa was more than willing to fill the void. The Pisan aquilin appeared in Pisa in 1272 at a market rate of 26 local pennies. Yet its earliest occurrence in the Lucchese documents is a year earlier, in 1271.[21] The fact that Pisa sent only 0.8% of her total monetary obligation to Rome in aquilins argues that there were perhaps few of them in actual circulation at home. Be that as it may, the proximity of Pisa to Lucca virtually assured the ready movement of the latter's coins in Lucchese territory. The 42.6% of Lucca's 1296 return paid in aquilins is to some extent reflected in the Lucchese private documents. In each instance where they are mentioned, aquilins take their place in a mix of heavy coins. In a loan contract of 1271, the money-changer Luccerius Castracanis advanced £76 *in denariis de auri grossis et aquilinis grossis de argento* to one Gulielmus *filius* Ubaldi *porcari de Tumba pro facienda mercadantiam*;[22] in two contracts of 1273, the merchant-banking company of the Bettori accepted investments *ad partem lucri* of £400 *bonorum denariorum lucensium denariorum parvorum in denariis crossis auri et aglinis tante valentie* and £380 *bonorum denariorum lucensium denariorum parvorum capitalium in denariis crossis auri lucensibus et florentinis et argenti aglinis tante valentie*;[23] in 1287, fourteen aquilins were part of another loan, which also included ten florins, twelve Venetian groats and two *gros tournois*, made by one Jacobus *quondam* Gulielmi Opithi, otherwise known as Malaconia,[24] to the merchant Margaritus *quondam* Cacciaguerre Spoletini; from 1284 comes a contract reflecting the purchase of ten points of raw silk for £50 *bonorum denariorum lucensium parvorum ... in aquilinis de argento tantum valentibus* at an exchange rate of $32\frac{1}{2}$ Lucchese *denarii* per aquilin.[25] Unfortunately we do not

[20] AC, LL 33, f. 107, 31 March 1268.

[21] David Herlihy, *Pisa in the early renaissance* (New Haven, CT, 1958), 197 cites a reference to a Pisan *grossus duorum solidorum* equalling 24 local pennies dated 3 September 1263, and then a series of references, beginning in 1272, to the *aquilinus grossus argenti* valued at 26d. Pisan but slipping to 33d. Pisan by 1279. Peter Spufford, *Handbook of medieval exchange* (London, 1986), 48, includes the groat of two soldi in his list of aquilins. Whether these were the same coins is, however, problematical.

[22] AC, LL 36, f. 21, 7 January 1271.

[23] AC, LL 36, f. 23. AN, notary Paganello di Fiandrado, f. 77, 23 September 1273; f. 16v, 28 January 1273.

[24] AN, notary Filippo Spiafame, f. 11, 11 January 1287.

[25] AN, notary Bartolomeo, Tegrimo and Fulciero Fulcieri, f. 346, 26 June 1284.

know the relationship between the Lucchese penny and the Lucchese groat, and therefore we cannot know if the aquilin were indeed a coin inferior to the *grossi*. We can, however, be sure that these few references represent but the tip of the iceberg of aquilins moving into Lucca – in exchange for florins – to fill the gap created by the dwindling supply of Lucchese groats.

So, also, Venetian groats served to compensate the presumed shortage of gold and heavy silver coins in Lucca. As in the case of Pisa, the references to Venetian *grossi* in the notarial documents are sporadic but nontheless suggest a substantial influx of these pieces – a flow reflected in the tithe of 1296. The first indication of a *grossus* of Venice in Lucca dates from 1230, when the partners Boiardus *quondam* Moriconis, Juncta *quondam* Viviani and Juncta *quondam* Bornetti exchanged £100 *denariorum lucensium* for £8 *de Venethianis grossis*, evidently to be used in a business venture in Venice.[26] Some years later, in 1236, £25 Venetian groats were deposited in the sacristy of the Lucchese cathedral – a form of hoarding suggesting their esteem in Lucca.[27] In 1238, three loan contracts survive which involve Lombards trading Venetian *grossi*, while in 1243 a Lucchese innkeeper deposited 20s *grossi veneziani* with the money-changer Genovese Anticus.[28] These early examples seem to me to be the casual traces of Venetian or Lombard visits to Lucca rather than the consequence of significant specie transfer. Towards the end of the century, however, the Venetian coin enters Lucchese business channels. Venetian *grossi* are included in the previously mentioned loan of 1287 to the merchant Margaritus Spoletini.[29] On 11 January 1297, a Lucchese notary and an associate borrowed £62 *bonorum denariorum lucensium ad parvos* made up of Venetian groats, rated at 28d Lucchese per *grossus*, and Bolognese groats exchanged at 17d Lucchese per *grossus*.[30] Also in 1297 a Lucchese silk merchant routinely borrowed 40s in *grossi veneziani* from two other merchants.[31] Thus, again, only the tip of the iceberg is revealed to us, but unlike the situation regarding the aquilin, it is clear that Venetian coins were moving to Lucca to settle balances of payment. Louise B. Robbert has recently estimated the volume of business of the Lucchese in early fourteenth-century Venice, either from commerce, banking, artisanal activities or a combination thereof, to have been 285 935 ducats – this is big business with big returns, and these profits, or a part of

---

[26] AC, LL 5, f. 87v, 27 November 1230.

[27] AC, LL 11, f. 10v, 25 February 1236.

[28] AC, LL 11, f. 159v, 21 January 1238; LL 11, f. 235, 8 August 1238; LL 11, f. 257v, 5 November 1238; LL 17, f. 17, 19 March 1243.

[29] See note no. 23.

[30] AN, notary Filippo Risichi, f. 174.

[31] AN, notary Filippo Risichi, f. 242v, 6 July 1297.

them, had ultimately to find their way back to Lucca.[32] Apparently, in order to repatriate profits, Lucchese actually shipped coins to their native city. I have found in the notarial materials only one reference to a banking connection between Lucca and Venice. In this instance, the Cardellini Company appointed two of their number, Arrigus Cimacchi and Bendinellus Cardellini, as agents . . . "*ad mercandum pro ipsis sociis et quolibet eorum et eorum vice et nomine in civitatibus Venetie et Janue et ubique lucam ad omnibus personis . . . etc.*" and even this leaves it uncertain whether either of the designated procurators actually put in an appearance in Venice.[33] It seems to me that this lack of a routinized banking link between Lucca and Venice goes far in explaining the presence of such a conspicuous quantity of Venetian *grossi* gravitating to Lucca.

These, then, were the principal foreign coins apparently circulating in thirteenth-century Lucca. As a kind of appendix, however, I will at this point simply mention the other types of coins that I have encountered in the Lucchese notarial materials. From Lombardy we find indications of money of Parma, Mantua and Cremona along with *imperiales*, either of Milan or the Tyrol, but each with such infrequency as to make them, for our purposes, insignificant. Rounding out the list are references to the *perpero* of Constantinople, *provinois* of Rome, one trace of the Neapolitan carling and one appearance of the Florentine silver guelph.

It is clear that in the above discussion we have been dealing in large measure with a string of hypotheses and as yet unanswered questions. It is to be hoped, however, that further work on both published and unpublished sources can put the matter of the movement of coin, bullion and credit in medieval Tuscany in a more complete perspective than I have been able to do in this brief essay. I would conclude by emphasizing a point made in passing on one or two occasions above, to wit, the relationship between foreign exchange banking and the movement of coin. It is my contention that where the services of international or inter-city exchange bankers were unavailable – or unnecessary, as between Lucca and Pisa or Lucca and Florence – specie physically moved back and forth to balance trading accounts, as in the case of Lucca and Venice. Where, conversely, such services existed, as they did at the fairs of Champagne, international balances

---

[32] Louise B. Robbert, 'I Lucchesi ed i loro affari commerciale a Venezia al tempo di Castruccio Castracani' in: *Castruccio Castracani e il suo tempo: convegno internazionale, Lucca, 5–10 Ottobre 1981* published as *Actum Luce*, 13–14 (1984–85) 190. On the consistent fineness of the Venetian *Grosso*, and hence its widespread acceptability, see the same author's 'Monetary flows – Venice 1150 to 1400,' in: *Precious metals in the later medieval and early modern worlds*, ed. J.F. Richards, (Durham, NC, 1983), 53–77, and Frederick C. Lane and Reinhold C. Mueller, *Money and banking in renaissance Venice* (Baltimore, 1985), 257–68.

[33] AN, notary Bartolomeo, Tegrimo and Fulciero Fulcieri, f. 186, 3 March 1284.

were settled by transfers of credit by exchange instruments and little specie or bullion was moved over long distances. This, I would argue, is why we find relatively few coins of Troyes and none of Provins or Paris showing up in the monetary structure of late thirteenth-century Lucca.

# INDEX

This index includes both the text and notes, but it excludes the Foreword and most references to modern authors. Persons are indexed under their family name if known (e.g. Guidiccioni, Aldibrandino f. Paganini). If a person has been identified by three names – personal, father's, and grandfather's – it is assumed that the last has become a family name. However, if a person is identified by only two names, he is entered under the one that is most distinctive (e.g. Bonrami, Arrigus *but* Soldanus f. Gerardi), unless the patronymic has plausibly become a family name (e.g. Guidiccioni, Betto). Because such rules are necessarily arbitrary, it is recommended that the user search under all known names of an individual. Relationships are made explicit only when this has been expressly indicated, in which case the abbreviation *f* stands for *filius/filia* (son/daughter of) and *m* for *marita* (wife of).

Personal names in the text are sometimes in Italian, sometimes in Latin; this index generally reproduces the text form but collects multiple references under the Italian family name.

abstinence, sexual: X 531, 534–5
Accepanti family:
 Giovanni: V 137
 Jacopo: V 137
accounting: VIII 166; X 532; XII 1, 3; XIII 822, 824, 827
Adiuti, Bonaccorso: VI 69
administration: XII *passim*; XIII 822, 826
agents: I 472; II 28
agricultural produce: I 468
Alamanni family:
 Nicolao: VIII 172
 Puccius: VIII 178
Albertini, Bruneto: IV 153
Albertinus: I 467
Aldibrandini, sons of: I 461
Allafossa: V 135
Allucci family:
 Johannes: VIII 177
 Rustichellus: III 24
Alluminato f. Comparetto: III 32
Alucci family:
 Lucieptus f. Johannis: VIII 177
 Rustichellus: VIII 177
Amadore, Rainerius: XIV 256
ambassadors: III 33; XIV 248; XV 322, 324
Ammanati company (Pistoia): XII 2
Ancona: I 475–6

Anselm, bishop of Lucca: VII 35
Antelli, Alessio: I 467
Antelminelli family: I 475–6
Antelmini, Ubertus: VIII 177
Antonino, saint: XIII 829
Antraccole: V 138
Antwerp: XIII 822
*apotheca, see* shop
*appoderamento, see* poderial system
aquilin (Pisan coin): XVI *passim*
arbiters: XII 6–7; XIV 257
archdeacon: IX 64
Ardicione Malisti: VIII 173
Arezzo: XIV 246–7, 258–9; XV 320, 322, 324; XVI *passim*
Argilliere: X 529
Arnolfi family: II 12
 Andruccius f. Benectonis: VIII 178
 Orlandino: IV 148–9; V 128
 Pierus f. Benectonis: VIII 178
 Simus f. Benectonis: VIII 178
 Vannes f. Benectonis: VIII 178
Arnolfini family:
 Arrigus: VIII 176; XI 365, 375
 Tacus: VIII 176
Arras: VI 72
Arringhetto, Amata f. Giovanni: V 138
artisans: I 467–8; VIII 158
Arzuri, *see* Azuri
assessment (*estimo*): V 131–2

For Product Safety Concerns and Information please contact our EU
representative GPSR@taylorandfrancis.com Taylor & Francis Verlag GmbH,
Kaufingerstraße 24, 80331 München, Germany

Printed and bound by CPI Group (UK) Ltd, Croydon, CR0 4YY
08/05/2025
01864404-0001